THE HIDDEN NORTHWEST

ROBERT CANTWELL

THE HIDDEN NORTHWEST

J. B. Lippincott Company

Philadelphia & New York

To my brothers

JAMES LEROY CANTWELL

CHARLES HARRY CANTWELL

U.S. Library of Congress Cataloging in Publication Data

Cantwell, Robert, birth date
    The hidden Northwest.

    Bibliography: p.
        1. Northwest, Pacific—History. I. Title.
F851.C27   979.5   72–1306
ISBN–0–397–00871–6

Acknowledgments

I am greatly indebted to Andre Laguerre, managing editor of *Sports Illustrated*, for having encouraged the writing of a number of articles for that magazine which became the source of several chapters in this book. I also owe a debt to Ray Cave, assistant managing editor, for his perceptive editorial assistance, and to Miss Christiana Walford, of the magazine's research staff, for her professional scrutiny of much of the manuscript and her creative suggestions and insights. John Cantwell, director of reference of the Public Record Office in London, and Miss D. M. N. Folland, of the Grey Coat School, were most helpful in my research into the early life of David Thompson.

In the Northwest itself I am especially indebted to: Nevan McCullough, Enumclaw, Washington, whose knowledge of the Cascade forest is unsurpassed, and to his friend Hollis Day, Tacoma, who made possible a horseback trip into the Cascade Mountains; George Weyerhaeuser, president, and Bernard Orell, vice-president, Weyerhaeuser Company; Joshua Green, Seattle; Murray Morgan, the historian, Tacoma; Emmett Watson, of the *Post-Intelligencer*, Seattle; Mrs. Dolly Connelly, Port Townsend, Washington; John Leland Hanson, Kelso, Washington; August Hanson, Castle Rock, Washington; Mrs. Kathryn Bowers, Tacoma; Miss Edna Breazeale, Mount Vernon, Washington; and Martin Schmitt and Edward Kemp, of the University of Oregon at Eugene.

Bil Gilbert of Fairfield, Pennsylvania, and Robert Waldrop of Wash-

5

ington, D.C., provided the canoeing experience that made possible a trip down the Canoe River of British Columbia. Mr. John Siecker, of the United States Forest Service; Mr. Clarence Pautzke, then chief of the Fish and Wildlife Service; and Dr. Loyd Royal, then director of the International Pacific Salmon Fisheries Commission, provided statistical material as well as practical assistance.

The late Stewart Holbrook, a tireless collector of Northwest lore, urged me many years ago to write this book. The late General Andrew McNaughton, former chief of staff of the Canadian Army and for many years chairman of the Canadian section of the Boundary Waters Commission, freely gave me his time and discussed developments on the Upper Columbia River from the Canadian point of view with a friendly informality I shall always gratefully remember. The reference staff of the library of the University of Washington at Seattle unearthed material at my request, as did the staff of the Oregon Historical Society in Portland, Oregon. Many complex arrangements were simplified by Miss Toni Huberman, secretary; and Miss Lucy Lowe worked with great patience and care in typing the manuscript in several drafts. George Stevens of Lippincott gave these drafts the benefit of a lifetime of editorial experience and a deep knowledge of the Northwest and its literature.

In a work of this sort, based in part on camping trips spanning many years, one meets literally hundreds of hikers, outdoor families, and campground neighbors who contribute to it by being part of the scene itself. If their names are omitted from this list, it is not from a lack of appreciation of the help they gave or because I underestimate the unvaried friendly reception I met with. Also in such acknowledgments as this it is customary to refer to the help given by one's wife. In this case the help was so unfailing that the book could not have been written without it. My wife drove most of the way across the Oregon Trail from Kansas to Puget Sound, and again across Canada following David Thompson's journey to the Columbia, and put up with camping, hiking, library research, and long discussions of a region which was really very remote from her own Southern background with uncomplaining attention, incidentally contributing an interest that in many portions of the book makes it virtually a collaboration.

Contents

Part One

I

The Rain

I

Rain and the scent of cedar were intermingled; life on the Northwest Coast was possible because there were cedar trees there. Unlike other wood, cedar splits into long, straight boards. The Indians inserted wooden wedges into a crack in a log, placed sticks to widen the crack as they drove the wedges deeper, and produced smooth boards as much as 3 feet wide and 15 feet long. These were lashed around poles to form the walls and roof of a house; and when the house was moved, the boards were towed behind a canoe to a new home site. While the Spanish mariners struggled with storms off the coast, the Indians were sheltered in these dry portable houses hidden in the woods on the banks of rivers.

Rain meant the arrival of salmon. There were salmon runs in the spring, but the big fish, the Chinook, lay in salt water until early fall, waiting for rains to swell the small inland creeks where they spawned. Usually it was evening, nearly dark, when word spread that the salmon were running. You could see them coming upstream, enormous shapes in the rainy twilight, with a torpedo rush, a burst of speed, as the salmon jumped at the base of a falls. Sometimes they fell back, stunned, as the falling water hit them, drifting downstream as other

Further information about many of the events, people, and places in this book, along with sources, can be found in the Notes and References section on page 291.

dark shapes raced past them to jump in turn. There was a wild ex-
hilaration about that scene.

The woods, dark green recesses of fir and spruce and cedar, were
unchanged from summer to winter; there were few hardwoods whose
leaves turned in the fall. Then you might come upon salmon spawning
in some creek in a pool scarcely larger than the fish. They broke the
surface with an idle, rolling, turning movement, unalarmed if you came
within a few feet of them; or suddenly, with belated terror at an intrusion they had ignored for hours, they shot through the rapids below
the pool, sending up zigzag, whiplike sheets of spray. The magic was
never-failing. The little streams that flowed quietly throughout the year,
so familiar they were scarcely named or noticed, were all at once revealed to have a life of their own, as if the life in their clear, cold
depths became for a time visible on the surface; they would never be
altogether lacking in interest again.

And always the rain falling. Rain hummed and buzzed in the woods,
little rivulets trailing around the moss on the forest floor. Glassy sheets
of water formed in depressions in the saturated ground, miniature ponds
through which the grass seemed enlarged and magnified by the water.
The first thing reported about the Northwest Coast was rain. The
legend of a unique land, one where it rained all the time, began with
Bartolomé Ferrelo, a Spanish mariner who approached the coast of
southern Oregon in February, 1543. The Weather Bureau subsequently
determined that February rainfall in that area reached as much as 25
inches, but Ferrelo needed no such exactitude. He turned about and
sailed south; there were no further Spanish voyages recorded for sixty
years, and then none for a century and a half.

Sir Francis Drake, carrying several tons of Spanish gold and silver in
the *Golden Hind,* sailed into the north Pacific thirty-six years after
Ferrelo. He reasoned that the Spaniards would not follow him there.
He calculated that by June, 1579, he reached the 48th parallel, which
would place him off the mouth of the Hoh River on the Olympic
Peninsula. The weather was so violent he decided to take his chances
with the Spaniards. Historians have doubted that he was as far north
as he thought, but his notes on the weather make it plausible. On the
west side of Mount Olympus, which rises 8,000 feet a few miles inland
from the mouth of the Hoh, the annual precipitation is 250 inches, the
highest in the United States; east of the mountain, only 20 miles
distant, the average rainfall is only 15 inches a year.

The checkerboard pattern of Northwestern weather, with rain at one
place and clear skies a short distance away, was a condition that mariners could not imagine. An explorer who claimed to have sailed these
seas without encountering incessant rain was dismissed as a fraud. This

was a Greek navigator named Apostolos Valerianos, also known as Juan de Fuca, who in 1596 in Venice met an Englishman, Michael Lok, a merchant and the English consul at Aleppo. Juan de Fuca, who wanted to get into the service of England, told Lok that four years earlier he had been sent to the Northwest Coast by the viceroy of Mexico. He found a broad passage—later known as the Strait of Juan de Fuca—which led to that inland sea later known as Puget Sound. Nothing came of this mysterious Greek's project, except that his story appeared in a new edition of Hakluyt's voyages by Samuel Purchas, a work more famous because in it William Shakespeare found inspiration:

> And all for some strange name he read
> In Purchas or in Holinshed

as James Joyce wrote in *Chamber Music*. Spanish archives produce no record of Juan de Fuca or Apostolos Valerianos, or any account of the voyage he claimed to have made. And yet Captain George Vancouver eventually located the strait only a few miles from where Juan de Fuca said he found it. De Fuca said there were many islands in the inland sea, and Vancouver found many islands in Puget Sound. If de Fuca fabricated his account, he had for his sources only the reports of previous explorers, and these stressed the rain and storms. He did not. He stressed that he had not been paid by the viceroy of Mexico, Count of Santiago, Marquis of Salinas, Luis de Velasco, which was why he was trying to get into English service. (The viceroy had troubles of his own. He was the son of the previous viceroy, the one known as the Liberator, whose enlightened policy toward the natives had brought about a revolt of Mexican grandees. Royal investigators from Spain were in Mexico, trying to get to the bottom of the matter, and began by instituting a reign of terror in which more than records were lost.) Juan de Fuca's failure to mention the rain could have been evidence that he was merely telling the truth. The rain on Puget Sound amounts to only 30 inches a year, or about half as much as the Count of Santiago would have experienced in his native Santiago, Spain.

After nearly two centuries the Spanish tried again, in the *Santiago*, commanded by Juan Perez. In 1774 the *Santiago* reached a point on the west side of Vancouver Island in what became British Columbia, but Perez was afraid to land: the weather was too bad. The following year the *Santiago* was sent north again, this time commanded by Bruno Heceta and carrying ninety-four men. The little schooner *Sonora*, with twelve men under the command of Juan Francisco de Bodega y Quadra, sailed with the *Santiago*. The two ships reached the Olympic Peninsula—not long after the battle of Bunker Hill, incidentally—on the morning of July 11, 1775. The Spaniards knew land was near, though they could not see it in the rain. At eleven o'clock the sun came out briefly. Close at hand, as though a curtain were raised, they saw dark, tree-covered hills and snow mountains beyond them. The skies darkened, the rain fell and the scene vanished as though a curtain had fallen.

The wind and the sea rose so powerfully the *Sonora* was almost driven ashore. In the storm that followed, the schooner could not keep the *Santiago* in sight. The next morning the ships were discovered to be 18 miles apart and about 10 miles from land. They tried to sail together along the coast but in the rain and darkness spent most of the time searching for each other. Lights were hung and rockets fired from the *Sonora,* but there was no answer from the *Santiago.* Three days passed, until on July 14, 1775, the ships came together again. They were near a great headland where tumbled rocks broke the waves around it, not far from the mouth of the Hoh River. They were also at one of the rainiest places on the entire coast; at that point rain falls on two hundred of every 365 days of the year. Inland, beyond the gray, crumbling cliffs, the trees rose in columns hundreds of feet high, among the oldest, largest and most enduring of living things on the planet. The rain forest was a survival from the age of dinosaurs and flying reptiles, a form of life that persisted in this area where rain and warm winds created a condition akin to the weather of a geologic age whose other growths had been extinct for millions of years.

The captains decided that the weather was too savage to risk sailing near the coast. Antonio Mourelle, the pilot of the *Sonora,* who wrote a book about the expedition, noted: "The men were much fatigued by the violence of the weather." During the council nine Indian canoes approached the ships. The Indians held up pieces of iron and furs to indicate that they wanted to trade the furs for metal. In so doing they created another historical mystery, for no traders were known to have been there. But the sign language was clear, and the sailors ripped the hinges from their sea chests and exchanged them for furs over the side. At some point three men from the *Santiago* went ashore to erect a cross and bury a bottle with documents claiming the land for Spain. They were not molested, and the *Santiago* sailed away. On the following morning seven men from the *Sonora* went ashore in the schooner's only boat to fill water casks. As they pulled their boat up on the sand, a horde of Indians, about three hundred by Mourelle's estimate, rushed from the woods and butchered the men around the boat. Two escaped the first attack but were drowned in the surf. The Indians ripped the boat apart for scraps of metal.

Only Mourelle, a cabin boy, two seamen and Captain Bodega y Quadra remained on the schooner. They fired the ship's only gun in the direction of the savages. The shot fell short. They loaded muskets and waited as canoes approached the *Sonora*. The Indians plainly did not know what guns were; they came on until their canoes were filled with their dead. The *Sonora* sailed to search for the *Santiago*. This time the ships came together at a barren island the captains named Isla de Dolores, the Island of Sorrows, later known as Destruction Island, beginning the practice of giving somber names to Northwestern landmarks.

Bodega y Quadra wanted Bruno Heceta to give him thirty men so he could punish the Indians. Heceta refused, and he was right. The forest back from the shore was a labyrinth of hidden paths in which the men would have been massacred in minutes. Heceta did provide six men to serve as crewmen on the *Sonora*, and the schooner sailed north, exploring as far as the southern coast of Alaska before returning to Mexico. Heceta himself gave up without exploring at all; forty-four of the men on the *Santiago* were sick. As Heceta sailed south he passed the mouth of the Columbia River and noted the color of river water in the ocean, but he sailed on without entering the river and in twelve days was in tranquil Monterey Bay in California. The image of the Northwest was that grim: land only two weeks north of the Spanish settlements was unknown when the Spaniards had been in California for centuries.

II

Captain James Cook reached the Northwest Coast three years after Heceta and made his landfall in February, 1778, on the coast of southern Oregon. Rain was falling. The sea was stormy. He saw a point of land and named it Cape Foulweather. The storm drove him out to sea. He approached the coast again near the northernmost point of the Olympic Peninsula. Another promontory attracted his attention, and he called it Cape Flattery. "There was a small opening which flattered us with the hope of finding a harbor," he wrote. "It is in this very latitude where we now were that geographers have placed the pretended Strait of Juan de Fuca. But we saw nothing like it, nor is there any possibility that any such thing ever existed." Cook had been with Wolfe at Quebec; he knew what an expanse of rock lay between the Atlantic and the Pacific, and he knew that even if the inland sea and the River of the West existed they could not be the Northwest Passage for which he searched. And nothing less would satisfy him. Cook was training a young midshipman, George Vancouver, as his personal charge, and Vancouver was a navigator of genius, but he absorbed Cook's views. And that cost Britain sole possession of the Pacific Northwest.

The Spaniards reached Oregon only fifty years after Columbus discovered the New World, only thirty years after Balboa discovered the

Pacific. But for three hundred years no settlement was built on the
Northwest Coast. And the first did not come from Europe; it came
from what Walt Whitman called the true Old World—the Far East.
The first settlement of the Pacific Northwest began in a maze of Oriental intrigue. The first Northwestern settlers were not driven by a
need for religious and political freedom, as were John Winthrop and
the Massachusetts colonists, nor were they visionary gold seekers like
Cortez and his conquistadores. They came from Calcutta. Northwestern
history began in an Oriental world of dark turbaned figures, among
English, Indian and Portuguese merchants engaged in projects of unfathomable complexity designed to get around the East India Company's monopoly on trade with the Far East. They were plotters as
well as merchants, and as the first town was hacked out of the Northwestern woods, they evoked the melodrama of Wilkie Collins's *The
Moonstone*, something having to do with stolen idols, unknown drugs
and Hindu thugs and assassins.

Wherever John Meares belonged, if he belonged anywhere, it was in
some such setting. He was an English adventurer, merchant and sailor,
only thirty-two years old in 1788 when he began the first colonizing
venture in the Northwest. The practical cover for his operation was the
trade in the fur of the sea otter. Some of Captain Cook's sailors had
purchased a few of these for iron nails and had sold them in China
for $60 apiece. In 1785 an English trader named James Hanna secured
more sea-otter furs on the west shore of Vancouver Island, sold them
in China and repeated the operation the next year. Two captains who
had been with Cook also sailed to the Northwest and picked up 2,552
sea-otter skins, which they sold in China for $54,875. Until their time,
Russia had had a monopoly on the trade, dating from 1728 with the
explorations of Vitus Bering and continuing with those of Georg Wil-
helm Steller and Alexander Baranov. Meares first sailed from Bengal in
1786 with two ships, the *Nootka* and the *Sea Otter* (or so he said),
and along the coast of Alaska secured enough furs to encourage his
backers in Calcutta to support a bigger enterprise—that is, to dominate
the Northwest Coast of North America.

Meares was somehow associated with Captain Charles William Barclay, who in 1787 reached the Northwest in command of the *Imperial
Eagle*. Barclay sailed under the flag of Austria to avoid legal entangle-
ments with the East India Company, which theoretically controlled all
trade in the Pacific Ocean. Barclay's voyage had some movie-scenario
interest because his young wife accompanied him and supposedly became the first white woman in the Northwest. In a queer reenactment
of the tragedy of the *Sonora*—Mourelle's book on the expedition had
been published in England—Barclay reported that he anchored near

Destruction Island and sent six men ashore to fill water casks, that Indians rushed from hiding and killed the men and that the *Imperial Eagle* sailed on. Barclay's account leaves the reader marveling at the way history repeats itself, or at the way history books repeat other history books.

Barclay returned to the Orient, and Meares then sailed from the Portuguese port of Macao. His expedition was equipped with two ships, false papers, flags and dummy captains supplied by a Portuguese partner. In the event the ships were stopped and questioned, these were to pretend they were in command while Meares and the captain of the other English ship pretended to be clerks. (Those Shakespearean comedies in which characters were always disguising themselves were by no means unreal in Northwestern history.) Meares was a master publicist. His sumptuous book, *Voyages made in the years 1788 and 1789, from China to the northwest coast of North America,* summoned up a forest land as mysterious as the bazaars and back alleys of Calcutta. For three months and twenty-three days he sailed across the winter ocean and at last, on May 11, 1788, "saw the long-wished-for land of America . . . a ridge of mountains whose summits were hid in snow."

Rain again, and storms; the early explorers could not say enough about them. "That night was a dreadful one; such heavy gusts and squalls of wind succeeded each other that we were prevented from carrying any sail. Those squalls brought hail and snow with them; and, towards midnight, it blew a perfect storm." Meares left a small force to erect a settlement at Nootka, a harbor which Cook had found on Vancouver Island. He traded along the coast and recrossed the Pacific with a shipload of furs. His backers now gave him four vessels, and he again sailed for the Northwest, this time with seventy Chinese carpenters and a prefabricated schooner built in China to be quickly assembled on the other side. He stopped at the Hawaiian Islands and picked up several native wives for each workman. The idea was that the Chinese workmen should not become homesick, and a steady supply of half-Chinese children should provide a dependable working force.

At Nootka the Chinese workmen quickly assembled the prefabricated schooner, which set out at once to trade for furs. They also built a small fort and several houses and constructed another schooner, using wood from the nearby forest. Meares now had six vessels coming and going from a port which few people knew existed and which was believed to be in a land as bleak as any on earth, where it rained all the time. It was Meares who concluded that Juan de Fuca had been right. Sailing south from Nootka, he came upon an opening off the southern tip of Vancouver Island. "The strongest curiosity impelled us to enter this strait," he wrote, "which I will call by the name of its original discoverer, Juan de Fuca." Bad weather drove him out to sea. Eight days later he was near the mouth of the Columbia River. Heceta had reported the legendary River of the West at this point, but Meares wrote, "We can now with safety assert there is no such river." He named the headland he saw there Cape Disappointment and the bay at the mouth of the river Deception Bay.

III

Captain Robert Gray of Boston was then sailing north toward Nootka in the sloop *Lady Washington*. Gray, thirty-three years old, was a little-known mariner, a descendant of *Mayflower* pilgrims, one of two captains in an expedition financed by Boston merchants to enter the sea-otter trade. The merchants gave overall command to John Kendrick, who sailed in the larger ship, the *Columbia*. The ships were not sailing together. On August 14, 1788 (a month after Meares decided the River of the West did not exist), Captain Gray anchored the *Lady Washington* about 30 miles south of Tillamook Head, which is south of the Columbia. Gray had a personal servant, a Negro named Marcos Lopius. While the men were on the beach, Lopius was somehow "employed in cutting grass down to the boat." There were apparently two different parties of Indians on the shore, one in a village back of the sand dunes and another visiting and trading with the sailors. Lopius "carelessly stuck his Cutlass in the sand. One of the natives seeing this took the favorable opportunity to snatch it at first unobserved and run off with it. 'Twas the hollowing of our people that first roused our attention . . . the Black boy had followed him in spite of everything they could say to the contrary."

The sailors ran to the Indian village and offered rewards if the boy was released. These were refused. The Indians wanted the men to go into the village after him but they were afraid to do so. Instead, the sailors pushed aside the brush that obstructed their view and saw "a large groop of natives in the midst of which was the poor black." He called to the men for help, "saying he had cought the thief." At this the main body of Indians left the sailors, ran into the village and "instantly drenched their knives and spears with savage fury on the boddy of the unfortunate youth. He quitted his hold and stumpled but rose again and staggered toward us but having a flight of arrows thrown out hit his back he fell within fifteen yards of me and instantly expired while they mangled his lifeless corse."

Gray named the place Murderers Bay. (It became known later as Tillamook Bay.) He sailed on to Nootka, arriving in time to watch the Chinese workmen launch the schooner they had built. He traded along the coast, finding sources of furs that Meares had overlooked or ignored. At one point Captain Gray personally traded an old chisel, worth a few cents in Boston, for sea-otter skins he sold in Canton for $8,000. When the weather grew cold, the English traders at Nootka sailed for the Hawaiian Islands to spend the winter, but Gray remained nearby, in a hidden cove so secluded that it remained unknown for another century.

Spain claimed all the land washed by the Pacific Ocean. It was hers by right of Balboa's discovery. The Spanish claims to the north Pacific were based on voyages of Bartolomé Ferrelo and Juan Perez and Bruno Heceta that went back far beyond Russian, English or American voyages there. And fragmentary evidence in the way of wrecks, Spanish coins and trade goods on the Oregon coast indicated that Spanish traders had operated in unrecorded voyages as well. On the other hand, Spanish explorers had never reported anything to justify a struggle for control of the region. But in that chaotic period at the beginning of the French Revolution the Spanish government had to make at least a token demonstration of sovereign rights, and in May, 1789, a small Spanish force from Mexico occupied Meares's post at Nootka and erected fortifications.

Meares's ships were, for the time being, allowed to trade. When they returned to Nootka loaded with furs, they were seized as prizes and sent to Mexico. Meares called this piracy. He fought his case in London so effectively that war was threatened between Spain and England. The Spanish government secured a promise of alliance with Austria, in the event of war, and was working for a similar alliance with France in negotiations that were broken off by the French Revolution. The dispute over Nootka had a more important historical consequence in the beginning of American and British understanding over the Northwest: the British government secured from the United States a promise that it would not aid Spain in the event of war. The diplomatic cooperation between Britain and the United States in the Northwest that started then continued for more than half a century, however antagonistic the two nations were in other areas.

Gray and John Kendrick met at Nootka in the spring of 1789. Kendrick was in no hurry to return to Boston. He exchanged ships with Gray, who sailed the *Columbia* to China, sold the furs and continued around the Cape of Good Hope, arriving in Boston in August, 1790. Gray was the first to carry the American flag around the world, and he was welcomed with a parade and a reception by Governor John Hancock. Gray's achievement stood out all the more strongly because of Kendrick's conduct: Kendrick never paid a penny to the owners or gave an accounting of any kind. After sham sales and reported ship losses, he emerged as a shipowner in his own right. He remained in the Pacific, visited Japan and had a flamboyant career until his accidental death—he was struck by a cannonball while exchanging ceremonious salutes with a British vessel.

Gray remained in Boston only six weeks. He married, got a new group of backers and sailed on the *Columbia* in September, 1790. By that time it was already evident that the Spanish government was going to abandon its claim to Nootka and with it Spanish claims to the north Pacific. The Spanish treaty with England was concluded on October 28, 1790. (The Spanish government paid Meares extravagantly for his losses, perhaps as much as $663,000, although the sum was variously reported.) The withdrawal of Spain had the extraordinary effect of leaving Russia and England poised against each other in the Northwest, even while they were allies in Europe, with Russia consistently operating to prevent the establishment of any English port on the Pacific Coast, and England consistently making concessions and adjustments with the United States to permit American, rather than Russian, expansion in that area. As for the Chinese workmen and their plural wives, nothing more was heard of them or of the docile working class Meares expected them to produce.

The formality of receiving Nootka from the Spanish authorities was given to Captain George Vancouver, now a distinguished British naval officer in his own right. The Spanish officer who was to surrender the post was Juan Francisco de Bodega y Quadra, last heard of fifteen years before as captain of the *Sonora*. Vancouver conducted a leisurely scientific expedition in the South Seas before sailing for the Northwest. A navigator of almost unparalleled accuracy, he reached Oregon on April 26, 1792, precisely where he calculated that he would: Cape Foulweather.

The surf broke with great fury around the bay. The evening was weighted with dark, gloomy weather. Vancouver prudently remained at sea. But the weather deceived him. He awakened to a serene blue sky. No rain fell. A fine fresh wind blew from the south. No one had ever before reported such a thing in the Northwest. With a steady wind, Vancouver raced his ships, the *Chatham* and the *Discovery*, northward. There was no reason for him to do so except elation at the end of the bad weather. Vancouver admitted it; he wrote that he sailed on because he was "desirous to embrace the advantage of the prevailing wind and pleasant weather."

That was understandable, but it cost England control of the Columbia and with it Puget Sound and dominance of the entire north Pacific coast. The only real claim of the Americans to the region lay in Captain Gray's discovery of the Columbia River, and there was no

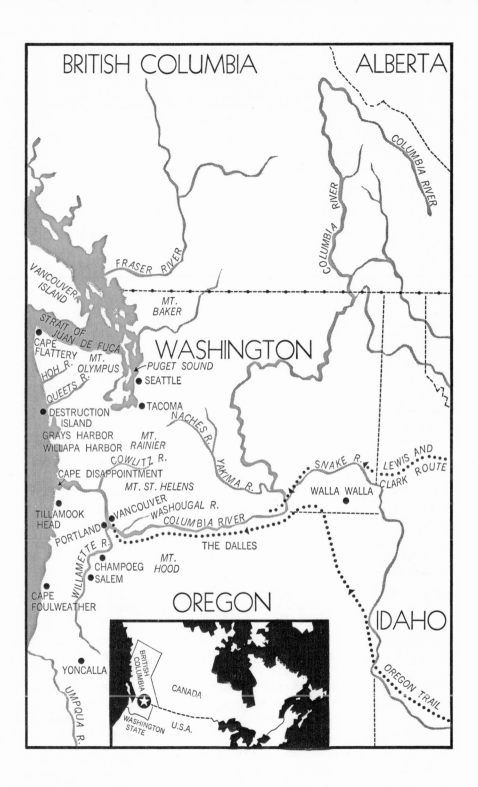

reason, except the fresh breeze, why Vancouver should not have discovered it before him. Vancouver's racing ships must have come very
near the mouth of the Columbia, for he saw the entrance of Willapa
Harbor, only 27 miles north. Just after daylight the next morning
Vancouver saw the jutting headland and scattered offshore rocks at
the southern end of the Olympic Peninsula. He named it Point Grenville after "the Right Honorable Lord Grenville." By a curious historical transformation, later works on Northwestern history placed the
massacre of the men of the *Sonora* (previously placed a day's sail
north near the Hoh River) at Point Grenville. The reasoning is plausible, but as with other scenes of historical events, its unlikelihood
becomes evident on the spot. The little Moclips River flows into the
ocean there, but it is so small that at low tide its waters sink into
the sand without reaching the waves.

It was curious that Captain Vancouver raced past the mouth of the
Columbia only to pause at Point Grenville, but that was his course.
He sailed on, and at dawn on April 29, 1792, he reached Destruction
Island. Here was a landmark which was virtually unmistakable. Destruction Island is not really an island. It is a big, barren rock about
5 miles off the coast midway down the Olympic Peninsula. But it is
the only island along the coast.

There Vancouver found the American ship *Columbia*, with Captain
Robert Gray in command. Why was Gray anchored off Destruction Island? Gray's experience with the weather, strangely enough, was
the opposite of Vancouver's. There was no storm for either of them
at the moment, but while Vancouver reported that he had been sped
north by pleasant breezes, Gray reported that he had been driven
south by storms and was now resting after the ordeal. But no matter
—the two mariners met with a timing that could not have been bettered if it had been planned. Vancouver sent a young officer, Lieutenant Peter Puget, to the *Columbia* to confer with Captain Gray and
in so doing gave Puget a degree of immortality, for Puget won Gray's
confidence, so much so that by seven o'clock that same morning Gray
was exchanging information with Captain Vancouver himself. Gray
told Vancouver that the Strait of Juan de Fuca, which supposedly did
not exist, was only some 20 miles north, and when Vancouver, as a
result, discovered an inland sea beyond the strait he named it for the
obscure lieutenant whose tact had made its discovery possible.

Gray then sailed southward. He kept close to the coast and came
to the indentation a few miles south of Point Grenville later known
as Grays Harbor. The entrance of the harbor was no more than 8
feet deep. The *Columbia* drew 6 to 8 feet. But the weather was fine,
and at high tide Gray risked it. He found himself in a large enclosed

bay fed by a good-sized river, the Chehalis. He named the harbor Bulfinch Harbor, in honor of the Boston architect who was one of the backers of his voyage, and questioned the Indians about a river bigger than the Chehalis. They directed him one day's travel south. High tide that night—May 10, 1792—was at seven thirty. Gray crossed the bar without trouble and sailed along the coast all night. At four in the morning he saw the headland that Meares had called Cape Disappointment. Rounding this, he came upon the bar of the Columbia. The current of the enormous river, 4 miles wide at this point, struck the ocean waves with a fury that gave rise to legends second only to the legend of rain. But Gray experienced no trouble whatever in crossing the bar and wrote, "We found a large river of fresh water, up which we steered."

On his part Captain Vancouver was astonished to find himself in the clear blue sea he called Puget Sound. He sailed among small islands whose white gravel beaches were backed by tree-covered hills. East and west were ranges of snow-covered mountains, and in the southern distance was the highest mountain of all, rising into the clouds from sea level in an almost unbroken sweep of rock and snow. He named the great peak for his old friend Admiral Peter Rainier, who thereby achieved greater fame than he had during his entire service in the Royal Navy. Vancouver was elated by his discovery. He wrote of the most delightfully pleasant weather, of forests reaching as far as the eye could see, alternating with parklike meadows elegantly adorned with clumps of trees, where deer were playing in great droves and where the explorers landed to gather gooseberries and wild roses. "A picture so pleasing," Vancouver said, "could not fail to call to our attention certain delightful and beloved situations in Old England."

IV

Two hundred and fifty years had passed since Bartolomé Ferrelo's voyage; Vancouver's praise was the first given the region. And for a long time Vancouver was alone in his enthusiasm. Alexander Mackenzie, the first man to cross North America, dismissed the scenery of the Northwest in a sentence: "Mountains and vallies, the dreary waste, and wide-spreading forest, the lakes and rivers, succeeded each other in general description."

Mackenzie began his great overland journey on May 9, 1793, while Vancouver and his men were still exploring the Northwest Coast. Mackenzie was young, perhaps only twenty-eight years old, possibly a few years older; conflicting dates given for his birth add to many other mysteries in his life. He was born in Scotland, and shortly be-

fore the American Revolution, when he was about ten years old, he
was sent to New York City. There he lived with an uncle of whom
nothing is known except that he was called Ready Money John. It
appears that Ready Money John led a comfortable if not easy life,
for during the Revolution the boy was sent to the safety of school
in Canada. Young Mackenzie spent nine years in the wilderness as a
fur trader and in the summer of 1789 made his way to the Arctic
Ocean, following the gigantic northward-flowing river that became
known as the Mackenzie River. He saw the ice pack beyond the narrow band of open water and reported that no Northwest Passage
existed through there. He journeyed to London with his findings, but
his inability to make accurate calculations of latitude and longitude
hampered him, or, as he said, "I made myself but little known during
my residence in London the Winter 1791/92."

Returning to Canada, Mackenzie went into winter quarters on Lake
Athabasca, north of where the city of Edmonton was later built, and
prepared to travel directly west through the Rockies to the Pacific. His
party consisted of ten men: himself, his assistant, six French-Canadian
canoemen and two Indians.

But before going on with Mackenzie's dislike of the Northwest
scenery and the weather, it is necessary to diverge from strict chronol-
ogy somewhat to explain the extraordinary importance of his remarkable assistant. His name was Alexander McKay, and he appears and
disappears in Northwestern history with a persistence that would be
unbelievable if it were not so thoroughly documented. First, McKay
unquestionably accompanied Mackenzie on his heroic venture; there
is evidence enough as to that in Mackenzie's repeated complaints (in
print) about his uselessness. Then, after the great journey, while
Mackenzie was knighted and became wealthy and famous, McKay
returned to the forest and married a part-Indian girl, to emerge from
his Canadian obscurity as an international figure when John Jacob
Astor placed him in charge of the fur traders in the founding of
Astoria. Finally, McKay died under mysterious circumstances while
that fort and trading post at the mouth of the Columbia was being
built; but through his family his influence continued in Northwestern
history long after his own time, for his widow Margaret married Dr.
John McLoughlin, a young Scottish physician newly arrived in the
Canadian wilderness. After the merger of the North West Company
and the Hudson's Bay Company, Dr. McLoughlin was given charge
of the Hudson's Bay posts on the Columbia and for more than twenty
years ruled almost single-handedly a region as large as France and
Spain, and where his authority extended over British and American
settlers alike. There was yet another aspect of Alexander McKay's

influence on Northwestern history; he became the villain, or one of the villains, of Washington Irving's *Astoria*. McKay's life symbolizes something of the hidden Northwest, one of its elusive characters known vaguely for an association with someone else, and scarcely heard of in his own right.

Mackenzie overshadows him, but not to the point of oblivion. Mackenzie and McKay and the eight other men set out for the Pacific on May 9, 1793. They followed the Peace River and the Parsnip River, tributaries of the Mackenzie, to their headwaters in the Canadian Rockies in northeast British Columbia. They reached the Continental Divide on June 12, 1793. At the base of a precipice they came upon a small lake which was the source of the Parsnip River. An Indian path only 817 paces long led to another lake whose outlet, barely large enough to float a canoe, flowed west to the Pacific. They had crossed the height of land, of enormous importance in those days of water travel in determining boundaries, and perhaps of special significance in this case if the charter of the Hudson's Bay Company was interpreted to give the Company control only of lands whose rivers drained into Hudson's Bay.

The weather was cold and raw. Mackenzie spent sixty-five days west of the Continental Divide, and forty-five of these he described as rainy, stormy, foggy, cold, cloudy, wet, showery or a combination of several of these. Near the Quesnel River in central British Columbia, rain fell for ten days in a row. When the rains stopped, the trees continued to drop rainlike moisture. Drenched, miserable and convinced that Mackenzie was crazy, his guides tried to desert. Mackenzie had to stay awake at night, his gun in his hand, to keep them from going back. He believed that McKay, worse than useless, was secretly urging the guides to desert so the journey would be abandoned. Coming out of the Rockies, Mackenzie had to turn southward along a great river (which he thought was the Columbia but was in fact the Fraser) or continue directly west through the Coast Range to the ocean. He decided to keep on going west. He went down the Bella Coola River that flows into the Pacific about 200 miles north of Nootka Sound; one of Vancouver's officers was in fact exploring in the area. Traveling alone ahead of his men, Mackenzie reached the Pacific on July 22, 1793. It was the only day on which he said the weather was pleasant.

Too many new worlds had been discovered; there was a latent wish not to find anything more. Over the reports of explorers on land or on sea there lay a sense of disappointment, an unlocalized pain of vast distances more important than anything to be found beyond them. William Shaler, a young New England mariner, exemplified it in his book, *Journal of a Voyage between China and the Northwest Coast of North America,* a decade after Mackenzie's journey. As Shaler approached the Northwest Coast, he was awed by the sight of mountain ranges rising above magnificent amphitheaters covered with evergreen forests. Nearer the shore he could see open plains beyond the wind-shaped trees. In the far distance, rising high above the continuous mountain ranges, were the great isolated peaks of Mount Rainier and Mount St. Helens and Mount Hood. Shaler steered for the mouth of the Columbia. He waited eight days, but "the rapid current of the great river, meeting the swell of the westerly winds, that have the whole sweep of the ocean from Tartary to the American coast, forms a bar at the mouth, which is always difficult and sometimes dangerous to cross. . . . The weather was so tempestuous I never dared attempt crossing the bar, on which the sea broke with horrible fury."

Simon Fraser in 1805, a year after Shaler turned back, crossed the Rockies in Canada and made his way down the Fraser River to tidewater. "I scarcely saw anything so dreary and dangerous in any country," Fraser wrote; "whichever way I turn my eyes, mountains upon mountains whose summits are covered with eternal snow."

In the fall of that same year Meriwether Lewis and William Clark and their men came down the Columbia to its mouth. On the evening of November 7, 1805, they could hear the sound of the breakers. "Ocian in view! O! the joy!" Clark jotted in his notebook. He could not really see the ocean from where he was, and his elation soon vanished. "We spread our mats on the ground," he wrote, "and spent the night in the rain."

Rain was still falling the next morning. The men were given time off to dry their clothes. But more rain fell the following day, an all-day rain, with gales from the sea. The third day Clark wrote: "We are thoroughly wet with rain, which did not cease during the day; it continued violently during the night." The fourth day the rain fell in torrents. The wind drove great river waves against the shore. The rain loosed stones on the hillside that rolled upon their camp.

On November 12, about three o'clock in the morning, "a tremendous gale of wind arose, accompanied by lightning, thunder and rain; at six it became light for a brief time, but a violent rain began which lasted through the day." And that night "it rained without intermission." Clark's diary entry for November 16, 1805, began, "The rain, which has continued for the last ten days without an interval of more than two hours. . . ." The following day he wrote with dawning horror: "*Eleven* days rain, and the most disagreeable time I have experienced. . . ."

Theirs was the most stupendous anticlimax of all exploring adventures. They had struggled for 4,000 miles across North America, upstream against the Missouri's terrible current, through the Rockies where they overcame dangers of fatigue, madness, Indians, rattlesnakes, grizzlies and hunger, meeting all hazards with a gallantry and courage that made their achievement one of the finest in exploring history, and found when they reached their destination they were in a land like the bottom of a well. They were in fact in a kind of meteorological well, a cylinder of saturated air; with monstrous ill luck they had landed in one of the rainiest parts of the region in the wettest part of the year. In absolute terms the rainfall is not so great there, averaging only 96 inches a year, but 65 of those inches fall in two months. Clark suspected the truth. He believed that if they went inland, to the falls of the Columbia which they had passed coming down the river, they would find a drier climate, and he was right. The annual rainfall there is only 19 inches, or about half that of the rain along the Atlantic Coast. But the hope of meeting a ship kept them near the coast and in the rain.

On Sunday evening, December 1, 1805, the winter rain began in earnest. Thereafter rain fell every day for thirty-one days. "Scarce a man can boast of having been one day dry since we landed in this place," Clark wrote. They built their stockade in the rain. With marvelous military genius the captains prepared the place against every danger except the one they actually faced—the rain. The camp was hidden in a forest of fir and spruce, on what they called Elk River, later Lewis and Clark River—a big square enclosure, with cabins lining two walls, the barracks of the men on one side, the separate cabins of Lewis and Clark on the other, with the storehouse between them. It was located so high above the surface of a river that the river might rise 50 feet a night—which seemed altogether possible—and not wash it away. In the rain the men toiled up and down the slippery bank to the river. The muddy ground turned into a morass under their feet, a compound of clay, sticks, bark and twigs, with muddy streams between mudholes sluicing down the hill. In the rain the hunters went up Elk Creek, and while they almost always returned with meat—the company consumed more than 150 elk—they also returned drenched.

And in the rain the captains decided to start back east overland. Their reason was that game was becoming scarce. When the salmon run began and promised ample food, they decided to leave anyway. "The Indian village was filled with rejoicing today," Meriwether Lewis wrote, "at having caught a single salmon, which was considered the harbinger of vast quantities in four or five days." He did not want to take a chance on having so much food that leaving would be unnecessary, and ordered the men to prepare the canoes for the journey back up the Columbia.

As they started work, a violent rainstorm drove them inside. For five days the rain was so fierce that no work could be done. On March 20, 1806, Lewis wrote, "It continued to rain and blow so violently today that nothing could be done to forward our departure."

Three days later Clark wrote, "This morning proved so raney and uncertain that we were undetermined for some time whether we had best set out." But suddenly the sky cleared. They wasted no time. By one o'clock in the afternoon they were on their way. In their hasty leavetaking they bought an Indian canoe rather than attempt further repairs on one of their own. When they reached the Columbia, they became lost in one of the alder-lined channels along the bank. An Indian they knew saw their trouble and hurried after them to set them right. A minor crisis developed. In their hurry to get away it seemed they had stolen his canoe. Not precisely stolen it—they had bought it from another Indian, not knowing the other Indian did not own it. Lewis felt the whole matter was too difficult to make clear to the savage mind. He gave the aggrieved red man an elk skin, because, he wrote, there was "no time to discuss the question of right."

In the five months that Lewis and Clark were in the Northwest there were only twelve days without rain, and six of these were cloudy. When they left the stockade (March 23, 1806), Clark wrote: "In this place we wintered and remained from the 7th of Decr. 1805 to this day . . . we have lived as well as we had any right to expect, and we can say we were never without 3 meals of some kind either pore Elk meat or roots notwithstanding the repeated fall of rain which has fallen almost constantly." Clark intended to count up the number of days on which rain had fallen, but he was too tired of the whole subject to finish his calculations. He left blank spaces in his diary to be filled in later but never got around to filling them. His conclusion read: ". . . notwithstanding the repeated fall of rain which has fallen almost constantly since we passed the long narrows on the of Nov. last, indeed we have had only   days of fair weather since that time."

V

Meriwether Lewis prepared a summary of the expedition's discoveries in a letter to Jefferson. He did not stress the rain. His report was not precisely secret but was intended for influential Americans in the government and elsewhere. One copy reached Canada and was read with interest in the office of the North West Company. Another copy evidently reached Russia. But the copy that had the greatest effect was that sent to John Jacob Astor. In 1807, soon after he received it, Astor began plans for a fort and trading post at the mouth of the Columbia—a project of extraordinary daring and imagination in which Astor had the support of President Jefferson and which the American government at that time could hardly have undertaken officially without arousing international disputes.

But Astor worked in a puzzling fashion. He recruited fur traders from Canada, and at their head, as has been said, he appointed the unfortunate Alexander McKay, who had reached the Pacific with Mackenzie a decade before Lewis and Clark. McKay was by no means a well-known figure such as Mackenzie had become. His part-Indian wife, however, was a forceful and intelligent woman of great influence on him and on others; her father was a fur trader named Wodin, her mother an Indian and she herself was educated in a convent of Ursuline nuns in Quebec. She bore McKay four children and one of these, Tom McKay, accompanied his father on the Astoria expedition, remaining in the Northwest after the expedition failed to become a friend and adviser of the early American settlers.

Astor sent the Canadian fur traders, together with the working force to construct the fort, to the Northwest on the *Tonquin*. He placed the ship under the command of Captain Jonathan Thorne, late of the United States Navy, with a reputation gained in action against the Barbary pirates. Astor also dispatched a land party of sixty men under Wilson Price Hunt, which was to cross the Rockies and join the party from the *Tonquin* on the Columbia; and while the planning and administration of this party was also perplexing, it was the disaster of the *Tonquin* that inspired the one great work that fixed the image of the Northwest as a land of unbroken forest gloom—Washington Irving's *Astoria*, a masterpiece oddly compounded of unenlightening fact and penetratingly imaginative fiction, but above all an unforgettable picture of a cold, remote, stormracked and inhospitable land.

The facts on which the tragedy was based are meager. Astor for some reason divided authority between Captain Thorne and Alexander McKay. Command of the expedition at sea went to Thorne, of course, but McKay was given command of the fur traders and had authority when trading with the Indians. Since the ship would necessarily be anchored near shore while the traders conducted their business, conflict between the two leaders appeared almost inevitable unless one or the other, or both, possessed unusual tact and skill. Both Thorne and McKay were hotheaded, imperious and jealous of their authority. Thorne in particular was almost obsessed with naval discipline and during the long voyage around Cape Horn was affronted by the casual shipboard manner of the first mate, Fox, an old merchant sailor who was on good terms with the Canadian fur traders.

Eight men were lost crossing the bar at the mouth of the Columbia River. After landing the work force to build the fort at Astoria, the *Tonquin* sailed to begin trading for furs and was never heard of again. A report, supposedly taken from an Indian who served as an interpreter for the fur traders, was to the effect that the ship was blown up, with the loss of everyone aboard. The story was that while the *Tonquin* was anchored near an Indian village, and trading was under way, the quarrel between Thorne and McKay came to a head and the Indians, as a result, were allowed on board. At a signal each Indian attacked the man nearest him. The dying survivor, or survivors, set fire to the powder magazine. Ross Cox, who had been a member of the Astoria expedition, published the story in *The Columbia River* in 1831, with many details it seemed unlikely an Indian interpreter could have supplied. In any event, the loss of the *Tonquin* made Astor's project a failure from the start. The post at Astoria was surrendered to the British during the War of 1812 without opposition, and when peace was signed and the post returned to the Americans, Astor sold it to the North West Company. The result was to give the British a more complete hold on the region than they had had before Astoria was built.

In his old age Astor wanted to give his side of the story. Washington Irving had recently returned to the United States after fifteen years in Europe, and Astor proposed that Irving write a book about the Astoria venture, with Astor's assistance and financial aid. Irving on his part was searching for a subject that would be compatible with his literary position. He was the first American writer to have become internationally famous; he was a graceful and sociable old bachelor, accustomed to good living in London and Paris and Madrid; he was a sophisticated observer of international intrigue who brought into his historical works the insight into court ways provided by his duties as ambassador. And he had a genuine interest in the wilderness. Soon after returning to the United States he went with an exploring party to the prairies of what later became Oklahoma, an interesting but difficult journey, surprising for one of his sedentary habits; the unknown West had stimulated him without giving him a concrete subject for a major work. In addition he knew a great deal about the fur trade. In his early years he had often visited in Montreal; he was intimately acquainted with the North West Company partners, lived in their homes and had been invited to go with them on their wilderness journeys. He regretted all his life that he had not done so. Irving had then been engaged to marry Matilda Hoffman, whose mother was a member of the great Ogden family of New York. (The Ogden family divided during the Revolution. One branch remained in New York and the other settled in Canada, where its members became prominent in the fur trade. Peter Skene Ogden, whose father was born in New Jersey, grew up in Canada and became one of the most notable of the North West Company explorers in the Rockies and in the Pacific Northwest.) Matilda Hoffman died on the eve of her marriage to Irving—who remained faithful to her memory all his life— and Irving's early interest in the American wild was broken by his foreign service in Europe.

Irving accepted Astor's offer to write the complete story of the Astoria venture. The old merchant's private papers were given to him, and he lived at Astor's mansion while he studied them. His nephew, Pierre Irving, was hired to winnow the documents. Events made *Astoria* of immediate political importance. By the terms of the treaty of peace after the War of 1812, the United States and Great Britain agreed to hold the Pacific Northwest in joint occupancy, open to the settlers of both nations. (The United States proposed adding Russia, which then claimed the Northwest Coast, but the Czar was an absolute monarch who could not permit any such dilution of his authority, and Russia made separate treaties with Great Britain and the United States.) The treaty of joint occupancy with Great Britain was ratified in 1818, with a provision for renewal in ten years. Russian claims varied from time to time, once reaching as far south as San Francisco Bay; and while they were eventually limited to the southern boundary of Alaska, the fear of Russian encroachment remained constant in both Washington and London. That fear was intensified in 1821, when the Holy Alliance was still strong, after the Czar issued an extraordinary ukase forbidding all vessels except those of Russia to approach within a hundred miles of the Northwest Coast. Distrust of Russian intentions lay back of the American foreign policy that culminated, late in 1823, in the Monroe Doctrine, and when the treaty of joint occupancy came up for renewal in 1828, the cooperation of Britain and the United States in the Northwest was extended for ten years more.

Joint occupancy was an innovation in international dealings. In a later period of history, when nationalist habits of thought were less compulsive, it appeared a bold and original contribution to the vexed question of sovereignty. And insofar as the early settlers of Oregon were concerned, it worked exceedingly well: both Britons and Americans were better off under two governments than the citizens of either country were when they were under only one. But the treaty of joint occupancy had a peculiarly unsettling effect on political theorists in the Eastern states. Who really ruled the country? Who was in charge? Who would collect taxes, grant licenses, issue regulations and do all

the many things required of the officers of towns, counties, states and
the Federal government? The apparent irrationality of a dual government in Oregon, or of a joint government, or of no government, with
the citizens of two nations intermixed and equal, aroused an almost
frenzied determination to impose on that distant Northwestern land
such orderly and logical patterns of government as political theorists
enjoyed in that society which was moving toward the War Between
the States.

As 1838 approached, it was proposed that the treaty be renewed
indefinitely. It was in this intellectual atmosphere that Irving wrote
Astoria. He made it a tragedy of divided authority. Who was to be
in charge, Captain Thorne in command of the *Tonquin* or McKay in
charge of the fur traders? Because no one had clearly defined authority, the entire company perished. Irving raced through the book with
almost shocking speed. He began writing in the summer of 1835,
finished the book in only two months—an amazing achievement in
view of the complex material he had to assimilate and organize—
and saw it published, a popular success in both the United States and
England, in the fall of 1836.

Among Irving's works, *Astoria* is a flawed creation from the start,
the saddest work among the classics of American literature, and yet
a truly great work in its boldness and originality and in the single
vivid image that it leaves in the mind of the reader of the tragedy of
a storm-racked land. Nothing lightens its gloom. The old-grandfather
chuckles of Irving's prose style, suitable for "Rip Van Winkle," were
grotesquely inappropriate for a story of a violent episode in the struggle of nations. The suave generalizations, the worldliness and weariness
distilled from years of work in the courts of monarchs and from longer
years of study of the times of Columbus and Ferdinand and Isabella,
were equally misplaced. It was no longer possible for Irving to comprehend anything simple. But almost inadvertently the image of the
Northwest came through, to shape national thought on the region and
work an influence on American literature as powerful as that of anything else Irving wrote.

Irving recognized at the outset that, if he could make the character
of Captain Thorne understandable, the other mysteries of the expedition of the *Tonquin* would fall into order. He concentrated on his
creation of Thorne as a single-minded commander, stern and unbend-
ing, his sense of authority gradually lacerated until he became, in the
end, the embodiment of a possessed and demented will. Those trivial
disputes during the long voyage became successive attacks on his
authority. He read darker and darker motives into each dispute with
McKay. The careless manners of Fox became in his inflamed mind
indications of a planned mutiny. And what of McKay? Was he con-

sciously provoking Thorne to create a crisis that would leave him in command? Irving made no attempt to get at the psychological complexities of McKay as he did with those of Thorne. He pictured McKay as a master of delay and pettiness, a pompous and almost comic figure, always insisting on his rights, a masterly intriguer (who makes one think of all the bureaucrats and court officials Irving must have known in Europe) rather than a fur trader who—whatever else might be said about him—was still one of the first two men to cross the continent of North America. Irving did not go into the results of McKay's action in taking his son Tom with him on the *Tonquin*. He did not note that Tom McKay, left an orphan at Astoria at fourteen, survived as a fur trader, explored the Northwest when there were only a handful of white people scattered through it and was, at the time Irving was writing *Astoria*, one of the leading figures of Oregon and a friend of the American settlers who were then beginning to arrive in considerable numbers.

Tom McKay was already a Northwestern legend, so much so that it seems inconceivable that anyone writing of the region at the time could have left him out of the account. He was a tall, wiry individual who walked with a limp as a result of one of the many wilderness accidents of his life, a great teller of tales who had a sort of formal beginning to his accounts of the unwritten history of the land. "It rained, it rained," he began. "It blew, it blew." He held the Americans spellbound with stories of his experiences—such as the time he led a party from the Columbia River to the Olympic Peninsula to try to rescue three Japanese sailors who had been blown across the Pacific and were held captive by the Indians—which appeared to be incredible. In later years Tom McKay was held to be a teller of tall tales and finally was known only as a great liar, but the first American settlers to reach Oregon remembered him differently. "There was an air of strangeness about him," one of them said, "and he was a very good and amazing person."

But no hint of such complexities enters Washington Irving's account of Tom McKay's father. Alexander McKay appears in *Astoria* only as a foil to Thorne, a foolish troublemaker, comic in his self-importance, until the horror of his death darkens his story with the somberness that lies over the whole tragedy of *Astoria*. The climax comes early in the book, when the *Tonquin* reaches the mouth of the Columbia on March 22, 1810. A hard northwest wind sends furious surges over the bar. It is late in the afternoon, but Thorne orders Fox to take soundings. The whaleboat is old and leaky, and Fox, alarmed, asks that he at least be given experienced seamen to go with him. Thorne interprets the request as another reflection on his ability. Perhaps, in his inflamed mind, he thinks to bring to a head any mutinous movement, if one exists, before the landing. Perhaps he wants to repay Fox for what he considers discourtesies he has endured. Or perhaps he merely wants to kill him. More likely he is unsure in his handling of the ship and in doubt about the bar. He seems strangely unaware of the many accounts that then existed by captains who had crossed it.

Whatever his reasons, his next move is criminal. He orders three French-Canadian canoemen into the whaleboat with Fox. The canoemen are neither deep-water sailors nor sophisticated fur traders; they are white-water experts, who were to be used in river travel, and know nothing whatever of the ocean. Fox says Thorne is sending them to their death. The Canadian fur traders also protest to Thorne, with results that might be expected. Fox makes a final plea to his captain, with tears in his eyes. Thorne is adamant. It is nearly dark by the time the whaleboat sets out. The horrified men on the *Tonquin* watch it rise and fall among the huge rolling waves; then it disappears.

The next day Thorne sends a pinnace to search for the whaleboat, but it cannot be seen. Thorne is unmoved. He orders another crew into the pinnace to take soundings where the whaleboat disappeared. This crew consists of one experienced seaman, a sailmaker, a gunsmith and two Hawaiian Islanders. The pinnace is in trouble while still in sight of the *Tonquin*, and the men try to return to the ship. The boat overturns. Thorne makes no attempt to help the men. A storm is building up, and he sails the *Tonquin* out to sea.

The seaman and the sailmaker are drowned when the pinnace goes over. The gunsmith and two of the islanders swim to shore, but one of the islanders dies of exposure. When the weather clears, the *Tonquin* crosses the bar without trouble, picks up the survivors and lands the party that is to build Astoria. The ship then sails north to trade, though McKay leaves his son behind.

Difficult as it was for Irving to make Thorne and McKay into plausible characters, the mystery of the end of the *Tonquin* is a greater test of his genius. No one really knew what had happened on the *Tonquin*. But Irving could visualize it clearly. He saw the ship anchored in a remote and desolate cove, and there McKay—or *his* McKay, as he was sure McKay must have been—invites the Indians on board to trade, if only as a cynical test of where Thorne's authority ends and his own authority begins. It was easy for Irving to imagine what Thorne would do: he kicks the Indian chief off his ship.

And now the question of divided authority has to be settled. McKay had charge when the *Tonquin* was trading. He had right on his side; Thorne was making it impossible for him to trade. The Captain Thorne that Irving imagined reacts by washing his hands of the whole business and telling McKay to do as he pleases. McKay placates the offended chiefs by welcoming them aboard the next day. The Indians scatter around the deck. McKay is dealing with the chiefs and savoring his moment of triumph; the crewmen are trading with the braves; the Indian women, in canoes, are waiting below the ship; and Thorne is pacing the deck in silent fury.

At a signal every Indian attacks the nearest man. Knives are drawn and tomahawks swung and the crew butchered. Thorne and McKay are killed within sight of each other and their bodies thrown overboard to be mutilated by the women in canoes. The ship's carpenter, wounded and dying, crawls below deck. In agony, with the savages celebrating on the deck above him, he sets fire to the powder magazine, and the red roar rises above the forest to end the story. Now, none of this could be known as factually true, but the fate of the *Tonquin* settled into history as Irving imagined it to have been. There is no other example in American literature of a myth accepted as historically true, solely on the basis of an imaginative re-creation of its supposed events.

The message of Irving's great book is that the dream of a world of united states is an illusion. Some one person has to rule. There has to be a final authority: a captain on his ship, a government with its powers, a sovereign on his throne. More specifically, the dual citizenship of the Northwest is impossible.

Astoria was not only influential in shaping the national view of a region. Irving's portrait of the implacable Captain Thorne, sending man after man to his death, was the first of many portraits of demented commanders in serious and popular American literature: Captain Ahab in *Moby Dick*, Wolf Larsen in *The Sea Wolf*, Captain Queeg in *The Caine Mutiny*, down to thousands of mindless sticklers for military protocol leading endless squadrons of cavalry to their death in movies and television. The climaxes of *Astoria* are double: first, the calm, lucid, dignified craziness of Thorne ordering men to drown on the bar of the Columbia, and second, the rivalry and the mutual contempt of Thorne and Alexander McKay as they stride the deck, watchful of each other and inflexible in insisting on their rights, up to the moment the savages slaughter them both. No, the image that Irving communicated in *Astoria* was unforgettable. But the conditions for its national acceptance had been laid down long before. The way was prepared by explorers' reports of incessant storms, by Mourelle's account of the murder of the men of the *Sonora*, by Meares's mysterious plots, by Lewis's and Clark's winter of endless rain, by the image of islands of destruction, capes of disappointment, harbors of murderers and bays of calamity. Only some such tragedy as that which Irving told in *Astoria* was appropriate for the world of wind and rain that men far less imaginative than Washington Irving believed existed at the far end of their unknown continent.

II

The River

I

    The best place to study the history of the Pacific Northwest was the Students Room of the old Canadian Public Archives building in Ottawa. It was open all night. The Public Archives of Canada were eventually housed in a modern building of their own, but before the transfer they occupied part of an office building behind Parliament House, in an area where offices and gardens gave way to residences and commercial structures. To an American visitor that portion of the archives dealing with the Pacific Northwest was a revelation, not only for the documents unavailable elsewhere but because these documents contained so little of the reports of storms and rainfall found in the morose American records.

    If one convinced the authorities that his scholarly qualifications were authentic, he received a pass which enabled him to go in and out of the Students Room any hour of the day or night. There was a short walk through the grounds around the government buildings, an area totally uninhabited in the evenings. No lights burned in those offices to indicate that some grave emergency was being dealt with. Only scholars passed that way. The pass was given up to a guard whose desk blocked the entrance to an elevator. The elevator inched up past dark floors to the Students Room at the top, the only lighted space, a big bare room with windows on both sides, long plain wide tables, straight chairs, and piles of books and papers ranged before the students who, at any hour, could be found there. There may have been other nocturnal pleasures available in Ottawa, but no one who worked in the Students Room was concerned with them. People arrived unnoticed, worked on their papers, took notes and disappeared before one noticed they had gone. A few elderly men seemed to be regular customers, or to be held in great esteem, for their books and packets of documents were placed at their accustomed places without their asking for them. More often late arrivals gave the impression of having come in after finishing work on a night shift somewhere to continue their studies of Canadian history.

Around midnight the last attendant left, having brought from the archives enough documents to keep the scholars busy until morning. The Students Room was silent, except for occasional creaking footsteps as someone went to the shelves for additional source material, and for an odd, good-natured interruption at sunrise, when people gathered at the windows that faced east, where they exchanged sardonic comments about the subjects of their studies or, to a newcomer, expressed polite interest in his work. But suddenly there were early morning arrivals on hand—bright-eyed, freshly shaven scholars, who displayed energy even in opening their briefcases, and who set about taking notes with an air of confidence as the students who had worked through the night wearily put away their papers and left.

The Students Room was ideal for the study of history because of its hours, but it was particularly good for the study of the history of the Pacific Northwest. Northwestern history was entangled with ideology in the United States from the start; even the amount of rainfall there was a matter of political dispute, and what the region was really like, and what should be done about it, were questions whose answers involved the admission of free states or slave states into the Union. And as a result the contents of the Canadian archives had the advantage of clarity, in the freedom of English observers from slanted or tendentious writing. Also, in the bins behind the Students Room were photostats of the unpublished journals and the field notes of David Thompson.

Thompson has been called the greatest geographer known to history— or the greatest land geographer, or the greatest natural geographer, as hedges against criticism in this controversial field. Whether he was or not, he was certainly the finest geographer to explore the Pacific Northwest. And his journals, big, black-bound, ledgerlike books, written with a beautifully clear handwriting and enlivened with his eccentric spelling and punctuation, evoke the Pacific Northwest with an immediacy and an accuracy found in no other explorer's writings. Thompson's notes preserved in a cold storage of unpublished freshness the spirit of the

Northwestern wilderness at a time when no other white man had seen it.

David Thompson was born in London on April 30, 1770. So much is known because his birth is recorded in the Register of Births and Baptisms belonging to the Parish of St. John the Evangelist, on Smith Square, London, and the book survived the bombings in the Second World War. An entry on page 137 of Volume II reads:

Born, April 30, 1770, David Thompson, son of
David Thompson, by Ann, his wife, baptized
May 20, 1770.

His father, according to family tradition, was a Welshman named David ap Thomas (meaning David, son of Thomas) who changed his name to Thompson after settling in London. Sixteen pages farther on there is another entry:

Born, January 25, 1772, John Thompson, son of
David Thompson, by his wife Ann, baptized
February 16, 1772.

There is something peculiar about this second entry. The name of the father that was originally written on the line has been erased. The name of David Thompson has been written over the erased place in black ink, different from that used in the other entries in the book, and in a different handwriting from that of the other entries. It is impossible to make out the name that was erased. It could very well have been David ap Thomas, and the correction the Anglicizing of the father's name. But the record of burials in St. John's Church has also been preserved, and this records David Thompson, the father of David and John, the husband of Ann, as among the burials for February, 1772. This entry is likewise in conspicuous black ink, entirely different from the other entries on the page—the same black ink used to record the birth and baptism of John Thompson, and obviously written at a different time from the other entries. Whatever the significance of these alterations, the important matter in the life of David Thompson, the future explorer, was that his father died when he was two years old and his mother was left to care for him and his newborn brother.

She somehow cared for David for five years; the next record of his life appears when he was seven. On Tuesday, April 28, 1777, the directors of the Grey Coat School in London assembled to consider new admissions to the school, and Mr. Abraham Ackworth "was this day pleased to present David Thompson to be admitted. . . ." The Duke of Newcastle was pleased to present Samuel James M'Phearson with the same object. His Grace, the Duke of York, presented a boy named William Vaux. Five others presented the names of three other boys and two girls. All seven applicants were accepted. One of the directors who voted to admit David Thompson to the school was Jeremy Bentham, the philosopher, who lived nearby. The business of admissions did not take long. Most of the discussion of the directors concerned the salaries paid the teachers. The master of mathematics throughout the seven years that David Thompson attended Grey Coat School was Thomas Adams, who received a salary of £7 a year and his room and board.

The school, on Grey Coat Street near Westminster Abbey, was originally part of a hospital, a royal foundation started in Queen Anne's time. It then had about a hundred students (who lived in its building) and a staff of ten people, including a cook and a laundress. In a secluded, almost hidden way the Grey Coat School was beautiful. The school building itself, with wide, stone-floored halls and low-ceilinged rooms, surrounded a big grass-and-stone-paved courtyard and playground, shaded by trees (still standing almost two centuries later) that were old when David Thompson played there. The students wore uniforms: knee breeches and white stockings and gray coats for the boys, and flaring dresses and white stockings for the girls, so much being known because two quaint wooden figures, dating from Queen Anne's time, survived the bombings of London in the Second World War. David was being prepared for a career in the Royal Navy, which accounted for the emphasis on mathematics in his schooling. He was studious, read a good deal—*Robinson Crusoe*, *The Arabian Nights* and *Gulliver's Travels* were his favorite books—was not recorded for any misdoings and won a medal for being the best mathematics student in the school. The Grey Coat School was part of Westminster Abbey, and the schoolboys generally played in the Abbey itself, among the tombs of poets and heroes.

He wanted to be in the Navy, worked with that end in mind and took it for granted that he would follow a naval career. His greatest heroes were naval heroes. But he was not taken into the Navy, and in his later years he was at pains to emphasize that it was not because of any lack of desire on his part, or of a failure to qualify: the reason was that the Navy was greatly reduced after the American Revolution. He was instead apprenticed to the Hudson's Bay Company. Service in the Canadian wilderness was not regarded as a privilege in a seafaring nation at that time. David's schoolmate Samuel M'Phearson ran away rather than go into the service of the Company. At the quarterly meeting of the directors on March 30, 1784, the master of the Grey Coat School reported that "Sam'l M'Pharson, a Math boy, elop'd . . . & is not returned. The said Sam'l M'Pharson was one of the boys intended for the service of the Hudson's Bay Company. . . ."

David was more tractable; a later entry read:

On the 20th May David Thompson, a Math boy
belonging to this Hospital, was bound to the
Hudson's Bay Company, and the Treas. then
paid Mr. Tho's Hutchins, Corresponding
Secretary to the said Company, the sum of
five pounds for taking the said Boy Apprentice
for seven years.

He sailed for Hudson's Bay nine days later. Stationed first at Churchill Factory, then the Company's major post, he worked as a clerk and at fifteen was transferred to York Factory to assist the elderly governor of the Company, Humphrey Morton, "in the writings." The following year David was moved farther inland to serve William Tomison, the Company's senior officer in North America. In 1787, at the age of seventeen, David made his first long Western trip, into the then little-known area of Saskatchewan. He was trained by Philip Turnor, an outstanding explorer even in Canadian history, and learned well; apart from a broken leg at the age of eighteen, caused by an overturned sled, he had no serious accidents in 50,000 miles of wilderness travel.

His apprenticeship ended in 1791, and he was given a three-year contract at £15 a year, increased to £60 three years later. At that salary he was a surveyor, and in addition to map making he located trading posts and trade routes and looked into sources of furs. He was, however, still involved in the routine work of trading for furs. These were the years in which Mackenzie and McKay crossed Canada to the Pacific, and the period in which the North West Company expanded into a dynamic organization that overshadowed the ancient Hudson's Bay Company. Thompson's interest in exploration, especially exploration of the unknown West, amounted to a passion, and difficulties arose with his superiors because he was charged with neglecting business to explore. He made up his mind to leave the Company when he was told that no further surveys could be sanctioned "however the countries yet unknown."

He left on a Sunday morning in May, 1797, at Reindeer Lake. The official in charge there notified his superiors in London:

This morning Mr. David Thompson acquainted me
with his time being up with your Honours, and
thought himself a free-born subject and at
liberty to choose any service he thought most
to his advantage as to quit your service and
enter the Canadian company's Employ.

The North West Company gave him freedom to explore, and he made a great deal of the opportunity, surveying more than 4,000 miles of unknown country in ten months. He went south to the Missouri

River in the Dakotas, and in what became Minnesota he found what he thought was the source of the Mississippi. He also covered the area where the city of Winnipeg was later built. Alexander Mackenzie praised his work, saying that Thompson had accomplished more than the North West Company officers expected him to do in two years. Early in 1799 he made a long trip up the Saskatchewan River to Slave Lake and up the Athabasca River. He descended the Churchill River to the North West Company post at Isle à la Crosse. This was a strategic post at the extreme frontier, near the divide that separates the waters flowing into the Arctic from those that flow into Hudson's Bay.

There, on June 20, 1799, Thompson married Charlotte Small, the half-Indian daughter of one of the original partners of the North West Company. He was then twenty-nine years old; his wife was fourteen. Her father, Patrick Small, was a relative (and the heir) of Major General Small, who had fought as a captain with the British forces at Bunker Hill. Patrick Small was given two of the twenty shares when the North West Company was organized. He himself had married an Indian woman at Isle à la Crosse in his early fur-trading days and raised a large family of half-Indian sons and daughters. He had, however, inherited wealth, in addition to his enormous profits of the North West Company, and retired in 1791. At that time his daughter Charlotte, who became Thompson's wife, was only six years old.

Thompson's was a genuine marriage; his children were baptized, and he and his wife remained a devoted couple throughout their long lives. Their first child, a daughter, was born on the second anniversary of their marriage. They were then living at Rocky Mountain House, a new North West Company post, established near the eastern base of the Rockies—the most remote Western point reached by the fur traders. It had been built by John McDonald, another figure of consequence in North West Company history, a slight, energetic and able Scotsman, intensely religious, a Roman Catholic—Thompson was a Church of England man—who was connected with Thompson by marriage: McDonald had married Patrick Small's daughter Nancy, two years older than Thompson's wife.

In the month that his daughter was born, Thompson made his first attempt to get through the Rockies that rose like a wall on the west. He and James Hughes, with whom he was also connected by marriage— Hughes's daughter was married to Charlotte's brother, that is, Patrick Small's son—headed a party of seven men, with an Indian guide who claimed to know a pass at the headwaters of the Saskatchewan River. Thompson was trying to locate a route to the Pacific south of that followed by Alexander Mackenzie. In the narrow canyons near the headwaters their Indian guide failed them; he could not locate the pass.

"He led us to steep rocks," Thompson wrote, "and we had to return."

Thompson had gained the favor of Alexander Mackenzie. But in the tangled affairs of the North West Company that great explorer was at odds with Simon McTavish, the richest man in Montreal and the dominant figure when the North West Company was organized in 1784: he owned eleven of the original twenty shares. (Simon McTavish's friendship for Patrick Small and for Major General Small led to Patrick Small's partnership.) After McTavish the dominant figure in the North West Company was William McGillivray, his nephew. And McGillivray in turn was connected with the kind of clan, or network of relatives, that was formed around the children of Patrick Small; his wife was the sister of John McDonald. On July 6, 1804, McTavish died suddenly in Montreal on the eve of a meeting of the partners of the North West Company. His death left McGillivray the leading figure among them. When the directors met, four days after McTavish's death, they elected David Thompson a partner also.

Thompson continued to work in the Western outposts. The immense unmapped area west of the Rockies had taken on a new importance because of the Louisiana Purchase in 1803, the implications of which were only beginning to be realized, and assumed an even greater importance when Lewis and Clark set out on their expedition in 1805. In the summer of 1806 Jacques Finlay, a Canadian known as Jaco, scouted a route through the Rockies from the East to the West. He worked under the direction of John McDonald. His route was not far from where Thompson and Hughes had failed to locate a pass five years before. Finlay followed the Saskatchewan River into a canyon north of where the resort town of Banff was later built. He turned south along the eastern edge of the Continental Divide. His task was merely to cut a trail and, at a great river which was reported to lie east of the Rockies, build canoes for Thompson's party to use the following summer.

While Jaco Finlay was going west through the Rockies, the Lewis and Clark party was going east after its damp winter at the mouth of the Columbia. In the wilderness that later became Montana, Meriwether Lewis and eight of his men left the main party to explore other and, it was hoped, easier routes through the mountains. They rode far north, almost to the point where the border between the United States and Canada was eventually drawn. There Lewis and his men fell in with a group of eight Blackfoot warriors. Lewis was not alarmed by this small party, but he suspected they might be the advance unit of a larger force. The Indians and the Americans camped together. The usual night guards were strengthened. It grew cold during the night, and the Indians moved nearer the fire. At dawn one group of Indians rushed to free the Americans' horses. The others tried to make off with the guns. One Indian was stabbed and killed when he grabbed a rifle. Lewis shot and mortally wounded another. The remaining six Indians fled. The Americans recovered all but one of their horses and rounded up twelve horses the Indians had left behind.

This happened on Sunday morning, July 27, 1806. The place was about 300 miles south of where Jaco Finlay (and, a year later, David Thompson) crossed the Rockies. Expecting an immediate pursuit, Lewis and his men rode 80 miles before dark on that day, wearing out their horses, and then rode 20 miles by moonlight, until they passed through a herd of buffalo whose movements wiped out their tracks. They rejoined the main party without further incident and, in fact, as the party was nearing Missouri River travel again, the worst of the trials of the expedition were over. But the results of the tragic incident—the only violence in Lewis and Clark's crossing of the continent, and the first bloodshed in the wars of the United States Army and the Plains Indians—were disastrous; the fighting that began there went on in one form or another for eighty years.

II

Early in the spring of the next year Thompson began preparations to cross the Rockies and build a chain of posts in the river valleys between their western slopes. He worked with great secrecy to avoid alarming the Indians, to evade rival traders of the Hudson's Bay Company, and to anticipate American advances into the Pacific Northwest which were expected to follow Meriwether Lewis's great achievement. In the North West headquarters at Fort William, on the western end of Lake Superior, Thompson was given a copy of Lewis's report of his findings— that historic letter which also stimulated Astor to found Astoria. Thompson copied Lewis's letter and also copied out Vancouver's description of his explorations of Puget Sound. But he made no such elaborate plans as had these explorers. He sent ahead of him an ordinary working force of five men, under Finian McDonald, a redheaded giant 6 feet 4 inches tall, who traveled up the Saskatchewan in canoes, outwardly no different from any North West Company trading party. They were instructed to camp deep in the mountains and wait for Thompson to join them.

He himself set out from Rocky Mountain House on May 10, 1807, with his wife and three children. The eldest, Fanny, was then seven, a son, Samuel, was three, and Emma was an eleven-month-old infant. The family traveled with three North West Company employees and ten horses. Their route was along the Continental Divide, where peaks nearly 12,000 feet high rose sharply in the west. An easier pass (where the Trans-Canada Highway was later built) was only 25 miles south, but Thompson was anxious to avoid Indian trouble, and the higher and more rugged route was hidden and unused. To his surprise the Indians seemed to have vanished from the region. He surmised they had moved south because they expected war with the Americans. Exaggerated reports of Meriwether Lewis's conflict with the Blackfeet had reached Thompson; he believed that Lewis had killed the Indians in cold blood, and he thought the Indians were assembling to attack the next Americans to appear.

The snow at the height of land was too heavy to attempt a crossing. Thompson camped his party for two weeks. They were between the glaciers later known as Freshfield Icefield and Wapta Icefield, 2 to 3 miles apart, in a maze of pyramid-shaped peaks. "The rushing of Snow down the Sides of the Mountains equalled the Thunder in Sound," Thompson wrote. "Scarcely an hour passed without hearing one."

When the snow melted, the party moved on along the headwaters of the Saskatchewan until they dwindled to a small stream. At two o'clock in the afternoon of June 23, 1807, they came to another small stream flowing westward. They followed it down as it descended through canyons to the west slope. This was where Jaco Finlay had marked a trail, but his trail was useless. In one day they made only a mile and three-quarters. They scrambled back and forth across a mountain torrent, sliding down steep pitches and plunging into thickets on the stream bank. The stream became a river, later known as the Blaeberry, and after five days of slow descent they found that it emptied into a powerful river, a hundred yards wide, flowing due north through a valley that varied from 1 to 12 miles across.

This was the Columbia, the great River of the West, but they did not know it, nor could they see how, with its northward flow toward the Arctic, it could reverse its course and become the river that Lewis had seen far south. In the warm midsummer days the valley was secluded and windless, pale grass and reeds along the river edge and dark evergreen forests above them edging back to the base of the mountains that rose steeply on both sides. Behind them were the Rockies that seemed to be a solid wall, two miles high; ahead of them, across the Columbia, the peaks of another range rose humped and awkward-looking, three-quarters of the way to their summits, and then soared to knife-edged flint pyramids, with flat snow planes on their sides—a sea of mountains, a range that was old and weathered before the Rocky Mountains had emerged from the sea. Thompson called them the Nelson Mountains after Admiral Nelson; later generations renamed them the Selkirks.

The canoes that Finlay had left were useless. Thompson's party went slowly up the river—that is, traveling due south—along its wavering banks. Ten miles above the Blaeberry a big river, the Kicking Horse, poured into the Columbia with terrific violence. But for the most part there were only small streams cascading into the Columbia through narrow gorges or curving through groves of trees into the narrow plain. There were more than a hundred such streams in 50 miles. As they moved toward its source, the great river became narrow and clear. A lake about 6 miles long, later called Lake Windermere, lay enclosed by grassy hills, and the river, where it poured from the lake, was only 30 feet wide, deep and cold and with a steady flow, fed by brooks and springs. Another small, swift-flowing stream connected with a lake still larger, a lake without a visible source, later named Columbia Lake. This was the true source of the Columbia. Willows and pines lined the lakeshore. To the east, open rolling country extended to the distant Rockies. On the west was a massive rounded mountain he estimated at 12,000 feet—Mount Nelson was Thompson's name for it—with snow and glacial ice far down its sides. Herds of wild horses grazed on its slopes. In less than three hundred years "these amazing creatures"—his term for them—had spread from Cortez's Mexico to find their way through the mountains to this wild sanctuary. From their number he guessed that the winters were mild and there were no predators.

Southward, like a notch in the sight of a rifle, was an opening between the Selkirks and the Rockies that reached far down into American territory—or into territory then unclaimed, but which the Americans were entering. But Thompson's interest was concentrated on the river. "This is a fine sheet of Water," he wrote of Columbia Lake, "deep, clear, without reeds." The sources of other rivers were diffused in rills and brooks and swamps, until it was difficult to determine the parent stream, but here was a great spring-fed lake "from which issues its wild rapid Stream . . . its descent is great."

The descent of the river is great indeed; it falls more than half a mile in its erratic 1,250-mile course to the sea. The natural power of the river is beyond calculation, but its power to chain men's imagination has been even greater. The Columbia has always been a river of destiny, shaping history by its legend before it was known to exist in reality, generating claims to international boundaries before anyone even knew where it ran. Thompson was awed by the river whose source he had discovered. "Many reflections came to my mind," he wrote on one occasion. "A new world, in a sense, lay before me." And at another time, in a philosophic mood, he wrote:

Here among this stupendous and solitary wild, covered with eternal Snow and Mountain connected to Mountain by immense Glaciers, the collection of Ages on which the Beames of the Sun makes hardly any

Impression. . . . One is tempted to enquire what may be the volume of water contained in the immense quantities of Snow brought to, and lodged on, the Mountains, from the Pacific Ocean, and how from an Ocean of salt water the immense evaporation is constantly going on in pure fresh water; these are mysterious operations on a scale so vast the human mind is lost in contemplation.

He could not, of course, know the course of the Columbia, though he guessed at it with remarkable accuracy. The river runs due north for 232 miles after leaving Columbia Lake and seems headed for the Arctic Ocean. At the northernmost point of the Selkirk Mountains, at a place later called Big Bend, the river turns sharply west and then south. Between Columbia Lake and Big Bend the Columbia picks up the flow of 160 creeks and rivers. The elevation of Columbia Lake is 2,657 feet above sea level. At Big Bend it is 1,950 feet above sea level. Near the bend itself, where the river flows through a gorge, the rapids are almost continuous, but there are no falls on the upper river. The Columbia rather creates a kind of gigantic flume as it races through the dense woods that come down to the water's edge. Rounded or bowl-shaped stones half the size of a man's head line the banks as though hammered into place. Below the stone walls formed by these are narrow beaches of overlapping stones, beyond which the water is deep; and the river itself is free of boulders, nothing checking the rush and weight of the water. A thousand miles from the sea the Columbia is around 500 feet wide, more than 12 feet deep, surging at 12 miles an hour. In the 465 miles that the river flows in Canada its volume is increased by 474 creeks and rivers; at what became the international boundary it is 2,000 feet across, and still 1,300 feet above sea level.

At the headwaters of the Columbia, less than a mile from Columbia Lake, across a gravel plain covered with saplings, another river, the Kootenay, flows south, a river so powerful that when Thompson put a canoe in it "the waters make a hissing sound, as if full of small icicles." In other words, these two great rivers were flowing side by side, but in opposite directions, perhaps the most baffling problem, in an unmapped country, that a geographer ever faced. No river system on earth contains anything like the perplexing relationship of these two streams. The Kootenay, flowing south, curves inland and flows through 400 miles of mountain country before heading north into Canada again to form 80-mile-long Kootenay Lake, whose outlet joins the Columbia, the two rivers, separated by only a few hundred yards at Columbia Lake, going their separate ways for nearly a thousand miles before they come together.

Thompson was not the only traveler to feel the mystery of the Columbia or to sense something of lasting importance freighted along its dark wild passage. High in the mountains its power is startling, "filling

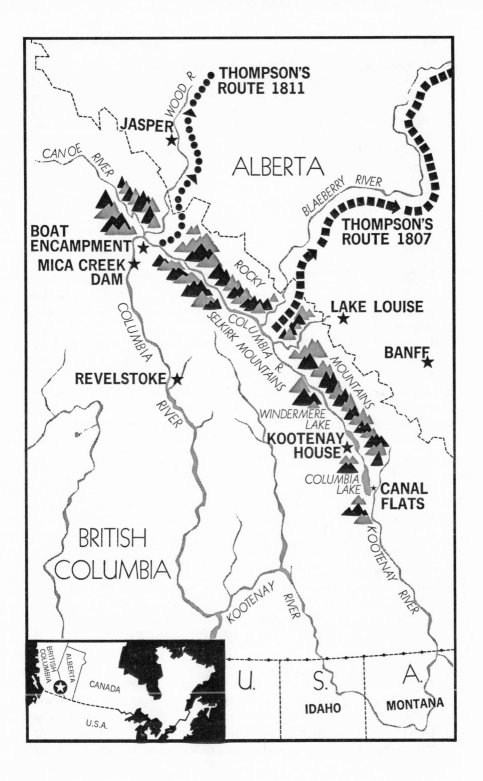

THOMPSON'S
ROUTE 1811

WOOD R.

JASPER

CANOE RIVER

ALBERTA

BLAEBERRY RIVER

THOMPSON'S
ROUTE 1807

BOAT
ENCAMPMENT
MICA CREEK
DAM

ROCKY

COLUMBIA

COLUMBIA R.

SELKIRK MOUNTAINS

LAKE LOUISE

BANFF

REVELSTOKE

COLUMBIA

RIVER

MOUNTAINS

WINDERMERE
LAKE

KOOTENAY
HOUSE

COLUMBIA
LAKE

CANAL
FLATS

BRITISH

COLUMBIA

KOOTENAY RIVER

KOOTENAY RIVER

BRITISH
COLUMBIA

ALBERTA

CANADA

U.S.A.

U.   S.   A.

IDAHO   MONTANA

the mind with awe," as the botanist David Douglas wrote. The river is rarely turbulent; the water seems to slide down an incline, the smooth stones offering scarcely more resistance than so many ball bearings. The air along the riverbanks vibrates with its power. On the upper Columbia it is easy to believe a statement that otherwise seems incredible: the fall of the Columbia contains a third of all the water power produced by all the rivers of North America.

III

The first weeks of Thompson's stay on the Columbia were discouraging. He built a house at the southernmost point of Columbia Lake, but by the time it was finished the weather was warm and the game disappeared. His men put nets in the lake and in the Columbia "but found to our great mortification not a single fish in them." They lived on berries and wild swans. In the midst of this crisis, on August 10, 1807, a party of visiting Indians told Thompson his settlement was doomed. They said a big force of Americans—forty-two men in all—was building a fort at the junction of the Snake River and the Columbia, a few days' travel to the south. The Indians said that the Americans were going to build a chain of forts all the way down the Columbia to its mouth.

Thompson never learned where the Indians got their information, or misinformation. There was no American party on land within a thousand miles. It was true that the St. Louis fur trader, Manuel Lisa, was then on his way to the Rockies with a small force, but he planned only to reach the Yellowstone River on the far eastern slope of the mountains. An American ship, the *Quatamozin* of Boston, happened to be on the Columbia River near the sea; it had been trading along the Northwest coast since 1806, and in July, 1807, while Thompson was building his post, the *Quatamozin* spent two weeks on the lower river. But neither the far-distant land party of Manuel Lisa nor the shipload of Boston traders could be considered builders of forts along the Columbia. The only notable fact about the Indians' rumor was that it came at a moment when Thompson's party was already discouraged by a near famine.

They remained, foraging for whatever food they could find. Salmon suddenly appeared in Columbia Lake, big fish, each weighing about 25 pounds, and five were speared the first day. But that brought another hazard. Indians generally raided after the salmon runs began, so they would not have to carry food. Every running stream was then a larder. Thompson's house was open to attack from the east. The Rockies in that direction were relatively low and easy to cross, and the Indian tribes east of the mountains were numerous and warlike. They were the Piegans, a northern branch of the Blackfoot. Long years of contact with the fur traders had equipped them with guns. They made a practice of crossing the Rockies in sudden merciless attacks on the Kootenay Indians on the west side, who, of course, had as yet no access to traders and no firearms. To get beyond the reach of such a foray, Thompson moved to the west side of Lake Windermere, where he put up a three-sided stockade, protecting four small log houses, on a terraced slope above the lake. He called it Kootenay House and prepared it for defense and laid in supplies for the winter.

Between the Russian fort at Sitka in Alaska, built five years before, and the Spanish mission on San Francisco Bay, almost two thousand miles apart, his was the only white settlement. To the south of his cabins there was no settled region nearer than New Mexico and, to the southeast, none nearer than St. Louis, some 1,800 miles distant. His post was in an area of two million square miles uninhabited by white men, the only civilized household in a region five times the size of the original thirteen American colonies. Thompson said they lived "in tolerable comfort." Game reappeared when the weather grew cool. The men brought in deer, antelope and mountain sheep, storing the meat in the low glaciers of the Selkirks.

A few Indians from the Piegan tribe appeared from east of the Rockies. Two women were with them, indicating that it was not a war party. Thompson feared they were spies for a larger party to follow, and he was alarmed when groups of wanderers appeared, until forty Indians were camped nearby. He invited a few of them to come inside the stockade, at different times, to show them the strength of the walls. He had no hope of preventing an attack by the threat of punishment if they wiped out his party. They knew there were no white people near enough to punish them. But they would recognize from the strength of the stockade that the defenders could inflict very heavy casualties before they were all killed.

He did not know it then, but a war party of three hundred Indians, a combination of several tribes from east of the Rockies, had assembled only 20 miles east of his post. The war party was commanded by three chiefs who, fortunately, were suspicious of each other. One of the chiefs had traded with Thompson earlier and knew him to be fair and honest, a factor that probably prevented the destruction of Kootenay House. The war party sent two men to Thompson, ostensibly on a friendly visit but with the real purpose of discovering the size of the force defending the stockade. Thompson invited these two newcomers into the house and showed them how well the Canadians were prepared for defense. During their visit two Kootenay Indians arrived with furs to trade. The Kootenays were no longer defenseless. Thompson provided some of them with guns, eventually trading twenty guns. "Their eyes glared on the Peagans like Tigers," Thompson wrote. "This was most fortunate."

He understood that the Piegans would think that the visit had been staged for their benefit, that he had made a pact with the Kootenays to supply them with guns in return for their help in defending the post. The Kootenays had suffered too much from the raids of the Piegans; there was no fear that they might join the other Indians in a joint attack after they were armed. Thompson gave his Piegan visitors many presents to take back to their chiefs. As soon as they left, he prepared for an immediate attack. But it did not come. He learned in later years that when the two spies reported to the war camp, the younger warriors demanded war at once, or at least pretended to want war in order to undermine the older chiefs. The older chiefs were uncertain. They did not like the idea of fighting the Kootenays, now armed and eager for vengeance. And they were impressed by Thompson's presents. In the end the decision came down to the one chief who had earlier dealings with Thompson east of the Rockies. He had no quarrel with Thompson and decided against war.

The weather was growing colder; the Rockies were now white, and the Indians from the plains had to return east soon before the passes were blocked or made difficult by snow. As a precaution, Thompson stationed part of his small force at the first house he had built on Columbia Lake to guard against a surprise attack through the mountains. It was under Finian McDonald, Thompson's friend and companion for many years. But there were no signs of the Piegans, and in fact Kootenay House, which remained in existence for years, was not threatened again.

With the departure of the Indians, and food again plentiful when the deer returned with cooler weather, Thompson went on taming horses. Part of the big herds on the slopes of the mountains, the horses collected to graze on the wide pastures back from the shores of Lake Windermere, only 2 miles from the stockade. The scent of man appeared to disturb and yet attract them. When he approached, they "appeared at a loss what to do; they seemed inclined to run away, yet remained. Their nostrils distended, manes erect, and tail straight out, prancing and snorting about in a wild manner." He marveled that a horse with a rider could always overtake another horse, tame or wild, without a rider. He and his men chased them on horseback, selecting the horse they wanted and following it in relays until it was exhausted. "As these hills are covered with short grass," he wrote, "and very little wood, we easily kept them in sight. It was a wild steeple chase, down hills and up others."

His first wild horse was a fine iron gray. The human odor was so terrifying to the animal that at first contact the skin of its head was contorted. He kept it tied between two tame horses. In the stockade itself he tied the animal near his house, where it would become accustomed to people. Soon it was tractable and liked to have Thompson pass his hand across its nostrils. It was then easily broken to the bit and saddled, and he used the gray to run down and capture others.

IV

Someone, somewhere, knew of Thompson's whereabouts. In December, 1807, two letters were delivered to Thompson at Kootenay House by an Indian. They created one of the most baffling mysteries of early Northwestern history. They were, or seemed to be, intercepted letters, containing new United States Army regulations prohibiting persons other than citizens of the United States from trading with the Indians. One was dated July 10, 1807, and the other September 29, 1807. One was sent from an American army post called Fort Lewis, Yellow River, Columbia. There was no such post. One letter was signed by Captain Zachary Perch, commanding officer, and the other by Lieutenant Jeremy Pinch. No officers with these names were ever in the service of the Army of the United States. And no regulations of the sort contained in the letters were ever issued.

Where could they possibly have come from? For years Northwestern historians brooded over the enigma. Thompson himself disregarded them. He may have thought that the fabricated regulations were genuine, for he tended to believe that Americans were capable of any deceit or foolishness, but he was sure there were no Americans near enough to enforce them.

In the spring he left Finian McDonald in charge at Kootenay House and explored and traded along the Kootenay, going south, to what became Glacier National Park in Montana and into Idaho, and north to Kootenay Lake, before rejoining Finian McDonald to take the entire company east over the Rockies. It was now June, 1808, and on their eastward crossing the weather remained fine. The venture had been remarkably successful, even though they had lost several packs of furs in the Kootenay floods. Tragedy threatened at the headwaters of the Saskatchewan, when they prepared to leave camp on the morning of June 19, 1808. One of the horses broke away while its pack was being tied and raged through camp among the terrified children. Thompson killed it, almost the only instance in his journals in which he acted on impulse—he described it in his diary, but left it out of his narrative of his western travels. "One of the horses nearly crushing my children," he wrote, "I shot him on the spot and rescued my little ones." Later he decided that the horse was not vicious; the pack had been tied in a fashion that frenzied it.

The next morning there was another alarm. When the party set out, his older daughter, Fanny, could not be found. She had merely strayed away from camp, but an eight-year-old girl lost in the wild country was a terrifying thought, and the difficulties of the party were increased because Mrs. Thompson was then seven months pregnant with her fourth child. Fanny was found, and that same day the party reached navigable water at the eastern end of the defile. The canoes that Finian McDonald had hidden the year before were still there, and in good condition. The Saskatchewan was high, a wide, green river whose current was racing eastward at ten miles an hour. They started at sunrise. Some of the party took the horses overland to Rocky Mountain House. Thompson and his family and three of the men and an Indian hunter rode in a canoe. The current caught the long gray craft and drove it forward into the Canadian prairies with the speed of a galloping horse. There was no attempt to paddle, except to steer the canoe away from rocks. Waves formed, and the water foamed high around boulders and fallen trees whose roots had lodged in the riverbed, but the high water leveled the rapids. They sped along at the edge of turbulent passages, bursting through standing waves that sent torrents of water over the canoe, and by midday the mountains were far behind them. The river was widening through the low hills but still flowing fast. Every few miles another fast-flowing mountain stream joined it to give new impetus to its current. About four o'clock in the afternoon the current suddenly slowed, and the paddles were used for the first time. Three hours of paddling took them another 15 miles.

They came to a limestone cliff about 50 feet high on one side of the river, with a sandy beach before it, that made a natural campsite. They beached the canoe and began their separate tasks. Thompson started a fire, his customary duty at the end of a day of travel. The men gathered wood. A kettle was placed on the fire, and they rested before the evening meal. Thompson wrote in his journal his reckonings of latitude and longitude. He usually jotted notes beside his columns of figures, such things as "moose plenty" or "willows budding." This time he wrote, "All safe on shore." He noticed one of the Indians sitting with his hands on his knees, his head bowed in his hands, and thought he was sick. He asked, "What is the matter?"

The Indian looked at him. "I cannot make myself believe that we have come here in one day," he said. "It must be two days, and I have not slept."

When Thompson finished his observations, he calculated they had covered 132 miles that day.

V

In the years between 1807 and 1812 Thompson crossed the Rockies repeatedly, establishing a chain of trading posts in Idaho, Montana and eastern Washington, and was in charge of the Columbia district of the North West Company. His achievement in this respect was remarkable, but it was obscured in later years by the controversy that developed over British and American claims to the Columbia River. In the fall of 1810 Thompson was placed in charge of a party of twenty-four men which was to cross the Rockies and establish additional trading posts. Little credit was given his genuine accomplishments because his critics insisted that he had failed in his major task: to build a British post at the mouth of the Columbia before Astor's men on the *Tonquin* could reach there. No orders directing him to build such a post were ever found, and Thompson at no time gave any indication of being engaged in a race to get there before Astor's men. But in retrospect a case could be made that he had failed to take the steps that would have secured Oregon and Washington, and perhaps Montana and Idaho as well, for Great Britain.

A party of twenty-four men was far larger than his usual trading party. As was customary, this force went on ahead into the mountains. Thompson traveled some time later with his partner and friend William Henry, who was also a notable character in North West Company history. The twenty-four men started to cross the Rockies by the pass that Thompson had previously used, which had become the main travel route of the North West Company to the Columbia district. On their way to join them, Thompson and Henry met the men coming back. They reported that the Indians refused to let them through. This was the first interference offered by the Indians to Thompson's passage through the mountains. If Thompson was responsible for failure at any point, it was in not investigating the report, or in not forcing a passage through despite the Indians. His brother-in-law, John McDonald, the following year crossed by this same pass without interference. But Thompson accepted the report without question and set about finding another route.

He took a few of the men north, leaving the Saskatchewan and crossing to the Athabasca, only 150 miles in a direct line but much farther by river and mountain travel. Moving upstream on the Athabasca, they came to the Whirlpool River, a small tributary that dropped steeply from the Rockies. Their way up the Whirlpool was through narrow defiles with mountain slopes on both sides. It was now winter. The temperature dropped to 20 degrees below zero on December 29, 1810, when they set out for the final climb. Thompson had eight men, three horses and sixteen sled dogs. The snow was so deep the horses could not travel through it and were sent back to a winter camp where William Henry was in charge. At higher altitudes a new fall of soft snow left the dogs floundering helplessly. They were sent back with the horses, and the men struggled ahead with their packs. There was enough food: on New Year's Day, 1811, they killed two woods buffalo and a mountain goat. Their pass led along a narrow river for 30 miles, with the mountain later known as Mount Hooker, 10,782 feet high, on the side, and a 9,000-foot peak on the other, their glaciers nearly touching.

They reached the height of land, not quite 6,000 feet, on January 10, 1811, and made camp at the base of a glacier. Immense tracks in the snow that looked like the footprints of a giant alarmed the men. Thompson was sure that they were the tracks of a grizzly, enlarged because the outlines had melted and then frozen again, but the men thought they were the tracks of one of the prehistoric monsters that were then believed to have survived in the Rockies. They kept by a great fire and to reassure themselves talked about the brilliancy of the stars that seemed to be almost within reach overhead.

A glacial wall almost 2,000 feet high rose in a glassy-green expanse only a few hundred yards from their camp. In the distance, to the west, the land sloped away to what Thompson was sure must be the valley of the Columbia. A half mile of steep descent took the men to the timberline. A small brook was visible there, dropping to the west. The frozen creek bed fell away sharply and became the channel of a river, later known as Wood River. The weather was warmer. Game was plentiful; they killed two moose as they entered the woods. The trees, even near the timberline, were large, some of them more than 6 feet through. The route down from the heights zigzagged back and forth across the river, crossing it seventeen times on one day and thirty-seven times the next.

The men wanted to turn back. Thompson's name for the Wood River was the Flat Heart, "from the men being so dispirited." In a week of slow travel the party reached a point where the Wood came out of its deep canyon and poured into a wide plain to join a wider river, undoubtedly the Columbia. Thompson had reached the Columbia at the precise point where the river rounds the Selkirks at Big Bend and turns west and south, an amazing demonstration of geographical instinct, and he had done so in the dead of winter, in the first winter crossing of the Rockies recorded.

The plain was covered with huge cedar trees 12 feet in diameter, and spruce and fir trees even larger, as much as 15 feet through, rising 200 feet or more to their first lofty branches. There was only a light snowfall here, and the air was warm. The party tried to continue downstream beside the Columbia. It was now frozen, except at the strongest rapids, and often there was no room for passage along the riverbanks. The effort was exhausting, and after several miles the men refused to go farther. Thompson himself was not sure where the river would lead them, and returned to Big Bend. He next tried to lead them upstream to the protection of Kootenay House. Here, however, was another geographical paradox. The most violent passage of the Columbia in its entire course is in the few miles upstream from Big Bend. The river pours through a narrow chasm at what later became known as Surprise Rapids—a great cleft in the rocks, the aftermath of some ancient earthquake that split the mountains and, draining a former lake, formed the Columbia itself. So the way upstream was infinitely more difficult than the downstream attempt had been. The dense forest and the tangled underbrush beside the river made winter travel impossible. The very mountains remained unclimbed there for more than a century, not because they were difficult to climb but because the problems of approaching them were as difficult as those of any other mountain range on earth.

Three rivers converge at Big Bend: the Columbia, the Wood, and a river flowing from the north that Thompson named the Canoe River. A short distance above the Big Bend itself, on the banks of the Columbia, the men built a cedar cabin and prepared to spend the winter there. They were surprised to find the days mild and the snowfall light. They were in a warm belt, where warm currents from the Pacific, funneling along the Columbia, are boxed in at the bend of the river and create a pocket of mild weather surrounded by icy mountains. (The average winter temperature there is 5 degrees warmer than it is a hundred miles south, and the snowfall is two feet less.) The Canoe River was never frozen. Deer and moose were plentiful. Elsewhere the deer were walled into yards as the snow accumulated. They formed clearings where they fed as the first snow fell, and later snows formed high banks on the edges of these, confining them to frigid yards where wolves slaughtered them. But in the comparatively open woods of the Canoe River valley they had freedom of movement all winter. "Our hunting grounds are the Canoe River and its banks,"

Thompson wrote. "The snow is much wasted and in this fine valley the Moose Deer can move freely about."

He worked at building boats to float down the Columbia. The bark of the birch trees growing west of the Rockies could not be used to build the kind of birch-bark canoes used elsewhere for travel throughout Canada and the northern United States. Dugouts carved from a single cedar log, after the Indian fashion, were beyond their skill as wood carvers. Thompson built wooden frames, like those of birch-bark canoes, and cut thin sheets of cedar, lacing them together in the way that softened sheets of birch bark were laced to make canoes east of the Rockies.

They did not inspire confidence among his small force. Three men decided to leave the company and go back over the mountains. After they left, Thompson sent two others after them, with letters of explanation, and a request for men and supplies, to William Henry in the winter camp on the Athabasca. There were now only two men remaining with Thompson in his camp which, because of his boat-building venture, he called Boat Encampment.

The two men he had sent to William Henry returned with help and two sleds loaded with goods and provisions. By that time the weather was often pleasant. On the morning of March 11, 1811, Thompson waked to find the skies clear, the mountains visible a great distance away. At two o'clock, when the temperature reached 32 degrees, he saw "a white-headed eagle"—a bald eagle. The next day small birds were everywhere. Ten days later the country was warm and sunny, the temperature ranging between 40 and 50 degrees. The river was rising rapidly, as much as 3 inches overnight.

Just at that time, on March 23, 1811, Captain Thorne on the *Tonquin* was approaching the mouth of the Columbia. It was while Thompson was preparing to start down the river that Thorne sent two boatloads of his crew to their deaths at the bar. Ice on the river, and a sudden storm, delayed Thompson's departure. With the few men he had, travel directly down the Columbia was out of the question; he had to go upstream to Kootenay House to get more men from the posts he had established earlier. He was, in fact, already too late if his purpose had been to beat Astor's men. By the time he left Boat Encampment, on April 17, 1811, a shore party had landed from the *Tonquin* and was at work on the fort at Astoria.

As soon as Thompson left the sanctuary of Boat Encampment, the weather became cold and disagreeable. The snow was 3½ feet deep along the banks of the Columbia, where they dragged their boat and struggled over fallen trees. On the heights above them "the Country every where is yet like the depths of winter." They had 90 miles of desperately hard travel to the mouth of the Blaeberry—"the Rapids may be said to touch each other, and most of them dangerous, full of large Rocks or Stones, with cascades of Water, very strong." Then there was relatively easy progress to his old post at Kootenay House, through a spring landscape with willows budding and great flights of wild geese. He raced down the Kootenay to the posts he had established in Idaho, added four men to his party and with these crossed overland to the Columbia with a pack train of thirteen horses.

He started down the Columbia below Kettle Falls on July 3, 1811, and reached Astoria eleven days later. The fort had been building for four months. The *Tonquin* had sailed on its trading voyage, but its loss was not then known. Washington Irving in *Astoria* wrote, "Mr. Thompson could be considered as little better than a spy in the camp. . . ." Ross Cox, the author of *The Columbia River*, who was in Astoria at the time, said:

> In the month of July, Mr. David Thompson, astronomer to the North-West Company, of which he was also a proprietor, arrived with nine men in a canoe at Astoria, from the interior. This gentleman came on a voyage of discovery to the Columbia, preparatory to the North-West Company forming a settlement at the entrance of the river. He remained at Astoria until the latter end of July, when he took his departure for the interior, Mr. David Stuart, with three clerks and a party of Canadians accompanying him, for the purpose of selecting a proper place on the upper parts of the river for a trading establishment.

Thompson made a few short trips from the fort itself. He wrote of the Willamette Valley: "The whole of the River is very beautiful and rich Country and happy Climate." His men wanted to see the ocean. From the size of the waves on Lake Superior they had expected great waves on the lower Columbia and were disappointed at its smooth surface. The day after their arrival he led them across the river and climbed a hill from which they could see the breakers. There at last they were convinced that the Pacific Ocean was bigger than Lake Superior. "On the shores of the Ocean," Thompson wrote, "the agitation of the sea is constantly breaking against the rocky shore in great surges. . . ."

He was back at Boat Encampment in mid-September, 1811. William Henry was on his way over the Rockies with supplies, but he had not arrived, so Thompson left a letter for him at the cabin and poled up the Canoe. He found it a small but beautiful river, "its breadth 30 yards, the water clear over a bed of pebbles and small stones. It flowed through a bold rude valley, of a steady descent, which gave to this River a very rapid descent without any falls; yet such was the slope of its current that by close examination I estimated its

change of level to be full three feet in each 120 feet." After five days
of quiet and leisurely travel, messengers arrived with word that William Henry had reached Boat Encampment; Thompson and his men
raced back down the river, covering in six hours what had taken days
of travel upstream.

Thompson's life work was nearly over. He made one more trip
across the Rockies in 1812, traveling to the posts he had set up in
Idaho and Montana. He also explored land that was new to him,
journeying as far south as the place where the city of Missoula was
later built, and there he turned aside to study the route of Lewis and
Clark through the mountains. But he was increasingly involved in the
administration of the Department of Columbia of the North West
Company, sometimes in disagreement with the partners over policy;
and the North West Company itself was entering a period of crisis
in its struggle with the Hudson's Bay Company. Astoria was taken by
the British in the War of 1812, and the American fur-trading posts
in the Northwest were given up and subsequently sold by Astor to the
North West Company—Thompson's brother-in-law John McDonald
being sent from London to take possession of Astoria itself. Under
these conditions there was little opportunity for exploration. Such op-
portunities as remained were further reduced when something close
to armed warfare broke out in the wilderness between the Hudson's
Bay men and those of the North West Company.

Canadian history is often hard going for someone not a native of
Canada, for much of it deals with the ramifications of the Hudson's
Bay Company that remained a powerful influence in Canada and
nourished a blameless view of its own past. The rise of the North
West Company when its ancient rival was stagnant and nearly bankrupt had been astonishing; the sudden rejuvenation of Hudson's Bay
was no less so. (At one point the North West partners decided not
to buy the older company, thinking they were going to get its property
in any case after it failed.) One powerful factor in the revitalization
of Hudson's Bay was Thomas Douglas, the fifth Earl of Selkirk. In
his childhood the ancestral home at the mouth of the River Dee had
been shelled by John Paul Jones during the American Revolution—
Jones planned to capture the Earl of Selkirk—and the young lord
grew up with a hatred and fear of the United States that dominated
his later life. In 1807 Lord Selkirk married the daughter of one of
the largest shareholders in the Hudson's Bay Company. He was influenced in his view of Canada by Colin Robertson, a former North
West Company official (who had been discharged, incidentally, by
John McDonald), and his projects were on a heroic scale. By 1810
Selkirk virtually owned the Company. In 1811 the Company gave him

title to a tract of land, as large as a European nation, that extended over Saskatchewan and Manitoba and south over North Dakota and Minnesota. Selkirk launched great colonizing ventures, first in eastern Canada and later on the prairies, in order to offset the emigration of natives of the British Isles from the United States. The colony, located on the prairie where Winnipeg was later built, met hostility from the French-Canadian employees of the North West Company, and their antagonism, already evidenced in armed battles in the woods, came to a bloody climax in the battle of Seven Oaks in 1816, in which Governor Robert Semple of the Hudson's Bay Company and twenty of his twenty-seven men were killed. Selkirk himself died in 1820, at the age of forty-eight, and in 1821 the British government ordered the North West Company to merge with Hudson's Bay.

Thompson was not temperamentally equipped to take part in these bloody doings. The takeover wiped out the positions of many of his friends as well as his own. The names he had given to places he had first explored were often changed; the Nelson Mountains became the Selkirks. He retired to a farm near Montreal and, apart from service when the United States–Canadian boundary was explored, did no further exploring. His children settled in eastern Canada, some of them becoming government employees. He read a great deal, wrote the great *Narrative of His Explorations in Western America, 1784–1812* and was remembered as having been quiet and uncommunicative, though he enjoyed the visits of his grandchildren and liked to take them out at night and teach them the names of the stars. Washington Irving, while writing *Astoria*, visited him and tried to buy his papers, but Thompson would not sell them, and they apparently did not get along very well, for Irving's comments on Thompson were sparse and grudging. Thompson died on February 10, 1857, his wife three months later. There was no newspaper account of the death of "this greatest geographer . . . whose work is unparalleled in the history of North America."

VI

Thompson epitomizes the hidden Northwest: he was among its most original and creative figures, but one who was ignored in its history and whose contribution was not diffused into the stream of its popular culture. Reading Thompson's field notes in the silence of the Students Room in Ottawa gave one the impression of looking at old-fashioned photographs made on glass plates, with their bright unvaried light, sharp outlines and unsparing images. He left thirty-nine volumes of his journals as well as the long *Narrative of His Explorations*, and while the crucial volume of his journal for the year 1811 disappeared, he also left eleven volumes of his field notes, and among these were his notes for 1811. None of his work was published in his lifetime. In 1888 Joseph Burr Tyrrell, a Canadian geologist who had worked a good deal in the Canadian Rockies, first called attention to Thompson's achievements in a paper published in the *Canadian Institute Proceedings*. Dr. Tyrrell could find no likeness of Thompson, an unusual circumstance in itself, since the walls of Montreal were almost festooned with portraits of individuals connected with the fur trade. He did, however, locate an elderly man who had known Thompson, and who described the explorer as a stocky man, with squarish features and black hair cut in short bangs across his forehead. He said Thompson resembled the steel engravings of John Bunyan that used to be found in old editions of *Pilgrim's Progress*.

Dr. Tyrrell's labors in bringing Thompson's achievements to light were almost unequaled in historical scholarship. He bought Thompson's papers and spent about twenty years retracing Thompson's path through the wilderness, checking his diaries and field notes against the localities he wrote about and identifying the persons with whom Thompson had been associated. His findings were incorporated into a magnificent edition of Thompson's *Narrative*, published by the Champlain Society of Montreal in 1916.

The book was, however, limited to 550 subscribers, and while scholars quarried it, Thompson's name was still unknown to the general public. Only the Thompson River in British Columbia was named for him, an important and often beautiful river but one which, oddly enough, Thompson himself had never seen. In 1922 the first public ceremony honoring Thompson's memory was held, and in 1927 a stone was erected marking the site of Kootenay House. Eleven years later Thompson's original post on the banks of Lake Windermere was set aside as a historic monument. There followed a period in which Thompson came to be regarded almost with veneration. This was particularly the case with American writers, and especially with scholars in the Northwest, who prized him not only for his practical achievements, magnificent as they were, but for the human qualities that shone through his writings, his sagacity and humor, his love of humanity and his common sense and ceaseless interest that invested the most remote part of the world with a sense of life that carried timelessly through the years.

A reaction against his reputation set in, especially among English writers, culminating in the work of Arthur Morton, who dismissed the praise of the explorer as sentimental and attributed deceit and cunning to Thompson throughout his life. The burden of the attacks on

Thompson was that he lacked both the singleness of purpose required to achieve the ends of empire and that hardness and inflexibility found among genuine historic figures which would have carried him past whatever Indian threats lay in his way across the mountains. Morton's work suffers from an unfamiliarity with the perplexities of the river systems that Thompson had solved. It gives the impression of having been derived from the study of maps in a library rather than from knowledge of the mystifying terrain itself. But Canadian scholars who followed Morton's lead were familiar with the most obscure of Thompson's contemporaries, and the least-known of the wilderness areas about which disputes raged, and characteristically backed up their research with canoe trips into the wild which were enough in themselves to place at a disadvantage any commentator who opposed their views.

In 1962 Professor Richard Glover of the University of Manitoba published a new edition of Thompson's *Narrative*, limited to 750 copies. He duplicated, in a sense, the amazing labor of Tyrrell in an earlier generation; but where Tyrrell had found, all over Canada and in the Northwest, only impressive evidence of Thompson's genius, Glover reversed him, page by page, with a systematic denigration that makes the book a monument of scholarly hostility, perhaps unprecedented as an expression of dislike by the author of an Introduction for the book he introduced.

The entire work was, in Glover's view, "a tissue of falsehood and misrepresentations." The burden of the charge against Thompson was that he had failed to reach the mouth of the Columbia and establish a post there before Astor's men arrived to build Astoria, but there were many less momentous accusations brought against him as well. For example, Thompson wrote that as an apprentice he saw the young employees of the Hudson's Bay Company come in after a winter in the wilderness and, in gambling and drinking, lose in a night the earnings of a year's work; he decided not to drink or gamble. "Every festival of the Church of Rome," he wrote, "was an excuse to get drunk." Professor Glover interpreted this to mean that Thompson suffered from "that common Puritan disease—consciousness of his own virtue." Another sign of the same failing was Thompson's refusal to permit alcohol to be taken to the Columbia district for trade with the Indians. Ordered to do so, he loaded the whiskey kegs on pack horses in such a way that, in crossing the mountains, the kegs jammed against the rocks and the liquor was spilled. He then sent back a report explaining what he had done and added that the same thing would happen to other kegs of whiskey sent over the mountains. This was only one instance of Thompson's differences with the feudal generation of fur barons, but it involved something more than a Puritan conscientiousness of virtue. The use of liquor to debauch or destroy troublesome Indians was on an epic scale. Thompson's father-in-law, Patrick Small, on a single expedition to a tribe of Indians near Detroit after the American Revolution, took with him no less than 3,000 *gallons* of brandy—enough to immobilize a city, let alone a tribe of Indians who had no experience in its use, and to whom intoxication in the dead of winter often meant death.

Personal and religious differences, the conflict of the Hudson's Bay Company and the North West Company, partisan emotions involving rival fur traders with whom Thompson was often at odds, and the enterprise of the Hudson's Bay Company in later years in promoting a kind of scholarly public-relations account of its own history—all this influenced the revised opinion of Thompson's accomplishments. He was acutely conscious of the dangers that faced Britain's North American colony after the Revolution and was insistent on the discipline that would be necessary if the dangers were to be overcome; his awareness in this respect alone set him apart from the reckless, hard-drinking, openhanded fur traders whose image in popular Canadian culture was nurtured in the way that the legendary cowboy figures in the American picture of the West. Thompson did not fit in with the gallery of Canadian wilderness heroes. Since he did not belong to the recognized type, whatever he did was questionable; since he had failed to fortify the mouth of the Columbia, other neglect was probable. When Thompson left the Hudson's Bay Company, to mention one instance, a considerable sum of money—£227 5s—was left to his credit on the Company books. Professor Glover wrote of this:

> In acting as he did in 1797, Thompson not only deserted employers who had consistently treated him well, but he also ran away from a large sum of money. . . . The Company continued to manage this for him, as it had done in the past. While in their service he directed them to make various payments to his mother, and over the next five years they went on making a succession of doles to her, till the accounts record the final entry 1802 Aug. 12, the balance paid his mother Eliza Evans this day £13-9s-11d. How Thompson supported his mother after this, if he supported her at all, is a question which it seems impossible to answer.

What makes the question even harder to answer is that his mother was not Eliza Evans, but Ann Thompson. On the record the Company gave Eliza Evans almost £40 a year, a very substantial living in a time when a schoolmaster received £7 a year—unusually generous, also, since the Company at that time was in a condition approaching bankruptcy.

But criticism of Thompson along such lines was subordinate to the great charge against him: he failed to secure the Columbia River for

Britain when he could easily have done so, and his failure cost Britain dominance of the entire North Pacific coast. A typical comment was this: "Thompson's conduct after his canoes were stopped in 1810 suggests that under the stress of such anxiety his nerves had reached the breaking point." The argument was that Thompson could have built posts along the lower Columbia in the years between 1807 and 1810, that he could have led his party of twenty-four men to the mouth of the river in the fall of 1810 and constructed a Canadian outpost there before Astor's men arrived on the *Tonquin* in the spring of 1811. In fact, Thompson never had enough men in the years before 1810 to build such a post so remote from his source of supplies and reinforcements. Meanwhile Lewis's report on the lower Columbia—the only source of information about it—greatly overestimated the number of Indians there, but even so there were enough to overwhelm any party Thompson could have raised.

And on the face of it, any notion that a race was under way between the Americans and the Canadians to reach the mouth of the river was absurd—not because of Thompson's conduct, but because of the conduct of the Americans. If Thompson's delay was puzzling, that of Astor's party was inexplicable. If Thompson was guilty of neglect of his opportunity, what could be said of the neglect of the Americans to build posts on the lower river after Lewis and Clark's expedition in 1805? If Thompson was slow in crossing the Canadian Rockies in winter, what could be said of Astor's party under Wilson Price Hunt, which began organizing in 1809 and reached Astoria in February, 1812? Or, if the race was urgent, what could be said of the *Tonquin?* Astor's company was chartered in 1809, and the *Tonquin* finally sailed in September, 1810. When it reached the Hawaiian Islands in February, 1811, the ship was detained for twelve days with visits, ceremonies, feasts and the accumulation of supplies, normal enough procedure after a long voyage around Cape Horn but hardly the course of a party in a race to reach the Columbia before its Canadian rivals. It would appear that the contest between the Canadians and the Americans, if it existed at that time, was one of determined effort *not* to get to the mouth of the river first.

For a century and a half the Big Bend country where Thompson spent the winter of 1810 remained almost unchanged. Then in the fall of 1964 work began on a great dam to be built across the Columbia at Mica Creek, 18 miles downstream from the Big Bend and Boat Encampment. The building was on an enormous scale; the dam was to be 2,500 feet across and 645 feet high (scaled down from an original plan of 850 feet), submerging the place where Thompson built his cabin under 600 feet of water. This was the place where, in his words, he had felt that a new world lay before him. That comment was characteristic of the visionary and prophetic note that suffused his writing but which, in his case, was combined with a meticulously accurate description in detail: he wanted to note everything he could about that new world. It was curious—now that the region was to be changed for all time—that his description of what it was originally like remained almost the only detailed account of it.

No one followed his lead. A few hunters and prospectors passed that way, and there was a little logging close to the river, but the land was essentially unchanged up to the very moment it was to be submerged. No one even wrote of it. The Canoe River remained unexplored. It was going to be wiped out before it was discovered—except, of course, for his notes of discovery in his notebooks preserved in the Students Room.

Thompson was exceptional among Northwestern explorers in many ways, but he was unique in sensing that the region was important enough to warrant a detailed study of every part of it. From the time of his first crossing of the Rockies to the last, he saw the Northwest as a land of promise, a keystone in the structure of nations whose future involved them all. The isolation of the region, the sense of its distance from the Old World that oppressed other explorers, did not affect him at all; it was part of what he liked about the country. The gloom and the depression that lay over the writings of Mourelle and Meares and Mackenzie and Meriwether Lewis and Washington Irving, the all-but-universal emphasis on storms and dark skies and forbidding woods and impassable mountains, were altogether lacking in Thompson's writings: they were replaced by his intense interest in specific features and by an almost uncannily accurate closeness of observation. He noted the time of the arrival of birds, counted the flocks of migrating ducks, measured the depth of rivers and estimated the speed of their currents, and noted temperatures, changes in the weather, cloud formations and direction and velocity of winds. He riveted each observation to a specific place by his sighting of the sun and the stars to determine latitude and longitude, and later surveyors with instruments more accurate than his corrected his figures only slightly—unimportant differences, for the most part, for he usually located his points with reference to some natural feature, a mountain or a great rapids, that established where he was for people who could not calculate latitude and longitude. He had above all a sense of locality, of the particular qualities and features of each place, a sense doubly meaningful in the Northwest, where the variety of country found within a few miles was a unique quality of the whole region.

He loved the Northwest, and it is a commentary on the culture of that region that his writings remained unpublished for more than a century. In a sense he had little to say to people who were primarily concerned with exploiting the country. With all his hardheadedness there was something childlike about David Thompson, as there was about the poet William Blake; reality for him meant the tangible world of rivers, rocks, rapids, trees, sandbars, rain, clouds, snow, heat and cold, food, shelter and the ways of people and horses. Every river was an engrossing subject for study, and every mountain pass a marvel in itself. Towns and trading posts were temporary or unimportant, appearing and disappearing, or so changing their character as to be unrecognizable; the real world was the land of trees and rocks over which he made his pilgrimage, like Christian in *Pilgrim's Progress*, equipped with his primitive surveying instruments and noting latitude and longitude on his way to the timeless reaches of eternity. His work has more meaning to a society bent on preserving what it can of the world of nature. Stepping out of the Students Room, into the gardens behind Parliament House, the morning light on those old Canadian rosebushes could make a shiver run up your spine.

III

The United Government of Oregon, Great Britain and the United States

---

I

Gloomy as was the American vision of the Northwest Coast, it had a powerful appeal to the imagination of Easterners. The very word "Oregon" was an intellectual force. No one knew where it came from. Oregon was a name for the Columbia, the River of the West, and may have been the result of a misunderstanding of a Spanish phrase, but it was too apt and too fitting to have been an invented term, and it took hold as the symbol of a tangible reality. William Cullen Bryant expressed a common feeling when he wrote in "Thanatopsis":

> Where rolls the Oregon, and hears no sound,
> Save his own dashings—yet the dead are there . . .

The dead were there, at the mouth of the river, in a place so lonely the thought of endless unheard waves evoked it with a solemn finality. So live, the young poet told his fellow Americans,

> that when thy summons comes to join
> The innumerable caravan, which moves

66

> To that mysterious realm, where each shall take
> His chamber in the silent halls of death,
> Thou go not, like the quarry-slave at night,
> Scourged to his dungeon, but, sustained and soothed
> By an unfaltering trust, approach thy grave,
> Like one who wraps the drapery of his couch
> About him, and lies down to pleasant dreams.

Would the unfortunate seamen of the *Tonquin* have been comforted by the message of the poem? Could they have climbed down to a leaky boat, at the order of a demented commander, to go to their death with the composure of sleepers lying down to pleasant dreams? Still, the poem was a brave one, and to him who in the love of nature held communion with her visible forms, the poet invoked an unfaltering trust that accepted without question the terror and promise of an American destiny. That destiny included conquering a continent whose very dimensions were unknown, something that F. Scott Fitzgerald had in mind when he wrote that "for a transitory enchanted moment man must have held his breath in the presence of this continent, compelled into an aesthetic contemplation he neither understood nor desired, face to face for the last time in history with something commensurate to his capacity for wonder."

Coleridge planned a Utopian colony on the banks of the Susquehanna because the name of the river seemed to him to be beautiful. Hall Kelley had a more concrete dream: he wanted to found a new republic of civil and religious freedom "in the dark and cruel places about the shores of the Pacific." Kelley's capacity for wonder was unlimited. By some instinct he knew that the reports of a wholly inhospitable wilderness in the Northwest must be false, and in default of firsthand information he decided that Oregon was, on the contrary, a land of fertile valleys, beautiful mountains, rushing rivers and a benign climate. Kelley was the son of a New Hampshire physician, a descendant of an old New England family. He was born in 1790. At the age of fourteen he suddenly developed an impairment in his speech. He stammered helplessly, especially when he wanted to say something to someone he regarded as superior. He came to believe that he was slow in understanding. After two years the worst of his handicap disappeared, but he always retained a diffidence and a natural shyness that made his ventures into public affairs seem heroic.

He grew up to become a good-looking, even handsome individual, with a quiet and thoughtful air. He eventually received his degree from Middlebury College, and finally from Harvard as well. He married a well-to-do Boston girl who died after bearing him a son. That was in 1816, and it was during the next year that Hall Kelley's vision of Oregon came to him in the form of a religious mission. The religious motive was to promote Christianity in those dark and cruel places on the other side of the continent, and the practical side called for obtaining from Congress a grant of land on the Columbia River for three thousand colonists.

In the meantime Kelley filled in for an ailing Boston schoolteacher and turned out to be a surprisingly good teacher himself—almost the only practical accomplishment in his life. He taught for five years, became the master of a school and was a prolific author of textbooks. He was married again, this time to the daughter of a Boston family with considerable property. He also "became involved in difficulties" with the usher of his school. The local school board upheld him. Josiah Quincy, the mayor of Boston, set up a special committee to inquire into the dispute. The committee upheld the usher and discharged Kelley. The reasons were not given to history, but Kelley himself was sure that he knew what lay back of them: sinister enemies were alarmed by his plans for his Oregon colony.

These enemies, in his view, worked with great skill and malignancy. They were behind the lawyers who brought continual lawsuits and received court orders to seize his property. They influenced newspaper editors to ridicule the Oregon colony. They spread slanders and hired thugs to intimidate him. They broke into his house. They stole his luggage. Masked as recruits to the Oregon colony, they made off with the colony's assets. A textile mill near Boston into which he put his money went bankrupt. He lost his property in Boston itself. His second wife, who bore him three sons, turned against him. He was convinced that both his commercial losses and his domestic unhappiness came from the operations of international agents who were determined to thwart his grand design.

As a matter of elementary fact, his Oregon plan did reach into a very touchy political world. The treaty of joint occupancy was in force in Oregon; the rights and privileges of the citizens of one nation were respected by the government of the other. The ultimate disposition of the region would depend on the wishes of the people who lived there. Joint occupancy lasted for twenty-eight years. In that interval there were, in historical terms, no significant difficulties in its operation in the Northwest. A territory the size of Europe (apart from Russia) was governed and settled almost without dispute; indeed, no part of America was settled so peacefully.

The Alaskan boundary and the withdrawal of Russian claims to Oregon were settled by treaties in 1824, and during that year Hall Kelley began promoting the Society for Encouraging the American Settlement of the Oregon Territory. His most important recruit was Nathaniel Wyeth, a wealthy ice dealer, who, while he first became interested in

Oregon as a result of Kelley's campaign, saw possibilities of individual gain that Kelley did not, and possessed practical experience and administrative ability that Kelley conspicuously lacked. Kelley's own progress was slow. Help from Congress was delayed; the cooperative colony was implicitly antislavery. Representative John Floyd of Virginia urged Congress to support an American colony on the Columbia, but it was to forestall British settlement there, unhampered by idealistic considerations. (A committee of Congress was set up, but took no action.) The treaty of joint occupancy was renewed in 1828, and in that year, at last, Kelley secured from Congress a grant of land for settlement in the Oregon country. At the moment of victory the matchless cunning of his adversaries was revealed. His name was omitted from the bill, and only the name of a rival proslavery promoter of another colony was included. The next day an amendment corrected the oversight, but Kelley remained convinced that powerful enemies were working against him. It is easy to get an impression that the opposition to Kelley existed largely in his own mind. Still, the measures taken to discredit him and his project seem disproportionately agitated. One typical reply to the Oregon colony was a burlesque movement started in Boston to colonize the State of Maine. Kelley's supporters dropped away. Nathaniel Wyeth set out for Oregon in 1831 with his own company, taking five men who had originally signed up with Kelley but leaving Kelley himself behind.

It was not until the winter of 1832 that Kelley was able to start for Oregon, and by that time he was entirely alone. After fifteen years of constant struggle he expected there would be some kind of ceremony at his leaving. Instead his wife and sons and other relatives stood about, stony-faced and silent, as he began his great adventure. Five lawsuits having to do with his unpaid bills were pending against him. He disregarded them; they were typical obstructions created by those determined to prevent the building of a new world in Oregon. It was said he was leaving his wife and family without means of support. He felt the charge was ridiculous; his mother-in-law had an annual income of $12,000, some part of which she should be devoting to the Oregon crusade.

So the possessed schoolteacher moved in a roundabout way across the continent. He went to New Orleans, then to Mexico City, and finally across the deserts of Sonora and Arizona until he came to a small town near San Diego—a dangerous journey that the most intrepid mountain man would not have undertaken alone. By the time Kelley arrived there he looked like a Mexican. He was dressed in Mexican garb, wearing a white slouch hat, a blanket cape, and leather trousers with red stripes down the sides.

Ewing Young was in the town, and Kelley proposed that Young ac-

company him to Oregon. Ewing Young was one of the most celebrated of the mountain men, of equal stature with Kit Carson, Jim
Bridger, Jedediah Smith, Hugh Glass and Joseph Walker in that
heroic generation, but he instantly rejected Kelley's invitation. Oregon
had a reputation for savagery even among the mountain men. Jedediah Smith, one of the bravest and most far ranging of them, had led
a party of fourteen men into southern Oregon to trap beaver; they
were tricked by Indians who pretended to be friendly, and only four
escaped. And that attack came after Smith had successfully faced
savages and other wilderness terrors throughout the Rocky Mountains
and the southwestern desert. Smith found a refuge at the Hudson's
Bay post on the Columbia, the Company sending a party to punish
the murderers, but Oregon retained an evil reputation among the fur
trappers.

Young was as brave as any of them. He was the first to trap beaver
in Arizona, leading a band of forty men (among them the young Kit
Carson at the start of his career) into the Apache Indian country
when it was unmapped and unexplored. Young also trapped and
destroyed a party of Apaches, starting the wars of the Apaches and
the Americans that lasted until the surrender of Geronimo in 1886.
Since Arizona was Mexican territory, and Young was not licensed by
the Mexican government, his activities there were illegal. He hid his
furs in the mountains, rode hard to Santa Fe, secured a license from
the Mexican governor, collected his furs and wound up a year of
trapping, Indian fighting and fast traveling with a profit of $24,000.

Hall Kelley was a character such as Young had never encountered
before. He was well-educated, soft-spoken, quietly determined and,
with all his frequent foolishness, had an elemental common sense and
a courage that even a mountain man could respect. On his part Kelley
wrote that Young was remarkable for sagacity, enterprise and courage.
He added owlishly that after Young's years in the wilderness "he had
lost, perhaps, some of the refinements of manners once possessed, and
had missed some of those moral improvements peculiar to Christian
civilization."

Kelley was accustomed to rebuffs. He rode north alone and camped
near Monterey while he sounded out the Mexican governor of California, and the Americans living in the area, about help for his Oregon
colony. None wanted any part of it. While Kelley was pondering his
next move, Ewing Young suddenly joined him, with five men driving
ninety-two horses. The mountain man had changed his mind. Kelley
and his horses were added to the party, which moved north at once,
traveling fast. Beyond the last Mexican settlement they were met by
nine men driving fifty-six more horses.

Meanwhile the Mexican governor at Monterey sent a schooner to the Hudson's Bay Company post at Vancouver on the Columbia River, warning that Hall Kelley and Ewing Young were on their way to Oregon with horses they had stolen from California ranchers. The Company distributed notices warning all settlers that Young and Kelley were horse thieves, and no one was to have any dealings with them. Well on the way into the wilderness, four of the nine newcomers left Young's party. That still left twelve well-armed men and around 150 horses and mules. The five who remained of the nine strangers were tough characters—tougher than Young's original force of five men. Three were ex-sailors who had deserted their ships. The other two were professional Indian killers. They had spent the previous year with Joseph Walker's band. Walker was the most mysterious of the mountain men. He too was a brave and tireless explorer, the first to cross the High Sierras and to explore the Yosemite country, but his reputation as a paid destroyer of Indian camps wiped out the record of his achievements in other respects. Washington Irving, who after his long years in Madrid was in a position to know, wrote that Walker was secretly allied with Mexican authorities. Irving gave a detailed account of one of Walker's raids in which his Mexican associates rode down defenseless Indians, lassoing them and dragging them behind their horses to their deaths. The two members of Walker's band now riding with Young spoke freely of their work destroying Indians. "They spoke often of the black flag," Kelley wrote, "and the rifle and the arsenic."

North of the San Joaquin River the party came upon an Indian village where all the men were away. Young and most of the party rode on. The newcomers remained to rape the women and rob the tepees of whatever of value they could find. Some sporadic firing by Indians followed, but Young's party was not attacked. They now approached the region where Jedediah Smith's men had been murdered. Seven Indians, unarmed and bent on placating the whites, approached Young and his men, who waited with their rifles ready. While still some distance away two of the Indians stopped, afraid to come any nearer. Five approached steadily, showing they were unarmed, until they were within ten feet of the guns.

According to Kelley's account, one of the horse thieves who had joined the party said to Young, "These are the damned villains. They ought to be shot."

"Yes," Young replied.

The shots were fired at once, and all five Indians killed. The two who had remained at a distance ran.

Kelley's horror was evident in his expression. He saw Young looking at him sharply. "Well, Mr. Kelley," Young said, "what do you think of this?"

Kelley knew that if he made a wrong answer he would be shot in turn. After a moment he said, "We must protect ourselves in the wilderness among hostile Indians."

It served for the moment. The party rode on. Kelley expected to be killed. On one occasion he saw one of the thieves raise a rifle and aim in his direction, but Young intervened, and the man did not fire. Shooting Kelley seemed unnecessary. He was so ill he could barely remain on his horse. As they went on through the mountains, he grew weaker every day, dazed and stupefied, and it was only a question of time, in his own mind and in the minds of his companions, until he would be unable to keep them in sight.

By the time they reached the Umpqua River in southern Oregon he was too weak to travel any farther by horse. In his misery and sickness there was only one ration of comfort, which he could hardly bring himself to accept, and that was his discovery that his original vision was not irrational. The weather remained fine. The silent forest, the glimpses of snow-covered mountains through the trees, and the meadows glowing with flowers told him he had been right: Oregon was a land of infinite promise. And here, to Young's embarrassment and to Kelley's relief, a party of civilized wayfarers came into sight. Each year the Hudson's Bay post on the Columbia sent a party to California. This one was led by Michael La Framboise, a French-Canadian of long experience and heroic reputation, who also possessed a common humanity not always found among the fur traders. La Framboise was trading with the Indians for furs on his homeward journey. He was not following the direct route up the Willamette Valley but was circling to the Indian tribes along the coast. He hired an Indian to take Kelley by canoe down the Umpqua, where La Framboise would meet him later and take him to the post at Vancouver.

Kelley's health improved magically as soon as he got away from the horse thieves. The Umpqua, one of the most beautiful rivers in the Northwest, raced in almost constant white water, through prairies covered with blue camas flowers and then into a dense forest where game abounded, as in a game preserve, because the Indians would not hunt there, believing it haunted. The Indians displaying "a wonderful skill descending rapids," carried Kelley 40 or 50 miles to a camp near the mouth of the river.

Out of the valley of the shadow Kelley awakened to the knowledge that he had always been right: "no part of our country surpassed this in beauty of scenery, fertility of soil, and other natural advantages." The Hudson's Bay party moved slowly northward over prairies broken only "by isolated hills, heavily wooded, and presenting a lovely contrast to the sea of grass and flowers from which they spring." He could not record all the marvels he saw: the cataracts of wilderness streams, the hidden waterways lined with groves of great trees, the snow-covered mountains that rose in tranquil majesty above their dark timbered foothills. He had come to the end of his traveling. He felt that his work was over: his vision was justified, his hardships repaid. In a daze he reached the Hudson's Bay post at Vancouver where, uncomprehendingly, he found he was considered a horse thief.

Dr. John McLoughlin, the chief trader, received him kindly because he was ill but made it plain that he did so for no other reason. McLoughlin was fifty years old, an imposing, iron-willed Scotsman with some medical education, though his practice had never been extensive. In his early years McLoughlin had been overshadowed by his brother David, who, after being graduated from the medical school in Edinburgh, settled in Paris and became one of the most famous physicians in Europe. John McLoughlin became only a resident physician for the North West Company in the Canadian wilderness. As has been said, he married Margaret McKay, the widow of Alexander McKay, and one of their four children, Tom, sailed to Astoria with his father at the age of fourteen.

Margaret was a forceful and intelligent woman, and she and McLoughlin remained closely united despite the fact that she was nine years older. During McLoughlin's service with the North West Company the conflict with the Hudson's Bay Company reached the stage of wilderness killings and battles that culminated in the battle of Seven Oaks. McLoughlin's part in the battle was unclear, but he and his uncle, Alexander Fraser, a prominent North West Company official, were among those charged with Governor Semple's murder. While they were on their way to trial, their canoe overturned on Lake Superior. One of the accused, believed to have been the chief suspect, was drowned, and with his death the case against the others was weakened. McLoughlin was acquitted of the murder charge. When the British government ordered the North West Company merged with the Hudson's Bay Company in 1821, McLoughlin, in the redistribution of posts that followed, was transferred to the Columbia River district, then the most remote in all the Company's enormous terrain. He was greatly pleased with his new surroundings. "For mildness and salubrity of climate," he wrote, "this is the finest portion of America for civilized man."

By the time Hall Kelley arrived at Vancouver, Dr. McLoughlin had perfected his control over a complex operation that included not only the chain of outlying posts and the basic fur trade but a highly organized river transport on the Columbia, ocean shipments to England, and the building of large wilderness farms raising produce for Russian trading posts in Alaska. McLoughlin could exercise almost complete control because the Hudson's Bay Company had the exclusive right to trade in all the region in the latitude of Hudson's Bay. Goods could be bought only at the Company store, and no settler could buy anything unless he could prove that he had a personal need for it—a measure intended to prevent settlers from trading with Indians on their own. True, Oregon was far south of the latitude of Hudson's Bay. But the treaty of joint occupancy gave equal rights to both British and American settlers, so the Company could operate there as it operated elsewhere in Canada, and Americans could settle there; however, if they did so, there was no place where they could secure goods if the Company—which meant McLoughlin—refused to sell to them.

Hall Kelley and Ewing Young were banned from the main post at Vancouver on the Columbia because the Mexican governor of California had accused them of being horse thieves. Young was furious not only with the governor of California but with Kelley. He moved restlessly around the Willamette Valley, trying one project after another, always frustrated because McLoughlin would not sell him supplies. Hall Kelley's case was different. Explaining that he could not allow Kelley within the Company stockade, McLoughlin gave him an empty house in the adjoining village. The house and the shed alongside it had been used for cleaning fish and game, but it had formerly been the home of a respectable workman, and Kelley did not mind living there. But as his health improved he wondered why he was so studiously avoided. Each day his meals were sent to him from the officers' table. He was isolated as thoroughly as if he had been the carrier of some dread communicable disease. He ate his solitary meals with the painful knowledge that other Americans were dining and living hospitably with officers of the Company.

His clothing had grown shabby during his long desert travels. His white slouch hat was stained and out of shape, his blanket cape worn, and his red-striped leather trousers shapeless and odd looking. He was not locked into his house and theoretically was free to come and go as he pleased, but outside the post there were few places he could go without the Company's assistance. One letter reached him. Ewing Young wrote to tell him that he would kill him if they ever met again. The mountain man now held Kelley responsible for all his trouble for having induced him to travel to Oregon.

Each day Dr. McLoughlin entertained a brilliant group of Americans at the officers' table in the main post. Included among his guests was Thomas Nuttall, an ornithologist. The American Philosophical Society had sent him west with the Wyeth party. Nuttall was then thirty-eight years old, shy and self-effacing, the author of the encyclopedic *A Manual of the Ornithology of the United States and Canada*, published the preceding year. Nuttall added two birds during his stay in Vancouver, the Nuttall's poor-will, or *Phalaenoptilus nuttallii nuttallii* (to use the name which Audubon gave it when Townsend sent him a specimen), and the olive-sided flycatcher, or Nuttall peewee, a bird notable for its powerful whistled call.

With Nuttall, as his Philosophical Society associate, was John Kirk Townsend, then only twenty-five, far more enterprising and active than Nuttall, who sent to Audubon seven new species, including the Townsend chipmunk, the Townsend thrush, the Townsend fox sparrow, the Townsend warbler and the Townsend surf bird, a plover he discovered while exploring around Cape Disappointment. Townsend would have had another discovery credited to him had it not been for an unfortunate happening. He found a previously unknown reptile. He preserved it in alcohol to take it back East with him. A hard drinker named Thornburg, a tailor who had come across the plains with Nathaniel Wyeth, found the bottle and, undeterred by the snake inside, drank the liquor. (Townsend told this story to the Reverend Samuel Parker, another erudite American visitor to the Hudson's Bay post. Parker included it in his book, *Journal of an Exploring Tour Beyond the Rocky Mountains*, which he published in 1838 after he returned to the Eastern states.)

Still another distinguished traveler joined the company. This was John Ball (Dartmouth, 1820), whose interest in the West was stimulated because his New Hampshire neighbor, John Ordway, had accompanied the Lewis and Clark Expedition. Ball was also keeping a journal. The *American Journal of Science* published it the following year.

There was some plausibility in Dr. McLoughlin's excuse to Kelley that he did not have room for another guest. But could Kelley not at least have eaten with the others? Not one of them visited him. Their explanation, offered later, was that they were afraid of incurring McLoughlin's displeasure, and McLoughlin had the power to terminate their scientific studies at any time by withholding the help of the Company.

On his part, McLoughlin enjoyed the delicate balancing act that his position made possible. He was a friend of the Americans (and he actually aided many of them, so much so that the Company eventually tried to collect $60,000 from McLoughlin for goods which it claimed he had advanced to needy Americans on his own and charged to the Company), and he was also the ranking representative of Great Britain who could demand new powers and supplies in order to be able to counteract the American invasion. McLoughlin also enjoyed being able to mediate between the conflicting groups within his own Hudson's Bay subordinate officers at Vancouver. He called them the Philosophers and the Patriots. The Philosophers believed in the treaty of joint occupancy and held the arrival of American settlers to be inevitable, therefore urging a policy of accommodation and friendliness; they looked forward to a future of cooperation and the prosperity of both Britons and Americans. The Patriots demanded the absolute exclusion of the Americans from the British settlements and the active discouragement of further American arrivals. Both policies were followed at different times —sometimes one, sometimes the other, often in violation of the Hudson's Bay Company's own traditional practices. The Company, for example, had always trapped furs sparingly in a particular area to permit fur-bearing animals to reproduce; but in Oregon, before the waves of American emigration began, the Company systematically stripped the country of all the animals its trappers could capture in order to prevent American newcomers from getting a start in the fur trade.

The charter of the Hudson's Bay Company gave it all the powers of government, including the power to declare war, though not against Christian nations. The Company probated wills, administered justice, and pursued and imprisoned criminals. Those accused of serious crimes were sent to Quebec to be tried; lesser offenses were punished with fines or imprisonment in the local guardhouse. There was no comparable agency among the Americans. There were no United States officers of any kind in Oregon and only two American institutions. In 1835 the Reverend Jason Lee established a Methodist mission for work among the Indians near what became Salem, Oregon, some 60 miles south of the Hudson's Bay post at Vancouver on the Columbia, and Dr. Marcus Whitman, the following year, built another mission near Walla Walla, some 200 miles east. About seventy Americans scattered around Oregon included a few farmers, some former fur traders, and several members of the expedition that had crossed the continent with Wyeth. On a second expedition Wyeth reached Oregon shortly before Hall Kelley, but he happened to be away on a fur-trading venture of his own when Kelley and Ewing Young came in from California.

Dr. McLoughlin's position was scarcely threatened by Kelley, but with a mysteriously willful obstinacy he ordered that no one should have any contact with Kelley, and his orders were kept. For five months Kelley did not have a visitor. If he had been eccentric and fanatical before this time, he was unbalanced afterward. The most remarkable aspect of his strange half-imprisonment was that he himself seemed to accept it as a sentence he somehow had to serve. His lack of defiance was bewildering. He looked out from the dooryard of his house onto the Oregon countryside he had worked so desperately to reach; he read, wrote in his notebook and waited. But how long he waited! It was not until February, 1836, that he nerved himself to approach McLoughlin. He dressed himself as carefully as he could and walked from his house to the stockade. With a regard for civilized usage he called at McLoughlin's office rather than his private quarters.

It was the great moment of his Oregon adventure. He was as tense as he had been when the horse thieves were trying to kill him. He knocked, and an underling opened the door. He asked to see Dr. McLoughlin. He was told that McLoughlin was busy and could not see him. Before he could explain his needs the door was slammed in his face. He returned to his cabin.

The next morning something even more startling happened: he had a visitor. His door was pushed open without ceremony. Nathaniel Wyeth appeared.

"Well, Kelley," said Wyeth, "how did you get here?"

How, indeed? Kelley was too agitated to answer him. He could not remember what else was said, but he recollected that Wyeth made some abusive remarks and suddenly left. Kelley never saw him again. On his part Wyeth wrote in his journal: "In the morning made it to Vancouver, and found there a polite reception, and to my great astonishment Mr. Hall J. Kelley. He came in co with Mr. Young from Monte el Rey and it is said stole between them a bunch of horses."

Kelley's door was unlocked; if he wanted, he could leave at any time. Feeble health and the lack of any money and his inexperience in the wilderness imprisoned him. To his credit the Reverend Jason Lee called on him during a visit to Vancouver; otherwise—aside from the meals regularly left for him—he might not have existed. The winter wore on. In his loneliness Kelley was sustained and soothed by the validity of his great vision of Oregon. The weather remained mild. The forenoons were clear and sunny; the afternoons often ended with showers or light drizzly rain. The murmur of rain on the roof was music, the true sound of this world, a low, steady, cheerful, friendly drumming on the shingles. The schoolteacher wrote in his diary as he listened. This was the time of the year when all explorers had reported savage storms. But there were only three light snowfalls during the entire winter. The coldest day of the year came near the end of February, and then, for a brief period, the temperature dropped below freezing. Rain had fallen, and as the air grew colder, ice formed and the rough stockade and village were transformed. "For a few hours," Kelley wrote, "houses, trees and fields sparkled with an icy covering."

That was the only cold day. Spring came with a succession of clear, cool, sunlit days. He began to leave his cabin and walk down the banks of the Columbia toward the ocean. In April a Hudson's Bay ship arrived with supplies, and Dr. McLoughlin offered Kelley a chance to return home on it. He also gave Kelley £7. The ship, long delayed, eventually got him to Boston, where Kelley found less interest in Oregon than there had been when he left. He settled in the town of Three Rivers, Massachusetts, apart from his family, and began petitioning Congress for recompense for the hardships he had endured, a practice he continued until his death in 1874. An early Oregon writer said of him, "Unappreciated and misunderstood, by some called a fanatic, by others a crank, and by the Hudson's Bay Company a horse thief, the ghost of Hall Kelley appears and disappears through the shifting scenes of Oregon's strenuous history with such kaleidoscopic presentment as almost to baffle description." And a pioneer historian wrote, "We envy none who can look upon the story of Hall Kelley with contempt." He remains a sort of haunting half-memory, a puzzled visionary, glimpsed rather than seen, riding alone with murderers in the mountains or sitting on the banks of the great river of the West in the bright spring days and planning a new kind of world to come into being on the dark and cruel places about the shores of the Pacific.

II

It rained, it rained; it blew, it blew. "The days are very short," James Gilchrist Swan wrote in *The Northwest Coast*, "and the settlers find it difficult to pass off the long, stormy nights, unless with the aid of books." By 1841, five years after Kelley reached Oregon, there were three hundred books in the region. They were passed from family to family, and read and reread. Before long it became necessary to organize a system for their distribution and to secure more. The first government of Oregon was a circulating library.

In his own way Dr. John McLoughlin stimulated a love of literature. He had no objection to the American newcomers as farmers, cultivating their few acres, or as missionaries, teaching the Indians and preaching to them; and indeed, under the treaty of joint occupancy, he could not legally oppose them. But it was prudent for the American settlers to spend the winter nights reading or working at household crafts rather than engaging in actions that McLoughlin might interpret as threats to his rule. A circulating library was harmless; as the historian Edmond Meany wrote, "Surely all could agree on this." Nor did McLoughlin discourage joint actions by the Americans that spared him trouble, as in the trial of an American for murder. In 1835 Thomas Hubbard, a gunsmith who reached Oregon with Nathaniel Wyeth, shot and killed the hard-drinking Thornburg. The American settlers served as a jury to try Hubbard. Thornburg had been living with an Indian girl. He treated her brutally, and when she left him, Hubbard protected her, and she moved into his cabin. The evidence indicated that Thornburg, insanely drunk, went to Hubbard's cabin to kill him and reclaim the girl. Hubbard was acquitted.

There was a division among the Hudson's Bay men between the Philosophers and the Patriots; there was also a division among the Americans between the missionaries and the mountain men. Ewing Young wanted an open defiance of McLoughlin and the Company; the missionaries wanted the cooperation of all the white people in their great cause: to educate the Indians and prevent, in Oregon, the Indian wars that darkened American history everywhere else. Young's standing with all parties was somewhat compromised by the charge that he was a horse thief. To clear his name, he issued a detailed statement of his possessions, which, however, did not greatly inspire confidence in him. Young said that when he started for Oregon with Hall Kelley he had seventy-seven horses and mules, and that these were all his own—none had been stolen. His personal crew of five men, and Kelley, had twenty-one horses. That made ninety-eight horses and mules. But the Young party arrived in Oregon with 154 animals. Young explained the difference by saying that when the nine newcomers joined the expedition on the way they had fifty-six horses. "Whether they bought them, or stole them," Young said, "I do not know."

Having thus cleared things up to his own satisfaction, Young wrote to the governor of California demanding that he retract his accusation that Young was a horse thief. That alarmed official hastily did so. There was now no reason for Young to be excluded from the Hudson's Bay post, but McLoughlin continued to keep him out on general principles. Young retaliated by threatening to build a gristmill and a distillery and produce liquor for the Indian trade. The threat was a serious one, not only to the Company but to the missionaries. David Thompson had kept the North West Company from bartering liquor in the Northwest at the beginning of the fur trade there, and a later agreement with the American Fur Company to the same end had been continued by Hudson's Bay. The Indians secured some whiskey from trading vessels, but there was nothing like the wholesale debauching of troublesome tribes that had taken place east of the Rockies. The Reverend Jason Lee and the American settlers consequently addressed a formal request to Young, asking him not to build the distillery and offering to pay him, from their own slight resources, what he would have earned by it. Young replied in a dignified statement, generously abandoning the plan and refusing the money, and taking the occasion to try to unite the Americans against McLoughlin.

There were not only Patriots and Philosophers among the English. Peter Skene Ogden did not fit into either category, and his habits of mind made him skeptical of classifying people in any such fashion. Ogden's standing as an explorer and a mountain man was not surpassed by anyone on either side of the border. He was one of the first traders in the mountains of what became Idaho and Montana, the first to transverse the Humboldt River, one of the first white men to reach Great Salt Lake, and the first to explore eastern Oregon. His literary interests were evident in a remarkable book, *Traits of American Indian Life and Character*. He was married to an Indian woman, and his standing with the Indians was as high as that of anyone in the Northwest. He was a hearty, sociable individual. He had family ties with influential citizens in the United States, and in his personal dealings with the settlers he tended to appraise them as individuals regardless of their native country. It was an indication of a new order of things when Ogden was made governor of the Columbian district of the Hudson's Bay Company. McLoughlin still ruled his own post at Vancouver, but Ogden had none of McLoughlin's doctrinaire convictions about the way to treat the Americans. So far as Ogden was concerned, the settlers who were looking for homesites were free to do so and were to be considered friends if they were peaceful and neighborly. He was, however, ironic about McLoughlin's policy of discouraging farmers and welcoming American scientists such as Townsend and Nuttall. He said Townsend and Nuttall arrived in Oregon bearing letters of introduction from the President of the United States, shot all the birds on the Columbia River and were a perfect nuisance.

Confused reports of what was happening in the Northwest aroused interest in Washington, and late in 1835 the Secretary of State sent a secret agent to investigate. The agent chosen was William Slacum, a purser in the Navy. He was instructed to visit the British settlements and, without arousing suspicion, report secretly on what was being done. Slacum was in no hurry to set out. He waited so long that he was able to visit Hall Kelley after Kelley's return to Massachusetts, and it was almost two years after his assignment before Slacum finally reached Oregon. There, in a move which would certainly have surprised Kelley, the secret agent allied himself with Ewing Young in a profitable commercial venture. Young formed the Willamette Cattle Company. Slacum chartered a schooner and with Young and a small group of settlers sailed for California. There they bought cattle and returned to Oregon driving 630 head. No accusations of cattle theft followed Young on this occasion, though observers noted the animals were lean and had been driven hard by the time they reached the Willamette Valley. Returning to Washington, Slacum turned in a report that greatly exaggerated the extent of the Hudson's Bay Company operations in the Northwest.

The Company's posts were not large, but they were strategically located. On a map the area open to settlers appeared to be limitless; in fact the trees were so big and the forest so continuous that the accessible farmland was small, since a lifetime was required to clear a farm in the woods. Only in widely separated areas, along the Willamette or near Puget Sound, were there broad level meadows, ringed by trees but free of trees on their surface, prairies that were covered with grass and flowers and had the appearance of cultivated ground. The Company wanted to monopolize these islands of treeless ground. The largest of its subsidiaries, the Puget Sound Agricultural Company (established over the objections of the old guard of the Company, who believed farming beneath the dignity of the ancient company of adventurers), covered 167,000 acres and was enormously profitable, with a business of supplying food to Russian fur-trading posts in Alaska.

The Company also maintained small posts in Oregon proper but gradually abandoned them as Americans settled along the Willamette; its main operations were north of the Columbia River. The cattle that Ewing Young brought from California multiplied in the Willamette pastures; within four years the herd was a large one, and Young was the richest man in the region. He died on February 15, 1841, with no known heirs. The Hudson's Bay Company ordinarily probated wills in the area that it controlled, but in this case the Americans were unwilling to entrust the disposition of Young's estate to McLoughlin and the Company. Two days after Young's death the American settlers met near Young's grave and elected a judge with probate powers. While they were about it, they also elected a committee to frame a constitution for Oregon and draft a code of laws.

Most of the employees of the Company were French-Canadians and Roman Catholic in religion (most of the officers were members of the Church of England, or Scottish Presbyterians), and in an effort to win support for the proposed government the Americans elected a Catholic priest, Father Francis Norbert Blanchet, chairman of the committee to draft the constitution. After six months a second public meeting of the Americans assembled to hear the report of the graveside committees. Father Blanchet resigned, saying the constitutional committee had held no sessions. It happened that the United States Exploring Expedition, under the command of Lieutenant Charles Wilkes, was in the Northwest at the time, and an American settler was elected to the constitutional committee and instructed to confer with Wilkes and McLoughlin about the formation of a provisional government.

McLoughlin was, of course, opposed, and Wilkes advised the settlers to take no action. The practical problems were formidable. The new government could hardly declare its independence, in the way the original thirteen colonies had declared themselves independent of Great

Britain. Here there were two countries involved, and if the people of Oregon became independent of one, they could not expect to be independent of both. Nor could the new government enforce its laws without running up against the treaty of joint occupancy that gave equal rights to the settlers of both Great Britain and the United States. Obviously, the citizens of the new government would necessarily swear allegiance to Oregon, but over and beyond that, would they also swear allegiance to the United States of America, or to the Queen of England, or to both? These were questions not dealt with by political theorists. And what would happen in foreign relations? Were Oregon citizens to be loyal to London or to Washington in *their* dealings with each other?

For two years after the graveside meetings the formation of a governmental organization of any kind was abandoned, but the circulating library flourished. It began with the three hundred books the emigrants had brought to Oregon but was then formally established as the Multnomah Circulating Library, with one hundred members and a membership fee of $5. Only $100 was sent east to buy more books. There now existed a continuing active organization of the settlers, the first such in the region, whose operations extended beyond literary affairs—"a quiet and adroit maneuver," Edmond Meany called it. As an offshoot of the library, a debating society served as a meeting place for the settlers in matters of their common interests.

Meanwhile the probate court tried to locate Young's heirs and to care for his cattle, though it had no money with which to operate. The cattle were preyed on by wolves and perhaps appropriated by people as well. Neither the circulating library nor the debating society had the power to levy taxes, but the wolf committee elected in the winter of 1843 was authorized to do so. Bounties were set—$5 for a cougar, $3 for a wolf and $2 for a bear—with the money to be raised by collection from the settlers. It was also hoped that the French-Canadian employees of the Hudson's Bay Company, who were indifferent to the circulating library, might be attracted by the bounty payments and thus drawn into the public meetings.

But if measures could be taken to protect cattle, why could they not be taken to protect people? At one of the wolf meetings a committee was elected to consider measures for the military and civil protection of Oregon. On May 2, 1843, the settlers met at Champoeg to hear the committee's report. Unexpectedly, the meeting was packed with French-Canadian employees of the Hudson's Bay Company, and in a move that took the Americans by surprise a resolution was introduced at the outset opposing the formation of an Oregon government. As a rule the French-Canadians voted as a unit against whatever the Americans favored, or against what they believed the Americans favored, and in this case, in the midst of confusion that was heightened by the fact that many of them did not understand English very well, they voted *for* the establishment of a government—the question having been put in a negative resolution—when they thought they were voting *against* it. The confusion increased, and it was decided that the only way to settle the matter was to have a division that everyone could understand. All those who favored a government were to walk to one side of a field, and all those opposed were to walk to the other side. When the heads were counted there were fifty-two on the side of the government, and fifty opposed to a government being organized. The committee was instructed to draft a constitution and to present it to the settlers at another meeting at Champoeg in two months' time.

Halfway across the continent another historic development dwarfed the action of the Oregon pioneers: the first large wagon train left Independence, Missouri, on May 22, 1843. There had been small covered-wagon parties before, but this one was enormous—120 wagons, with horses, mules, oxen and several thousand head of cattle, and 260 men, 120 women and 602 children. The newcomers, when they reached Oregon, would outnumber the American settlers and the Hudson's Bay employees who were already there.

There was something rushed about the efforts of the Oregon people to get their government functioning before the newcomers arrived. On July 5, 1843, at Champoeg the settlers adopted the constitution. There was to be no governor: the executive power was placed in a three-man committee. There were no taxes: the government was to be financed by a membership fee. Slavery was prohibited. The constitution incorporated the Northwest Ordinance, the Declaration of Independence, the Constitution of the United States and the laws of the territory of Iowa, since one settler happened to have a copy of the Iowa laws.

The wagon train moved slowly across Kansas and Nebraska, northwest along the Big Blue and the Little Blue to the Platte River, then overland to the Sweetwater and into the Rockies. The cattle were driven bunched up behind the last wagon, with guards on all sides to prevent straying. One of the guards of the livestock was Jesse Applegate, a thirty-two-year-old schoolteacher who had been working as a surveyor in Missouri. Applegate was entranced by the country. Travelers before him wrote of crossing the continent in recitals of horror and hardship; he found it a great adventure. It seemed to him akin to the prehistoric or the Biblical tales of the migration of peoples. His post in the wagon train was a humble one, but he gradually emerged as the expedition's leader and its historian. He liked to watch the long disorderly herd of cattle—"that vast square column," he wrote in *A Day with the Cow Column in 1843,* in which all colors were mingled, moving here and there briskly, as impelled by horsemen riding furiously in front and rear. But that picture, in its grandeur, in its wonderful mingling of color and distinctness of detail, is forgotten in contemplation of the singular people who gave it life and animation. No other race of men, with the means at their command, could undertake so great a journey; none save these could successfully perform it, with no previous preparation, relying only on the fertility of their invention to devise the means to overcome each danger and difficulty as it arose.

He described their alarm when the emigrants came to "a deep river, with no tree upon its banks," and the narrow defiles in the Rockies where they had to take lumbering wagons "where even a loose horse could not pass."

But the weather remained good, the grass was abundant and the transcontinental passage was made almost without loss. On the Columbia itself a boat overturned and two boys were drowned; they were the sons of Applegate's brother. In Oregon the settlers spread out over the Willamette Valley, and Applegate found himself at once drawn into the work of the newly formed government. He was a student of the old Federalist writers, and their influence showed through the operations of the new state that had come into being. The treaty of joint occupancy was still in force, so subjects of Great Britain and citizens of the United States had equal rights, and what the provisional government amounted to was that they could also become citizens of Oregon if they paid a $5 membership fee. But the difficulties were not so grave as they seemed to be. A new constitution was drawn up during the winter. Even an oath of allegiance was drafted. All officials of the government swore to support the laws of Oregon, insofar as these were consistent with their duties "as a citizen of the United States or a subject of Great Britain." The foreign relations of the new government were defined:

> As descendants of the United States and Great Britain, we should honor and respect the countries which gave us birth, and as citizens of Oregon we should, by a uniform course of proceeding, and a strict observance of the rules of equity, justice and republican principles, without party distinctions, use our best efforts to cultivate the kind feelings, not only of our native countries, but of all the states or powers with whom we may have intercourse.

Applegate was a tall, lean, absentminded individual, always reading and studying, the father of a large family, a successful rancher and a pathfinder of genius. There was something Lincolnian about him, and Lincoln who, a little later, was offered the governorship of Oregon Territory but turned it down at his wife's request, would have been at home with Applegate and his neighbors. But Applegate's story belongs later in this account. He became a central figure in *John Brent*, a novel by Theodore Winthrop that became extremely popular during and after the Civil War, the prototype of innumerable Western novels. During his first winter in Oregon, Applegate won the friendship of Peter Skene Ogden and persuaded Ogden to have the legislative measures of the Oregon provisional government accepted as law by the Hudson's Bay Company. With that decision a government of dual citizenship really began to function, and the vision embodied in the treaty of joint occupancy took on living reality.

III

The second large wagon train bound for Oregon left Independence in the spring of 1844. It included eighty wagons and some 800 people, with 225 of these the heads of families or men able to bear arms. Elections were held after one day on the trail, and Cornelius Gilliam was elected to command. He was thereafter referred to throughout his life as General Gilliam. Michael Troutman Simmons, a thirty-year-old Kentuckian, was elected second in command and was thereafter invariably referred to by pioneers as Colonel Simmons. Somewhat unusually for a man of his background, for he came of a Kentucky family of slaveowners, Simmons was opposed to slavery. He had left Kentucky, where his family operated sizable plantations, to build a gristmill in Missouri.

A short distance along the way Simmons resigned his post but remained in charge of a portion of the emigrants who chose to stay with him. Gilliam was "a man generous and brave," said John Minto, one of the company, who became the historian of the 1844 train, "but had not, I think, the elements of discretion that would enable him to control all the elements of his company." The wagon train continued in two segments, but because of disputes with Gilliam, effective leadership of much of the column passed to Simmons on the way.

Simmons was on terms of personal friendship with George Washington Bush, who had been a slave in Louisiana. Bush somehow acquired his freedom and became wealthy as a fur trapper and a Hudson's Bay trader in the Rocky Mountains. He had been to the Pacific before, but by the northern route through Canada. Bush's wealth was in cattle; he had become a cattle trader in Missouri. With his German-born wife and five children, Bush joined the 1844 wagon train because laws banning free Negroes from Missouri had been passed and he feared the confiscation of his property. He did not know that Oregon, in an effort to win support in Congress, had passed a similar measure. "Not many men left a slave state as well-to-do," said John Minto, "and so generally respected." Bush told Minto that, if he did not have a free man's rights in Oregon, he would put himself under the protection of the Mexican government in California.

The 1844 crossing was as successful as the previous one had been, accomplished almost without loss. At the Columbia River most of the emigrants—220 of the 225 men able to bear arms—turned south to take out land in the Willamette Valley. Simmons and four other families, and three young single men, remained on the north shore of the Columbia River. There were thirty persons in all in this splinter group, including George Washington Bush and his family. They were the first American settlers to locate north of the Columbia, or more exactly they were the first Americans the Hudson's Bay Company permitted to settle on the north side. They camped on the Washougal River, which flows into the Columbia a few miles upstream from the Company post at Vancouver. Throughout the winter they worked cutting cedar shingles for sale in Hawaii. In the spring of 1845 Simmons led a small party of the men on an exploring trip to Puget Sound. They were looking for a place for a permanent American settlement. The Company had never permitted such ventures before. Officially, its policy was unchanged. But with the founding of the provisional government of Oregon a new spirit of international cooperation at the level of everyday life was, for the time being, in effect. Moreover, Peter Skene Ogden was favorably impressed by the newcomers. He said that during the winter they had conducted themselves in a most neighborly, friendly manner and ordered the Company posts to extend Simmons credit, except for such goods as might be traded to the Indians for furs.

On the way to Puget Sound one member of Simmons's party, John Robinson Jackson, was attracted by a site at Cowlitz Prairie, about midway between the sound and the Columbia River. He built a cabin and cleared a farm there, becoming the first American to settle permanently north of the Columbia. Jackson's bold action was carefully studied by the Americans to see if the Company created any difficulties—his farm adjoined the huge Cowlitz farm of the Puget Sound Agricultural Company—but there were none; the English were faithfully adhering to the laws of Oregon insofar as they were consistent with their duties as subjects of Great Britain. And Jackson, an Englishman who had become an American citizen in Illinois, was an able pioneer, honest and hospitable and industrious.

Simmons and the rest of his party continued north, two days' travel over prairies, to the point where the Deschutes River enters Puget Sound. A small, fast stream, the Deschutes flows across a tableland

and drops 80 feet in a series of falls, chutes and terraces into a sheltered bay. The river could provide power for a mill, whose products could be loaded into deepwater ships at the base of the cliff. What was even more important in considering a site for a settlement, there was no Indian village where the river entered salt water. The falls were at the very mouth of the river, and were too steep for salmon, and Indian villages were ordinarily built where they could benefit from the salmon runs.

This was an ideal site for an American settlement. Its only drawback was that the second largest Hudson's Bay post, Nisqually, was only 10 miles away across an arm of Puget Sound. Nisqually was the richest of the Company's properties in the Northwest. The post, a big stockade with gardens and pastures around it, with warehouses and living quarters enclosed behind high log walls and a gate that was locked each night, stood on the top of a cliff on the north side of the Nisqually River. The Nisqually formed on a glacier on the northwest side of Mount Rainier and in a steep, 50-mile descent ran through the largest and most fertile of the treeless prairies north of the Columbia. The Nisqually farm of the Puget Sound Agricultural Company extended all the way from the sound to the Cascade Mountains, 30 miles distant. Where it entered the sound, the Nisqually cut a wide delta known as Nisqually Flats, a swampy, brushy expanse covered with small trees and laced with winding channels, a haunt of waterfowl.

The Hudson's Bay post at Nisqually (and to some extent the great farms of the Puget Sound Agricultural Company) was largely the creation of Dr. William Fraser Tolmie, who modified McLoughlin's authoritarian rule even more than did Ogden. Tolmie was born in Scotland and was graduated from the University of Glasgow medical school in 1832, when he was twenty years old. A severe illness made his future in Scotland dubious, and with some doubt that he would survive, he joined the Company to serve as a physician and surgeon in the Northwest. His genius was recognized even in his youth: the Arctic explorers George Back and John Richardson advised him before he set out. Tolmie carried Alexander Wilson's *American Ornithology* with him on his voyage around the Horn, read deeply in Oriental history and geography to prepare for the fur trade with the Far East and, after stopping at the Hawaiian Islands, carried dahlia bulbs and other flowers to plant around the posts in the wilderness. He was the first to try to climb Mount Rainier; he collected native plants, studied bird life, studied geology and found coal deposits, and collected Indian legends. His first act when he took charge at Nisqually was to discontinue fur trade on Sunday. He called the Indians together and through an interpreter explained why he was doing so. "I explained the creation of the world," he wrote in his diary, "and the reason why Christians and Jews abstained from work on Sunday, and had got as far as the Deluge in sacred history, when we were requested to stop, as the Indians could not comprehend things clearly."

Such was the head of the Company post on whose goodwill the Simmons party would depend. They could not have found a more sagacious neighbor. Tolmie not only endorsed the beliefs that were embodied in the Oregon constitution; he served in the Oregon legislature. In the fall of 1845, when Simmons finally began construction of his settlement, Ogden and Tolmie continued their aid to the Americans, Ogden furnishing the crank for a gristmill that Simmons built on the Deschutes, and Tolmie providing supplies and employment at the post itself for some of the men in the American company. The new settlement became known as Tumwater and was adjacent to where the state capital was later built at Olympia. Not all the original thirty members (including children) located at Tumwater. The Negro, George Bush, settled with his family at Bush Prairie, a few miles away. But as the first community of Americans north of the Columbia, Tumwater had some historical importance. If the disposition of the region was to depend on the wishes of the people who settled in the Oregon country, the American claim rested on the people in Tumwater, for they were, except for Bush and Jackson, the only ones.

The Company had been too successful in its efforts to discourage settlers. There were no Americans there before the Simmons party, but there were no British settlers either. The Company belatedly settled some of its former employees on farmlands, but they were outnumbered by the few American arrivals. But the Company was not risking a mass migration following Simmons's lead. It was almost taken for granted that when the boundary between the United States and Canada was ultimately decided, the Columbia River would be the point of division. When that happened any American settlers north of the river could not expect the British to honor their land claims or to credit them for the improvements they made on their property.

Simmons was undisturbed by fears of any such eventual confiscation. He erected a sawmill, as well as a gristmill, and became the leader and spokesman for the few Americans who ventured north. The provisional government of Oregon, to exercise some sort of administration over these settlers, appointed a board of commissioners to represent it. Simmons served on this, along with James Forrest, the manager of the Cowlitz farm of the Company, and Sir James Douglas, who in 1846 followed McLoughlin as head of the Company's post at Vancouver. In the summer of 1846 the British government unexpectedly abandoned its claim to all the territory north of the Columbia River and agreed to a settlement of the boundary along the 49th parallel. With that event Simmons's property became valuable, as its title was secure, and American settlers rushed into the Puget Sound region. For Simmons himself, however, the period of prosperity was phenomenally brief.

Simmons was my Grandmother Cantwell's father, and in my childhood we were occasionally required to go to Tumwater for some celebration honoring his memory, or for family reunions. They were not very festive occasions, and the story of Simmons's life, despite some heroic achievements, was imbued with a distinctive sort of Northwestern melancholy. As the founder of the first American settlement in what became Washington State, his photograph was frequently published, revealing a kind-looking man with a light beard and mustache, regular and sensitive features and an expression of sadness in his eyes. The family gatherings took place in midsummer, on a Sunday, and often revolved around my grandmother's brother, Christopher Columbus Simmons—so named because he was born on the Columbia River after his parents crossed the plains—who was honored at appropriate intervals because he was the first white child born in the region. And he was a noble figure of a pioneer patriarch, with a long white beard, kindly features and a benign pride in his fine beds of Olympia oysters on the tide flats of Mud Bay.

Around him were other members of the Simmons family named after heroes. Simmons's own brother was Andrew Jackson Simmons, but the names that Simmons gave to his sons were those of patriots less temperamental and more sagacious than Old Hickory. There were George Mason Simmons, named for the author of the Bill of Rights; Francis Marion Simmons, for the brilliant, untaught and kindly Swamp Fox of the Revolution; David Crockett Simmons, for the honest and outspoken wilderness hero; and Benjamin Franklin Simmons, for the philosopher. Their names seemed to invest them not precisely with the qualities of the great men they were named for but with a sort of unreality which made them not so much living relatives as people one read about in textbooks. We were led from one venerable figure to another, in particular past an array of elderly women in black crinkly dresses, and loudly introduced, or rather identified, someone shouting into an aged ear, "He's Catherine's grandson!" or some other indication of distinction within the family circle. The strain of melancholy visible in Simmons's portraits seemed to have been handed on to his descendants, or to be attributed to them if it was lacking, and we somehow got the impression, as one ancestor after another looked us over, that we had failed to brighten their outlook on the world.

We rarely saw these relatives except at such times; they seemed to materialize briefly once a year from whatever historical period in which they had their real being to examine the rest of the population in the hope that someone in the later generations would duplicate the achievements of a better and more prosperous time.

The truth was that the family was overwhelmed with reverses almost as soon as Michael Troutman Simmons became wealthy. As the earliest American settler, Simmons held a number of important posts, including that of the first representative from Washington elected to the legislature of Oregon when Oregon Territory was created. A certain impracticality in his nature, evident in his commercial dealings, was evident also in his disregard of political realities when he made himself the advocate of the cause of the Negro pioneer George Washington Bush. The law of the Oregon provisional government, enlightened in most respects, called for the expulsion of all free Negroes within six months after notice was served on them, or a punishment of thirty-nine lashes, repeated at six-month intervals until the offender left. Also, the procedure for claiming land, while extremely generous, was limited to white people. The racial provision threatened Bush's title to his land claim on Bush Prairie. Simmons put through the legislature a measure that specifically exempted Bush from the racial provision of the law and later secured an act of Congress confirming Bush's title. Simmons's political opponents—he was an antislavery Democrat—charged that he was paid by Bush to render these services, but that was not the case; he acted from principle.

And by that time Simmons had himself become wealthy. During the California gold rush, lumber in San Francisco sold for as much as $1,000 a thousand board feet, and Simmons's waterpower mill could cut some 3,000 board feet a day. The boom was short-lived; steam sawmills were rushed into operation, and $200 a thousand board feet became a common price, dropping within three years to $35 a thousand. Simmons sold his mill to Captain Clanrick Crosby, a Maine sea captain, for $35,000.

Captain Crosby is identified in some Northwest histories as the great-grandfather of the singer Bing Crosby; in fact he was Bing Crosby's great-grandfather's brother. Captain Nathaniel Crosby (the ancestor of the singer) was a sea captain who settled in Portland, Oregon, and prospered there, after which a shipload of his relatives— no fewer than thirty persons—followed him from Maine. Captain Nathaniel then moved his shipping business to Hong Kong, where he died, and it was his son, also named Nathaniel, who returned to the United States and settled in Tumwater, where Captain Clanrick Crosby was established.

In the meantime Simmons invested the $35,000 he received from Clanrick Crosby in a brig, the *Orbit*, which was in Puget Sound with a cargo of general merchandise. One of the partners for whom the cargo was intended had died, and Simmons was persuaded by the survivor to take over the dead man's share. The owner of the townsite of Olympia, Edmund Sylvester, gave Simmons two town lots with the understanding that Simmons would start a store there. Until this time all goods had to be purchased through the Hudson's Bay Company, and it was still necessary for a purchaser to prove that he had a need for goods before he was allowed to buy—the old provision to prevent trade with the Indians and to provide a means of discouraging unwanted settlers.

As the only place where people could buy without restriction, the store prospered as greatly as had Simmons's lumber business before it. The supercargo of the *Orbit*, a young man named Charles Hart Smith of Calais, Maine, became manager of the store. He sailed with the *Orbit* to San Francisco, sold its cargo of lumber at a profit, bought supplies and returned to Tumwater. The fresh goods were sold through the Simmons store so profitably that Smith was considered a financial genius; it was predicted that he would become a financial power on the Pacific Coast. The *Orbit* was again loaded with lumber, and Smith, carrying all the available cash of the business, again sailed to San Francisco to buy more merchandise. In California Smith sold the lumber, but he also sold the *Orbit* and disappeared, taking with him, in gold, some $60,000 of Simmons's money.

IV

Simmons's financial disaster was followed by a family tragedy. During his brief period of wealth other members of his family, most of them living in Illinois, set out across the Oregon Trail to join him at Tumwater. The party was headed by Israel Broshears, a former Mississippi River pilot who had married Simmons's sister Catherine. The party was large and well-equipped, with new wagons, strong teams of oxen and considerable livestock. They set out early in the spring of 1850 but moved very slowly. They were handicapped in various ways. Samuel Ryder, who had married another of Simmons's sisters, Susannah, was almost helpless; his sight was failing, and he was now virtually blind. Simmons's mother, an elderly woman, had remarried after the death of Simmons's father, and she and her second husband, Austin Morton, were not strong. Beyond Fort Kearney, Nebraska, on Friday, June 7, 1850, the party was stricken with cholera, and seven members died.

A physician, Dr. David Swainson Maynard, was traveling on his mule to the goldfields. Maynard kept a diary of his western trip. "Find plenty of doctoring to do," he wrote of June 7. "Stop at noon to attend some persons sick with cholera. One was dead before I got there and two died before the next morning. They paid me $8.75. Deceased were named Israel Broshears and William Broshears and Mrs. Morton, this last being mother of the bereaved widow of Israel Broshears. We are 85 or 90 miles west of Fort Kearney."

Maynard had attached himself to a wagon train, making himself useful while his luggage was carried in one of the wagons and he rode on his mule. The train to which he was attached moved on while he remained with the Broshears party. He was with them from noon until dawn the following morning. "Left the camp of distress on the open prairie at half past 4 in the morning," Maynard wrote in his diary. "The widow was ill in both body and mind. I gave them slight encouragement by promising to return and assist them along. I overtook our company at noon twenty miles away."

The hired man who had been traveling with Susannah Ryder and her husband fled the Broshears camp for fear of the pestilence. The passing wagon trains refused to stop. Mrs. Broshears tried to get help to bury the dead; in later years she remembered only that her main concern was to bury the bodies deeply so the wolves would not get at them. She was then thirty-three years old, accounted a beautiful woman, a reputation the photographs taken in her old age support, but slight and rather frail. Her brother-in-law Ryder could not help her, and her stepfather, Austin Morton, was dying. Late in the day she managed to hire some men to dig graves that were deep enough, and then, incredibly, the party again moved on.

They had gone only a few miles when Maynard, coming back, met them. "Went back and met the others," Maynard wrote in his diary —that is, the survivors of the Broshears party—"in trouble enough. I traveled with them until night. Again overtook our company three miles ahead. Made my arrangements to be ready to shift my duds to the widow's wagon when they come up in the morning."

This he did and was soon in charge of affairs with the remnants of the Broshears party. Maynard was then forty-two years old. He was short, 5 feet 4 inches tall, but muscular and powerfully built. He became a figure of prominence in the Northwest, the founder of the city of Seattle, its first physician and its wealthiest citizen. The story of his life as written by Thomas Prosch, a respected Northwest historian, had it that he was born at Castleton, Vermont, on March 22, 1808, though no record of his birth could be located there. He attended the local school and studied medicine under Dr. Theodore

Woodward, professor of surgery and obstetrics at Castleton Medical College. No record of his attendance could be found in that institution, which subsequently became the medical school of Middlebury College. In 1828 Maynard married Lydia Rickey—no record of this marriage could be located either—and soon thereafter moved to Ohio. There, according to his story, he became one of the founders of Cleveland Medical College, the first in that city, later the medical school of Western Reserve University. Again, no record of a Dr. David Maynard could be found in the archives of that institution. In about 1837 (again according to Maynard's story) "he became responsible for another man to the extent of $30,000. The business failed, and in the wreck Maynard was financially ruined." He lived in obscurity in Ohio for the next twelve years. With the discovery of gold in California he began to plan to get away. "In coming to this determination he was moved also by the disaffection of his wife, whose nagging and fault-finding had become well-nigh unendurable."

An inability to find birth records or educational records does not mean they do not exist, or that further research might not unearth them; still, the lack of documentation of any kind in Vermont, together with a similar lack in Ohio, is at least unusual. The only concrete evidence of Maynard's life before his meeting with Mrs. Broshears that I was able to locate was an entry in the 1850 census. There a Dr. David Maynard and his wife and two children were counted in the town of Carlisle, Ohio (later a part of Elyria), on September 27, 1850. But by that time, according to Maynard's diary, he reached Simmons's home at Tumwater and delivered to the pioneer his widowed sister. "We were received with that degree of brotherly kindness," he noted in his diary, "which seemed to rest our weary limbs, and promise an asylum for us in our worn-out pilgrimage."

It had indeed been an arduous journey, 120 days of unbroken toil, characterized by ailing oxen, shortages of food and water, long drives by moonlight, the increasing hostility of Mrs. Broshears's sister, Susannah Ryder, at the doctor's attentions to her sister. Maynard was in charge of everything. He hired a helper, George Benton (a nephew of Senator Thomas Hart Benton), met by chance on the way; he paid the ferrymen at river crossings; he sold Mrs. Broshears's cattle for $110 to pay for flatboat passage for the party down the Columbia River; he bought himself a horse for $55 (it was stolen before he could bring it to the camp) and long before the Rockies were crossed Mrs. Broshears left all decisions to him. If, as Maynard insisted, he gave up his own plan to go to the goldfields only in order to aid Mrs. Broshears, he revealed a concern by a physician for the well-being of a patient scarcely to be matched in the annals of medicine.

Simmons was less grateful than Maynard expected him to be. He paid the doctor $100 for helping his sister across the plains. The doctor set out on a canoe trip on Puget Sound to locate a coal deposit. He sold his claim and then settled in Olympia; he had no reluctance to work at manual labor and through the spring of 1851 worked cutting wood to be sold in San Francisco, paying his passage there in that manner.

He was now more than unwelcome at Simmons's settlement at Tumwater. Mrs. Ryder threatened to shoot him on sight. As Maynard's biographer put it:

> Mrs. Broshears soon found herself to be in high favor with the bachelors and widowers. Her people speedily saw the trend of affairs, and they tried to direct it into quarters to suit themselves and their own ideas of propriety and of personal desirability. Knowing that Dr. Maynard was a married man, from his own admissions, they disapproved of the bent of inclinations shown by him and their widowed sister. They made suggestions of other men, introduced them, and did what they could to break up the contemplated alliance between Maynard and Mrs. Broshears. They restrained her somewhat of her liberty, and prevented her going with him when they could.

In California Maynard conferred with Senator John Weller, a vehement proslavery politician who defeated General John C. Frémont for election to the Senate that year. Maynard had known Weller in Ohio. Four years younger than Maynard, Weller was born in Ohio, received his degree at Miami University in that state, studied law, and was elected to Congress in 1839 for the first of the three terms that he served as Congressman from Ohio. Weller enlisted at the start of the Mexican War, rose through the ranks from private to colonel, and after his return to Ohio ran for Governor, narrowly missing the Democratic nomination in 1848. He started a law office in San Francisco during the gold rush, beginning a political career that led to the Senate in 1851 and to the governorship of California six years later. Weller was an aggressive and implacable opponent of the Free Soil and antislavery movements, an accomplished conspirator, and an advocate of a proslavery Pacific republic. He was remarkably well financed also. He showed Maynard a chest full of gold so heavy that Maynard could not lift it.

When Maynard returned to Olympia, he had enough goods and capital to start a store. Edmund Sylvester, owner of the Olympia townsite, who was a friend of Simmons and had given Simmons the land for his store, discouraged rivals from starting competing businesses. When Lafayette Balch, another historic figure in the territory, unloaded a shipload of goods at Olympia, Sylvester made impossible terms for Balch: Edmond Meany in his *History of the State of Washington* wrote that Sylvester "was afraid the opposition might injure Simmons's store." Maynard now received the treatment that had been given Balch. "The other dealers," said Maynard's biographer, "made it as unpleasant for him as they could. In the end they got rid of him."

Maynard moved his goods to Steilacoom, where the Army had built a small post. He remained there only a short time. David Denny, a young member of a family that had located in Oregon, had built a cabin on a point of land near where the city of Seattle was later laid out, and on November 13, 1851, a schooner landed twelve adults and twelve children to form the nucleus of a settlement. They called the place New York, after the city, in anticipation of future greatness, but presently added the Indian word Alki, meaning "by and by." The point was too exposed to be a good townsite, and in February, 1852, three of the settlers staked out adjoining land claims on the sheltered side of the bay in what became Seattle itself. In the meantime Maynard had been directed to the same site by an Indian chief, Seattle, who had recently been baptized by the Roman Catholic priest, Father Modeste Demers. Maynard reached the site of the future city in March, 1852, a month after the first settlers. His supply of goods made him a welcome recruit, and the boundaries of the claims that had been tentatively staked were adjusted to make room for Maynard's claim; he had by all odds the best location in the area. The site of the town was shaped like an hourglass, with a narrow neck of low land separating the steep hills of the business and residential districts from the tide flats and industrial areas to the south. Maynard's land took in most of this narrow portion and controlled access to the north and south. His land was also on a level expanse that fronted the sound and, as such, was the logical location for both docks and a railroad terminus.

Maynard worked with remarkable speed and energy. He surveyed and laid out a townsite of fifty-eight square blocks, with eight lots in each block, and a public square on one boundary. He named the streets, including one named for Senator Weller, and called the town Seattle. In October, 1852, his friend Henry Yesler, also from Ohio, settled at the edge of Maynard's claim and built a steam sawmill, Maynard adjusting his boundaries to provide room for Yesler's mill. Operating his store, running a blacksmith shop and also practicing medicine, Maynard sold town lots for almost nothing or even gave them away, a practice that led to ridicule at the time but that actually stimulated the growth of the town and helped it to become the largest settlement on the Sound. The land that Maynard disposed of in this fashion was in the southern half of his claim, in the more level portion; the hilly portion to the north, which ultimately became the downtown business district of Seattle, was not divided into lots and remained in his wife's name after the southern portion had been sold.

Maynard was in a curious dilemma as a property owner. In taking out 640 acres as a married man, he automatically conferred the title of half his land to his wife. The land law of Oregon, passed on September 27, 1850, provided that a man who had been a resident of Oregon on or before December 1, 1850, was entitled to 320 acres on his own account, and if he was married at the time, or became married within one year—that is, by December 1, 1851—his wife would also be entitled to 320 acres. Maynard arrived at Tumwater on September 25, 1850, in ample time to qualify.

There had been great uneasiness among the settlers as to whether Congress, after Oregon became a territory, would validate the land titles granted by the Oregon provisional government. Congress, however, accepted the Oregon donation land claims, but in so doing Congress made a distinction between the settlers who reached Oregon before the gold rush and those who came during it or later. A settler could take out his 640 acres as a married man provided he had lived there before December 1, 1850. That is, Maynard could have had an unequivocal claim to what became the most valuable real estate in the Northwest, but in that case half of his property would have belonged to the wife he had left in Ohio.

By the fall of 1852 he was a political figure of some importance, and when a convention was held to petition Congress to set aside Washington Territory as distinct from Oregon, he was one of the delegates. They met at Monticello on the Cowlitz River, later the site of Longview. The convention informed Congress that there were now three thousand inhabitants in the region (doubling the actual figure) and argued that Oregon as then constituted was too large to be administered. Since the Oregon legislature supported them, their memorial to Congress was accepted almost without debate, and Washington Territory was thus created.

The settlers returned to their cabins after the convention. Maynard went on to Oregon, where he petitioned the legislature to grant him a divorce. He stated that he married Lydia A. Rickey in the State of Vermont on August 28, 1828, and that they resided in Vermont until 1834, when they removed to Ohio, where "Lydia still resides." Maynard further stated that he and his wife continued to live together until the spring of 1841, that in April of that year, on returning home after visiting a patient, at about ten o'clock in the night, he "found his wife lying with a certain John Helmrick in an obscene manner—that the undersigned had previously doubted her chastity, but had never seen anything positively confirming his suspicions, at which time the usual relations existing between man and wife ceased."

Maynard mentioned in his petition that he wished to bring his two children to Oregon. There was a discrepancy between the dates he gave for their birth and that given in the census of 1850. The census gave the year of Henry Maynard's birth as 1831, the petition 1830; the census listed Frances Maynard's year of birth as 1838, and the petition for divorce made it 1837. The bill was introduced by Isaac Ebey, one of the first settlers on Whidbey Island in Puget Sound, a renowned pioneer figure who was later beheaded by Haida terrorists from Vancouver Island. Ebey presented the bill as a personal favor to Maynard, although he spoke against it because of his opposition to divorce in general. The bill aroused grave misgivings on a point about which the early settlers were most sensitive: land ownership. Maynard's ground for divorce was the alleged act of adultery of his wife. No proof was offered, nor was any defense by the wife requested by the legislature. The right of legislatures to grant divorces, though often questioned, had been affirmed by the Supreme Court, which held that the marriage contract was not a contract in the sense that the Constitution prohibited laws impairing the obligation of contracts.

But in Oregon, and especially in Maynard's case, a divorce involved the wife's claim to 320 acres of the 640 acres that the husband had taken out as a married man. Unmarried, he could have had only half as much. The effect of the divorce was to take the wife's half and present it to her former husband. As Mrs. Maynard's lawyers later said, "Here was an act of the legislature, passed without notice to her, before she had ever been to Oregon, and when no cause of divorce as against her existed. . . . Here was an act done which disposed of the wife's dearest interests, in her absence, without her knowledge, against her will, and without inquiry." And as Maynard's biographer wrote rather chillingly, it was evident that Maynard "could have anything he asked for that the legislature could give." If he used this power to secure something more than a divorce, no record of it remained. His bill of divorcement was passed on December 10, 1852, and on January 15, 1853, he and Mrs. Broshears were married. Andrew Jackson Simmons represented the family at the ceremony, the rest of the Simmons family remaining opposed.

V

Simmons's fortune continued to decline as that of his new brother-in-law improved. He gave up his store in Olympia and his original homesite at Tumwater, eventually moving to a farm near Cowlitz Landing, a day's travel from the settlement he had founded. He was again in the wilderness. He retained his standing with the old settlers and was referred to as the Daniel Boone of the territory, but he was out of place with the new arrivals, such as Maynard, and especially with the proslavery arrivals from the Southern states. General Isaac Stevens, the first territorial governor of Washington, appointed Simmons his chief Indian agent and praised him highly as "one of the oldest settlers, if not the American pioneer . . . a kind, frank, confiding man, of excellent judgment, and strong sense."

But words of that sort became rare. At one time the territorial government of Oregon had tried to honor him by naming a county where he had first settled Simmons County; he asked that it not do so. His rejection of the honor was not a pose; he was genuinely indifferent to public notice in the face of the work he hoped to do. (The county was named for James Thurston, the territorial delegate to Congress, who died on his way to the capital.) There was now little likelihood of any such offer's being repeated. The era of goodwill that came with the formation of the provisional government was already part of the remote past. No one recollected that there had been a time when American backwoodsmen and British officials served on equal terms in the same legislative body. Even more remote was the self-discipline, or the spirit of accommodation in matters of everyday life, that dual citizenship made necessary. All that remained was a vague sense of the old days as a time when the pioneers worked together—"people helped each other out"—and that time was indulgently regarded as the sentimental vaporings of the older generation about the past, or ridiculed as never having existed at all, by the hard-driving members of the shrewd and aggressive generation that had displaced them.

What gave Simmons a remnant of his former standing was his mastery of Indian languages and his knowledge of Indian psychology. In May, 1849, he warned Dr. Tolmie that Patkamin, a Snoqualmie chief, was planning an attack on the Hudson's Bay post. His warning was dismissed as alarmist. Patkamin was indeed on the warpath, but he was seeking war with the Nisqually tribe. At that time four American settlers were employed by the Company in building houses outside the Nisqually post—the Company was improving its properties in preparation for the cash settlement for them provided by the treaty of 1846—and they continued to work even after Patkamin appeared with his men at the gates of the post. Patkamin went inside and began a lengthy oration demanding that the white men leave the country, while his warriors milled around the gate. A gun was fired by accident. The Indians tried to storm the fort with their chief still inside. The gates were closed—on the Indians, but also on the American workmen. Four were shot and two were killed, before a cannon fired from the fort ended the attack. Patkamin went unpunished. He had a perfect alibi; he was holding council with the whites when it happened. He became known as a crafty and dangerous individual (it was oddly out of character that he acted as Maynard's guide when Maynard searched for coal deposits soon after he arrived at Tumwater), but Patkamin personally somehow always avoided responsibility for events. Only his brother and a lesser chief of the Snoqualmies were hanged for the murder of the Americans.

As Governor Stevens's agent, Simmons played a major part in the series of treaties with the tribes west of the mountains that the governor concluded in 1854 and 1855. The many treaties between the Indian tribes and the United States government were less than perfect, and a number of them were appalling; the only defense that could be made for them was that other countries treated subject peoples even worse. From the time of George Washington's first treaty with the Delaware Indians, each tribe was regarded as a separate nation, a difficult situation at best, but particularly so in the Northwest, where many tribes were little more than separate families or loosely connected bands. But insofar as any Indian treaties could be said to have been good, those which Governor Stevens made, and which Simmons had a principal part in negotiating, were the best. Their merit was not only in their generosity but in their application of civilized principles: they were the only Indian treaties ever made by the government that outlawed human slavery.

That principle applied only to the four treaties made by Stevens in the region where Simmons was the Indian agent. The clause outlawing slavery was not included in other treaties made by Stevens with tribes east of the Cascade Mountains. The first of the four was concluded at Medicine Creek on December 26, 1854, with the Nisquallies and eight other tribes and bands in the southern Puget Sound area. The practical provisions included a large reservation, an annual payment of $32,500, and the right of the Indians to fish at their accustomed places. (Indians in the Puget Sound region ordinarily owned fishing sites on the rivers, usually in the shape of cedar houses that were occupied by the family during salmon runs, and these were often far distant from the main community or tribal ground and thus outside the boundaries of the reservation.) But the important innovation in the Medicine Creek treaty was Article XI. It read: "The said tribes and bands agree to free all slaves now held by them and not to purchase or acquire others hereafter."

Virtually all Indian tribes kept slaves—usually other Indians or, in the South, some Negro slaves. None of the treaties previously negotiated by the government with the Indians contained antislavery provisions. The Medicine Creek treaty appears to be the only action by the Federal government freeing slaves before the Emancipation Proclamation during the Civil War. The treaty aroused intense antagonism in Washington. It outraged Jefferson Davis, then Secretary of War, who systematically undermined Governor Stevens's position in the capital, but it was nevertheless ratified in the last days of Franklin Pierce's administration. The Medicine Creek treaty was followed with another containing the same antislavery provision, with the Duwamish and other tribes near Bellingham Bay; a third treaty, with the Clallam and other tribes along the Strait of Juan de Fuca; and a fourth, with those along the Pacific Coast. Ratification of these treaties was held up by the Senate, but they were eventually ratified on the eve of the Civil War.

James Gilchrist Swan, author of *The Northwest Coast,* was present at the treaty-making with the Coast Indians and left a casual glimpse of Simmons on that occasion. The camp was on the bank of the Chehalis River about 10 miles from Grays Harbor, with fourteen white men and some 350 Indians—Chinooks, Chehalis, Quinault, Satsop, Cowlitz and others. A 3-acre expanse of ground was cleared to form a square, in which one great tree served as the backlog for a huge camp-fire. The tents and wigwams of the Indians were ranged around the square, each tribe allotted a separate space. Governor Stevens's tent was near the river, with the tents of the other whites around it. On tables, and on frameworks of poles, were carcasses of beef, mutton, deer, elk, along with salmon, wild geese, ducks and other game. The Indians were cheerful—"the best feelings prevailed among all"—and as the proceedings were delayed waiting for other chiefs to arrive, the white contingent made it a social occasion. "There were some tales of a wild and romantic nature told at that camp," Swan wrote, adding that Sidney Ford, the first judge, and Colonel Simmons did their part. "Old frontiersmen and early settlers, they had many a legend to relate of toil, privation, fun and frolic. . . ." Swan made their accounts sound like ancient history. In fact they were talking about things that had happened eight or nine years before.

The hostility focused on Governor Stevens by Southerners in the national capital spilled over on Simmons as well. During the brief and suicidal Indian war in Washington Territory in 1855 and 1856, Simmons was an aide to Governor Stevens and was able to perform services as an Indian agent that prevented the spread of the conflict—services which, however, were violently misrepresented in Washington and led to an investigation of his conduct of the Indian agency. The war began with the murder of Andrew Bolon, a special agent to the Yakima Indians (Simmons's opposite number east of the mountains), by a Yakima Indian named Qualchin—Loolowcan, in an alternative spelling— who was the son of Owhi, the principal Yakima chief. To show his good faith, Bolon had gone alone to confer with the Yakimas. Loolowcan volunteered to escort Bolon home after the conference. On the way he shot Bolon in the back, cut his throat, killed his horse and tried to burn both bodies to hide his crime. An Army force of eighty-four men sent to punish the Yakimas was driven back. After this reverse, while troops from Steilacoom moved east of the mountains, Indians attacked isolated homes of settlers in the White River valley near Puget Sound, killing eight and kidnapping the infant child of one household.

The violence spread irregularly, culminating in the tragicomic attack on Seattle on January 26, 1856, by a force under Chief Leschi of the Nisquallies and Owhi of the Yakimas. The city was defended by the sloop of war *Decatur* (whose commander was Guert Gansevoort, a cousin of the novelist Herman Melville), and one of the consequences of the battle was an intensified conflict between Governor Stevens and Seattle citizens (including Maynard) over control of the volunteers. Simmons in this case had disparaged the seriousness of the danger to the city. He was primarily concerned with preventing the spread of the conflicts and in avoiding provocations that could lead to a general war against all the Indians indiscriminately. (The attack on Seattle was a raid conducted by a relatively small element of hostile Indians in the hope of involving other tribes and bringing on such a war.)

One of the most dangerous of possible causes was a practice in which hostile bands hid in the reservations of the Indians who remained at peace. The peaceful Indians did not or could not expel them; the war party among the Americans demanded armed invasions of the reservations to get them out. In this crisis Simmons persuaded the peaceful Indians to leave the reservation and move across Puget Sound to its western shore. He did so on the strength of his personal promise that they would not be attacked by white people or be involved in the crossfire of the white belligerents and the Indian war parties. With no other guarantee, and with no military protection, men, women and children left the reservation for temporary campgrounds. In all, some five thousand peaceable Indians crossed to the west side of Puget Sound and lived in camps there while the war went on elsewhere.

An investigation of Simmons's conduct as Indian agent was subsequently ordered from Washington. The investigator assigned to look into his doings was a celebrated secret agent, John Ross Browne. Born in Dublin, Browne was a medical-school dropout and a newspaper reporter in Louisville who came to the notice of officials as a shorthand reporter of the debates in Congress. His work there led to his becoming a confidential agent of the Treasury. His first undercover assignment was to investigate United States revenue officers in California during the gold rush. On his way to the goldfields, newspaper stories were published announcing that he had been fired. He arrived in California, however, in time to be hired as the shorthand reporter of the debates at the constitutional convention in that state. There was intense national interest in the convention because of the question of whether California would or would not prohibit slavery. Browne gathered his transcription of the debates in the convention into a book. It earned him around $10,000. He subsequently became an author of books of adventure, such as *Etchings of a Whaling Cruise* (the subject of Herman Melville's first work of literary criticism, and one of the sources of inspiration of *Moby Dick*) and *Adventures in the Apache Country*.

Browne became an investigator for the Bureau of Indian Affairs, looking into the operations of Indian agents. Their corruption was a national scandal, so much so that Browne declared the rarest object on earth was an honest Indian agent. Browne was so distinguished in his field that it was, in a sense, a distinction to be investigated by him. The charges against Simmons were vague. It was alleged that he was never present at the central Indian agency. Another charge was that he was illiterate, and, while untrue, this accusation frequently appeared in Northwestern history as fact. Browne traveled through the Indian country around Puget Sound after the Indian wars. He wrote a laudatory report of Simmons's work. "It would be difficult," he said, "to find a more suitable person to conduct the office of the agency." Simmons's personal qualification, as Browne saw it, was that he had known the Indian chiefs for fifteen years, longer than any other American. He was on friendly terms with them as individuals. As for his absences from the office, it was an indication of his hard work rather than otherwise: "Mr. Simmons is necessarily absent much of the time," Browne wrote, "on official visits to various parts of the Sound." In spite of Browne's report Simmons was ultimately removed as Indian agent, but by that time his career was nearly over, and he died in poverty on November 15, 1867, at the age of fifty-three—plainly an honest Indian agent.

VI

In a remarkable contrast to Simmons's career, Maynard prospered for fourteen years. As Seattle grew to become the largest Northwestern city, his land grant became increasingly valuable. Thomas Prosch pointed out that Maynard was "the first professional man, first official, first employer, first real estate seller, first merchant, first in and of a great number of movements and undertakings of business, social and public character." He started the first hospital in Seattle. In his prosperity he studied law, was admitted to the bar and actually practiced for a brief period. His qualifications as a physician were subject to much curious speculation. His medical instruments were conspicuously evident (and eventually wound up in display cases in the local historical society), despite some uncertainty as to his medical background. His biographer wrote that as a physician Dr. Maynard depended "on pleasant surroundings, a cheerful atmosphere, confidence on the part of the patient, the alleviation of pain, fresh air, sanitary conditions, and occasionally a bit of pardonable deception." In all respects Dr. Maynard was undoubtedly able to provide the last of these. He had, however, begun to drink heavily, though he nevertheless retained his medical reputation, his supporters saying that Maynard was a better doctor when he was drunk than the other physicians in the city were when they were sober.

The disaster that struck him came in an unusual fashion; it followed the issuance of a certificate clearing his title to the ownership of most of downtown Seattle. In 1868 the district register of the general land office in Olympia issued such a certificate to Maynard and his wife, something that would normally have been done years before. Half of the original land claim was granted to Dr. Maynard and half to his wife, Mrs. Catherine Simmons Broshears Maynard. In so doing the certificate automatically went to the commissioner of the General Land Office in Washington for approval, usually only a formality. Two years passed. The commissioner noted that the name of the wife was different from that on the original claim and assumed that the first Mrs. Maynard had died. (So fixed did this belief become that Hubert Howe Bancroft, in his *History of the Northwest Coast*, denounced Maynard as a fraud for listing his first wife as dead, though Maynard had not done so.) Before clearing the title, it had to be determined if the woman who was supposed to have died had left heirs. In that case, they would be entitled to her 320 acres.

Hearings began in Olympia in 1872 to determine the real owner of the land. The effect on Maynard's contemporaries in Seattle was immediate. Much of the land had changed hands several times. To some extent all land titles in the city were endangered, and even if one's own property was clear, the mix-up threatened to involve people in lawsuits over adjacent and disputed land. Everything combined, wrote Thomas Prosch, "to create much commotion in Seattle. The people chiefly concerned did not know what to do or how to protect their rights and save their landed possessions. The whole procedure was regarded with disfavor, and those engaged in it were viewed with suspicion."

Maynard and his second wife did not appear at the hearings. They were represented by attorneys. However, the first Mrs. Maynard, formerly Lydia Rickey, was discovered living in Wisconsin, and she traveled to the Northwest to claim her half of Seattle. Maynard enjoyed the sensation that her arrival caused. She lived at the Maynard home during her stay in the Northwest. "I am going to give the people here a sight they never saw before," he said. "I am going to show them a man walking up the street with a wife on each arm."

The townspeople, however, did not enjoy the spectacle; they had too much at stake. The original claim divided the property into two portions, 320 acres to Maynard and 320 acres to his wife. Maynard had sold or given away all but two lots in the portion in his name, but much of the wife's portion was intact. The land office in Olympia ruled that the first Mrs. Maynard, as Maynard's wife at the time he took out his claim, was entitled to the wife's 320 acres. The decision was a fresh shock to Seattle property owners; many of those who had previously paid Maynard for their land now went to the lawyers for the first Mrs. Maynard and bought it again to make sure their titles were clear. But in the fall of 1872 the commissioner of the General Land Office in Washington reversed the officials in Olympia and decided that neither woman was entitled to the land, and the unfortunate purchasers who had twice paid for their lots had nothing to show for their money.

The decision ultimately came down to Columbus Delano, Secretary of the Interior in Grant's administration, who shortly thereafter resigned under fire because of corruption in handling Indian affairs. Delano also decided against both women. Maynard's first wife could not have it; she had never been on the land. His second wife could not have it either for, while she had been on the land during the prescribed period, she had not been Maynard's wife at the time he claimed it. The land was therefore thrown open as public land for entry and sale. Maynard died on March 13, 1873, two weeks after Delano's decision was announced. The lawsuits over his property went on until 1887, when Seattle had a population of forty thousand.

Uncertain ownership forced the city itself to move north, away from the level land of Maynard's original land grant. As a result Seattle was built on hills that sloped steeply into Puget Sound. This meant that long streets were cut on the hills—streets that paralleled the waterfront—and these were connected by side streets so precipitous that any steeper grade would have made them sheer drops. Where Maynard had his home and office, and where he planned a beautiful public square, became the Skid Road, the most famous red-light district on the Pacific Coast, except for the Barbary Coast of San Francisco. Maynard Street and Weller Street and the other avenues that Maynard had named after his friends became a maze of whorehouses, saloons and gambling houses. For half a century the crimes of violence that periodically disrupted Seattle's political life were planned in the labyrinth of the

Skid Road. As late as 1934 the kidnapping of George Weyerhaeuser, heir of the family that dominated the Northwest lumber industry, was planned in a house of ill repute on Fir Street. The railroad stations were built on Maynard's original land grant—there was no other level land convenient to the waterfront—and the L. C. Smith Building, whose forty-two stories made it the tallest west of Chicago, stood on the boundaries of Maynard's land, but the area itself remained blighted.

As such it attracted the attention of Japanese bargain hunters. The Japanese colony in Seattle, built around shipping lines, owned substantial business interests in the city, including banks, insurance companies and shops, and the Japanese also had a monopoly on the truck-gardening business, owned most of the small grocery stores, and provided manpower for all the section crews on the railroads and the superintendents of apartment houses. After Pearl Harbor it was discovered that the Japanese had purchased virtually all the land in what had been the Skid Road and Maynard's old land claim—Seattle had become the largest Japanese city outside Japan itself. The location was strategic, for the ferry system that led across Puget Sound to the Navy Yard at Bremerton had its docks on the waterfront. Moreover, the Japanese-owned property straddled the neck of the hourglass-shaped property and thus dominated passage between the business and residential area on the hills and the industrial area on the tide flats. The Japanese inhabitants were hastily removed to concentration camps after Pearl Harbor, and the disappearance of some $30 million in Japanese assets during the transfer led to postwar actions by Congress which were almost as confused (and lasted almost as long) as had been the legal struggle for Maynard's property in the first place.

In my own childhood, despite Maynard's importance in the family history, we never heard Maynard's name mentioned. We were dimly aware that Michael Troutman Simmons was a respected figure, though we never heard of anything he had done, because he was one of the people who lived in the old days before life had become as interesting and comfortable as it was in our own time, but of the scandal of Maynard and Mrs. Broshears there was no mention whatever. One reason may have been that the second Mrs. Maynard lived to great age, becoming one of the last survivors of the earliest group of pioneers in Washington. She continued to live in Seattle for part of each year, and in the earlier years, before she was forced to sell it, she converted the lower floor of the old Maynard home into a library or reading room. She remained a frail-appearing and delicately featured old lady, but she was in fact sturdy and self-reliant; each summer she crossed the Cascade Mountains on horseback alone to live for a few months in Ellensburg, a practice that mystified other relatives, even while they admired her independence, for she continued to do so while she was in her seventies. She was regarded by younger generations as a source on the history of Seattle, but in this respect she was unsatisfactory to the people who tried to question her. "She does not care much for new people," Thomas Prosch wrote, "and once in a while resents their intrusion in plain words and striking manner."

In all this period nothing whatever was known of what had really happened along the Platte River, or how it had come about that she had left Illinois with one husband and appeared at Tumwater with an unknown man who turned out to be married to someone else. Thomas Prosch, then a young newspaperman (his paper ultimately became the *Seattle Post-Intelligencer*) won her confidence. She wanted to clear Maynard's reputation of the legends that had grown up about him and, to some extent, about her. She loved him, and she still loved his memory; she told Prosch there was no better man on earth than Dr. Maynard, that he was uniformly honorable, helpful to others to the point of self-sacrifice, a man who had failed only because he was too trusting of other men. At last, in 1906, Prosch published a book, *David S. Maynard and Catherine T. Maynard, Biographies of Two of the Oregon Immigrants of 1850.* The work also contained Maynard's diary and, in addition to its publication as a book, appeared in full in Volume I, Number 1, of the *Washington Historical Quarterly*. For the first time the tragedy on the Platte, and the story of Maynard's meeting with the stricken company, became public knowledge.

In the summer of 1939 my wife and I drove across the Oregon Trail, insofar as it was possible to follow it by car, not with any intention of checking on the truth or untruth of Maynard's account but in order to see what remained unchanged in the country the pioneers had crossed on their way to the Northwest. We set out from Independence, Missouri, where a grove of oaks at the edge of the town then formed a parklike clearing where the covered wagons once assembled. There is no highway where the Oregon Trail itself ran. The wagon trains followed a long diagonal across Kansas and Nebraska, while the modern roads run along section lines, in checkerboard patterns. Historical markers and maps culled from emigrant journals made it relatively easy to follow the general course, not with mile-by-mile exactness but from point to point: if we lost the trail briefly, it was possible to locate it again by proceeding to the next town that had been a settlement on the trail.

Most of the way was through thinly settled farm country. Long stretches were altogether uninhabited. Much of the region was unchanged from what it had been a century before. It was a beautiful route, full of surprises in how different it was from what reading

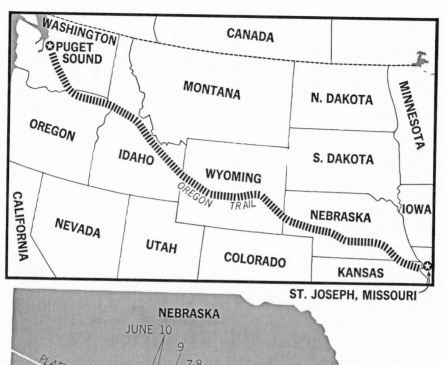

WASHINGTON
PUGET SOUND
CANADA
MONTANA
N. DAKOTA
MINNESOTA
OREGON
IDAHO
WYOMING
S. DAKOTA
CALIFORNIA
NEVADA
UTAH
COLORADO
NEBRASKA
IOWA
KANSAS
OREGON TRAIL
ST. JOSEPH, MISSOURI

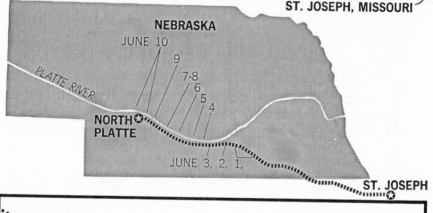

NEBRASKA
JUNE 10
9
7-8
6
5
4
PLATTE RIVER
NORTH PLATTE
JUNE 3, 2, 1,
ST. JOSEPH

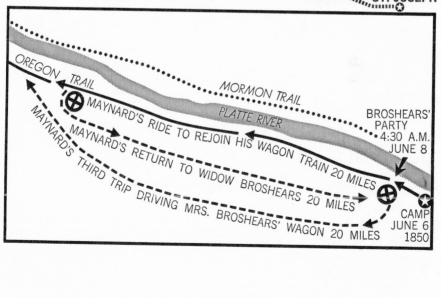

OREGON TRAIL
MORMON TRAIL
PLATTE RIVER
MAYNARD'S RIDE TO REJOIN HIS WAGON TRAIN 20 MILES
MAYNARD'S RETURN TO WIDOW BROSHEARS 20 MILES
MAYNARD'S THIRD TRIP DRIVING MRS. BROSHEARS' WAGON 20 MILES
BROSHEARS' PARTY 4:30 A.M. JUNE 8
CAMP JUNE 6 1850

about it led one to expect—not a dry wasteland, but, in the first few hundred miles, deep green hills and oak groves, clear streams and small ponds and lakes, and then limitless levels of prairie, still unfenced. The days were warm and mild, the light winds billowing the long grass in changing silken patterns. Almost daily there was one short torrential thunderstorm, with rains so violent the water struck with the roar of a falls. The storms cleared as suddenly as they came. Pools lay in sheets over the fields, evaporating almost visibly under the sun, while in the distance there were the lightning-lit clouds of another storm.

The Oregon Trail crossed the Platte River near North Platte, Nebraska, and went into the Rockies along the Sweetwater. There were in 1939 no improved roads after one left the Platte, and often no roads at all, sometimes no more than two ruts in the grass leading to some isolated ranch house or ranger station. We rarely met another car or saw anyone on the way. The only stopping places were occasional stores where a country road intersected some dim remnant of the trail. It was hard going in a car over dirt roads, and the innumerable short, steep hills made one conscious of how difficult it must have been for oxen to haul covered wagons along a way that can be driven only in low gear. In some places, especially at the eastern approach to South Pass, it was a little dangerous by car because the road was only a narrow dirt shelf along a crumbling red-stone cliff. But the principal impression created by recrossing the Oregon Trail was of the enormous extent of country covered and its amazing variety: South Pass itself, a wide, low passage between distant peaks, where the road was no more than a traillike path, barely discernible under the sage, with deep ruts on both sides left by the thousands of covered wagons that passed through there; the ghost town of Atlantic City, on the east side of the Continental Divide at the crest of the Pass, with some old log cabins, two inhabitants, and a spring whose waters flow to the Gulf of Mexico, while Pacific Springs, a mile west, drains into the Pacific Ocean.

It was a deserted world. The only time it was ever populated was when the wagon trains went through. The cool air and the pungent scent of sage at nightfall and the absolute silence heightened the sense of distance from the east and the west. Beyond South Pass numerous indistinct side roads branched off, creating constant uncertainty as to which to follow, and low ridgelike hills, up and down, 10 feet, 20 feet, 30 feet, called to mind what painful up-and-down progress they must have meant for teams. Beyond the Green River lay dry, broken, treeless, rocky country, with gaunt rocks that made the land appear to have been twisted out of shape and hardened; near the

Snake River was the land of boiling springs and geysers, where the country seemed to be intoxicated, with rivers jetting from canyon walls or pouring from underground where they had no business being, reeling through a landscape that had lost its way. Then there was the sudden transition to greenery at Emigrant Hill on the Oregon border, with huge, cool stands of pines and open ground from which one could look out over forested hills that ended in a blue haze on the western horizon.

The place where Maynard met the Broshears party was almost midway between the start of the Oregon Trail and its terminus. The site was on the south bank of the Platte River opposite the town of Cozad, Nebraska. The flat prairie land ended there. About a mile to the south lay a maze of steep, crumpled, green hills and deep canyons impassable for oxen and wagons. The Oregon Trail that elsewhere might be miles wide here funneled into a narrow strip along the Platte, though the river itself was hidden by a belt of trees. There was nothing grim or spooky about the place where Mrs. Broshears buried her dead, but in the early morning it had a spectral air: the sunlight across the flatland to the east washed up against the trees and hills like footlights projected upward while the earth was still in shadows.

> The widow was ill in both body and mind. I gave them slight encouragement by promising to return and assist them along. I overtook our company at noon twenty miles away. Went back and met the others in trouble enough. I traveled with them until night. Again overtook our company three miles ahead. Made my arrangements to be ready to shift my duds to the widow's wagon when they came up in the morning.

Many years after 1939, when it became known that no records of Maynard's early life existed to corroborate his story, a second trip to that part of the Oregon Trail seemed necessary, this one to check on the truth or the untruth of his account. The land was still unpeopled. During the Second World War huge tracts south of the Platte were farmed, but the farms were operated from a distance, so no farmhouses were built; it was cultivated but still deserted. Now it was possible to pinpoint more exactly where Maynard had been. At first glance his story seemed incredible. He wrote that he had remained with the sick and dying from noon of one day, all through the night, until dawn. Then he rode forward 20 miles to catch up with the wagon train with which he had been traveling. Then he rode back 20 miles—or nearly 20 miles, for Mrs. Broshears could not have gone far after burying her dead—or 40 miles in all, after a sleepless night. And now after joining Mrs. Broshears he rode forward with her at least another 20 miles, for he reported that the Broshears train came within 3 miles of where his wagon train had stopped. He then rode forward an additional 3 miles to make arrangements for shifting his duds to the widow's wagon the next day. Two days without sleep and more than 60 miles of hard riding were involved—or perhaps more, if his wagon train had continued on after his first meeting with it.

"Yes, he could have done it," said Judge Samuel Dietrich, president of the North Platte Historical Society. There had been trouble with a gang of teen-agers the night before I arrived in North Platte, and I had to interview the judge and ask his opinion in intervals between his court sessions trying the offenders. The jail cells were filled with them. Judge Dietrich was the great authority on emigrant crossings of the Platte River. He grew up on a farm on its banks and in his youth made a hobby of digging out of the sands the covered wagons that had mired and had been lost trying to cross the river. As floods swept over them, or the current changed, wheels or wagon tongues would become visible above the sand. The wagons were seldom intact, but Judge Dietrich would take a good wheel from one, or part of a frame from another, and thus reconstruct entire wagons. They were dotted around the area in parks and public squares.

My questions to Judge Dietrich had to do with where Maynard could have crossed the Platte. He wrote that it was 51 miles west of the place where he met the Broshears. If that was true it meant that he had ridden 60 or more miles on the day in question, but perhaps there were crossing places lower on the river, which would mean that the distances were not so great as he thought they had been.

"He could have done it," Judge Dietrich said, showing me the various places where the river could have been crossed. That is, he could have ridden the 60 miles he said he rode and still have crossed at the usual crossing place. Judge Dietrich's demonstration took so long that I was afraid I was imposing on him and delaying his return to his court. "No, that's all right," he said, referring to the prisoners in their cells; "they're not going anywhere."

He pointed out the difficulties of travel over the Oregon Trail that the emigrants accepted as a matter of course. Those records contained experiences far more trying than an all-night and an all-day ride. They contained instances of hardships and feats of endurance much more difficult than anything Maynard reported. "It would have been hard," he said, "but he could have done it."

The second Mrs. Maynard died shortly after Maynard's biography was published. The strain of melancholy that seemed to be a heritage of the Simmons family was evident in a photograph of her taken shortly before her death and, in her case, at least, seemed not unwarranted by the experiences she had endured. It was combined with a strong sense of independence that was also a family trait. I knew personally only two members of the pioneer generation of which she was a part—my grandmother and her sister Charlotte, who married a stepson of John Robinson Jackson. They were much like the portrait that Prosch drew of Mrs. Maynard. Like her they were quiet and reserved, and they possessed "a strong and clear sense of past events and people." Unlike her, they had the sociability that developed as they raised their families. In my own childhood the pioneer women were considered somewhat commanding by the townspeople, but in our own relations with them they were so unfailingly generous and kindly that it was impossible, half a century later, not to think of them with affection. Their pride was certainly evident, but they were also simple and good-humored, content with very little and perhaps too proud to give any indication of whatever bitterness they may have felt at the greater material success of the people who had triumphed on the land their families had cleared.

Like most of the women of the pioneer generation, they were constantly planting things. They seemed always to be tending flowers and fruit trees and shrubs and berry bushes, a practice that dated from the successful transplanting in the new region of plants that had been carefully transported in the wagon trains. There was a good deal of interest among the pioneers in the well-being of such growths that had not been found in the country before the Americans arrived. Sometimes a kind of ceremony was involved (though no notice was given of it at the time), such as the planting of a magnolia tree, not ordinarily found in the Northwest, when a grandson married a Southern girl. But the gesture was not even mentioned until the tree reached substantial size several years later. Those pioneer women, to some extent, seemed to feel that they owned the country, or had some sort of claim to it, something that always irritated people who came to the Northwest in later migrations. More than any of the others, the second Mrs. Maynard retained a certain imperious air, and in her case, in the absence of legal titles, the impression was somehow communicated that the place really belonged to her, if only because of the difficulties she had experienced in order to get there.

IV

The Easterners

I

In six months in Panama he crossed the Isthmus six times. He went back and forth from the Pacific to the Atlantic like a prisoner pacing his cell. He had a job of some sort with the Pacific Mail Steamship Company, whose offices were on the second floor of an old Spanish building in Panama City, but he had no regular duties, and no one made things easier for him by giving him tasks to do. Sometimes, carrying his revolver, he helped unload gold that came into port on the Pacific Mail steamers from California. He stood guard on the beach or rode in a rowboat offshore while the natives stripped and carried through the surf the boxes of gold, weighing 70 to 100 pounds each, to be loaded on mules for the trip to the Atlantic side. But that was a volunteer task to keep himself occupied.

At the age of twenty-five Theodore Winthrop was an active, restless, ambitious newcomer to Panama, to whom inactivity became increasingly burdensome. In March, 1853, he quit his easy and well-paid job—$1,800 a year, plus good food and luxurious lodgings—and sailed for San Francisco, saying he was going to visit the goldfields. After a few days in California he left on April 24, 1853, for the Pacific Northwest, planning to gather material for a book about this region that was then prominently in the news.

He sailed on the Pacific Mail's steamer *Columbia*. A fellow passenger was Jesse Applegate, who, after ten years in Oregon, had become a prosperous rancher and a political leader. Winthrop could not have found a better guide to show him the Northwest. If Winthrop was unimpressed by his good fortune, it was because encounters of this sort happened so frequently in his travels as to be almost commonplace.

Theodore Winthrop was the sixth in the line of descent from John Winthrop, the governor of the Massachusetts Bay Colony, and both his father's family and that of his mother, among the most renowned in New England—Jonathan Edwards was in her family line—linked him to people of influence wherever he traveled. He was born in New Haven, Connecticut, on September 28, 1828, the son of Francis Bayard Winthrop, a lawyer who had failed as a merchant in New York; he was wiry and muscular, slight and a little below average height, with thin, regular features, light blue eyes and brown hair, an engaging, attractive individual who made friends easily and whose fortunate acquaintances were by no means dependent on his family connections. But they shaped his views and inclined him to take for granted a meeting he might otherwise have valued more highly.

The *Columbia* steamed north along the coast; Winthrop recovered from a brief seasickness, and his literary ambitions, dormant for a long period, revived. "I wish to write a truly American style," he wrote, "good and original, not imitated." Green and ochre hills that came down to the sea in southern Oregon made him wonder what lay beyond them, deep, unmapped valleys where Applegate and a few pioneers were building their settlements. When the ship entered the Columbia River, Winthrop began keeping a diary: he tried to capture in words the swell and roar of the breakers at the mouth of the wide river, the high wooded bluff above the grand and lonely shore, the brilliant white cone of Mount St. Helens that came into sight as the ship moved upstream, and everywhere the sense of the sunless forest that lay beyond the bold and surf-beaten coast.

The vision of a great book was forming in his mind. He wrote in *The Canoe and the Saddle,* published after his death:

> The Oregon people, in a climate where being is bliss—where every breath is a draught of vivid life—these Oregon people, carrying to a new and grander New England of the West a fuller growth of the American Idea, under whose teaching the man of lowest ambition must still have some little indestructible respect for himself, and the brute of the most tyrannical aspirations some little respect for others, carrying there a religion two centuries further on than the crude and cruel Hebraism of the Puritans; carrying the civilization of history where it will not suffer by the example of Europe—with such material that Western society, when it

crystallizes, will elaborate new systems of thought and life. It is unphilo-
sophical to suppose that a strong race, developing under the best, largest
and calmest conditions of nature, will not achieve a destiny.

He had an opportunity to share in that destiny. The *Columbia*
reached Portland on April 29, 1853, and Applegate invited Winthrop
to join his small group of pioneers in southern Oregon and begin a
new life. But Winthrop was not ready to break so completely with
his past. Applegate set out on a three-day ride up the Willamette Valley to his ranch; Winthrop remained in Portland, then a featureless
town of two thousand people, with the stumps of big trees still standing in its muddy streets. "There is a heartiness and rough sincerity
impressed upon people by the kind of life they lead in these new
countries," Winthrop wrote to his sister Laura. "An easy hospitality,
given and received without ceremony, is a thing of course. In a few
minutes I shall turn in between the blankets of my host, Mr. Malcolm Breck, who has a large store and business here."

II

Unfortunately, some of the hearty and hospitable pioneers had
smallpox, and when Winthrop resumed his travels, he carried the disease with him. In his letters home Winthrop described Applegate
without mentioning him by name; he now named Malcolm Breck
without explaining his connections. Identifying Breck would have
meant something to his family. During the preceding years Winthrop
had worked for William Henry Aspinwall, the founder of the Pacific
Mail Steamship Company, the principal owner of the Panama Railroad and then famous as the richest man in New York and one of the
richest men in the world. Breck was Aspinwall's brother-in-law. Before
he went to Panama, Winthrop was employed by Aspinwall for minor
personal tasks that required discretion, while nominally working as a
clerk in the office of the Pacific Mail Steamship Company. He lived
in the Aspinwall home much of the time. He escorted Mrs. Aspinwall
to social functions when the financier was away, as he often was, tu-
tored Aspinwall's son, Lloyd, and provided agreeable company for his
young daughters. Winthrop was an interesting companion and an
entertaining guest; even more to his advantage, he was the bearer of
a name of great social distinction. Not that the Aspinwall family
was unknown, but it was only in the lifetime of William Henry Aspinwall that it had become the most prominent family in the New
York merchant aristocracy. (William Henry Aspinwall's sister Mary,
for example, married Isaac Roosevelt, of Hyde Park. Their son James

married Sara Delano, and their grandson was Franklin Delano Roosevelt, the President of the United States some eighty years after the events herein recounted.)

Malcolm Breck was the younger brother of Mrs. Anna Breck Aspinwall, so much younger than the financier as to belong to a different generation. How often Winthrop had written to his mother that he was conducting Mrs. Aspinwall to another of her charitable events! And how often on summer Sundays, he had ridden with her on long carriage drives over the country roads of Staten Island! But no echo of the relationship appeared in Winthrop's travel letters home from Portland: Mr. Breck was merely a hospitable storekeeper. And in fact Winthrop's relations with his family were only fitfully confidential. He was spoiled as a child, a favorite of his mother, indulged by his sisters and accustomed to having his own way. His father was twice married; he had two sons by his first marriage and five children—three daughters and Theodore and a younger son—by his second wife. The death of Francis Bayard Winthrop when Theodore was twelve years old had a powerful effect on Theodore, so much so that he could scarcely remember anything that happened before his twelfth year. At fourteen Theodore entered Yale. He was dismissed at the beginning of his sophomore year for some unspecified offense; he said it was because he broke the windows in the rooms of a freshman.

His half brother by his father's first marriage, the Reverend Edward Winthrop, was an Episcopal minister in Marietta, Ohio, and Theodore was sent to him for a year of disciplined study. Unfortunate for everyone concerned, the experience was a psychological disaster for Theodore. His half brother was nearly twice his age, and applied an inflexible severity that was scarcely distinguishable from active dislike. Theodore's half brothers had grown up in different circumstances from the children of their father's second marriage. Their mother was the daughter of Moses Rogers, who was an extremely wealthy New York merchant; their boyhood home, in those early prosperous years of Francis Bayard Winthrop's life, was a mansion on Turtle Bay at the East River. It could hardly have been expected that a half brother approaching middle age would have had much sympathy for a boy of Theodore Winthrop's temperament, independent and self-contained, and growing up in a thrifty, genteel condition of greatly reduced circumstances. Theodore was active and athletic, fond of outdoor sports, especially skating and swimming, and a superb horseman. He was considered an exceptionally good-looking boy and was neat and clean, orderly in his habits, accustomed to withdraw from his family and read in his father's library—Francis Bayard Winthrop had literary tastes and, as one indication of the sort of books he liked, was one of the first readers to appreciate the stories of Nathaniel Hawthorne when Hawthorne was still unknown.

After a year with his half brother, Theodore was readmitted to Yale. In *John Brent* Winthrop gave some indications of his feelings about his half brother: he portrayed in that novel a well-nigh demented minister who ceaselessly tormented a boy because of misdoings that he considered to be sinful and "gave him to understand that he was a child of hell." In any event, Theodore had no further disciplinary trouble in college. He experienced a religious conversion and spent so many hours praying in his room that his sisters feared he was losing his mind. He had the closest of family ties with Yale: his mother's brother, Theodore Woolsey, was professor of classics there, destined to become president of Yale before Winthrop's graduation. Winthrop studied with obsessive zeal, was graduated with honors and, while beginning graduate studies, collapsed.

For a year he traveled in Europe, keeping notebooks, writing poetry and undertaking trips in search of health that would have felled a robust man. Nervous exhaustion, vague and unlocalized illnesses, stomach pains and recurring attacks of crushing despondency alternated with brief periods of feverish sociability and enthusiasm. Only his shortage of money kept him from visiting Turkey after he traveled in Greece, and long after he was expected to return to New Haven, he was still in Paris, running up tailor bills that embarrassed him years later.

During his European journey Winthrop visited his schoolmate Richard Hunt, whose father, Judge Jonathan Hunt of Boston, had established a Paris residence that became a center for American expatriates; the two sons of the family, Richard and William, were studying art, and Richard, who subsequently became famous as the architect of the mansions of the Astors, Belmonts, Vanderbilts and others, figured also as one of the characters in Winthrop's novel, *Cecil Dreeme*. It was during his visit with Richard Hunt that Winthrop first met Aspinwall. The financier had experienced astounding good fortune just at that time. Gold was discovered in California on January 24, 1848, and in April, 1848, before news of the discovery had spread to New York, Aspinwall chartered the Pacific Mail Steamship Company, which had a government subsidy for operating steamers on a regular schedule between San Francisco and Panama City, in effect a monopoly on shipping on the Pacific Coast.

President Polk's message to Congress later that year confirmed the report of the gold discovery, starting the gold rush of 1849, and Aspinwall, who was a wealthy merchant before this time, became overnight a commanding figure in New York financial affairs. A single one-way voyage of one of his four West Coast steamers from San Francisco to Panama made a profit of $70,000. Profits on this scale, however, evoked financial rivalry, and Aspinwall was involved in a merciless struggle with George Law, another dynamic millionaire. Law was a huge, corpulent, shabbily dressed man, coarse and bullying in his manner, remembered as one of the most unpopular individuals in the history of New York City; Aspinwall was kindly and courteous, "addicted to literary and artistic pursuits," in the language of the time. Law was a railroad builder and canal builder who went into the shipping business in 1847 when Congress first authorized subsidies for steamship lines carrying mail on regular schedules. Law started a line whose steamers sailed from New York to the Isthmus of Panama, with stops at Havana and New Orleans. In so doing he broke a virtual monopoly which the firm of Howland and Aspinwall held on trade with the northern ports of South America. With profits from trade with the California goldfields, Aspinwall set up a line of steamers to compete with Law's subsidized line on the Atlantic. Law retaliated by placing four steamers on the Pacific Coast, sailing between San Francisco and Panama City.

Aspinwall was associated with John Lloyd Stephens, a travel writer, adventurer and explorer and American secret agent, who had become the best-informed American about South America. Sent to Honduras on a confidential mission by President Van Buren in 1837—he was to explore a canal route, report on the effects of the emancipation of slaves in the British colonies, and find out why every American consular representative sent to Central America died on the job—Stephens returned to the region often. If he ever discovered why all the consuls died at their posts he never publicly revealed it, but he learned something he did publicize. He was the first explorer, if not the discoverer, of the Mayan ruins in the jungle, about which he wrote his great book, *Incidents of Travel in Central America, Chiapas, and Yucatan,* and he was on familiar terms with the members of the governments of the Central American republics. So he was able to secure from the Republic of Colombia a concession giving him the exclusive right to build a railroad across Panama. With Aspinwall's money, the Panama Railroad Company was incorporated in New York, Stephens becoming president. The railroad became known before the Civil War as "the single most profitable business in the history of commercial enterprise." As one indication of its profitable monopoly, for twenty years—until the completion of the Union Pacific in 1869—all the gold mined in California was carried on Aspinwall's steamers and over his Panama railroad, $750 million in all.

When Winthrop returned to the United States after his European tour, he began to work in the New York office of the Pacific Mail

Steamship Company and thereafter lived much of the time with the Aspinwall family in their summer home on Staten Island or in their new mansion, the most magnificent in the city, on University Place near Washington Square. At that time he was paid only the salary of a beginning clerk. His office duties were light: he copied letters or walked across the lower end of the island of Manhattan to deliver tickets to a connecting steamship line. But he was called upon to serve as Aspinwall's emissary in social affairs, especially those having to do with literary and artistic circles in which the financier was regarded as a patron of the arts.

Aspinwall's financial dominance was accompanied by tremendous risks; the cost of the Panama Railroad (on which some six thousand laborers were believed to have died while laying 47 miles of track) threatened him with ruin. Winthrop described him in *Cecil Dreeme:* "His gigantic schemes are the terror, the wonder, and the admiration of Wall Street . . . a large, handsome man, a little conscious in his bearing, but courteous, hospitable, open-handed, using wealth splendidly— in fact, my ideal of what a rich man should be."

When his struggle with Law had become critical, Aspinwall asked Winthrop to take his son Lloyd, and a nephew, to Switzerland to find a school for them there. This was in 1851, and Winthrop, who was then not quite twenty-four years old, found the responsibility a heavy one. His troubles were increased by "the indulgence and expectations of the boys." To his horror, no school in Switzerland would accept them. He went from one schoolmaster to another, "only to find," he wrote, "that his final judgment was against taking Yankee boys of that age; then beginning with another, with no better results. This has been very amazing to me." When he at last found a schoolmaster willing to enroll them, Winthrop returned at once to Aspinwall in New York, with nothing like the loitering in Paris that marked his first European trip.

In a scene in *Cecil Dreeme,* the narrator meets an aging financier: "He received me cordially. His manner had a certain broken stateliness, as of a defeated sovereign, to whom his heart says, 'Abdicate and die.'" Aspinwall did neither. He reorganized the steamship company, took Law into its directorate and removed his steamers from competition with those of Law in the Atlantic, in return for Law's removal of his steamers from the Pacific run.

Violent measures were foreign to Aspinwall's character, insofar as the public knew it. But violence attended his Panama ventures. His ships were wrecked and burned. The cost of replacement ran far above estimates. In 1850 a Howland and Aspinwall gold shipment was robbed of $150,000, and an express company had $100,000 in gold taken while crossing the Isthmus. The largest gold robbery, $250,000, took place in

September, 1851, about the time Winthrop took the Aspinwall boys to Switzerland. The Isthmus Guards, a secret law-enforcement agency organized by the Panama Railroad Company, hanged thirty-seven suspected members of the gang of thieves, without trial, on the promenade at Panama City.

Winthrop had planned some venture into Latin America; he began studying Spanish soon after he started work for the steamship company. But he was in the humiliating position of having to ask his mother for money for his lessons. For that matter, he depended on her for money for his clothes, for the old tailor bills from his Paris days and for expenses connected with keeping up his place in society. He was trusted by Aspinwall in money matters as well as family matters, to a certain extent—he bought paintings for Aspinwall's art gallery (open to the public) and was given a free hand in the bidding, though he bought prudently and cautiously, $300 for a Thomas Cole landscape being his largest purchase—but he still received only his clerk's salary from the steamship company. He left his card at fashionable homes on New Year's calls, and he knew many of the hostesses of the city through Mrs. Aspinwall, but any office boy could do the work that he was doing, and Aspinwall showed no inclination to advance him in business: Winthrop was still working, or more exactly not working, at the job he held at the start, while around him his contemporaries were on their way to fortunes.

Winthrop tried to make something of his work. He asked for an appointment as purser on a West Coast steamer. There pursers could acquire capital, carrying goods to ports where there were shortages and becoming partners of local merchants. Coal supplies were a problem in the Pacific, and Winthrop wrote to the famous geologist, Dr. Benjamin Silliman, who had taught him at Yale, to ask what he should look for on surface terrain that might imply coal deposits below.

Nothing came of that either. Aspinwall appeared to have forgotten his existence, though in the summer of 1852 Winthrop was more occupied than before in serving as Mrs. Aspinwall's companion and escort. His feelings were wounded when another fashionable young man told him that the Aspinwall girls joked about him and repeated his sayings as the witticisms of their private genius. It came to Winthrop forcibly: "I cannot conceive of any year being in most respects more disagreeable than this has been." On August 19, 1852, when Aspinwall came to his office, he found Winthrop's letter of resignation on his table. Winthrop asked leave to terminate his connection with the company if he could not be given work of some responsibility and promise of advancement.

After some reflection Aspinwall asked Winthrop to come to his office.

He expressed the highest regard for him, thanked him for the work he had done in the past and asked if he would accept a post in Panama rather than resign. Winthrop was taken aback but agreed. He had expected something better. He feared his mother's disapproval, for Panama was an unhealthful place. John Lloyd Stephens had returned to New York a month earlier, a dying man. Even without the loss of this formidable associate, Aspinwall would have found the fall of 1852 a critical period; Stephens's impending death made it disastrous. Stephens had pushed the railroad along as far as it had gone—fares alone on the uncompleted line brought in $7 million—and violence increased as the time approached for joining the rails. In September, 1852, the month Winthrop left for Panama, the paymaster of the Panama Railroad was attacked and robbed. Seven miners homeward bound with their gold were robbed and murdered on the trail to the railhead. Retaliatory action by vigilantes resulted in the hanging in Panama City of forty-one suspected members of the ring of gold thieves, without trial.

John Lloyd Stephens died in New York on October 10, 1852, and by the time Winthrop reached Panama the railroad affairs were more confused than ever. The cashier Winthrop had expected to replace decided to remain at his post. Winthrop was ignored, if not snubbed. His sister Laura said that "his situation was not altogether a pleasant one for a man of delicacy." Everyone knew, in her words, that he was in Panama only "by the kindness of Mr. Aspinwall, and his sincere desire to serve him." What everyone knew was that he was Aspinwall's pet, or his former pet, and Panama City was a long way from New York. Winthrop liked the Pacific Mail office, the huge rooms with thick stone walls and open rafters 30 feet overhead to leave space for cool air; he enjoyed riding every evening over the savannahs near the city; and he shared the excitement when the *Tennessee* steamed in from San Francisco with $2 million in gold and when the *California* arrived with a record shipment of $2.6 million. At such times he could force his way as a volunteer guard into the closely knit ranks of the local employees. But he had left New York in the hope of advancement, and at the end of six months he still had no regular job to do. His letters to Aspinwall were not answered. For a man of delicacy he endured for a long time a situation that appeared not so much uncomfortable as dangerous.

III

A heavy rain was falling the morning after Winthrop arrived in Portland. Instead of going to Fort Vancouver, a few miles away on the Columbia, as he had intended, he spent a restless day waiting for the rain to stop. He visited Dr. John McNulty, the physician of the Pacific Mail Steamship Company, an adventurous and somewhat mysterious individual who formerly practiced medicine in New York City not far from where Winthrop had rooms. In the spring of 1849 Dr. McNulty had organized the Colony Guards, made up of twenty-five men who, for $400 apiece, were enrolled and, "well-armed and provisioned, dressed in the United States Army uniform," started overland for California. The Colony Guards disintegrated before they reached Salt Lake City. Dr. McNulty made a grueling crossing of the desert, reached the goldfields by the Humboldt River route and by the middle of 1850 was practicing medicine and selling mining stock in Sacramento. He also became involved in promoting a town in the Pacific Northwest, offering for sale "the most desirable lots in Pacific City, at the mouth of the Columbia River, Oregon."

Dr. McNulty had smallpox. Indeed, shortly after Winthrop left Portland, the physician was stricken with the disease in its most virulent form, though Winthrop did not learn that until some time later. Winthrop had a letter of introduction to Colonel Benjamin Eulalie de Bonneville, in command of the United States troops for Washington and Oregon, at Fort Vancouver. Bonneville made him most welcome; he gave him quarters in his own house for several days. He assigned Lieutenant Henry Hodges of the Fourth Infantry, a sociable young officer, to escort Winthrop down the grassy terraced slopes from the Army post on the hill to the old Hudson's Bay post on the bank of the Columbia to take their stirrup cup with Peter Skene Ogden, governor of the Company. Hodges shared quarters with Captain Ulysses S. Grant, and Winthrop met Grant at that time. Another officer sharing Grant's quarters was Lieutenant Thomas Brent, who was commanding a small party of soldiers bound east through the mountains. Suddenly abandoning his plan to write a book on the Northwest, Winthrop decided to go with them. At The Dalles, the falls that marked the head of navigation on the Columbia, he went riding to explore the countryside, collapsed and could barely get back to the small fort the Army maintained there. His illness was diagnosed as smallpox, and he was quarantined, one of the officers giving up his quarters for him.

In his delirium Winthrop was haunted by a recurring dream. Vengeful Indians were trying to kill him for having introduced smallpox among them. After three weeks he emerged from isolation dazed and weak and seemingly in a different world. The soldiers under Brent had long since left for Salt Lake. The Columbia had flooded. Great sheets of water spread over the lowlands and subsided. The land seemed utterly deserted. Near Vancouver the smallpox epidemic had entirely wiped out one Indian tribe and almost exterminated another. The tragedy made a lasting impression on Captain Grant: the stricken Indians riveted themselves on his memory. He saw them trying to cure themselves in their steam baths—"It would kill every time," Grant wrote. Grant also remembered a Hudson's Bay physician who set up a hospital for the Indians "not a stone's throw from my own quarters, and saved nearly every Indian he treated."

Winthrop's shaky account was not so graphic. He wrote of seeing Indians "dying in crowds, almost every one who was attacked." His own fever was light, and his features were unscarred, but he had trouble getting his bearings again and was undecided as to what he should do. A Hudson's Bay boat came down the Columbia with a cargo of furs. The boatmen had come from Fort Colville, racing along with the powerful Columbia current, exhilarated by their great annual adventure and unwilling to stop before they reached the end of their journey. They packed all day around the falls of the Columbia and at five in the evening, with Winthrop as a passenger, started down the last miles. "The evening was most lovely," Winthrop wrote, "and after rowing awhile, at nightfall the Indians all went to sleep at the bottom of the boat, and we floated downstream all night by starlight. . . ."

At four in the morning they reached Vancouver. Winthrop now had to make some concrete plan of action. It was already June 5, 1853, or thirty-six days since he had arrived in Portland, and he had neither seen anything of the country nor had any experience more stimulating than the monotony of Panama. A part of Winthrop's indecision came from the conflicting impulses in his own nature: he wanted to reach into an unknown and unspoiled wilderness, in which he dimly felt that he saw some promise for the future of America, but he was also a citizen of the Old World, more deeply involved in social and intellectual stirrings than he acknowledged to himself and constantly drawn to it, despite the boredom and weariness he experienced in his years in New York or the feverish alternations of enthusiasm and dissatisfaction he had known in Europe.

More deeply, he was at odds with his family over an old familiar dispute in the Winthrop inheritance—the question of his religious faith. The religious fervor that alarmed his sisters in his college days was over: he had broken with the Puritan creed of his New England ancestors; and his relatives and friends in New York society, whose adherence to the Episcopal Church was an integral part of their social position in the city, were shocked and offended by his expressions of skepticism. Even those circles which were not notably devout and, indeed, often characterized by worldliness and unabashed greed, were nevertheless steely in an insistence on the outward signs of devotion, and though Winthrop sometimes went to church, occupying the

Stuyvesant pew in Grace Church when the family was away, he could not accept their division between the Christian ideals expressed and the kind of life that was lived and accepted and condoned. Nor could he accept the Puritan concept of sexual pleasure as sinful. He went through periodic sessions of despondency so shattering that they sometimes seemed to be evidence of some physical disorder as much as of psychic strain, and while he was too active and restless to be involved in anything like a prolonged struggle to find a religious faith, he nevertheless tried to come to grips with what he really believed, if only to avoid causing his mother the pain evoked by reports reaching her that he had become an atheist.

But at last he felt he had to write to her and tell her that he had neither faith nor any religious belief. To a descendant of the founder of the Massachusetts Bay Colony, it was a cruel admission. He was a good deal gossiped about. George Templeton Strong, the famous diarist of New York social and political life, another of Winthrop's distant cousins, reported that Winthrop had fallen upon evil ways, in addition to the social handicap created by his outrageous puns and his flippant antireligious witticisms: he had become "a lump of grim conceit . . . letting off gas about atheism and propounding horrible paradoxes." It was not enough, Strong said, that Winthrop had lost his own belief in God; he was becoming a missionary of atheism, trying to seduce his sister Laura and her husband to join him in infidelity.

Laura was Mrs. William Templeton Johnson, a charming, quiet and beautiful young woman who was closer to Winthrop than anyone else. He called her Johnny, a nickname occasioned by her enthusiasm for marriage after her own happy marriage to Mr. Johnson. Johnson was a stolid, good-looking and good-hearted young attorney who appeared to live in a state of bemused and modest surprise at the ardent poems she addressed to him celebrating their domestic happiness. She was, however, a naturally gifted poet, in the old tradition of household poets, expressing in candid and simple sonnets and lyrics the family joys of their Staten Island life, her adoration of her husband and her hatred of slavery. She wrote with a feminine directness and grace that made Winthrop's long philosophic poems seem no more than dim and wandering exercises in words. One of her sonnets might have been a commentary on her brother's intellectual bafflement with his emotional problems:

> Love is no iron fetters of the soul,
> But true election, freedom good and wise . . .

But for the most part her poetry was spontaneous and unstudied, its substance everywhere around her in the casual life of gardens, streets, music, the pain of illness in her children, her sympathy for a mother whose child had died:

> Oh, Father, pity thy poor child,
> Who cannot bear her burden long.
> Oh, lift the shadows black and wild
> In the dark vale, or make her strong.

Sometimes she put in a few words the questions that Winthrop struggled with interminably in his philosophic poems: words, she wrote, were the concealment of struggling thought—"silence must our refuge be at last." Or in moods of sadness she found music the ghost of happier hours. A glimpse of an unknown child seen for an instant led her to write:

> Depth on depth are in her eyes!
> Dark and liquid mine they meet,
> In a wilful strange surprise,
> Searching all the dreary street.

But her life was centered on her family, so much so that it was referred to cryptically by Winthrop in *The Canoe and the Saddle* when he wrote: "Our lives forever demand and need visual images that can be symbols to us of the grandeur or the sweetness of repose. There are some faces that arise dreamy in our memories, and look us into calmness in our frantic moods. Fair and happy is the life that need not call upon its vague memorial dreams for such attuning influence, but can turn to a present reality, and ask tranquility at the shrine of a household goddess." A hardworking household goddess was what Laura was, summed up in her later years in an anniversary poem to her husband:

> Thus I am evermore, as now, thine own,
> Still more and more thine own as years pass by,
> Life draws its sweetness but from thee alone,
> And pride forgets itself in ecstasy!

Winthrop confided in her, and the recollection of his doubts and forebodings remained to trouble her long after Winthrop himself had replaced them with others in his restless ventures and ambitions. In her memoir of her brother she wrote that Winthrop's feeling about the political collapse of the United States, or its near-collapse in those pre-Civil War years, was a factor in his alternations of despair and strenuous striving. The Fugitive Slave Law, she said, was a final blow to his belief that a new and just social order would come into being in the New World; he saw America, no longer the world's hope of freedom, drifting to disgrace and total ruin, a slave whip in her hand. The loss of religious faith destroyed his barriers against temporal defeats and errors; he could no longer hear, in his own phrase, "those great calming words without which life grows restless, and may not dream of peace."

These two gifted children of the Winthrop line were conscious of their heritage, but the ancestral figure who meant a great deal to them was not Governor John Winthrop, the source of family pride of their relatives, but the poet William Alabaster, who was a kinsman and contemporary of Governor Winthrop, a wayward and inspired man who responded differently to the struggles in England that led Governor John to try to found a new world in America. The poet Robert Herrick considered Alabaster the best poet of the time. He was indeed marvelously gifted, often suggesting an earlier Gerard Manley Hopkins, and somewhat like Hopkins also in his struggle to find religious faith and in the gnarled and cryptic lines in which he expressed it. But he was a man of his times as well, an intimate friend of the Earl of Essex, a court favorite, a Puritan who suffered for his beliefs in England, a convert to Roman Catholicism, a priest in Rome, ultimately imprisoned by the Inquisition for his questioning and ambiguous views. Then he somehow returned to England, where he ended his days as the rector of a country Church of England parish. "Alabaster" was a code word with Winthrop and his sister. It marked a distinction between those Winthrops who were aware of their kinship with the poet and those who were not, or who would not have appreciated the greatness of Alabaster's sonnets if they had known them. Winthrop's own poetry was generally without distinction, but passages in his intense prose, especially in *The Canoe and the Saddle*, sometimes echoed Alabaster's magnificent lines:

Long tyme hath Christ (long tyme I must confess)
Held mee a hollow Reede within his hands,
That merited in Hell to make a brande
Had not his grace supplied mine emptiness.
Oft times with languor and newfangleness
Had I been borne away like sifted Sand,
When sinn and Sathan gott the upper hand,
But that his steadfast mercie did me bless.
Still let me grow within that living lande,
Within that wound which iron did impresse,
And make a springe of bloud flow from thie hand:
Then will I gather Sapp, and rise, and stand
That all that see this wonder maye expresse
Upon this grounde how well grows barrenness.

A sense of loss characterized Winthrop's writing: the loss of hope for his personal career, surely, and for the future of the country, and more deeply than either the loss of religious faith that left him at the mercy of impulses and alternating periods of enthusiasm and despair. He did not know what he should do, or why he should do anything, beyond a determination not to return to his home and his old life without having come to terms with the inward forces that had driven him to leave them. The brief confidence that had generated his travels had ebbed. He rode through Oregon without knowing where he was going. Two days after his arrival at Fort Vancouver, and a brief visit in Portland, he rode slowly southward along the valley of the Willamette. He bought a mare, a fine animal that proved his ability to judge horseflesh still remained with him. He rested at noon in riverside groves, letting his horse graze. He bathed in some wild brook and slept under the trees before riding on.

On the west there was the Coast Range, a rough and desolate chain, and on the east the Cascades, with the giant snow peaks rising at almost regular intervals. All along the way the settlers who had taken out donation land claims lived a mile or so apart in rough shacks. They were afraid that the land titles granted by the Oregon provisional government would not be validated by the Federal government, so they did not improve their land. Their wealth was in cattle, grazing in natural pastures where small clear streams flowed into the Willamette, and wealth it was, for shipments of beef to California made them rich without working.

The women in these cabins were lonely, Winthrop wrote, glad to have a visitor and "captivated by talking of the trip across the plains, which almost all the Oregon women have made." After three days Winthrop crossed the Willamette where it turned east into the Cascades and rode another day to Applegate's farm. He unaccountably missed it, rode beyond and stopped for the night in a grove of oak trees. He put his horse to pasture, built a fire in a dead tree, ate an evening meal of dry biscuits and slept through a tranquil and starry night.

In the morning he retraced his steps to Applegate's farm, which consisted of a large log house and barn, five hundred head of cattle, fifty horses and a flock of sheep so large no one bothered to count them. The farm lay in a sheltered and windless valley, with a small stream that drove a gristmill. Applegate's daughter Rozelle wrote that her father had killed two bears and forty deer in the three years since he settled there. Applegate had eight children, the youngest a baby named Peter Skene Ogden Applegate in honor of his old friend of the Hudson's Bay Company.

Applegate had a simple solution for Winthrop's uncertainty: he urged him to settle in Oregon. But Winthrop became increasingly restless as his health improved. He rode about southern Oregon in the way he had crossed the Isthmus, though now his journeys, hundreds of miles long, led him to the goldfields. He made plans and rejected them, and sometimes seemed to be resisting some impulse even while he knew that, in the end, he would give in to it. With Applegate he rode down the Umpqua River valley along the river where Hall Kelley had traveled by canoe. Their way led past secluded farms like Applegate's, where one of his neighbors had brought across the plains the first thoroughbred in the Northwest, named Kentucky Belle. They visited Scottsburg, founded by one of Applegate's roadbuilding and pathfinding companions, where mule trains set out for the newly opened Siskiyou goldfields. Near the mouth of the Umpqua, the nearest port to those fields, there were traces of ancient trading unrecorded in history, in the shape of relics and trading goods from Spanish trading vessels centuries before. Winthrop sailed out to the Pacific from Scottsburg, a voyage of 20 miles down the river to the sea, perhaps to examine the harbor, though he gave no explanation for it whatsoever. Winthrop wrote that Applegate (he now mentioned him by name) "has nearly confirmed my intention of settling in the country." He wrote a little later that he had been given an opportunity to acquire a small fortune in a few months if he would settle in the Northwest. He was inclined to accept it, but for one obstacle: "If I had a home, a wife, something to fix me to a local habitation, I should most certainly establish myself here in Oregon."

IV

In the end he rode back to the Columbia, following an alternate route near the Coast Range. It was the beginning of his return to the Old World, and in retracing his steps one feels that he had always known he would return to it. He reached Vancouver again on July 11, 1853, to embrace whatever secret decision had been reached. This time he did not stay with Colonel Bonneville but went at once to the Hudson's Bay Company post—"where I am always welcome," he remarked obliquely. He wrote in excitement to his brother William: "I wish you could see the great 'brick' of these parts, Governor Ogden of the H. B. Co. and other bricks of the same;—certainly the nicest set of men whom I have had the good fortune to know, free and hospitable, full of fun and good sense. This Oregon is a noble country!"

Ogden had just published *Traits of American Indian Life and Character,* his first book—his only one, as it turned out, for he died the following year. He wrote it for the wife of Sir George Simpson, the head of the Company, because she asked him what life on the frontier was

really like. It was an interesting work but probably did not greatly en-
lighten Lady Simpson.

Colonel Bonneville was at a disadvantage in the area around Vancouver with this formidable wilderness hero. Bonneville was what his
contemporaries ridiculed as "a history-made man," meaning the creation
of writers of history, a publicity product. The guilty historian in his
case was Washington Irving. Born in France but raised in the United
States and educated at West Point, Bonneville had a generally undis-
tinguished military career that included a notably unsuccessful explor
ing expedition through the Rockies to the Columbia. On a leave of
absence from the Army, he secured private funds to back a party of 110
men and twenty wagons in the hope of making a fortune in the fur
trade. After going through South Pass, he established Fort Bonneville
(known among the fur traders as Fort Nonsense) on the Green River in
Wyoming, but he never occupied it. He sent a portion of his party to
hunt on the California coast, but after a luxurious winter among the
Spaniards the men returned to the mountains, their chief accomplishment, in the words of Edmond Meany, having been "the murder of a
number of poor Digger Indians in revenge for the theft of a beaver
trap," and a later encounter during which "half a hundred of these most
inoffensive of natives were slaughtered."

Washington Irving, when he wrote *Astoria,* drew on Bonneville's
diary and later was induced to write *The Adventures of Captain Bonneville,* in which he attributed to Bonneville deeds of daring, narrow
escapes, heroic rescues and adventures which had in fact happened to
Kit Carson, Jim Bridger and many other early trappers and traders. The
good captain seems not to have been at all disturbed in reading, in
Irving's account of his life, episodes of which he was personally unfamiliar, and as the book became enormously popular, Bonneville thereafter served in remote Army posts with great dignity and impressive
military bearing, bestowing on such visitors as came his way his genuine
hospitality and charm.

Captain George McClellan was also at the post at Vancouver. He
reached there on June 27, 1853, under orders from the Secretary of
War, Jefferson Davis, to explore the Cascade Mountains. He was now
assembling his force for one of the most baffling fiascoes in the history
of exploration. On July 11, 1853, Winthrop wrote to his family that the
exploring parties were just starting from Vancouver. "I should have
joined them if I had been on the spot when they were organized," he
said, "but now I do not think it best." Instead he set out for parts
unknown with the most notorious individual in the United States.

It was always Winthrop's fate to come upon celebrated people in odd
circumstances, but he never again equaled his meeting with Captain

William Howard in Vancouver. Howard was hiding out in the Northwest. He was the principal figure in the divorce case of Edwin Forrest, the greatest Shakespearean actor of his time, and his wife Catherine. Howard was a handsome, powerfully built man, generally silent in company and domineering and inflexible in his personal relations. Born in Maine in 1807, he was commissioned a captain in the Revenue Service when he was only twenty-one years old. He commanded the *Detector*, patrolling for smugglers, with a crew of seventeen men. At about the same time Howard became a friend of Edwin Forrest, two years older, who was even then a well-known actor.

After a year of routine duty, Howard was suspended from the Revenue Service for misconduct of a nature not specified in his official record. He hurried to Washington to state his case and was restored to duty. Otherwise his record for twenty years shows only a year's furlough, without pay, in 1835, during which he traveled abroad—nothing in his life, in fact, prepared him for the sensational developments that began in 1849.

Howard had lived well, staying at the Astor House when on duty in New York, which was much of the time. He was an inconspicuous member of the social and literary circle around Nathaniel Willis, a poet and editor who was the most influential figure in New York literary affairs; and he often stayed overnight at Forrest's home on West 22nd Street. Howard did not really belong in literary circles. He wrote nothing and gave no indication of intellectual interests. But he appeared and disappeared where one would hardly expect to find him: at the home of Anna Lynch, the most celebrated literary hostess of the period, an intimate friend of Edgar Allan Poe; or at parties for Mrs. Caroline Kirkland, the author of *A New Home: Who'll Follow?*—a gifted and charming woman, a friend of Winthrop's, who died while serving as a nurse in the Civil War. Howard was also often in the company of Richard Storrs Willis, a musician, the composer of the popular "Glengarry Waltzes" which led Stephen Foster to start writing music. Winthrop had known Richard Storrs Willis in New Haven, and Nat Willis was an old friend of the Winthrop family. One of Willis's early poems was written in honor of Laura Winthrop on her second birthday.

But literary and musical acquaintances could hardly have brought Captain Howard into national prominence. He became famous by way of his connection with the Forrests. Forrest's position as a theatrical figure, and his unusual temperament and history, increased national interest in the details of his domestic life, which were startling to begin with.

Forrest made his first stage appearance in Philadelphia when he was only eleven years old. He was gifted with a lightning-fast memory and was so precocious that he was a stage star in his own right by the time he was sixteen. He was an athlete, a good boxer, an acrobat skillful enough to perform with a circus, which he did at one time. At the age of twenty-five, about the time he first became friendly with Captain Howard, Forrest was internationally famous, earning $16,000 for eighty performances a year. By 1847 his earnings of $33,956 for 158 performances a year surpassed those of any British or American actor in previous history.

Forrest married Catherine Sinclair, daughter of an English musician, after an extended period of sowing his wild oats, and settled down to a more discreet life in a brownstone house in the Chelsea district of Manhattan. Mrs. Forrest, a tall, beautiful young woman of great poise, was not precisely a member of New York's intellectual circle but rather an occasional and honored guest at literary gatherings. Forrest personally took no part in them or, if there was a literary dinner in his own home, put in a token appearance before going to the theater. But Mrs. Forrest often entertained while Forrest was on tour.

During a London engagement Forrest became convinced that William Macready, his only rival in Shakespearean parts, was trying to sabotage his English appearances. Forrest took a box in a London theater and, while Macready was delivering Hamlet's instructions to the players, loudly hissed the performance, starting an international dramatic war. When Macready toured the United States, Forrest opened in the same cities in the same plays. He also hired supporters to bombard Macready with eggs and vegetables.

Mrs. Forrest tried to persuade Forrest to modify the language of one of his newspaper advertisements attacking Macready. Forrest accused her of taking Macready's part because of her English background. He ordered her to leave him. She refused. For three months they lived in the same house without speaking. At length Mrs. Parke Godwin, daughter of the poet William Cullen Bryant, asked Catherine to make her home with her family until she could establish a residence of her own. Catherine accepted gratefully; Mrs. Godwin's social position prevented any scandal that might have followed if she had been forced to return to England.

The day after Catherine left Forrest's house, William Macready arrived in New York. His first performance was broken up by Forrest's hoodlums. Macready canceled his American tour. Almost every literary figure in New York, from the aged Washington Irving to the young Herman Melville—270 names in all—petitioned Macready in newspaper advertisements not to give way to the thugs. Accordingly, on May 10, 1849, Macready opened at the Astor Place Theatre in *Macbeth*. Rioters had infiltrated the audience. When Macready spoke his first lines, they howled him into silence and began throwing heavy objects that forced him to ring down the curtain. The Astor Place riot followed; before it was over thirty-one people were killed and an unknown number, a hundred or more, were shot by members of the National Guard.

One month after the Astor Place riot Captain Howard was abruptly dismissed from the Revenue Service. The reason given was "to reduce the number of officers." It was well known that Howard was a friend of Forrest and his wife. To anticipate Mrs. Forrest (who planned to ask for a divorce in New York) Forrest hastily established a residence in Philadelphia and asked for a bill of divorcement from the Pennsylvania legislature. In a long bill of particulars Forrest accused Mrs. Forrest of misconduct with a number of men, but most specifically of adultery with Captain Howard. As a result of this circumstance, Mrs. Forrest's suit in the New York court was devoted to a point-by-point examination of the charges which were brought in Forrest's bill in Pennsylvania. Forrest was represented by John Van Buren, son of ex-President Van Buren, the leader of Tammany Hall, and Catherine was represented by Charles O'Connor, a political opponent of Van Buren, who was sometimes called the most distinguished lawyer in the city.

Apart from Captain Howard, there was no real case against Mrs. Forrest. She was charged with having been intimate with Nathaniel Willis (and Forrest, meeting the poet near Central Park, beat him to the ground), but Willis was aging and sedentary and of such tastes and inclinations that the charge was laughable rather than otherwise. However, servants offered explicit descriptions of Mrs. Forrest and Captain Howard in sexual intercourse, and these were widely published. In addition to the charge of adultery, Mrs. Forrest was accused of having encouraged Captain Howard's seduction of Anna Dempsey, a fifteen-year-old girl who had been a maid in the Forrest home. Van Buren brought Anna to the stand "to show the lewd and licentious conduct that was pursued in that house." Her testimony was not altogether convincing, but it was graphic and detailed. Not only were stenographic reports published in the newspapers; paperback books were hastily printed which, while limited only to what was said in open court, were more explicit and detailed than anything else then published relating to sex.

There was consequently a demand that Captain Howard be brought to testify, but he could not be found. Forrest's lawyers reported that they were told he was in the Sandwich Islands. In fact he was in Vancouver, Washington Territory, where Winthrop met him on July 12, 1853. (Mrs. Forrest was granted a divorce, with alimony of $3,000 a year, but Forrest appealed and successfully resisted paying anything for sixteen years. However, a new trial was expected, and the scandal had reached such proportions that Howard was well-advised to remain in hiding.)

He was promoting a coal mine on Bellingham Bay, only 18 miles from the Canadian border, over which he could easily make his way if necessary. He was at the point of leaving for his property, and he and Winthrop decided to travel together. (Before they left Vancouver, Winthrop made arrangements to travel east with the last government mail party of the year, which would leave in two months' time.) Winthrop and Howard traveled down the Columbia and up the Cowlitz to Monticello on the Hudson's Bay Company steamer. There, in Winthrop's words, they "took possession of the room of the H. B. Co's resident." At midnight they were awakened. Lieutenant William Petit Trowbridge, a young West Point graduate on his way to make studies of the tides at Cape Flattery, joined them. Winthrop wrote that he and Captain Howard, bothered by mosquitoes, "were glad to be awakened at midnight by Lieutenant Trowbridge, who was left by the steamer, and came down in a rowboat"—a mysterious comment, for if Trowbridge had been left at Vancouver, he could not possibly have reached there so soon.

In the morning the enlarged party started up the Cowlitz in a canoe with four Indian paddlers. The day was hot. The river was dark and deep, winding through wooded lowlands that reminded Winthrop of Panama—"fir trees, principally, some maples, alders, poplars and other water-loving trees"—and many mosquitoes. There were small rapids at Castle Rock, where the river swung in a wide bow around a rocky headland. The Indians abandoned their paddles for poles. They were soon making only two miles an hour against the current. Where the Toutle River comes in from Mount St. Helens, 35 miles away, the current became stronger, and a few miles farther on, where the Cowlitz turns east toward its source on Mount Rainier, the Indians gave up the struggle.

Horses were to have been awaiting the travelers there. But there was no sign of them. "We spent a tedious next day," Winthrop wrote, "waiting for horses, until the next evening, when we rode out to Jackson's prairie, 8 miles on his horses." Prairies that looked like cultivated fields and green pastures sloped away to the shadowy foothills and the silver peaks that became golden and rose-colored at sunset—"the immense bulk of Mount Rainier," Winthrop wrote, "the most massive of all—grand, grand, above the plain!" The travelers made their way through a stand of big trees, part of which remained a century later as a roadside park named for Lewis and Clark. The trail ran past the Cowlitz farm of the Puget Sound Agricultural Company, which now contained some 268 horses and mules, 6,777 head of cattle and 6,856 sheep; it became a repository of Hudson's Bay Company interest after the area passed to the United States.

At nightfall the travelers reached the cabin of John Robinson Jackson. Winthrop wrote that he had built a splendid farm, with "plenty of blackberries, huckleberries and raspberries, these last very fine." On his part, Jackson was interested in his visitors because of news he hoped to hear about the building of the transcontinental railroad— that is, the survey for the line to run from St. Paul to Puget Sound that was then being made by General Isaac Stevens and Captain George McClellan. "All the scanty population is alive with hopes and questions about the great Railroad and the exploring parties," Winthrop wrote. "Every man is confident it must pass through his place."

There still lay ahead of them a long trip to Puget Sound. They set out early the next morning, down sloping land to the valley of the Newaukum River. To the east the forests were continuous to the timberline of Mount Rainier, but there were small prairies, dry and dusty, near the Chehalis, a slow, dark river—Chehalis was an Indian word meaning "sand"—curving through cedar swamps to the Pacific. Winthrop and his fellow travelers rode through Mound Prairie, a mystery, a flat land covered with strange symmetrical mounds of gravel 8 feet high. When darkness fell they traveled by moonlight. At eleven o'clock they heard the sound of a falls. There was enough light so they could see the narrow Deschutes River, the dark outline of the sawmill and gristmill, and the steep drop of water over terraces and down chutes and, far below, the wide, still expanse of the inland sea. They were at Tumwater on Puget Sound, and they had ridden 52 miles that day to reach there.

Somewhere along the way Winthrop lost a week. He reached Tumwater, by his own account, on July 15, 1853. But he did not get to Nisqually, a day's travel distant, until July 24, 1853. Whatever happened to the missing week, he did not regret its loss. The day after arriving at Tumwater, he wrote, "Trowbridge and I, leaving Captain Howard to bring up the traps, started in a noble clipper of a canoe for Steilacoom, the United States fort. Paddled along against the tide. Indians took it easy; shot a duck and a polecat; pulled up a gigantic purple starfish; made a vocabulary of the Snooquamish language. Had a jolly time. Splendid sheet of water, with islands and nooks of bays. Mount Rainier hung up in the air."

Following his mystifying practice of arriving only after nightfall, Winthrop reached the landing at Steilacoom at nine o'clock that night. There was a small civilian store at the landing. The fort itself was 2 miles distant through the woods. It was only a collection of wooden houses and log cabins, which the Army rented from Hudson's Bay for $600 a year, a rental that exasperated the American settlers. "Waked officers," Winthrop wrote laconically. "Supper, and to bed."

Rumors of an impending Indian war made these after-dark arrivals even stranger, for if hostile visitors arrived as did Winthrop and Trowbridge, the post might have been in trouble. In any event, Winthrop reached the Hudson's Bay post at Nisqually by daylight. The fame, or the ill fame, of Captain Howard had preceded him. The Hudson's Bay Company required each post to keep a "journal of occurrences," and that at Nisqually carried this entry: "Sunday, July 24, 1853— Very warm. Captain Howard, accompanied by a Mr. Winthrop arrived from Vancouver. Captain Howard states that he is about commencing to work the newly discovered coal mine in Bellingham Bay. This is the Captain Howard of the celebrated Forrest divorce-case fame, and it is rumored that he is out here to be away when the case is again tried, he being an important witness. This is all table-talk, and very likely there is no truth in the report."

This entry was written by Edward Huggins, the Hudson's Bay Company clerk at the post. Winthrop wrote of Fort Steilacoom: "Barracks in a dry, barren plain; scanty trees. Today walked over to Fort Nisqually—a Hudson's Bay Company farm and station." It was a 10-mile walk, but at the end of it Winthrop's uncanny good fortune in meeting people at the right time continued. Dr. William Tolmie was at the point of starting for Victoria, in the Company's mail canoe, and invited Winthrop to travel with him. Victoria had become the Company's main post on the Pacific.

The mail canoe was a masterpiece. It was not a local product but was a war canoe acquired from those great sailors, canoe builders, oceangoing whale hunters and terrorists, the Haidas of Queen Charlotte Island far to the north. It was driven by eight paddlers and could carry three tons of cargo in addition to its passengers. Winthrop said it was superior to the finest clipper ship ever launched with a bottle of champagne from a modern shipyard on the East River in New York. The Indians recognized it from a distance: when it passed a bay where Indians were trolling for salmon, they stopped fishing and assembled around it. They had heard of the smallpox epidemic on the Columbia River and were frightened, begging Dr. Tolmie to vaccinate them. He did so in the canoe, each Indian paying him one salmon for the operation.

They sailed on. When the wind was against them, the Indians playfully propitiated it by giving it bits of meat or by making extravagant signs of subservience, pretending to back their paddles in the way it was driving. Dr. Tolmie talked about Indian legends. There were strange and disjointed narratives of supernatural events and beings, involving storms and sorcerers, figures made of enchanted cedar wood, seals that towed canoes to wild and unknown shores, gigantic salmon, wars between birds and dwarfs, monsters that breathed fire, trips to distant stars. There was a visitor from outer space who liked the looks of a girl on earth and who, when the women were all picking berries, carried her off to a distant planet. When her child was born, she returned to earth with the baby, on a rope she made of hazel-bush vines, and her lover, tearing his hair, loosed a shower of shooting stars. Unable to persuade his wife to return to him, he got the bluejay to help him, which the bird did by substituting an image of a boy carved out of rotten wood and carrying the child off to his father, the boy then becoming the sun.

When Dr. Tolmie reached Victoria, he lent Winthrop the canoe for his own use. Winthrop cruised around Vancouver Island, his course unclear. One morning when the air was fresh and a wind was blowing, the Indians thought it somewhat risky to set out. In the Strait of Juan de Fuca winds of 50 miles an hour sometimes sprang up almost without warning, knocking up 6-foot waves in a few moments. The squalls looked threatening. But the canoe went nobly over the swells —"just on the safe side of danger," Winthrop wrote. The Indians became wildly excited when big waves struck the canoe. They crossed the strait and glided suddenly into still water behind the islands. Here, too, Indians were trolling everywhere on the sheltered waters. The Indians began to sing—"a careless, jolly, happy race," Winthrop wrote, "amusing themselves with jokes and me with songs, some of which were pretty and original." One song so impressed him that he tried to make musical notations of it. When he put down the paper, one of the Indians picked it up and pretended to read the notes, the rest laughing uproariously.

They were a memorable crew of expert paddlers, whose names never ceased to astonish him. There was Unstu, who was also known as Hahal, or "Handsome," and Mastu, also called La Hâche. Two were members of the Haida tribe: Aituso and Nuckutzoot meaning "the Wolf." The others were Khaadza, Snawhaylal, Ay-Ay-whun, who was nicknamed A-wy, and a man called Paicks. Three women were among the company, Smoikit-umwhal, Tlaiwhal, and Sudzilaimoot. Smoikit-umwhal meant, roughly, "chief," and Sudzilaimoot meant, in effect, "shame on you," or something like that. One of the women was the wife of Edward Huggins, the clerk at Nisqually House; it may be that Winthrop was never far from the observation of the Hudson's Bay Company wherever he was. The native music they sang was lost. A century later ethnologists made recordings of Indian songs in the region, but by no stretch of the most elastic imagination could their keening sounds be described as Winthrop described what he had heard. Perhaps a period in Indian musical history had passed, or had changed as much as the white man's popular music changed from the songs of Stephen Foster to the popular music of a hundred years later.

Winthrop had lost track of time. He left Nisqually on July 25, 1853, and was in Victoria on August 4, according to his notebook. On August 15 he wrote to his mother from Victoria, describing a visit to Captain Howard's coal mine. For once his practice of arriving at night was unfortunate, for his paddlers somehow missed the entrance of Bellingham Bay, a body of water about 4 miles wide. "We landed in a deep, solitary, tarn-like cove, walled in by rocks and overhung by great pine trees. As the canoe entered, thousands of ducks rose from the water and flew screaming about, but the door was shut by the canoe; when we fired, the whole place was alive with echoes. . . . Then in the dim evening and by starlight we floated on, some paddling and some sleeping." In the morning the Indians took him up a river shrouded in almost tropical vegetation, where one of them had a salmon weir, and a fresh-caught salmon provided breakfast.

For another week he apparently remained with Howard, resuming his diary keeping when he left him on August 21, 1853: "Leave in Captain Howard's boat for Port Townsend at 8 A.M.; a calm pull against the tide." And now he was suddenly in a hurry. The government mail escort had to leave The Dalles by September 1 in order to get through the Rocky Mountains before the passes were closed by snow. That left Winthrop only nine days in which to travel the length of Puget Sound and make his way over Naches Pass through the Cascade Mountains. He had accumulated a packet of very interesting notes, he had learned the Chinook Jargon well enough to make himself understood by the Indians but he had nothing as yet to form the book he had hoped to write. All the way he had been in the company of well-informed and civilized people, no different from the people he had known in New York, filled with the same concerns and interests he had hoped to escape.

But now he was altogether on his own. He had first to go to Port Townsend to negotiate for Indian paddlers and a canoe to take him to Nisqually. Everyone he talked to warned him not to try to cross the Cascades alone. No one had done so. In particular he was warned not to travel with a solitary Indian guide, but he was confident of his ability to get along with the Indians. Even in the small matter of the time that he started his trip Winthrop betrayed his inexperience. Leaving Bellingham Bay with the tide against him, Winthrop could not reach Port Townsend that night. He camped on Smith Island, a small, isolated rock on the eastern expanse of the Strait of Juan de Fuca, a resting place for migratory birds, later a bird sanctuary. "Two fires and a moon rising," he wrote in his journal. "A star near the horizon looks like a comet."

Winthrop exaggerated his knowledge of the Indian tribes. The Indians camped at Port Townsend were members of the Clallam tribe, who were generally regarded as peaceful. Pioneer lore had it that the tribes east of the mountains, the Nez Percé, the Cayuse, the Spokane, the Yakima and Klickitat, were dangerous and warlike, the Coast Indians timid but treacherous. What confused the pioneer view was that in the period before Lewis and Clark the inland tribes, hunters and horsemen, were expanding their range into territory previously held by the Coast tribes: the Klickitats had moved west of the Cascades into the area along the upper Cowlitz River and on the Yacolt Prairie and had raided and established semipermanent camps in the Willamette Valley of Oregon. The notion that the Coast tribes were more peaceful was only relative. A tribe of Coos Bay savages gathered in a band of two hundred to wipe out Jedediah Smith's party. Farther up the coast of Oregon the Tillamooks murdered Captain Gray's servant; and north of the Columbia River, where the Chinooks, the Chehalis, the Quinaults and the Quileutes were ranged to the north end of the Olympic Peninsula, the savagery of the tribes that slaughtered the men of the *Sonora* was legendary. Farther north, in British Columbia and on Queen Charlotte Island, were the Haidas, master shipbuilders and carvers of totem poles, whose raids into Puget Sound were equally terrifying to the Indians and to the white settlers. Still farther north, in Russian Alaska, were coastal tribes referred to by the American settlers in Oregon as the Kakes, a term for remote and unknown people of great strength and violence. As late as 1857 a raiding party of these warriors, who traveled in war canoes that carried fifty persons, invaded Puget Sound and landed on Whidbey Island, where they murdered Isaac Ebey and beheaded him. A Hudson's Bay party forced the chief to surrender Ebey's head for burial; the legislature of Washington Territory, in expressing its thanks, placed the blame for the atrocity on savages from Russian America and absolved the Company and the Indians under its jurisdiction from having anything to do with it.

The notion that the Coast tribes were peaceful and the Plains Indians warlike was oversimplified. But the tribes that lived along the rivers and on Puget Sound were in permanent communities and to that extent could be controlled, or at least observed. It was possible for continuing relationships to be formed between the settlers and individuals of these tribes in a way that was difficult if not impossible

with those of the Plains, who were always on the move. The horsemen were impressive figures compared with the Indians on the coast
who lived by fishing, but their camps were miserable, huddled tents of
women and children, "small groups of wretched Indians," as Gustavus
Hines wrote in *Wild Life in Oregon*, "who are alternately shivering
with ague, and burning with fever, upon the brink of death." The
Indians on Puget Sound built permanent houses—that of Chief
Seattle was 100 feet long, and his brother inhabited one measuring
no less than 540 feet—and if they feared the intrusion of the white
men they also had reason to fear the raids of Indians who were less
settled and stable than they were.

In his *Traits of American Indian Life and Character* Peter Skene
Ogden held that white people were confused about Indians because
they attributed racial motives to them. If a white settler's family was
massacred by Indians, it was construed as evidence of racial hatred.
In fact it was evidence of savagery. In the wilderness such things happened all the time if one party of Indians came upon a defenseless
party of Indians. The killings that were atrocities if they were of
white people went unnoted if the victims were Indians. In their vulnerable position between the warriors on horseback from east of the
mountains and the raiders from the north in their war canoes, the
tribes along the shores of Puget Sound and the lower Columbia bore
out Ogden's views. By 1853 there were not more than 10,000 Indians
in all Washington Territory west of the Cascades, as opposed to about
20,000 in the tribes east of the mountains, and a case could be made
that the Coast Indians, in their dealings with white people, were not
more peaceable but simply weaker than the other tribes.

To James Gilchrist Swan the mistaken notion of the white people
about the Coast Indians went back to Meares, who claimed that they
were cannibals. A totally unjustified heritage of contempt was visited
on them by the white people. It was an axiom that their houses were
dirty. Swan found that they varied; some were clean and some dirty,
with as great a range as in the houses of white people in a city. They
were accounted treacherous. Swan wrote, "I have always found them,
when treated well, to be kind and hospitable."

Winthrop accepted without questioning the common view of a divided Indian world—miserable and cowardly savages, fish eaters, west
of the mountains; wild, dangerous but courageous and imposing warriors on the Plains in the east. His delay in reaching Port Townsend
strengthened his view. The town consisted of one house and a sawmill owned by white settlers, and an Indian settlement headed by a
Clallam chief known as King George. During the night before Winthrop arrived, there was a celebration of some sort. Winthrop counted

on King George to supply him with a canoe and paddlers. Instead he found everyone drunk or hung over from the party the night before. Unable to rouse anyone, and afraid of missing another tide, Winthrop lost his temper and kicked the Indian chief to try to arouse him. Fortunately he was wearing moccasins, and the Indian was undisturbed. But another Indian staggered up. Winthrop expected the Indian to draw a scalping knife, but the newcomer merely asked him for a drink. The incident provided the opening lines of *The Canoe and the Saddle*: "I have kicked a king!"

Leaving the lodge of King George, Winthrop met still another drunken savage. This apparition wore a faded frock coat, a battered top hat and shiny trousers crinkled at the bottom. The red paint daubed on his nose gave him the appearance of a decayed priest turned bartender. But he seemed to be less drunk than the others. He was known as the Duke of York, to distinguish him from his brother, King George. Fearful of missing the tide entirely, Winthrop bargained with the Duke of York to take him to Nisqually, promising him six Hudson's Bay blankets, worth $3 each. The Duke agreed, provided his wife could come as well. She was a young, sober, pretty, flat-faced woman, with a name that sounded like Chin Lin—Winthrop called her Jenny Lind. Winthrop paid another blanket for her passage also. At this an elderly helmsman demanded that his wife accompany them, but Winthrop refused. The canoe was an ancient and leaky craft, 40 feet long, with a red gunwale and a row of shells along the sides to ward off evil spirits. Three paddlers drove it, with the aged Indian steering in the stern.

As they were at the point of leaving, King George staggered from his lodge. He demanded that they stop at once. He had some justice on his side; it was his canoe. While he and Winthrop were arguing, the Indian whipped out a knife, waved it threateningly and passed out.

Winthrop at last got his crew under way. They had lost much of the tide, but a wind suddenly drifted in from the Pacific. The Indians hoisted a blanket sail, and they moved into the waters of Admiralty Inlet and the channels west of Whidbey Island. The Indians finished off a bottle of whiskey, paddled on, and presently the Duke of York uncorked another bottle. He handed it to Winthrop to pass forward and gave him a drink in a cup. Winthrop poured the drink overboard and kept the bottle. An odd, querulous mutiny followed, during which the Indians drew knives and picked up their rifles. It ended when Winthrop drew his revolver, and the Duke of York, after threatening to take the canoe back to Port Townsend and complaining they had not wanted to leave there in the first place, suddenly fell asleep.

The canoe drifted along, Winthrop giving a few strokes of his paddle to keep it on its course. The Duke of York's wife, who did not drink, remained awake, alert and watchful. Well into Admiralty Inlet, she aroused her husband, and the Indians, to Winthrop's surprise, awakened in good spirits, which increased when he fed them biscuits and kippered codfish, stopping for lunch near a lumber schooner. The afternoon was warm, sultry but not blasting, "as are the summer days in that far Northwest." He could see glimpses and the glimmer of snow on the Olympic Mountains, azure, luminous peaks, their blue slashed with silver. The wind from China had swept away the smoke of distant fires. A soft golden haze hung among the evergreens and toned the swarthy coloring along the rocky shores. They swept along through narrow straits, between piny islands, and by scattered bays where fleets might lie hidden.

When the tide turned strongly against them, they landed on a shingle beach. It was nearly sunset. Twilight was already spreading downward among the pines. Grotesque piles of blanched driftwood littered the shore. The Indians built up a huge fire and ate dried fish and hardtack, Winthrop taking some salt pork. After he brewed them some tea, and laced each cup with the whiskey he had confiscated, they became almost friendly. That whiskey must have had a narcotic effect, for they circled the fire and slept. Winthrop stretched out near them. He roused himself often to move a log into the fire. He was afraid—not afraid of losing his scalp, and not awake because of pebbles under his blanket or because the inextinguishable stars winked down at him through the ether, but afraid of missing the tide again.

An hour before dawn he wakened the Duke of York. Next he wakened the old helmsman and then the young paddlers. They dragged the canoe to the water and pushed off into the chill, starlit void. The red fire watched them as they sailed away. A pale lean moon was just lifting above the pines.

The tide of Puget Sound was racing into bays and coves and nooks, and at dawn a wind rose and sped them on. They landed for breakfast at a point where a giant cedar grew near the water. Winthrop was surprised when one of the paddlers, the man in the bow, a truculent blackguard he had thought him, brought him some huckleberries. Both the Olympic Mountains and the Cascades could be seen from the water. "Several tops sprinkled with snow in the Cascades are visible; at sunrise these are noble. . . . Moonlight, starlight, and the red dawn splendid over the smooth water." They passed to the west of Elliott Bay, where Maynard had founded Seattle the year before. Then they steered through the narrow deep passage on the west side of Vashon Island. Rounding the southern tip of Vashon Island, opposite where Tacoma was later located, they came to "a breadth of sheltered calmness." Winthrop, who was dozing, suddenly saw a white shadow in the water and lifted his eyes to see Mount Rainier:

> It was a giant mountain dome of snow, swelling and seeming to fill the aerial spheres as its image displaced the blue deeps of tranquil water. The smoky haze of an Oregon August hid all but the length of its lesser ranges, and left this mighty summit based upon uplifting dimness. Only its splendid snows were visible, high in the unearthly regions of clear blue noonday sky.

The Indians were singing. The Duke of York's wife led them, droning some drowsy air to which the paddlers responded with a disjointed, lurching refrain. Some of the songs had touches of sentiment or power. Most were grotesque combinations of guttural howls. But tones and strains of irregular originality surged up through their monotony. And sometimes gleams of savage anger flashed through the melody. They made Winthrop think of the teeth of a shark glimpsed while swimming in a bay in Panama. There was a queer variation in the singing. York's wife was singing the old French folk song popularly known as "Malbrouk." There was nothing remarkable in the Indians' knowing it, for the song was popular with the French-Canadian trappers of the Hudson's Bay Company. The French words told how Malbrouk had gone to the war. But York's wife sang:

> *Klatawah ocool polikely*
> *Klatawah Steilacoom*

which meant, "Go tonight—go to Steilacoom." Perhaps it meant they had made faster progress than expected, or perhaps it was a warning not to make another camp, but at any rate Winthrop urged the paddlers on through the Narrows, where the steep cliffs rose on both sides of the channel.

Strange Indians were lounging around the store at Steilacoom. They reported that a tribe of Yakimas from east of the mountains had arrived at Nisqually. The Duke of York and his companions refused to go any farther. The Yakimas were Plains Indians, like the Klickitats, lived by hunting, traveled by horseback and were great horse thieves and killers. Winthrop's original title for his book was "Clallam and Klickitat," which might be translated as "Fishermen and Thieves," though he admired the plainsmen more than the fishermen. The Duke of York explained that they dared not go on, because the horsemen from east of the mountains were cruel. *"Conway queesh nesika,"* he explained. "Cowards all are we."

"Fear naught, my cowards," Winthrop said, to reassure them. He led them, cringing and fearful, up the long weary climb from the wharf on the Nisqually up the cliff and then a mile across the plain to the stockade. He was a little ashamed of them when they begged to be allowed to sleep inside the stockade for fear of the Yakimas camped across the plain. He bought six blankets to pay them, as well as some rope and a pack saddle, two shirts, a spool of thread and some socks—$34.77 in all. In the morning they were gone.

V

Winthrop was shaking hands with Edward Huggins, the Hudson's Bay clerk at Nisqually, when a handsome Plains Indian, part white, rode up. He remained on his horse. He said he was a member of the tribe that had crossed the mountain. Advised by Huggins, Winthrop asked him to give the chief, Owhi, a message. He asked for an interview and said he needed horses and a guide across the mountains. The Indian rode away, and some time later, when Winthrop and Huggins were examining Huggins's garden, Owhi and his band appeared. The chief was a dark, distinguished old man—"a fine old Roman, cast in bronze." Winthrop asked him if it would be possible to cross the mountains to The Dalles of the Columbia. The old chief said that it could be done and pantomimed what it would be like, sold him a pack horse and two saddle horses and provided his twenty-year-old son, Loolowcan, to guide him.

The Indians were prosperous. They had already bought $400's worth of provisions from the Nisqually post. One of Winthrop's horses was a fine animal he called Klale, the Chinook word for "black," a plucky, wiry, intelligent animal he chose for his own use. The others were tough, hard-mouthed horses, one for the pack horse and the other for his guide.

Winthrop's negotiations with Owhi and Loolowcan were completed about three o'clock on the afternoon of August 23, 1853. As if on an impulse, Winthrop insisted on starting at once. He explained to Loolowcan that experienced travelers went only a short distance on the first day of a trip—the first camp should not be beyond the reach of anything that had been forgotten and left behind. He did not say that the unexpected start would put him ahead of any Indians proceeding in advance to lie in wait for him, if any intended to do so.

Winthrop's white informants were mistaken about the Indians he dealt with. Long after his trip (but before *The Canoe and the Saddle* was published) he was told that the Duke of York and King George had murdered white people, and he believed it, though the report was false. On the other hand, Owhi became one of the major leaders of the Indian war that came two years after Winthrop's meeting with him, and Loolowcan really was a murderer; he precipitated the war by his murder of the Indian agent, Andrew Bolon. But at the moment Winthrop was suspicious of the Duke of York, without reason, while trusting (or partially trusting) Loolowcan and his father.

Loolowcan was surprised at Winthrop's demand for an early start, but did not object. In three hours they reached a lake, later named American Lake, then passed Spanaway Lake and crossed a small hill in what later became the city of Tacoma. The mountains rose before them.

"I was going homeward across the breadth of the land," Winthrop thought. He was excited and eager, "with a lurking hope that I might prove new sensations of danger. . . . With the excitement of this large thought there came a slight reactionary sinking of the heart, and a dread lest I had exhausted onward life, and now, turning back from its foremost verge, should find myself dwindling into dull conservatism, and want of prophetic faith. I feared I was retreating from the future into the past."

By nightfall they had reached the cabin of a settler named Montgomery. He was away. His Indian wife, a comely, mild-eyed woman in a calico dress, fed them and let them sleep on blankets on the cabin floor, while the half-Indian children patrolled around them in the night.

Loolowcan tried to persuade him to give up the project. "My Indian boy is disheartened," Winthrop wrote in his diary, "but I bully him and persuade him to go on." He underestimated Loolowcan. He thought the Indian was merely homesick; he wanted to squat by a campfire and mutter guttural gibberish to other Indian youths "with matted hair, dusky skin, paint-daubed cheeks, low brows, and distinguished frowziness of apparel." More likely Loolowcan responded to glimmerings of conscience. He had enjoyed their wild ride across the prairie; he had revised his notion of this unusual white man, and he wanted to draw back from the murder which, after the traveler had been weakened by hardship, would normally follow near the end of the trail.

Winthrop slept fitfully. He was afraid Loolowcan would desert. He was up before dawn. A gray glimmer on the horizon deepened to violet. Clouds blazed, the sky grew azure and a golden light spread over the world. He wakened Loolowcan and they rode into a forest of tall firs. The morning wore on, but there was no thinning of the columnar trunks that blossomed into their crowns 300 feet overhead. The Indian had recovered his courage, but Winthrop found something disquieting in passing forever between roughhewn pillars that seemed to draw together behind him. "Before my courage was quelled by a superstitious dread that from this austere wood there was no escape, I came upon a river, cleaving the darkness with a broad belt of sunshine." This was the Puyallup, precisely as Owhi had described it. From an old Indian working a salmon trap there, Winthrop bought a salmon and twenty potatoes, paying four charges of powder and shot for them.

The trail led past where the towns of Sumner and Buckley were later built, on the road to Mount Rainier. At a small prairie two ex-soldiers, living in a tent, had taken out a land claim; otherwise they saw no one. The trail alternated between these small flowering prairies and deep forest. In the woods the shadows darkened early. From a bush by the trail there hung a fox-skin cap. It looked like a signal.

"It is my brother's," Loolowcan said.

Winthrop asked why his brother should be along their trail.

"How should I know?" Loolowcan said. "Indian come; Indian go; he somewhere, he nowhere."

Later he explained that his brother wanted to become a medicine man. Perhaps he had heard that Winthrop was going to the mountains. He wanted to go also, to see his *tamanous*, his guardian spirit, so he would become big medicine.

The mountain was sacred. There was no Indian name for it; the Indian term for "mountains" was *tacoma*, and Rainier was simply Tacoma, or the Mountain. Aspiring doctors among the Indians prepared for their professional careers, or discovered whether they were fitted for medicine or what rank they were to occupy, by subjecting themselves to long fasts in solitude, during which their particular *tamanous* became clear to them, and those who faced this ordeal on Rainier were believed to possess the strongest healing power. The mountain was also a sanctuary. Anyone who had committed a crime, even murder, could seek sanctuary there, and blood vengeance was not exacted by the dead man's kin.

Shortly before dark, in the gray light beside the trail, they came upon an Indian, armed with bow and arrows, standing motionless. He was Loolowcan's brother and offered Winthrop his hand with Indian courtesy. The Indian resembled Loolowcan but was shabbier and less impressive. He and Loolowcan talked so rapidly that Winthrop could not follow them. He wanted to go with them to the mountain. Winthrop privately doubted his qualifications to be a medicine man, but there seemed to be an element of sorcery in the way he had suddenly materialized beside the trail. Where had he been prowling? Where had he been lurking to watch them approach? How could he have

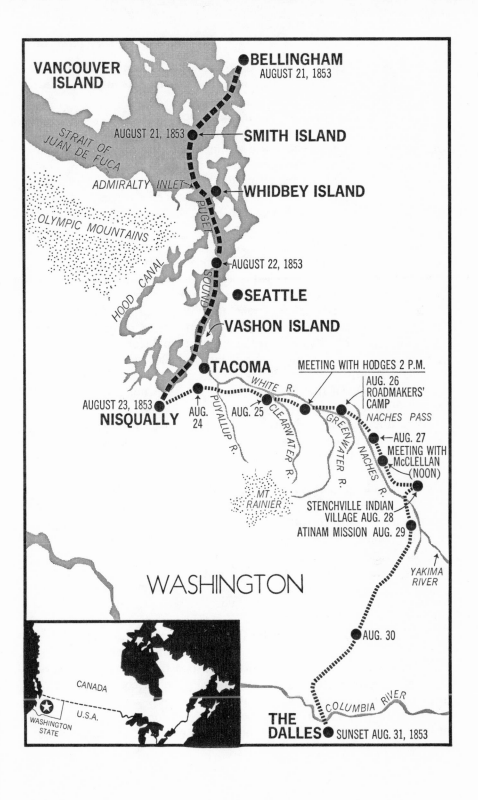

avoided being seen by them along the trail? "This amateur spy, this tyro magician, or whatever he might be, was unaccountable," Winthrop wrote.

They were near a small circular prairie beside the White River, an ideal campground. At Winthrop's direction Loolowcan built an upright gridiron of green elders and saplings, and Winthrop placed half his salmon on this, dividing the other half into two portions. One portion he fried, so everyone would have some food quickly. The other portion he wrapped in green leaves and baked beneath the ashes, putting potatoes around the salmon. He gave the Indians tea sweetened with sugar. They feasted enormously.

He crawled under his blanket. A cool breeze came down from the cliffs and snows of the mountain. The Indians were cheerful, laughing and talking until they laughed themselves sleepy; then they slept among the ferns. Night drew on. The sky was so starry clear and intelligible, and the forest so mysterious, that Winthrop found rest better than sleep. He lay awake watching the stars or, as he said, studying the clearness above the mystery. His last vision before he fell asleep was the eyes of Loolowcan staring at him and glowing, serpentlike. At midnight Winthrop awakened. He stirred and again saw the same look by the dim light of the fire. At dawn he saw the same eyes inspecting him still.

Winthrop announced his refusal to let the medicine man ride with them. He remained behind impassively. Indian manners, Winthrop wrote, were to ask for everything and never to be disappointed at getting nothing. He and Loolowcan rode along the trail that followed the north side of the White River, near where the highway later led to Mount Rainier National Park. The trees were now cedars, nearly as tall as firs but creating a different kind of forest, the branches growing almost to the ground. Fallen trees were everywhere. Winthrop's horse scrambled over them "like a cat, like a squirrel, like a monkey, like an acrobat, like a mustang." Sometimes the horse balanced halfway over a fallen tree fifteen feet through, and sometimes he clawed at a slope on his two hind feet, but Winthrop was never thrown.

They crossed and recrossed the White River, climbing ridges black with sunless woods. Then there was a short space where a party of white settlers had cut a road. This was a disastrous attempt to make a shortcut through the mountains so wagon trains could go directly from the Columbia to Puget Sound. The road was a mockery, impassable for covered wagons and all but impassable for two men on horseback and their pack horse. Winthrop and Loolowcan returned to the Indian trail.

"*Closche ocook,*" said Loolowcan. "Beautiful, this."

It was beautiful, an old winding trail that ran around great cedars into a silent forest. There were no bird songs or the hum of bees— there were no honeybees in the Northwest until the settlers brought them—though the morning sunshine was bright. Winthrop shouted aloud from a sense of well-being. "You talk with demons?" Loolowcan asked him anxiously.

No, he merely sang and shouted from happiness. He rode on hard, never resting. The trail dropped down to the banks of the river. Rounding a bend, he came upon a white man, in uniform, smoking a pipe. The soldier was a part of a unit under the command of Lieutenant Henry Hodges, of the Fourth Infantry. Hodges and Winthrop had last met at Fort Vancouver, when Winthrop was Colonel Bonneville's guest, and Hodges was assigned to take him to meet Governor Ogden of the Hudson's Bay Company.

Winthrop found Hodges himself sitting somewhat apart from his men, writing in a notebook. How had he come to be there? His presence was as unaccountable as that of Loolowcan's magician brother beside the trail. It was difficult for Hodges to explain. For that matter, it was hard for anyone to make clear. The reason went far back into the mysteries of pre-Civil War politics in Washington, D.C. When Millard Fillmore left the Presidency, one of his last official acts was to sign the bill setting up Washington Territory as distinct from Oregon, and when Franklin Pierce became President immediately after, one of his first acts was to appoint Major Isaac Stevens the governor of the new territory and instruct him to go to the Northwest overland, surveying a railroad route from the Great Lakes to Puget Sound on the way. Stevens set out with 240 soldiers, surveyors, engineers and naturalists and explored a zone of wild country 400 miles wide and 2,000 miles from east to west.

All this activity displeased Jefferson Davis, the Secretary of War, who did not want a railroad built across the northern United States. It spoiled his dream of a great confederacy of southern slave states. But he could not stop Major Stevens from finding good railroad routes through the high Rocky Mountains. Stevens was too energetic, able, industrious and honest to be prevented. Also, Stevens was opposed to slavery. Jefferson Davis's solution was brilliant in its simplicity. It was to determine that there was no possible railroad route through the low Cascade Mountains. Thus all Stevens's great work in locating routes through thousands of miles in the Rockies would be nullified by an inability to find any way through the last 20 or 30 miles of the Cascades. Accordingly, Captain George Brinton McClellan was appointed to complete the last portion of the survey for the transcontinental railroad. He would explore the Cascades while Stevens was on his way through the Rockies. While nominally under Major Stevens's command, Captain McClellan was instructed to report to Jefferson Davis directly. McClellan had no difficulty in persuading himself that the Cascade Range was indeed impassable. He took one look at the mountains and wrote, "There is nothing to be seen but mountain piled upon mountain, rugged and impassable."

McClellan hurried to the task of proving it with the energy and the organizational genius that later made him famous as commander of the Army of the Potomac in the Civil War. He reached Fort Vancouver on June 27, 1853, and spent twenty-one days assembling a force of 66 men, 73 saddle horses, 100 pack horses, and 46 mules. On July 18 he moved his force out of the fort, crossed a small stream and went into camp, having covered 1¾ miles. There they remained for three days. The pack saddles did not come up to Captain McClellan's exacting standards.

At the fort itself, Captain Ulysses S. Grant was weeding potatoes. Prices were so high that officers could not exist on their pay, and Grant and three other officers bought a worn-out team of horses from covered-wagon emigrants, restored the horses to health and planted a large tract in potatoes for their own use and for sale. The sight of officers of the United States Army weeding potatoes affronted Captain McClellan, who was always a stickler for discipline and appearance. (His dislike of Grant persisted so strongly that during the Civil War, when Grant's great victory at Fort Donelson changed the course of events, McClellan ordered Grant's arrest.)

Busying himself with the details of his expedition, McClellan was at last ready, on July 21, 1853, to order his men forward. The way led through country less wild than he had expected it to be. There were farmhouses and wagon roads through the flatlands and low hills. Past the wondering inhabitants of the farms, McClellan led his troops 6½ miles and again went into camp. The following day his party covered the same distance. In seven days after leaving Fort Vancouver they went 25 miles, ordinarily one day's travel by covered wagon. By July 31, 1853, McClellan was only 44 miles from Vancouver and was still about 200 miles from the mountains he was to explore. He was traveling at the rate of 3½ miles a day. If the emigrants in their covered wagons had moved at that pace, it would have taken them six years to cross the Oregon Trail.

But McClellan knew what he was doing or, more exactly, he knew what he was not doing. He was not finding a pass through the mountains, in deference to Jefferson Davis's wish that none should be found. The task was a hazardous one. The Cascades were threaded with Indian trails. At least eleven passes suitable for railroads existed. The Hudson's Bay Company drove its herds of cattle through Snoqualmie Pass, only 3,000 feet above sea level, with lower grades than those of the Alleghenies. Consequently Captain McClellan could not entrust the work to a subordinate. He had to not find a pass himself. He led his force from *west* to *east* around Mount Adams, far south of any possible route to Puget Sound, and then headed southeast, back toward the Columbia River, to camp at Goose Lake, which was far east of Vancouver, but still farther removed from the mountains. There he went into camp again, and it was not until August 11, 1853, that he again moved north toward the Cascades, over the dry plains country of grass and sagebrush.

And now the expedition moved fast, at least by its previous standards. On one day (August 16, 1853) the men moved no less than 14 miles, their record for a single day's travel. They were running out of food. By some miscalculation McClellan had brought along only three hunters to provide food for sixty-six men. Game was scarce in the plains, especially in midsummer. Fortunately there was a Catholic mission at Ahtanum Creek, near where the town of Yakima was later built. Two priests had long served there. The hungry travelers were kindly received by the fathers. Indian converts around the mission had large gardens and herds of beef cattle. McClellan was able to buy cattle from these Indians (he had been given an appropriation of $20,000, which he expended, as Thomas Prosch wrote, "in unknown ways"), and the men entered with a will into the task of butchering the cattle and jerking the meat to prepare for the next step of their journey.

Eleven days passed before McClellan was ready to begin exploring. His dilemma had become acute. Snow could be expected to fall on the mountains in September, but now, near the end of August, the weather remained fine. Unless McClellan acted—acted quickly—it would be impossible to not explore in the mountains, and in that case there was every likelihood that someone would discover a pass.

With the audacity that characterized his generalship in the Civil War, McClellan hit upon a bold expedient that no lesser military mind would have considered possible. He divided his force. One party he sent far north, toward the Canadian border, to look for railroad routes there. The Cascade Range, only 20 miles across in the south, was 80 or more miles wide there, and there was no possibility of a railroad pass being discovered in that area. Two other parties McClellan sent back to the Columbia River. Lieutenant Hodges, his quartermaster, a man who could be trusted to not accomplish anything—he was responsible for the initial delay caused by defective pack saddles—was sent over Naches Pass with twenty-six men and fifty horses. Hodges was ordered to proceed to Snoqualmie and secure food from the Army post there and return with it to McClellan. Naches Pass was known to exist, for it had been explored by a joint party of Americans and Britons from the Wilkes Exploring Expedition and the Hudson's Bay Company in the days of joint occupancy, but it was one of the most dangerous, difficult and beautiful of the passes through the Cascades and was impossible for a railroad route. The trail through Naches Pass climbed 1,750 feet in 3 miles and then went up a 500-foot incline in 1,000 yards. That left only McClellan with his personal escort to travel along the east side of the Cascade, in the area where many passes actually existed.

So here was Lieutenant Hodges, in the middle of nowhere, with twenty-six men and fifty horses crowding the wilderness where Winthrop had expected to meet no one. Hodges was surprisingly cool. He said that he could not ask Winthrop to have lunch with him, as he had no food to spare—in itself a violation of wilderness standards of conduct. Winthrop in *The Canoe and the Saddle* commented that McClellan was trying to flush a railroad out of the forest and had ordered Hodges to cross the mountains and bring back food, "lest dinnerlessness should befall the Hunter of Railroads."

While Winthrop and Hodges were talking, Loolowcan came up to say to Winthrop that they had a long ride before they would come to a place with good grass for a night camp. Hodges walked with Winthrop to show him where to ford the White River. "If, from his scanty stores, he could not offer hospitality," Winthrop wrote, "he would give me a fact from his experience of crossing the river, so I need not dip involuntarily into its deeps, and swallow cold comfort."

Winthrop and Loolowcan rode on. Deep in the wood they came upon an apparition, "a poor, wasted, dreary white horse, standing in the trail, too stiff to fall, too weary to stir." Winthrop tried to feed the horse some hardtack, but it could not eat. He thought he ought to kill it, but he could not bring himself to do so. "So I went on," he wrote, "disconsolate after the sight of suffering until my own difficulties along that savage trail compelled my thoughts from dwelling on another's pain."

Those difficulties grew worse. There was no grass for the horses. An open spot above the Greenwater River, a branch of the White, was bare. Loolowcan had expected to find pasture there, but the horses of Hodges's party had taken the grass. They hurried on, for darkness came suddenly. The road being cut by the settlers crossed the Indian trail. Misunderstanding Loolowcan, Winthrop followed the white man's road, which soon ended. There were only blazes on trees. Then the blazes stopped. "Dimmer grew the woods. Stars were visible overhead, and the black circle of the forest shut off the last gleams from the west.

Every obstacle of fallen tree, bramble and quagmire now loomed large and formidable."

At Winthrop's order, Loolowcan rode on to look for a campsite. Winthrop could hear him crashing through the brush; then there was silence. He was alone and lost. Moving blindly, he went on until he heard the rush of water over pebbles. He tied Klale and the pack horse and went forward on foot. The sound of the river led him down a slope, and suddenly, from behind the trunks of fir trees, he saw the gleam of a fire.

At the same instant he became aware of someone near him in the darkness. It was Loolowcan. "Perhaps not friends," Loolowcan whispered.

Winthrop told him—without regard to history, he said—that all white men were friends.

They went back for the horses and rode forward loudly. On the far side of the Greenwater a score of men were lounging around a huge fire. Several jumped up at the sound of the horses in the brush. Winthrop shouted, so they would not shoot, as he came into open ground. The horses dashed down the slope, splashed across the river and into the camp.

"I see a fire, and come to the road-makers' camp," Winthrop wrote in his journal; "picturesque scene among the lofty trees, by the rushing stream. In ancient times, these would have been robbers."

Later commentators sometimes implied that some of them *were* robbers, though of a different kind from the robbers who preyed on travelers in the Old World forests, robbing the government rather than individuals, and sure of being undetected because of their remoteness. There was a chance that, as Loolowcan whispered, some of them were not friends. But they greeted Winthrop warmly. He ate well: flapjacks and bacon and coffee. They waited for him to tell them who he was and where he was going. Loolowcan, fed but ignored, kept to the shadows.

One of the road builders was Edward Jay Allen, a sometime associate of McClellan, a New York-born engineer who had studied at Duquesne College in Pittsburgh. Ill with a throat ailment, Allen went west for his health and somehow became a delegate to the Washington territorial convention at Monticello in 1852. On the strength of his engineering education, Allen headed the road-building expedition, though he was then only twenty-two years old. Years later Allen wrote an account of Winthrop's arrival at the camp. It was not altogether convincing. As educated men, Allen said, they were somewhat apart from the general company. "A nearly all-night talk under the same blanket developed some tastes in common," Allen wrote, "and made me cognizant of his subtle companionship with nature, though I did not suspect his powers

of expression." Allen's memory was faulty, for he said he did not know
Winthrop's name and did not know who his visitor was until he read
The Canoe and the Saddle. But Winthrop wrote that he identified him-
self to the road builders, and he also, in his handwritten draft of *The
Canoe and the Saddle,* identified Allen by name.

Allen remembered that the road builders felt it was strange that a
white man should be traveling alone, in view of the unrest among the
Indians. They thought Winthrop should be prevented from going on.
"Regretfully I accompanied Winthrop on the trail next morning," Allen
wrote, "feeling that I was losing a link that temporarily connected me
with a fuller civilization." Allen said suspicions of the Hudson's Bay
Company lay back of the attitude of the men, but how they proposed
to stop him from going on was not indicated in Allen's account. Winthrop was anxious to be on his way. His horses were unfed, and they
climbed until noon before finding pasture.

> I had been following thus for many hours the blind path, harsh, dark-
> some and utterly lonely, urging on with no outlook, encountering no
> landmark—at last, as I stormed a ragged crest, gaining a height that over-
> topped the firs, and halting there for panting moments, glanced to see if
> I had achieved mastery as well as position—as I looked somewhat wearily
> and drearily across the solemn surges of forest, suddenly above their
> sombre green appeared Tacoma. Large and neighbor it seemed, so near
> that every jewel of its snow-fields seemed to send me a separate ray; yet
> not so near but that I could with one look take in its whole image, from
> clear-cut edge to edge. . . .
> No foot of man had ever trampled those pure snows. . . . Yet there
> was nothing unsympathetic in its isolation, or despotic in its distant
> majesty.

He rested and reflected that all through the Northwest there were similar scenes, not so grand as the one before him, but like smaller mirror
images: Mount Adams to the south, Mount Hood, and Mount St.
Helens, then a live volcano with a smoking summit; Mount Baker to
the north. In no older world, where men had tamed the earth to orderly
beauty, had they created a fairer garden. Nature had given the Oregon
people "the blessing and possible education of a refined and finished
landscape, in the presence of landscape strong, savage and majestic."

So Winthrop came to believe that new habits of thought and life
must inevitably develop in this land. He knew that in his own life there
were times of strain when calming influences, thoughts and memories
and dreams, were as necessary as breath. "Our lives forever demand and
need visual images that can be symbols to us of the grandeur or the
sweetness of repose," he wrote in a fine phrase. There are faces of people we love, or have loved, "that arise dreamy in our memories, and

look us into calmness in our frantic moods." And there are memories of scenes of nature that we remember, or can summon up, that touch us so deeply their meaning is infinite. As he studied the light and majesty of the mountain, "there passed from it and entered into my being, to dwell there evermore by the side of many such, a thought and an image of solemn beauty, which I could thenceforth evoke whenever in the world I must have peace or die."

The hardest part of his journey lay before him. Physical exhaustion was revealed in his vivid descriptions of the enjoyment of rest. A chain of connected prairies, sunlit and flowering, lay along the top of the world that formed the Cascade crest, a mountain paradise that remained almost unchanged a century after he passed that way. The horses fed in grass growing head high. He ate his lunch by cold springs, lying on green banks under a clump of evergreens, picking wild strawberries for dessert.

There was another eerie encounter with civilization deep in the wilderness. Under a huge tree across the trail Winthrop came upon a horse that was struggling under the branches. The animal had apparently slipped under the trunk and could not get out. It had on its flank the brand of the Army of the United States. Winthrop and Loolowcan freed it and added it to their string. Winthrop shot four grouse to provide an evening meal, and they left the woods for dry stony country east of the divide.

On the east slope of the Cascades the descent began with a 500-foot drop in a few hundred yards. Here the road crew had built a short corduroy road of knobby planks up the steepest portion, in anticipation of the covered wagons coming from the Columbia River. The incline was useless; the horses refused to step on it. Beyond this the trail ran along the edge of a cliff that curved inward below it. Leaning from his saddle, Winthrop could look directly into the Naches River. This was what he called Via Mala, where the trail became no trail at all, a passage barely wide enough for a single horse across flat stones and crushed-rock slides, bare of vegetation and burning in the sun. Difficult as was this narrow, slippery ledge, the descent beyond it was harder still, a sharp forward pitch to the bottom of the canyon. There the cliffs on both sides gradually closed in, and the trail again climbed, 1,000 feet this time, then followed a shelf so narrow that Winthrop could again look down on the Naches without leaning from his saddle.

The canyon widened and became a timberland valley. Winthrop and Loolowcan rode toward the river, with the silent relief of horsemen coming down from mountain heights to flat land. They stopped before they reached the river to make camp where a little swamp provided water. Winthrop fried some of the grouse to give them some food quickly. He roasted the others on an improvised spit, with a cone of pork suspended above the birds to drip on them while they cooked. Then they slept, and this time Winthrop made no mention of watching Loolowcan to see if the Indian remained awake.

The next day was Sunday, August 28, 1853, and they were on their way by five o'clock. About noon, riding into a thicket of hazelnut bushes, Loolowcan stopped suddenly and motioned for Winthrop to be silent. A white man stood on the bank, skipping flat stones across the river. The meeting with Hodges and the road builders had been surprising, and Winthrop was now prepared to accept anything; nevertheless, as he watched this solitary figure on the banks of an unknown river, in the middle of nowhere, Winthrop began to share the Indian's wonder at the ways of the white man. But he was glad to see him. In that remote world "an encounter by the wayside with a man and a brother was a fact to enjoy and an emotion to chronicle."

The stranger was equally surprised. Nowhere in *The Canoe and the Saddle* did Winthrop call attention to the fact that, if he and Loolowcan had been hostile savages, the people they surprised would have perished; no one had guards posted. But it was hardly necessary for him to point out the obvious. When he got to Fort Steilacoom at night, he had to pound on the door to waken the officers, something an attacking party could hardly be expected to do; when he met Hodges in the mountains, that officer was writing in his notebook; when he met the road builders, they were sprawled around their fire without defenses. But this individual skipping stones was beyond comprehension. He explained that he was a civil engineer with Captain McClellan's party, searching for a railroad pass through the Cascades, and rode off to tell McClellan of the arrival of visitors.

Winthrop suddenly felt extremely tired. He had made an almost incredible journey. Starting from the northern end of Puget Sound on August 21, 1853, he had gone the length of the sound and crossed the mountains seven days later. The August afternoon was hot. Winthrop's camp "for present nooning was a charming little Arcady, shady, sunny and verdant. Two dense spruces made pleasant twanging to the newly-risen breeze. . . . Rest in the shade of the spruces by the buzzing river was so sweet, after the severity of my morning's ride, that I hesitated for myself and for my unwilling mustangs to renew the journey." He cooked two grouse he had shot during the morning ride, while his Indian guide pastured the horses in a patch of wild peas.

After lunch, as Winthrop and his guide smoked their pipes, "the tramp of hoofs was heard along the trail, and, with the late skipper of stones and a couple of soldiers, Captain McClellan rode up. In vain, through the Naches canyon, had the Captain searched for a Pacific

Railroad. He must search elsewhere, along Snoqualmie Pass or other. . . ."
Winthrop took the occasion to return to McClellan the stray horse he
had rescued. McClellan pleasantly wished Winthrop well on the remainder of his journey. Winthrop wished McClellan well in his further
search for a railroad pass. McClellan then rode off, to investigate "some
other gorge, some purple cavernous defile for his railroad route."

McClellan could hardly have been glad to see Winthrop. He was
then twenty-six years old, rather short but powerfully built, with red
hair and a light red beard, reserved in his speech and with a habit of
staring directly into the eyes of a person he was addressing, which
people sometimes found disconcerting. He had been born into a wealthy
Philadelphia family, his father an eminent surgeon and his grandfather
the founder of the Jefferson Medical College in that city. He was a
military celebrity almost from the time he was graduated from West
Point at nineteen, for he went directly from the graduating exercises to
the battlefields of the Mexican War, where he served brilliantly as an
aide to General Winfield Scott. Triumphs over ill-armed Mexican
troops gave many unfortunate Southern officers a belief in the military
destiny of the Confederate States, but the men who made their repu-
tations in the Mexican War were largely Southerners—Jefferson Davis,
Zachary Taylor, Robert E. Lee, John Quitman, Braxton Bragg and
others—and the relative absence of comparable young officers from the
North gave an added sectional impetus to McClellan's reputation. After
the Mexican War he taught at West Point, perfected drills, wrote
military manuals and accompanied Captain Randolph Marcy in a survey of a southern route to the California goldfields.

He was meticulous, thorough, concerned about the well-being and the
training of the men in his command and fanatically single purposed.
He had nerve: at thirty-five, as commander-in-chief of the Army of the
Potomac, he refused to see President Lincoln when Lincoln arrived
unexpectedly at his camp. He had no fear of the Northwestern pioneers
who might criticize his work, or his lack of work. They were too far
from Washington to be influential. And according to Edward Jay Allen,
McClellan also distributed some of the $20,000 that had been given
him to friendly persons among the settlers. But Theodore Winthrop
appearing so unexpectedly in McClellan's camp was an unwelcome
visitor. Winthrop was the bearer of a famous name and had friends in
high places. Winthrop had grown up with Henry Hitchcock, whose
father, General Ethan Allen Hitchcock, was in command of the Pacific
forces of the Army of the United States; in fact, Winthrop carried
letters of introduction from General Hitchcock to Army officers in the
Northwest, though not to McClellan.

When McClellan rode off, Winthrop was seized with sudden misgivings. He did not express them directly—he rarely expressed anything directly—but with an oblique reference that might mean a great deal, or that might merely record a momentary impulse, he wrote: "On, on, with speed, was the lesson hinted to me by wind and water." Wind and water? For days "life had been its keenest, its readiest, its fleetest. . . . I had taken the risk, and success was thus far with me." Why, then, his sense of alarm, now that all danger seemed past, with soldiers unexpectedly around him? He put it down to a fear of overconfidence. Whatever it was, Winthrop got out of there fast after his meeting with McClellan. He rode on until long after dark, racing by moonlight, and spent no less than sixteen hours in the saddle that day.

VI

Winthrop was the first officer killed in the first battle of the Civil War. He was only then beginning to be known as a writer and left several partially finished books in manuscript, among them *The Canoe and the Saddle*, in which McClellan appeared incidentally, pictured with amiable irony as the great Hunter of Railroads, searching for them in the places where they were least likely to be found. In Winthrop's account, the meeting with McClellan was the last event in a chain of unreal happenings; he thought that if he had not become an experienced traveler, he "might have gone bewildered from phantasmagoria" —or, to put it simply, the craziness of events would have unhinged his reason. But hardships had stripped his mind of unessentials, and madness, he thought, comes from what is superficial.

He rode into a cloudless gale. The globe seemed to be whirling faster than the stars. He camped with Loolowcan in the shelter of the bank of the Naches, while the horses fed on the grassy plain above them. "So I had a night of weary unrest. The wild rush of the river and the noise of the gale ran through my sleep in dreams of trampling battalions—such as a wounded and unhelped on a battlefield might dream. . . . So I slept, or did not sleep, while the gale roared wildly all night and was roaring still at dawn."

Something, perhaps the arrival in his own country, perhaps the coolness of the meeting of Winthrop and McClellan, had a bad effect on Loolowcan. Now as they rode on, he turned more and more from "a half-insolent, half-indifferent, jargoning savage" to something increasingly wolflike. Riding ahead, Loolowcan suddenly veered from the trail and led Winthrop into a hidden and wretched Indian village that Winthrop called Stenchville. Loolowcan's pretext was that they could get fresh horses there. The crisis came with uncanny suddenness. Five armed Indians surrounded Winthrop. The Indians had horses to sell and pretended to bargain. But they doubled the price of the horses offered for sale each time Winthrop gave a price he would pay and contemptuously provoked a quarrel. In the background, as the quarrel developed, Winthrop could see the women and children scurrying away to hide in the brush near the village.

He remained on Klale, holding the other two horses as Loolowcan dismounted. Loolowcan demanded payment for guiding him to this point. Winthrop refused to pay anything unless Loolowcan guided him to The Dalles. Three of the Indians had rifles, one a knife, and the fifth a bow and arrows. One of the Indians grabbed at the reins of Winthrop's horse; Winthrop stuck his pistol in his face, and he dropped back. Winthrop rode away slowly, expecting an arrow in his spine. He did not believe the Indians would fire; they would be afraid of the sound reaching soldiers who might be nearby; but an arrow would be silent. He forced himself not to turn around. And he credited his escape only to the fact that soldiers were somewhere in the vicinity. Strangely, he bore the Indian no ill will for his treachery.

His portrait of Loolowcan is a masterpiece, perhaps the best of its sort in American literature, a bright, contradictory portrait of an almost likable savage "watching me with disloyal eyes from under his matted hair." There was something wolflike in his readiness and alertness, in his unerring memory and observation. He never for an instant lost his way and was always more cautious than any four-footed animal Winthrop had ever seen. He was wolflike in his hunger, his concern with his own food and his incomprehension of such human impulses and emotions as loyalty or gratitude. So powerful was Winthrop's sense of him as wolflike that in a blinding instant when the Indians surrounded him he thought of himself suddenly as a crippled animal at the point of being downed by wolves.

He was in fact weaker than he had suspected. He rode on rapidly and found an Army camp with part of McClellan's force. There he was directed to the Catholic mission, where he secured a reliable guide and rode on the last miles to the Columbia. He was conscious of a sense of inspiration lingering from his mountain vision, the awareness of knowing life at its fleetest, "a serene sense of new and large experience, and of some qualities in myself newly tested." But the physical strain of his ride over the Cascades left him with nothing but nerve to go on. After another long day in the saddle, a storm and a sleepless night, exhaustion felled him: "I was suddenly sick with a despair like death." While his guide scouted on ahead, Winthrop found himself lying in the sunlight in dry bunchgrass. He had fainted and fallen from his horse. He was roused to consciousness by a breath on his cheek as his horse bent over him. At night, beside a fire in a dead tree trunk, he was moved to a kind of Shakespearean soliloquy, and he found he could hear again those great calming words without which life grows restless, and may not dream of peace. Faith is instinctive, Winthrop wrote. Instinctive faith dies, and because without faith the soul dies, we must seek it, and perhaps wander for it far and not hopefully, as far, it may be, as the deepest forests on the remote and wild North-western Coast. He wrote in terms that echoed the poems of Alabaster:

> For early, thoughtful years and eras of ours are saddened and bewil-
> dered by the sting of evil, others' and our own; poisonous bigotries grapple
> with faith from its cradle; we are driven along the gauntlet of selfishness;
> love, the surest test of nobility, seems the most hopeless test, discovering
> only the ignoble; we dwell among comrades of chance, not choice, and
> cannot find our allies; know not any law of growth but the unreflecting
> stir about us. . . .

He reached The Dalles in time to join the government mail escort going east over the Rockies. The great adventure was over, and with it Winthrop's story virtually ended as well. His first misfortune was to volunteer as an unpaid member of an expedition to Panama when he returned to the East, leaving *The Canoe and the Saddle* unfinished. John Lloyd Stephens's original concession for the Panama Railroad provided that no canal would be cut across the Isthmus so long as the railroad operated; Lieutenant Isaac Strain was sent to Panama by the government to explore a new route. Strain's expedition was a series of disasters, costing the lives of seventeen men. Winthrop returned ill and disheartened and now faced the problem of making a living, thus further postponing work on his books. He set up an office and began to practice law in New York, remaining for a year; then his boyhood friend Henry Hitchcock, who was practicing law in St. Louis, invited him to become his law partner in that city.

His second misfortune was to affront his wealthy relatives and friends by becoming active in Frémont's campaign for the Presidency in 1856. A love affair with a young woman in St. Louis ended abruptly; while he was visiting his sister Laura in New York, his bride-to-be canceled their engagement. At odd moments, between his emotional crises, cam-paigning, practicing law and organizing wilderness parties to Maine, he wrote five novels and *The Canoe and the Saddle*. All his novels were rejected by publishers. At the beginning of the Civil War the *Atlantic Monthly* published his sketches of outdoor life, and his accounts of Army life in the same magazine were beginning to make him known as a literary figure in the early days of the Civil War.

He enlisted in the Seventh Regiment in New York and was assigned to duty in Washington with the rank of major. He had an interview in the White House with President Lincoln, usually referred to in those days as Uncle Abe, but, as he wrote wryly, nothing came of it: "In my uncle's house are many nephews." He conferred with the Secretary of War, the Secretary of State, and various Senators, and when he left Washington, it was with an appointment to serve as secretary to General Ben Butler, the Massachusetts politician who was in command of volunteers at Fort Monroe, Virginia.

Union forces held this strategic point near the mouth of the James River throughout the Civil War. At the time Winthrop was there, a large Confederate force was at Great Bethel, a few miles nearer Williamsburg, but there was an advanced Confederate position at Little Bethel, within striking distance of the troops at Fort Monroe. Runaway slaves in considerable numbers at first made their way to Fort Monroe. The Confederate troops at Little Bethel blocked their escape route. The plans for which Winthrop was responsible were directed toward destroying this outpost and forcing the Confederates back to the fortifications at Great Bethel. The troops engaged were largely New York units, one a company of German-speaking immigrant volunteers, the main body under the command of Colonel Abram Duryée, who had led the Seventh Regiment during the Astor Place riot. They were to march by night by parallel roads to be in position to overrun Little Bethel by daylight before it could be reinforced from the main Confederate force.

About midnight on June 9, 1861, when one of the New York companies passed near the German volunteers, they fired on each other. Any further movement was suicidal, but no effort was made to call off the operation. It went forward with a doomed and literal observance of the plans Winthrop had drafted, though the changed circumstances, with the Confederate outpost alerted and reinforcements coming constantly, made its operation more than ordinarily outlandish among plans for battles. Throughout the morning the fighting went on despite a general perplexity as to why it was not broken off, and at midday, shortly before retreat and when some Northern troops were already withdrawing, Winthrop led an assault with a handful of men on a Confederate battery. He was in advance of his men and was shot as he stepped on a log near the gun. The Southern newspapers reported that he was killed by a North Carolina drummer boy who had picked up a rifle lying nearby. The boy took Winthrop's watch from his body. Winthrop was buried where he fell, though his body was later delivered to his brother under a flag of truce. He was so far in advance that, had it not been for the specific details of how he met his death, a question might always have remained as to which side the bullet came from. His death was the major news event of the day in the North and was noted in Southern papers as well.

A century later something phantasmagoric and unreal still lay over that battlefield. Little Bethel is not far from the reconstructed town of Williamsburg, with its colonial houses and its innkeepers and shop-keepers in the costumes of pre-Revolutionary Virginia, with its wind-mill grinding corn meal and its blacksmith at his forge, and its lines of tourists moving slowly through the pleasant tree-shaded streets. The slice of American history that was so painstakingly reconstructed at Williamsburg makes the tangled briers and the sandy ground of the battlefield of Little Bethel seem miragelike and spectral. The battle seemed unreal in the North at the time, and there were editorial com-plaints that no inquiry was made into its conduct. Winthrop's death was a shock, a foreshadowing of the nature of the Civil War that lay ahead, something added to the usual tragedies of accidental deaths in warfare, a military mistake with overtones of mystery, or a revelation of incompetence on a scale so disastrous that treason could scarcely have accomplished more.

Winthrop became a Northern hero. His unpublished books were rushed into print. A critical discussion of his work belongs elsewhere in this account; here it is only necessary to say that fifty-five editions of his five books appeared between 1861 and 1876, and Winthrop was, for nearly a decade, one of the most popular of American writers. Then his fame evaporated almost as suddenly as it arose. Winthrop's novels have a bold narrative power, with flashes of sardonic wit and occasional vivid instances of characterization, but they rocket along with Eliza-bethan indifference to logic, involving disguises, mixed identities, fiend-ish villains, scandals, suicides and murders with the carelessness of dime novels. They are memorable, but in a one-dimensional way. One feels that their intricate plots are contrived and artificial, and at war with the acute intelligence that produced them. Sometimes Winthrop's nov-els seem hack jobs, hastily turned out in the hope of making money, but sometimes they seem to be serious works deliberately written in a cheap or popular form, carrying information or a message in melodrama aimed at the widest possible number of readers, and therefore con-sciously rejecting cultivated standards of literary excellence because the mass of readers did not share them.

Winthrop's novels were scandalous in their own time. They became an embarrassment to his critics, not only because of their homosexual overtones but because real people were so thinly disguised in them. Aspinwall was obviously an original of a major character in *Cecil Dreeme*, as was Richard Hunt, the architect. Less obviously the original of the villain in the novel was William Henry Hurlbert, famous as the wickedest man in New York, a dramatist, blackmailer, and a preyer on women, a violent Copperhead in the Civil War. Applegate was a hero of Winthrop's novel *John Brent*, a Western paragon who appeared like the Lone Ranger to rescue people from Mormons and Indians. In one sense Winthrop's novels were too deeply embedded in the unrecorded life of his age, with topical allusions to situations and characters whose significance was lost as the scandals they reflected were forgotten or covered up. Only *The Canoe and the Saddle* remains as evidence of his truly great promise. Topical allusions are in it also. Much of the queer, mannered prose of the book can be traced to the need to obscure its revelations. McClellan is a case in point. At the time the book was written McClellan was emerging as the most prominent Northern general. The glimpse of him in *The Canoe and the Saddle* is devastating, but only if one knows the story of his failure to find a pass through the Cascades: otherwise it appears only as a casual, mildly ironic sketch. Informed people could read Winthrop's books at one level, and the general public could read them at another.

McClellan missed every pass through the mountains. He reached the one to be known as Stevens Pass (where the Great Northern Railroad was later built) and reported there was no way through there. He was at Chinook Pass and at White Pass, later major highway routes through the mountains, and could see no possible opening for a railroad. He was at Cowlitz Pass, Carleton Pass, Hart's Pass, Cascade Pass, Cispus Pass and Twisp Pass and concluded there was no way through the Cascade Range except along the Columbia River. He added that there was no reason to believe there was *any* pass through the Cascades, not in the United States or in Canada, except one far in the north, at the headwaters of the Thompson River, more than 750 miles from the Columbia. (He could hardly have left it out, since its existence was already known.)

So McClellan concluded that his mission was accomplished. He felt that he had succeeded. He wrote that he had not lost a man. There had been no desertions or serious illnesses. The stupendous boldness of his lack of enterprise and his indifference to the reality of the country he wrote about became one of the mysteries in the life of that gifted and enigmatic officer. An observer bearing a less distinguished name might well have been dismissed as crazy for returning a report so obviously at variance with the facts. In particular, the country between Stampede Pass and Snoqualmie Pass is strikingly different from his picture of it; it is a parklike, pleasant area, later prized by vacationers but disparaged by wilderness enthusiasts and mountaineers because it is too easy. McClellan's explorations led into airy spaces of tranquil solitude, past an endless succession of cascading streams, over mountain meadows covered with windflowers and wild berries, through deer playgrounds, into shadowy cedar groves and along silver cliffs above deep blue lakes, where the old Indian trails looked out upon limitless expanses of velvet-green treescapes, with the serene snow peaks rising above them.

And even the Indian trails were generally easy walking. They were trade routes by which the Plains Indians east of the mountains reached the tribes along Puget Sound; and though they curved endlessly, they followed the summit ridges to minimize up-and-down travel with heavy packs. So they threaded back and forth from the east side of the summit ridge to the west side. McClellan passed from the east side of the summit ridge at Stampede Pass (where the Northern Pacific Railroad was later built) to the west side of the ridge and reported that there was no way through the mountains there. The report was a conscious falsehood. A century later one could stand at the summit of the pass and see the land lying in easy grades on both sides. McClellan came within three quarters of a mile of the summit of Snoqualmie Pass and turned back. He reported: "As far as the eye can determine, there is no possibility of effecting a passage in that direction." Governor Stevens, irritated at McClellan's deceptions, sent a civilian aide, Abiel Tinkham, over Snoqualmie Pass in midwinter. Tinkham reported a foot and a half of snow (McClellan refused to try the pass in winter, saying the snow reached 25 feet) and went through the pass without trouble from the east to the west, then repeated the passage from the western slope to the eastern prairie.

What McClellan had going for him was an intellectual concept, a myth of the old Oregon country as a wild and savage land, a myth so deeply rooted that it became stronger in forming national policy than the evidence of eyesight and physical reality. Whatever confirmed that legend was accepted without question, and whatever varied from it had to be explained and defended. The Northwest was a region whose history was shaped by ideology, by abstract and intellectualized notions of what was there; it was settled at a time when modern means of communication exercised their pervasive influence on the public mind. What made McClellan's false report possible was the prior belief that he was venturing into a bleak and inhospitable land. Years after his time the residue of that gloomy image still worked its profound influence. It contributed to the concept of the Northwest as a place without value of its own, or rather of a place whose primary value was as a source of raw material for more civilized and developed areas. To that extent the myth of elemental desolation served a practical purpose for the timber companies and the mining companies and the salmon fishermen who exploited the country; it made their operations possible, just as the myth of impassable mountains served the purpose of McClellan.

Winthrop's picture of the Northwest in *The Canoe and the Saddle* was a shocking reversal of the accepted view. The land was beautiful. It was as beautiful as any region on earth. The great river was the second most wonderful body of water known to man, second only to Puget Sound. The mountains surpassed the grandeur of the Alps. Winthrop found himself in the Northwestern woods. His wild ride through the forest was the high point in what a perceptive Scottish critic called "his life of innocent eccentricity." Somewhere on the way Winthrop found a faith that a new civilization would come into being there, in the midst of the Civil War and the ruin of the rest of the country.

This faith persisted in spite of the horror of the Civil War and the violence in the Northwest itself. Loolowcan, as has been said, was held responsible for having precipitated the Indian war of 1856 and 1857, by his murder of the Indian agent, Andrew Bolon. His father Owhi, who led the outbreak, gave himself up and was jailed for having broken a truce. Loolowcan came into the Army camp where Owhi was imprisoned during a council. He entered the camp at nine o'clock in the morning and at nine fifteen was hanged without a trial. Owhi was shot trying to escape. The Duke of York (who was incorrectly charged in *The Canoe and the Saddle* with having murdered a couple of palefaces after he left Winthrop) kept his tribe from joining the Indian war in that crazy and bloody business—"a good and faithful man," said the historian Elwood Evans, who knew him, "who doubtless saved many lives."

Captain Howard dropped out of sight for several years after his venture into coal mining on Bellingham Bay and his association with Winthrop. He was reinstated in the Revenue Service after the outbreak of the Civil War and commanded a Marine artillery unit that served with the Federal troops. After the war he inspected revenue vessels along the Atlantic Coast. After the purchase of Alaska in 1867 he was placed in charge of an expedition there on the steamer *Lincoln*. He was never called to testify in the Forrest divorce litigation.

Forrest never recovered the position he had held. He died in 1872, at the age of sixty-seven. His wife became an actress, married the drama critic of *The New York Times* and lived to old age on Staten Island, where she died in 1891. Peter Skene Ogden died at Oregon City in 1857. Dr. Tolmie retired to venerated old age on a farm on Vancouver Island. He married the half-Indian daughter of James Work, the chief factor of the Hudson's Bay Company, and their son became the premier of British Columbia. Edward Jay Allen served with McClellan in the Civil War and subsequently settled in Pittsburgh. He lived to great age and became an accomplished author, the writer of highly unreliable recollections of his Northwestern experiences. Lieutenant Hodges became Brigadier General Hodges. He next encountered Winthrop, after their meeting in the Naches Pass, at the Academy of Music in New York during an intermission of *La Traviata,* where Hodges told Winthrop of the death of Owhi. "He was hanged or shot last summer in the late Indian wars of that region," Winthrop wrote. "I regret his martyrdom."

The characters in *The Canoe and the Saddle* were real people, as were the originals of the characters in Winthrop's novels. But what sets *The Canoe and the Saddle* apart from Winthrop's other books is his conviction that the wilderness in some almost mystical sense promised salvation from the ruin of America by civil war. That process of finding himself was not a complicated psychological development. He discovered that he felt good, and that he liked to look at the mountains and the rivers, and that a return of hope was connected with his physical well-being and his response to the scenery. He saw that the greatest natural resource of the Northwest was its physical beauty, and from that insight he came to believe that the esthetic factor in mankind was a basic need, as essential as food and shelter. He did not attribute to the wilderness any magical properties that would heal the violence and disorder of life: it did not make people better in a moral sense, nor did it contribute any moral or intellectual superiority to the people who lived in the woods. The bitter history of the white people and the Indians was enough to prove otherwise—although Winthrop wrote, in a penetrating passage, that American thought on the Indians was confused by concepts of race, and these in turn were so deeply influenced by Negro slavery that Americans were unable to think rationally on racial questions.

The influence of the wilderness was not a moral force in itself; it was powerful for what it said of life elsewhere. Its simplicity threw into grotesque outline the tensions, the hysteria or the madness of much of what society took for granted, or accepted by habit, without thought; it helped to define what was really civilized in the civilized world. The education of the wilderness that strengthened or created one's power of discrimination was not study but enjoyment. No one ever evoked so vividly as Winthrop the images of a Northwestern summer—breaking camp an hour before dawn, a canoe moving out into the chill, starlighted void, a campfire burning on the beach; or the first glimpse of the Olympic Mountains seen from Puget Sound, with the pale blue and silver peaks luminous against the dark blue sky; or a trail through the giant cedar trees by the Puyallup River, where he felt himself to be passing forever between rows of identical pillars that closed behind him; or resting in a mountain meadow beside the Naches River, the horses grazing in grass so deep they did not have to bow their heads to eat. He remembered campfires—a salmon broiling, a grouse turning on a spit above a fire, the great blaze lighting the woods around the road builders' camp. He remembered riding over the immense waving prairies of eastern Washington, when a gale swept down from the mountains and the light and the wind met in an earth billow, the grass shaking like glittering spray. The hope that he placed in the land that had given him these things was a part of his being and, in his last months, when the sense of his own approaching death was strong, gave him a thought and an image that he could evoke "whenever in the world," he wrote, "I must have peace or die."

The scenes he summoned up are for all time a permanent part of the Northwest heritage. It was not a tragic land. In the older societies of the world, environment shaped or controlled man's growth; societies were driven or dominated by material needs; history was a record of the blind collisions of conflicting cultures that evolved differently in differing environments. Cultures were shaped by the fertility of the land, the kinds of crops, the amount of grain, the supply of water, the rigors of the weather, the sources of food—"the shape of the world has controlled or guided man's growth," Winthrop wrote. "The look of the world has hardly yet begun to have an effect upon spiritual progress."

The mountains of Europe and the eastern United States were unlike those Northwestern peaks, visible to sailors a hundred miles at sea, brilliant with snow, golden in the sunshine or silver in the moonlight. He remembered his own early travels in Europe, when he had walked alone along the streets of London, so moved by their age and associations that he was glad to find the green shade of Hyde Park, where he would lie down and pretend to sleep and let the tears flow. He remembered his emotion at the ruined arches of Rome, the narrow streets of Genoa or the rose-crowned hills of Malta, and the green wheat growing beside the temples of Greece. But the search for inspiration among a heritage of human institutions was a depressing business. When he climbed mountains in Switzerland, he found the scene there to be nobly rewarding, but the memory of it was clouded with recollections of Europe's swarming masses and a grim image "of such a mankind as has been made after centuries of opportunity." The Northwest was an unspoiled land, undarkened by a heritage of conflict or by rigid social forms or confined habits of thought that had come into being during an emergence from savagery.

So he came to believe that new forms of thought and life must develop in this land, and that the old promise of the New World, broken and frustrated elsewhere, would at last be realized here. A people molded by matchless scenery, strengthened by a benign climate, taught by the lessons of darker times, with their vision unclouded by their closeness to Old World history, would achieve their destiny. The influence of nature that played on them would be enduring, as he knew that the memory of his own life there would remain always with him— to remain with him and to be most meaningful in those moments when all other resources failed. He left to the Northwest a magnificent statement of its promise, seeing that promise not at all in material terms, never in terms of the growth of population or industry, but in the creation of new and better forms of life and thought that would result from the influence of an unspoiled world. It remained to be seen, in the next century or so, how much of that promise would be realized and how much of the land remain unspoiled.

Part Two

V

Salmon

I

A century may not be long enough to show the emergence of a new civilization, but it was certainly long enough to show signs of the decline of one. In the hundred years after Winthrop wrote, there were remarkably few indications of a great creative awakening in the Northwest; on the contrary, much of it was blighted in a way that suggested a determined effort to ravage the country before anything like a spiritual and cultural renaissance could take place there. In the late summer of 1961 I was in the Cascade Mountains not far from where Winthrop made his way over Naches Pass—not at the actual place; the weather unexpectedly turned too stormy to make it possible—and it occurred to me that it might be enlightening to take a look at the land he described in such eloquent terms and see what had happened to it, and what signs there were of those new systems of thought and life.

A major difficulty was that one scarcely knew where to begin. To start by examining the city of Tacoma, for example, to check on any indications of a new civilization arising among its pulp mills would be like McClellan's looking for a railroad pass in the regions where he was least likely to find one. Moving north from the southern extremity of Oregon, that area where Hall Kelley escaped from the horse thieves and where Jesse Applegate collected his library of 3,000 volumes, including all the Acts of Congress and the works of Macaulay and

Gibbon—and later the stamping ground of Ken Kesey, author of *One Flew Over the Cuckoo's Nest*, a novel of life in an Oregon insane asylum—no one could possibly consider Coos Bay and the towns around it as foreshadowing a new civilization. Moving inland there is Cottage Grove, which indeed had a remarkable, if short-lived, cultural fame: in 1920 the editor of the *Atlantic Monthly* discovered a girl from there, Opal Whiteley, who as a six-year-old child in a lumber camp was understood to have written an imaginative diary which the *Atlantic* published under the title of *The Story of Opal: The Journal of an Understanding Heart*—a book that became enormously popular and that created a sensation as well as doubts as to its authenticity. It appeared impossible that a six-year-old child could have been so conversant with Greek myths and Roman history as was the purported author of the diary, and Miss Whiteley ultimately fled to sanctuary in some Oriental religion in India to escape the effects of the publicity caused by her precocious literary efforts, eventually settling in England, where she refers to herself as H.R.H. Princess Françoise de Bourbon-Orléans. But such flickering signs of native genius could hardly have been what Winthrop had in mind.

Or, moving still farther north, there would be Salem, the state capital—"a village on one of those exquisite plains," Winthrop described it, "where the original oak trees have been left about"—a community that inspired a Northwest composer, Edward Finck, around the turn of the century, to try to write music with a truly native theme when he composed the "Salem Mazurka." Finck followed this with "Corvallis Polonaise," a composition inspired by Corvallis, the home of Oregon State College. There were for a period many songs expressing local and regional pride, such as "The Umpqua Is Calling for Me" or "Dear Little Webfoot Girl." But this sort of investigation could go on endlessly without turning up a trace of emerging native genius: one had to search elsewhere. Winthrop expected that it would take a long time for the Northwest to become civilized. He wrote to his sister of the feeling of grandeur connected with the mountains and the forests and the Columbia, which he called the great continental river, and said that sometime—"a thousand years hence"—the beauty of its shores, tended and cared for, would be wonderful. Perhaps he had in mind such mansions as the strange tower called Olana that his friend, the painter Frederick Church, had built overlooking the Hudson. There was one such castle eventually built on the Columbia. It was erected on the north side of the gorge where the river passes through the Cascade Mountains, the creation of Samuel Hill, the son-in-law of the builder of the Great Northern Railroad, an eccentric who was possessed by his admiration for European royalty, especially Queen Marie of Rumania, on whom he lavished a fortune in the way of special trains and other gifts, and who dedicated his castle with regal composure in 1926. But again the creation could hardly be called evidence of native genius.

And it appeared that a long time would be required, not merely for cultivated creations to come into being but to repair the damage to the physical beauty of the country that followed its settlement. Moving north from the Columbia, one came first to a gigantic wasteland of burned earth and black snags known as the Yacolt Burn, the result of a forest fire believed to have been the biggest blaze in recorded history. The fire that swept the Yacolt plain (where McClellan crossed so slowly on his way to the mountains) was merely the largest of a chain of sixty-eight fires which in September, 1902, broke out in the woods from central Oregon to the Canadian border; the Yacolt fire burned over 250,000 acres, and the pall of smoke was visible 40 miles at sea. Years afterward, when log supplies were short, the Yacolt Burn was quarried like a mine for the old logs that had not burned through but lay on the ground in their black charred shells, with sound wood remaining inside—reputedly the hardest and dirtiest form of logging ever known. But the damage done to the looks of the country by fires and storms was trivial compared to the work of the lumber companies. In little more than a generation they destroyed that landscape—strong, savage and majestic, as Winthrop called it—which he felt would inevitably work an influence on those in daily association with it. Or at least they destroyed the landscape in the more accessible regions, and if trees remained, it was because it was too hard and expensive to cut them down.

Nowhere in the art, literature or music of the Northwest can one find an echo of the amazing transformation worked by logged-off lands —unless a certain melancholy that pervades the Northwestern arts suggests its effect on the psychology of creative spirits. There was really nothing like the devastation left by the crews in the days of massive clear-cut logging. When they finished with the country, it looked like the pictures of trench warfare in the First World War. The huge stumps of the big trees bulged out of horizontal thickets of splintered debris left from their limbs, and from the smaller trees they brought down with them when they crashed; the earth was grooved with ditch-like scars where the logs had been dragged, and down these poured torrents of clay-clouded water after rains, staining all rivers within miles; gaunt snags stood here and there like monuments that had survived a bombardment. But the disaster areas were larger than any battlefield.

By the time the First World War ended, almost the entire region between Hood Canal and Grays Harbor was logged off, mile after mile of crushed and leveled forest, generally blackened with fires that swept the slashings after the loggers left—an abandoned, uninhabited, devastated land, unadorned except for billboards along the highway which, in a rather desperate bid for the tourist trade, read "Welcome to the Charmed Land."

It would plainly be impractical to search for signs of new approaches to the problems of human existence, new systems of thought and life, in those surroundings. One could only study the beneficent effects on human psychology of the scenery where it had not been so drastically altered. True, the growth of population in a century was very great. Joe Meek, a celebrated mountain man who had settled in Oregon, was the government's census taker in 1850; in the enormous area north of the Columbia River he counted 1,276 persons. In what was then Lewis County and its neighbor east of the Cascades—a stretch of territory running from the Pacific to the summit ridge of the Rockies in Montana—there were thirteen schoolchildren. The population of Oregon in 1850 was around 13,000, but it was admitted that not all of these were actually present, as fully half the males had gone to the California goldfields. By 1960 the population of Oregon was 1,768,687 and of Washington 2,853,214, and that the population was growing and would continue to grow was the primary evidence of the advance of civilization presented in all works on the Northwest, the obvious proof that the promise of the land was rapidly being fulfilled.

Most of these newcomers, however, were concentrated in the metropolitan areas around Portland, Seattle, Tacoma and Spokane and in the towns and smaller cities whose most outstanding characteristic was that they were remarkably like the small towns of the Middle West, and which in any case were so jammed in on one another that an inhabitant had to travel miles in order to see the scenic grandeur which Winthrop hopefully believed would slowly and subtly educate people in day-to-day association with it. What the inhabitants saw were cities and towns that never altogether escaped being incongruous and unreal in their setting, and which most often appeared temporary. All the ingredients of Midwestern cities were in them, the parking meters, the drugstore, the supermarket, the furniture store, the restaurant and the bar, the business block and the hotel, as though someone had made careful stage sets of typical American towns and set them up, like so many Potemkin villages, to give an illusion of growth and progress against an elemental wilderness, or against a wasteland of logged-off hills.

And temporary is what most towns were. A mill was built in the middle of a stand of timber, and a company town, usually named for the leading stockholder, was built around the mill, lasting until the trees were felled or the mill burned, both catastrophes to the local economy often happening about the same time. Under such circumstances as these it appeared unlikely that one should search for emerging signs of a creative awakening in the lumber industry, the major resource of the Northwest through the country in question. There remained spectacular projects, such as Grand Coulee Dam, three times the height of Niagara Falls, for some years the largest man-made structure on earth, but this huge enterprise could scarcely be cited as evidence of any native imaginative effort; it was conceived by the Federal government as part of some long-range planning of unfathomable complexity, and among its many benefits, apart from an increase in the population of ducks that inhabited new potholes formed by the seepage of water, was the creation of the large nuclear-power and hydrogen-bomb plants utilizing the electrical energy provided by Grand Coulee, and which could not be called creations of the native Northwest or signs of the emergence of a new kind of civilization there.

And yet some inheritance of the pioneer culture persisted. This most remote part of the United States developed the way the rest of the nation developed, except that it had fewer of the outward signs of a distinctive cultural life, such as had evolved in New England or in the Old South. In spite of the temporary air or the logged-off hills or the imposition of cultural patterns from older regions, a Northwestern society that was distinct and different somehow persisted. What confused its identification was that it seemed to have no independent or native expression in popular or sophisticated art. For many years the foremost novelist of Seattle was Elizabeth Champney, who wrote some forty books before she died in 1917, including such works as *Three Vassar Girls Abroad, Three Vassar Girls in England, Three Vassar Girls in France, Three Vassar Girls at Home, Three Vassar Girls in Italy, Three Vassar Girls on the Rhine, Three Vassar Girls in Russia and Turkey, Three Vassar Girls in South America, Three Vassar Girls in Switzerland.* These were richly bound and illustrated stories of adventure, spies and international intrigue, in the course of which older fellow travelers of the three little Vassar girls recounted the history and explained the political problems of the countries being visited. Their lectures were sometimes acutely perceptive, as in *Three Vassar Girls in Russia and Turkey*, published in 1889, in which an English diplomat tells the girls that "Herzegovina and Servia are really the spark in the great gunpowder mine which would shake all Europe but for the repressing hand of Great Britain." But it would be difficult to find works less immediately related to the environment in which they were written.

The novels and stories about Vassar and New York intellectual life written by Mary McCarthy, born in Seattle and the most gifted Northwestern novelist, are not different from those of other women writers from other sections of the country in the sense that they reveal a native

Northwestern character or viewpoint. Or in popular culture, the music of Bing Crosby, who grew up in Spokane, has no distinctive quality that associates it with the region where his family were pioneers; and John Reed of Portland, who began his literary career at Harvard with *Tamburlaine and Other Poems* and ended it in Russia with *Ten Days That Shook the World*, reveals in his writing no indigenous quality that could be traceable to the influence of the place, the people or the spirit of the region, and still less to the influence of those mountains and forests and rivers that Winthrop thought would inspire a better society than mankind had known before.

II

What remained as the likeliest part of the Northwest where the promise of an emerging civilization might be detected was precisely what had been there before: the uninhabited wilderness. And in spite of all that had been done to destroy it, the forested area was still very large. If the wilderness of British Columbia—itself larger than Oregon, Washington and California combined—was counted with the expanse of Northwest woods, there were vast regions of wilderness or semi-wilderness, islands of the unchanged past, in a sense, comparable to what the entire region had been a century before.

I was in the Northwest in 1961 to write about the Cascade Crest Trail, which starts at the border of Canada and follows the summit ridge of the Cascades through Oregon and Washington. I had no intention of covering all the miles of this rugged hiking and horseback path, but merely drove to the nearest point where it crossed a road, hiked a day to look at that part of the trail, and drove the next day to another starting point, hoping thereby to gain an adequate impression of it without having to carry a 50-pound pack its entire length. All I carried was a fishing rod. I did not fish much, but in the Northwest a fishing rod is a kind of safe-conduct pass, or identification card, and nobody carrying one is asked questions about who he is or what he is doing.

This pleasant kind of journalistic enterprise was interrupted in early September, 1961, when I agreed to go to the Horsefly River in British Columbia. After twenty years of trying, the International Pacific Salmon Fisheries Commission had managed to restore the sockeye salmon run to their original spawning grounds in the Horsefly. Many celebrated people, including governors, scientists, conservationists, biologists and the heads of fisheries departments, were expected to attend the ceremonies, and it was thought some press coverage would be appropriate.

The International Pacific Salmon Fisheries had no public-relations department. Arrangements were made by rather self-conscious biologists unaccustomed to handling such affairs. Mrs. Joseph Connolly, a correspondent for *Sports Illustrated* in Bellingham, Washington, had persuaded the magazine to have a representative on hand. It was her story; she had discovered it in reading official reports, and she had badgered officials to persuade them to invite the press. She had been ill, however, and Jack Olson, a writer for the magazine, was supposed to attend the ceremonies. He was on another story and could not go, and I was given the assignment because I happened to be in the Northwest.

I drove to Bellingham and met her in the home where she lived with her husband and young son, a tall, thin, pale woman whose neck brace gave her the appearance of some historical personage, Lady Jane Grey or Mary Queen of Scots, in a regal ruff. She was fearless. Because of her illness a sudden stopping of the car, or a fall, might have serious consequences, but she never flinched during the 600-mile drive up the Fraser River and along the Quesnel and the Horsefly, though cars, wagons and cattle constantly appeared on the road just ahead of us and forced us onto the shoulder to avoid a sudden stop; and when we at last came to the fisheries camp, she immediately put on a pair of waders and walked into the stream to watch the salmon despite the current and the rocks.

Forest fires had broken out all over the Northwest. Twenty-eight were burning in British Columbia, and others south of the border. The planes that had been expected to bring distinguished visitors could not land on the lakes: the pilots could not locate them through the smoke. Just before we arrived the telephone system had been taken over by the Canadian army and the Department of Lands and Forests; no telephone calls could be put through. Heat pressed down on the fisheries cabin on the banks of the Horsefly. The air was so still that dust hung like a curtain after a car passed on the road. The smoke was high and unbroken, filtering out colors and leaving everything on earth with the faded brown tint of old-fashioned, sepia-toned photographs. Aside from Mrs. Connolly and me, the only representatives of the press were two young men from a fishing magazine published in Vancouver. It could not be said that the scientists were glad to see us. A fish biologist, his face streaked with sweat, greeted us with a hollow voice, saying, "We've got Cokes on ice."

We walked upstream about a hundred yards to look at the river. It was filled with dead salmon. They lay on the bottom, white and leprous in the clear water. I knew that salmon died after spawning, and it took me a few minutes to realize that something was wrong; they do not die at once but float downstream, and some even live through the winter. But here there were hundreds, no, thousands. On the far bank a crew of young men with long poles like pitchforks were lifting the bodies from the water and throwing them up on the bank. There was a small haystack of them. In the dull, smoke-heavy heat the unreality of their movements, the rhythmic plunge of each pole into the water, the slow lift above the surface, and the toss of the salmon to the pile, was grotesque and irrational.

Bright-colored rubber boats had been inflated to carry people down the river so they could float over the endless lines of oncoming fish, and these boats were lying on stringy grass that was almost visibly turning into straw in the heat. A few worried officials of the International Pacific Salmon Fisheries Commission, in business suits, went through the motions of professional activity, conversing together, nodding, looking at charts, going back into the cabin; a few tense young fish biologists, in trim khaki clothes and wearing white helmets, directed a crew of local workmen, took water temperatures, brought in reports from downstream stations or from time to time drove off to the nearest town. They came back, dust-covered, with discouraging news to add to the catastrophe of the forest fires and the dying fish. No one was coming. The only visitors were the four journalists with dubious scientific credentials to report the occasion, and three commercial fishermen from Seattle who had taken a cabin near the town of Horsefly.

The sockeye, or red salmon, *Oncorhynchus nerka*, is a bright red fish weighing 6 pounds, on the average, and measuring about 24 inches in length, a hardy fish which, however, requires cold water for spawning and the water in the Horsefly was warm. The most abundant food fish of the Indians, salmon were largely responsible for their relative comfort: they had the highest standard of living of any North American Indians except the Aztecs. The sockeye appeared from the Pacific in the summer. Their numbers varied greatly, according to the productivity of the river systems in which they spawned. That is, they returned to their own spawning grounds after four years, but since they had gone to sea from different rivers, at different times, the incoming fish arrived annually, but each individual river received its salmon only at four-year intervals. Unlike Chinook salmon, which can be hooked and will strike at a spinner or other lure, the sockeye on its way to the spawning ground cannot be fished. Its digestive system atrophies, and it does not eat after entering fresh water.

Swimming only by day, and making as much as 17 to 33 miles a day against the current, the fish moved unerringly up the big rivers, into their tributaries, across lakes and finally to the small streams where they spawned, appearing punctually every fourth year. Some displaced fish whose timetable had gotten askew in centuries past appeared in the intervening years, but they were few in number and their lonely visitation was unlike the main run, which could be seen all along the way and filled the spawning grounds from shore to shore.

The Horsefly was only one of hundreds of such streams once used by the sockeye salmon, whose range extended from California rivers to those of the Arctic in Alaska. Heavy commercial fishing where the fish entered the rivers destroyed the runs completely in California and in most of Oregon and Washington, but the sockeye remained commercially important where they entered Puget Sound, and their greatest spawning area was in the rivers that flowed into the Fraser.

The Horsefly was one of the largest of these in terms of the number of fish it produced. It is part of the Quesnel River system in central British Columbia, forming about 500 miles from the mouth of the Fraser, and is a bright, short, shallow, crystal-clear little stream that springs from two branches on the slopes of Mount Perseus, a cone 8,361 feet high that the natives call Haycock Mountain. Its source is about a hundred miles west of the Canoe River that David Thompson explored in 1812, but is separated by uninhabited mountain country. The Horsefly flows 30 miles or so westward through deep wilderness and into a rocky chasm, heavily wooded on steep slopes that rise 800-odd feet above the water. The Horsefly at this point is 30 to 50 feet wide, and at the end of a dry summer about 4 feet deep. It is a noisy, wild, turbulent stream with beautiful coiling rapids that seem to wind and unwind as the stream is thrown from one side of the canyon to the other. As it emerges from its canyon, the river drops over a series of falls. The last of these drops 75 feet. Below the falls the river widens to 100 feet or more, slows down, warms up and flows with unhurried speed over miles of tranquil little rapids and riffles.

This is the spawning ground. It is ideal for the purpose of the sockeye salmon. The water is absolutely clear; the rocks on the bottom stand out as if magnified; the fish are as visible as if lights played upon them. Lodgepole pine line the banks, coming right to the water's edge, with grass-covered banks in any clear ground. The river is of even depth, width and flow for several miles, and then it settles to a lagoon-like slow-water course until it enters Horsefly Lake and then Quesnel Lake. In 1579, when Sir Francis Drake was approaching the Olympic Peninsula, the salmon were making their way to this perfect place for the fulfillment of their destiny. Sixty four-year cycles passed, and there was another great migration when David Thompson was building his chain of fur posts on the upper Columbia in 1809. Fourteen more generations of salmon had spawned there when certain happenings on the Quesnel River eventually stopped the run. For ages beyond recorded history, twenty-five times a century, the salmon had come to this particular place. They had been stopped, and now they had come back; it was an occasion calling for the presence of governors.

The run of 1857 was exceptionally heavy. The spawning fish churned up so much gravel that they uncovered gold. Five men who were prospecting in the area found free gold in the gravel near the downstream limits of the spawning ground. They picked up 100 ounces of gold in a week and started a historic gold rush into the interior. More gold was found on other rivers than on the Horsefly, however, and the river, notorious for the number of big black flies that gave it its name, also got a bad reputation for the false hopes it raised among the gold seekers.

But there was persistent, if intermittent, mining in the wilderness back from the river, and especially on the Quesnel River below Quesnel Lake. Every four years millions of salmon returned to the river, and at periodic intervals crowds of gold seekers worked the gravel of the Quesnel and departed. In 1888 it occurred to some forgotten promoter that mining would be easier if the flow of the Quesnel River could be stopped entirely and the gold extracted from the dry gravel that would be left in its bed. The Golden River Quesnel Company Limited was accordingly formed, and stock was sold. Work was started on a dam 763 feet long and 18 feet high at the outlet of the lake. The work went so slowly that the salmon runs of 1893 and 1897 were not impeded in the slightest. The dam was finally finished in 1898. In 1900 the company was bankrupt and the mining operation was abandoned.

The dam was left standing, its gates closed, in the hope that more investors would rush in to put their savings into Golden River Quesnel preferred. The 1901 salmon run turned out to be one of the largest ever recorded. Commercial fishermen who were netting salmon in the Strait of Juan de Fuca and at the mouth of the Fraser sold some 11 million sockeye salmon to the canneries, and millions more went on up the river, into the Quesnel, and were stopped by the dam on their way to the Horsefly. A small flume, no more than a foot wide, had been left for the run to go through. It was soon choked with fish, and most of the salmon died before reaching the spawning grounds, but enough got through to keep the cycle alive. The natural reproductive capacity of even a few salmon is tremendous, each female laying from three to five thousand eggs. In 1903 John Pease Babcock, an American who became British Columbia's first commissioner of fisheries, built a small fish ladder over the Quesnel dam at a cost of $4,104. When the salmon arrived in 1905—a small run, the offspring of the few survivors of the 1901 catastrophe—they easily got to the Horsefly. For that matter, too many salmon may actually reduce the number of fish produced, for the late arrivals at the spawning grounds, in laying their own eggs, destroy the nests made by those who came before them. The salmon in 1905 found uncrowded water and produced amazingly; in 1909, 4 million salmon reached the Horsefly. Only eight years after the cycle was nearly destroyed it was back in almost prehistoric abundance.

The next run, that of 1913, was the largest ever recorded. Some 35 million fish returned from the Pacific. Twenty-five million were caught by commercial fishermen in salt water, but 10 million started up the Fraser to spawn. One hundred and thirty miles up the Fraser there is a defile called Hell's Gate, a gorge 110 feet across at the bottom of an 800-foot canyon. The river, 100 to 200 feet deep, has a current of 25 feet a second. Salmon got through by making short rushes from relatively quiet pools formed by rocks and crevices on both sides, and by using the upstream eddies that projections create. In 1913 the Canadian Northern Pacific Railway and the Grand Trunk Railway were racing each other, laying tracks on opposite sides of the Fraser. Their blasting started slides that smoothed the banks of the river into a sort of trough, creating hydraulic conditions that the fish could not overcome. Babcock personally rushed up and down the gorge with buckets, carrying a few fish above the slide, but the races of salmon that were coming up the river in that particular year were virtually destroyed. The main sufferers happened to be the fish from the Quesnel-Horsefly system; there was no run in 1917; the cycle was broken; and the river was written off as a salmon producer.

About the time the Horsefly run was destroyed, apparently forever, a scientist at Stanford University, Dr. Charles Gilbert, discovered a method of identifying the home waters of salmon by their scales. Sockeye salmon are spawned in the gravel in riffles in streams which flow into a lake. They spend twelve days on their spawning grounds. Five days are spent preparing to spawn. The fish pair and select the right kind of riffle, with the precise kind of gravel required, and the right stream flow. Another five days are spent preparing the redd, the nest in the gravel. The female scoops this out, lying on her side and flapping her tail, the current carrying the sand away. Two days are spent spawning. The female hovers over the sand of the excavation she has dug, the male pressing against her and, as she deposits some of the eggs she carries, the male fertilizes them with his seminal fluid. The female now digs another nest upstream from the first, and the sand and gravel from this cover the eggs she has just laid, and so on, with several hundred eggs in each nest. Both the male and the female die after spawning, their weight reduced to only one third of what it was when they entered fresh water from the ocean.

The eggs develop under the gravel, safe from predatory trout, and the fry work their way to the surface of the gravel when the water warms in the spring. The fry are carried downstream to quiet water, collect in schools of minnows, and spend their first year in the lake which is invariably found downstream from the spawning grounds. As 3-inch fingerlings they move downstream to begin their three-year life in the Pacific. Their brains are programmed, every bend in the river and every rapid and obstruction implanted on some memory system that guides them on their reverse migration. Each scale of each fish is marked with a distinctive pattern that looks like a human thumb-print, but where a human thumbprint differs for each individual, the scale pattern of salmon differs for every lake. The patterns of each scale are not only like the human thumbprint; they resemble the rings of a tree and, like those of a tree, they are growth rings. When the fingerlings are in the lake, the scales are small, and the growth rings form a tight center, a small fresh-water nucleus akin to the con-centrated heart of a tree formed in its early stages of slow growth. After the salmon reach the sea, the scales grow larger and growth rings are added at the rate of seven a year, but only the tightly woven rings in the center tell where the fish originally came from. So fixed is the life pattern of the sockeye that a salmon caught in the ocean can be identified as having come from some particular stretch of riffles, and so destined to return to it, or die trying. Or, when the migrating fish enter fresh water in a confused and fast-swimming mass, it is possible to say that these are going to the Stuart River, or the Adams, or the Chilko or the Raft, or any of the other rivers and tributaries on the way.

Some time passed before any practical use could be made of Dr. Gilbert's discovery. In 1937 the International Pacific Salmon Fisheries Commission was formed to regulate commercial catches. Both Canada and the United States had laws intended to prevent the destruction of the species by limiting the number of fish that could be taken on their way to spawn, but their efforts were badly coordinated, and American fishermen were able to haul in their nets loaded with fish while Canadian fishermen were idle, and American fishing boats were tied up while Canadian fishing boats were coming in with so many fish it appeared that none would be left by the time the season for Americans opened. But at last the means existed for controlling fishing on both sides of the water, so that, in the case of badly depleted runs, the fish could be permitted to escape the nets and spawn. The actual procedure was complicated. Fingerlings were netted, and samples of their scales taken, as they headed down the rivers to the sea. Plastic replicas of the scales were made. These were filed in small loose-leaf notebooks, each page containing 115 replicas of scales and identifying them as coming from specific rivers. No means existed for controlling fishing on the ocean, but the fishing boats had to take their catch to canneries, and when the first salmon of the incoming migrants appeared on the docks, their scales were checked, and it was possible to see where the fish were headed. The life cycle of the salmon delayed the operation; it was necessary to wait four years to see if the identifications were right. But eventually the distinctions became clear enough, so that when the first salmon were caught by the offshore fishermen, it was possible to say that these were part of the migration headed for Bivouac Creek, Driftwood River, Forfar Creek, Felix Creek, Nechako River, Endako River, Nedina River, Thompson River, Seymour River, Big Silver Creek on the Harrison, or Birkenhead River on the Lillooet. There were none from the Horsefly, or not enough to worry about: by 1941 the run was finished there, with perhaps only a thousand survivors appearing irregularly on the spawning grounds that, in the past, twenty-five times each century, had had millions.

These last remnants were guarded. There were 2,000 commercial fishing boats ranging the waters between the United States and Canada. The days and hours on which they were permitted to fish were determined by the relative abundance of the migrating races of fish coming through. The ideal arrangement would have been to close the fishing grounds periodically, so that the best and strongest fish at the peak of each run could escape to their home streams. To stop all fishing would have been self-defeating; in a good year, one in which the rate of sea survival was high, streams produced more fish than they had room for, in which case the fish would overcrowd the spawning grounds, and many would have to be destroyed to prevent them from destroying the beds already spawned. The mouth of the Fraser River was a funnel toward which the migrating salmon moved, one run after another, at fairly well-defined intervals. The problem was a negative one, that of not inadvertently catching the last survivors from the Horsefly in the midst of one of the runs of salmon from rivers whose abundance permitted fishermen to take all they could catch.

The regulations were international documents. They were written in a strange mixture of diplomatic language and everyday fisherman talk. The high contracting parties, namely, the government of the United States, and the government of Canada, agreed that the taking of sockeye salmon should be prohibited in a specified period, such as five o'clock on the afternoon of a Wednesday to five o'clock in the forenoon of the next Monday, in all the area between Angeles Point in Washington and across Race Rocks to Williams Head in British Columbia. In this period it was hoped the threatened species could pass safely through and make it to the mouth of the Fraser River. The rebuilding process was slow and complicated by the four-year wait between runs to see if the experiment was working.

In the meantime great fishways were built at Hell's Gate on the Fraser where the slides had stopped the runs. In 1949 several thousand fish returned to the Horsefly, and the spawning grounds were taken over by the commission and improved and policed; in 1953 the run began to assume substantial size. Then in 1957, a full century after the spawning salmon kicked up gold on the Horsefly, the salmon returned in large numbers, at least 200,000 counted on the spawning grounds. Clarence Pautzke, then the United States commissioner of the Fish and Wildlife Service, said, "Imagine a race of fish destroyed not once, but twice, and still making a comeback. . . . No stream can be written off." The sockeye is not a game fish, but the restoration of the Horsefly, Pautzke said, "had a terrific impact with regard to bringing back runs of fish. . . . It points the way to the restoration of all species." Dr. Wellington Royce, a scientist at the University of Washington, wrote that the lesson was not limited to the sockeye; success on the Horsefly would make it "a model that may be followed with any species on any river."

In the summer of 1961 salmon from the Horsefly began to appear in the nets of offshore fishermen. Loyd Royal, the American-born director of the International Commission, said he had never seen fish in better condition. "No parasites," he said. "No sea lice." When the salmon began passing through the Strait of Juan de Fuca, it became evident that they were numerous; it seemed possible that a million fish were on their way to the spawning grounds in the last days of August or the first days of September, and four years hence, if all went well, their spawn would be returning in the enormous numbers that were there before that dam on the Quesnel River was built. Consequently commercial fishermen were allowed to take some 600,000, allowing about 300,000 to spawn.

III

Meriwether Lewis was almost the only explorer who did not marvel at the abundance of salmon. He was anxious to start home when the first fish were caught by the Indians in the Columbia in the spring of 1806. But almost all other visitors marveled at the salmon runs as a phenomenon unlike anything in the New World. John Jewitt, a survivor of the ship *Boston,* was enslaved by the Indians of Nootka in 1803 and held captive for three years. He watched the Indians capture salmon in their traps made of pine splinters—big contraptions, about 5 feet in diameter at the mouth and some 20 feet long—

and recorded that as many as seven hundred salmon could be caught in less than fifteen minutes. In *The Northwest Coast*, James Gilchrist Swan told how, in his early days on Willapa Harbor in 1852, while camping beside the north fork of the Palux River, he was awakened at dawn by the wild splashing of the salmon moving up the river. These were the big salmon, the Chinook, weighing up to 80 pounds, that came with tidewater in the spring. The Indians speared them or caught them in nets—big nets woven of spruce roots, up to 600 feet long and 16 feet deep—but the more abundant food fish was the sockeye salmon that ran from late August to early December, until "every river, brook, creek and little stream is completely covered with them."

Indian ceremonies at the arrival of the salmon varied from tribe to tribe, but the first fish was always an occasion for celebrations and rejoicing. Sometimes only the heart was taken, and the fish buried headed upstream so the salmon coming later would know which way to go. Elaborate precautions were taken to prevent a dog from eating the first fish to arrive; if a dog got the salmon's heart, the entire run would go back to the ocean. In some tribes the first fish was cut into small portions, and a portion given to each child. But in any case, the time when the salmon were supposed to arrive was always a time of tremendous anxiety and tension. Occasionally (as in 1827 on the Columbia) there was no run. Ordinarily the Indians lived through the winter on smoked or dried salmon. They traded over the mountains with packs of dried salmon, pounded together with dried blueberries (a food about which explorers left contradictory accounts, some liking it, and some complaining bitterly), and as the Indians were generally short of food by the time the first salmon were due, they feared more than anything that some ill-treatment given the first salmon would discourage the rest from coming up the rivers.

It was doubtless the white man's neglect of such elementary precautions that caused the rapid depletion of the fishing industry. In 1867, the first year of record, the commercial fisheries on the Columbia canned 4,000 cases of salmon, which hardly made any impression on the swarming millions of migrating fish. The next year 18,000 cases were canned. Two years later around 100,000 cases of canned salmon were shipped from the river. Three years after that the total was 250,000 cases. Four years later—that is, 1876—around 450,000 cases were shipped out annually. The peak was reached in 1883, when no less than 629,000 cases of salmon were canned. But at this point something happened; the white people evidently were inconsiderate of the salmon's feelings, or had forgotten to give portions of the first annual catch to the Indian children and old people, or had otherwise neglected the required ceremonies, for the catch suddenly plummeted. By 1889 fewer fish were caught on the Columbia than had been taken fifteen years before, and by the end of the First World War the sockeye salmon had all but vanished from Washington rivers, had disappeared from those of Oregon and California, and was found only in Canadian and Alaskan waters.

The tension of the white men gathered around the spawning grounds of the Horsefly in 1961 made one think of the anxiety in Indian camps in the days of the first explorers. Sockeye salmon will not spawn when the water temperature is above 55 degrees. The temperature of the Horsefly was above 59 degrees. Prolonged stay in warm water affects the gills of the fish with a bacterial disease called columnaris. The salmon move upriver in waves, with a relatively small early run far in advance of the main migration. On the Horsefly almost the entire early run, perhaps 130,000 fish, had died without spawning. These were the dead fish seen everywhere along the banks, in the bottom of deep pools, or lodged in riffles or in the limbs of trees that had fallen into the river. And now the main run was arriving. Usually fish on the spawning grounds are extremely active, darting in great lines, a hundred fish across, in formation so orderly they seem to have been drilled. Or they may race with what appears to be exuberance, hundreds of them in a pack, sending up spray five feet in the air and pushing before them a wall of water so high that they may be washed several feet up on dry land and frantically wriggle back into water.

But these incoming swarms of fish were torpid, turning and moving ceaselessly but languidly. Occasionally a female would begin halfheartedly to prepare a redd, then give it up. The river was hourly becoming more crowded. On the bank, near the cabin, two pathologists who had arrived, as we did, before the roads were closed because of the fires, were dissecting fish after fish, dozens of them, or perhaps hundreds of them, peering at organs and casting aside the dismembered carcasses, their white surgeons' coats stained and blemished and expressions of frustration on their features.

Perhaps to get us out of there, perhaps to imitate public-relations-department hospitality, the biologists took us to the Seattle fishermen for cocktails. Their cabin was raised on stilts, like all the cabins thereabouts, to escape floods, with steep wooden steps to a narrow porch, and a screen door, beyond which was a room lined with bunks. The fishermen were glowering in various stages of truculence. Behind their anger, evident in sardonic comments to the pale biologists, one sensed a hangover of old suspicions that the various regulations that had been issued to let the salmon pass through had really been for the benefit of rival Canadian fishermen. A successful catch meant about

$30,000; a bad season, nothing. But the fishermen recognized their duties as hosts and tried to make us welcome. We sat on the springs of the bunks and drank their whiskey.

The leader of the American fishermen, who resembled Ernest Hemingway and was somewhat like Hemingway in his violent social oscillations between friendliness and hostility, said, "For Christ's sake, get ice! Do something! You could dump a few tons of ice in the river!" The fish biologist said politely it was a good idea, but did we know how much ice would be needed to reduce the water temperature 5 degrees? Besides there were no ice-making facilities within hundreds of miles, and the roads were closed. The American fishermen construed this as a typical bureaucratic excuse for doing nothing. When something had to be done, you did it. The atmosphere grew unpleasant. It was lightened by a strange distraction. One of the fishermen had played football with Elmer Tesreau, nephew of Jeff Tesreau, the great pitcher of the New York Giants in McGraw's best years. Jeff Tesreau subsequently became the baseball coach at Dartmouth and the grand old man of generations of students. His nephews, Elmer and Louis Tesreau, grew up in Chehalis, Washington; I went to high school with them. Jeff Tesreau coached and prepared them like a pair of thoroughbred horses for great athletic careers. He got Elmer to Dartmouth as a freshman, but at the first frigid New England winter Elmer returned to the Northwest. The two brothers were perhaps the greatest football players ever seen—that is, when they were playing together. Elmer, though younger, was a year ahead of Louis, and while they were exceptional alone, they were unbeatable as a pair, both big, fast, brainy, perfectly coordinated and moving together as though they read each other's minds and anticipated each other's intentions. Their high-school teams, which never lost a game, were, except for the lightness of the line, probably the equal of college teams.

Elmer was pleasant, friendly, hardworking, a serious student; Louis was amiable, lazy, easily amused, with an enjoyment of life so pronounced that it was believed his premature appearance of age—he was nearly bald when he was in high school—was a result of the elaborate parties and entertainments which sportsmen from Seattle and coaches from eastern colleges and scouts for major-league baseball clubs were reputed to put on in order to recruit him for their teams. Louis was a great punter, in some games averaging 60 yards a punt, and was also a master of a now-forgotten art—dropkicking—though most games were so one-sided he was rarely called to demonstrate it. Neither Elmer nor Louis did as well apart as when they played together, though Elmer eventually won some degree of national fame as a costar of the All-American, George Wilson, at the University of

Washington. In the Rose Bowl game of 1925 with Alabama, Elmer functioned as a roadmaker for Wilson in the way he had previously opened the way for Louis, and the score at the end of the half was Washington 19, Alabama 0, a startling upset. But in the second half the entire Alabama team piled on Wilson, who was carried off the field. Elmer and the Washington team held on until the last few minutes, and then three long forward passes made it Alabama 20, Washington 19, the passes caught by Johnny Mack Brown, whose performance was so spectacular he became a hero of the Hollywood movie colony and remained there permanently as a movie actor.

The fishermen said that Elmer Tesreau had recently died. Louis Tesreau was dead. Now recollection of other gifted athletes whose lives had been short cast a pall over the gathering, none too jovial to begin with. But the catastrophe on the river was momentarily forgotten, and bickering over the International Pacific Salmon Fisheries Commission stopped for the time being. The fishermen decided to go back to Seattle. There was some question about the roads being closed, but they dismissed it; when something had to be done, you did it. We went to our quarters at a hunting lodge on Horsefly Lake, where the cabins prepared for our use, among all the empty cabins that had been expected to hold visiting dignitaries, stood in lonely isolation, as a visible reminder of all the guests who had not come to the party.

IV

In the morning the forest fire was within 3 miles of the commission's camp. A bluish-gray smoky haze lay over the lodgepole pines across the river. During the night the fire had destroyed a small lumber mill in the foothills southeast of the camp, and trucks loaded with people, belongings, trunks, clothes, animals and furniture passed by on the way to town. About 250,000 salmon were at the spawning grounds. Workmen were still methodically pitching the dead fish onto the banks. Occasionally there was a dense whiff of rotting fish, but less than one would expect; most of the carcasses were still lodged under water or in the shallows.

Walking downstream along the spawning ground, we saw the fish headed upstream in broken and waving irregular ribbons, sometimes only a few, thinly scattered, more often in large bands of several hundred. Their bright vermilion bodies, lighter red under the water, seemed to have the texture of rich, wrinkled Chinese silk. They were indifferent to people wading among them. They moved irregularly forward, one pair passing another, drifting back, passing ahead. There might be a small pool formed by boulders, with olive-colored rocks on the bottom and bubbles rising where the water flowed into it, with a dozen or twenty fish in it, the number fairly constant because some moved upstream as others came in from below. This same scene was repeated all the way across the river and all the way downstream for miles. The sockeye change color when they start for the spawning grounds, the bodies becoming a brighter red, the head taking a deep green color, very conspicuous when the fish is taken out of water but less so, under the water, than the brilliant red sides. Their movements were unhurried; they faced the shore on an angle at times, one side or the other, turning a little and drifting down, and coming back with a few strokes of the tail. In the water they seemed almost tubular in shape. The ones below a crevice in the rocks appeared to be waiting before entering the quieter pool; if they came on steadily, there would not be room enough to swim. Leaving the pool to go upstream, into a surge of foaming water, they moved in pairs, almost touching, one slightly higher in the water than the other, a slight, short, forceful rush, followed by another wait below another pool. Watching them became hypnotizing; it was like trying to watch a fluid.

Word spread that the salmon had gone into the gorge above the spawning grounds and were trying to jump the falls there to get to colder water. It was a hopeless effort. The first falls, a mile or so above the top reaches of the spawning grounds, was 20 feet high. Sockeye are said by biologists to be able to jump only 5 or 6 feet. And above the first falls there was another, 50 feet high, and above that the Horsefly raced through a narrow rocky flume for miles without a quiet stretch. But the salmon did not know that and were moving upriver to the base of the falls and throwing themselves into the air.

It was impossible to reach the falls by going up the river; we had to climb a ridge and follow a trail for about 2 miles, and then angle back to the falls. The trail was dry and powdery underfoot, with the dusty filmlike surface that is called duff, each footstep sending up a small gray explosion. Several hundred feet below, the river was visible through the trees, a thin silver line below the steep cliffs or the sharply angled slopes of shale and gravel that were held by thin foliage or small scattered trees. Near the point where the side trail led back to the falls we came on two teen-agers who were trying to dislodge a huge boulder and send it down the slope. To help in fighting the fires, crews of auxiliaries had been hastily recruited in Vancouver, men from the skid road, juvenile delinquents, and others who had little enthusiasm for fire fighting once they got into the woods. They were wandering about, trying to keep out of sight of the people who were supposed to be in charge of them. The two youngsters had a big pole, which they used as a lever, and were laboring to get it so placed that they could move this old gray rock, about the size of an icebox, so it would roll through the shale and, picking up material as it fell, start a landslide. When they saw us, they walked away, farther up the trail toward the fire fighters, swinging their arms widely, like kids who have been discovered writing something on a wall.

The thought of a landslide stopping the flow of the Horsefly at that time was enough to summon up the image of the final turn of the screw. But in fact the rock that had poised over the cliff for ages was pretty solid; it would have taken a blast of dynamite to loosen it. The trail down the side of the canyon was a long slant, sliding earth or gravel underfoot, passable only because there were small, deep-rooted trees that gave one a handhold. At the falls the canyon walls rose 50 feet or more. The fish could be seen about 100 feet downstream, moving slowly into the pool at the base of the falls. They were lost from sight in the turbulence of the water. Then they could be seen again, emerging with terrific velocity, poised for a moment against the falls before they dropped back into the water. The textbook entry that said these fish jump only 5½ or 6 feet seemed wrong. The strongest impression was of the difference in the height of the jumps. Every few minutes some particularly gifted specimen took off in a great soaring lunge into the atmosphere, her body flailing powerfully as she left the water, and settling into an upward glide twice as high as the majority of her leaping companions. I thought they jumped as high as 12 feet, but we finally agreed that perhaps 8 feet would be about right.

At the end of their first day at the falls the fish were jumping at the rate of 65 a minute. They fell back, stunned, drifted downstream and came back to leap again. Later on they were jumping at the rate of 130 a minute. There was no visible pattern in their movements. For several seconds there would be no fish in sight, then a dozen at once, crisscrossing each other or even colliding in the air. A big gray boulder the size of a freight car divided the falls. About one salmon in ten struck the boulder. Its top half was hot and dry, and the bottom half drenched with spray from the falls and the water left when the fish landed sideways against it. The salmon hit the rock with a sound like the crack of a .22 rifle, clearly audible above the roar and throb of the falls. Occasionally a salmon missed the falls and the rock entirely, just jumping in the air. More often one missed the falls but hit the rock, sailing at right angles with it, and remained partially lodged on a small shelf high above the water for several seconds— plainly outlined, big, misplaced, eerie. And while it hung there the fish were leaping tirelessly, one after another or a dozen at a time, all day long.

Except for the sound of the falls the woods were quiet. There were no birds. Tracks of bear were everywhere, but the bears were gorged and had vanished. There were no eagles, though these birds are said to follow the salmon and to be fond of the eyes of the dead fish. The hot, late-summer sunlight, filtered through the smoke, fell heavily on the motionless air, into a world that seemed drained and emptied of all life except the salmon moving steadily against the current to the highest point and the coldest water they could reach.

At one o'clock that afternoon the forests around the headwaters of the Horsefly burst into flame. We were visiting the farmhouse of Frank Jones, the only settler in the area, who had taken out a homestead on the Horsefly forty-eight years before. He had retired after leasing his lands to the Fisheries Commission. Farming had never been very profitable, but he managed to get by during the Depression by running a trapline 30 miles up the Horsefly River to its headwaters. "I was sitting on the porch here," he said, "when I saw it start. I've never seen anything like it. I saw it start at the base of Haycock Mountain about noon, and by one forty-five it was two thirds of the way to the top."

The road became a thick coil of standing dust from the trucks loaded with bulldozers headed into the mountains. Before nightfall some 30,000 acres were burning. The flames enclosed both upper arms of the river, from which the colder water had been flowing. When the fire came within a quarter of a mile of the falls, the salmon reacted to the warming of the water and stopped trying to jump. The atmosphere in the fisheries camp was like that in some Civil War headquarters that had received word of a final defeat. The smoke was so thick that the trees across the river were barely visible in the thick brown haze. There was a question of whether even the work of cleaning the river of dead salmon could be carried on; everyone was likely to be drafted to fight the forest fires. Ironically, word arrived of the official count from the watchers farther down the river: there were 303,000 fish counted up to that time.

A story went around that the fish were heading downstream. Migrating salmon, of course, go against the current; downstream swimming was almost a contradiction in terms. We walked about a mile down the Horsefly to where there was a pool of quiet water where the fish could be studied clearly. A grassy bank rose over the river at this point, opposite a white-gravel stream bed where, in high water, the river created another channel around a little island. A wall of dead fish, 5 to 10 feet wide and 100 feet long, was piled up on the bar, and the fisheries crew was still methodically lifting dead fish from the water and tossing them on the pile. I counted 110 fish in the pool directly below the knoll, and most of these were headed downstream. They did not swim downstream very far; they turned and came back, ceaselessly, and headed downstream in a dazed and confused manner, while more fish from above drifted down to keep the number in the pool roughly constant.

Someone asked Loyd Royal about the outlook for the next run, four years from now. He winced and said he would make no predictions of any kind. After a moment of silence he seemed to feel this answer was inadequate and said stoically, "The 1965 run is impaired. It may be so badly impaired there will be no fishing. . . ." The temperature of the water was 59 degrees; unless it dropped remarkably, there would be no spawning, and the salmon cycle on the river might be ended for all time.

The two young Canadians came by in the evening to invite the Americans to their cabin for a drink. Because no one had expected that it would be difficult to get to town, there were various shortages: some people had no liquor; others had no food. Mrs. Connolly, who had thoughtfully secured several steaks before the roads were closed, invited us to dinner. No one said anything about the salmon run. Like many other Canadians, these journalists were intensely interested in American politics and had strong opinions for and against individual politicians and particular parties and policies; they knew who had run against someone in the past, and what the issues had been, and were constantly asking for informed opinions about American politicians I had scarcely heard of.

After dinner the political discussions grew more headstrong. "I would be willing to become an American citizen," one of the young journalists said earnestly, as though he could think of no greater sacrifice, "in order to vote against Goldwater!" At that time Senator Goldwater was not a candidate for President and was known, if at all, as an obscure conservative from Arizona. How much popular support did the John Birch Society actually have? What did I think of the Hiss-Chambers case? My own feeling about Canada was that among the various advantages the United States possessed, in the way of climate, fertile soil, minerals, timber, oil and other aids to civilization, the greatest advantage of all was the presence of Canada on the north; if there had been a hostile nation there, the settlement of the West would have been impossible, or could only have come about after wars like those of France and Germany. But it could not be said that they seemed to feel Canada had similarly benefited from the presence of the United States on the south. It was rather that Canadian interest in broad issues and the minutiae of American politics stemmed from a vague mistrust in general, or an uneasy feeling that at any moment some dangerous trend might develop somewhere, and only by constant inquiry could Canada be forewarned.

They walked back to their cabin, guided by a dim flashlight that barely glowed in the smoky darkness. I slept on the lower half of a double-decker metal bunk from which the mattresses had been removed, spreading my sleeping bag and lying as close as possible to the open window. In the night I was awakened by a sensation that had become so infrequent I did not recognize it—it was cold. A cold, chill, damp air was somewhere in motion. There were unfamiliar sounds, the rattle of something on the shingles of the roof—it was rain. Outside the sky was light with gray, luminous rain clouds. The wind began to blow hard from the west and north, driving the fire back over the land it had burned. Then the rain began in earnest, huge drops that set up a high singing, buzzing sound in the pines.

In the morning the rain was washing in a beautiful, unbroken downpour that put a glistening, shiny light over everything. The green of the trees was a bright, fresh green, the walls of the cabins were brilliant with the water flowing over them, the rainwater draining in rivulets beside the trail left the rocks washed to sparkling jewellike browns and grays and blacks. The ruts and mudholes in the road were thick golden-yellow mud splashing with the heavy drops. The fires were out, or almost out; in any case the damp woods were so water-soaked that sparks could get no fuel in them. Rain was general over the Pacific Northwest, falling from the Rockies to the Pacific and from Alaska to the California desert, quenching in a day the fires that were out of control, or threatening to become out of control, and quieting the woods with a simple, effortless finality that no power on earth could duplicate.

On the mountains the rain fell as snow; the air was freezing, and the heights were blurred in the rain clouds. So the salmon run was saved, or at least the last few days of the run were saved. But the margin of time had come down to a matter of hours.

There was a sequel of sorts. The four-year interval between runs gave an interrupted air to history because no one really knew the results until the salmon began to return. A project was approved to run pipes from two high mountain lakes, whose waters were always cold, down to the spawning grounds to prevent another such catastrophe. But before the pipes could be laid, a question came up: was it certain that the heat of the water alone had caused the damage? The next run in 1965 was studied to find out. There was no party of visiting dignitaries this time, merely a crew of pathologists and assorted biologists and hydrologists, checking the fish and the water to see if some hitherto unknown agency had operated with such lethal effect. But none was discovered, and Congress ultimately approved an appropriation of $25,000 to pay for the United States' share of the cost of a pipeline survey.

The annual report of the International Pacific Salmon Fisheries Commission said, "The loss from warm water in 1961 was disastrous. Water temperatures are believed to be the highest for several decades." Nearly 200,000 fish died without spawning. And the remainder survived long enough to spawn only because that wonderful last-minute rain chilled the mountains. Still the river was saved, the cycle continued, and those returning fish were a reminder of the way that nature in general, and fish in particular, continue to surprise people no matter how close their observation of the ways of nature and of fish. The Horsefly was an object lesson that Theodore Winthrop would have understood. If the Northwest had not developed new systems of thought and life as he had thought that it would, it might still do so out of necessity, in order to restore at least a part of the natural wealth that a century of exploitation had destroyed.

VI

Tree Farms

I

On Friday morning, May 24, 1935, Miss Berg dismissed her
fifth-grade class for lunch at 11:45, and George Weyerhaeuser ran
down the hill from Lowell Grammar School in Tacoma and disappeared. He was wearing a green sweater with white stripes, brown
corduroy trousers, and white tennis shoes. His description was broad-
cast all over the nation: "Smiling, handsome face, with no distinguishing marks, slender, average height, dark, curly hair, brown eyes." Miss
Berg added: "An alert, obedient and brilliant pupil." He was nine
years old.

When George left school, he ran half a dozen blocks to Annie
Wright Seminary. The newspaper said he was supposed to ride the
rest of the way home with his older sister Ann in the family car, but
he just decided to walk home. Northwest lumber millionaires tradi-
tionally sent their sons to the democratic environment of Lowell
Grammar, but their daughters went to Annie Wright, an exclusive
girls' school whose most famous alumna, the novelist Mary McCarthy,
had been graduated a few years before. Lowell Grammar stood near
the crest of a hill overlooking Commencement Bay and Mount Rainier
on the east and, on the west, the magnificent blue and silver wall of
the Olympics. The students were the children of mill hands whose
homes were on the slope on one side, plus the boys from lumbermen's

mansions on Yakima Avenue, which local patriots claimed was the most beautiful residential street in the country.

George wanted to become a track star. He practiced broad jumping on his way to Annie Wright. Then he cut through the grounds of the Tacoma Lawn Tennis Club to the next street. A tan Buick was standing at the curb. A man grabbed George, put his hand over his mouth, dragged him to the car, dumped him on the back seat and put an old blanket over his head, warning him not to move or make any noise.

The car moved down the hill through midtown Tacoma, over the Puyallup River bridge, and was in wooded backwoods before George was missed at home.

In the desolate stumpland east of the rundown coal-mining town of Issaquah, the car stopped and the blanket was removed. There were trees all around. George could hear the sound of a river. The two men had put hoods over their faces before they took the blanket away. They told him to write his name on the back of an envelope, which he did. He was blindfolded and led into the woods across a running stream. He thought they were going to push him into the water.

Hidden in the woods was a deep pit, 3 feet wide, 6 feet long, covered with tin, braced with posts, lined with boards. George was lowered into this and, to ensure that he did not climb out, he was fastened to two heavy crosspieces by handcuffs, one on one arm and the other on a leg.

One man drove away to mail the ransom note and to ditch the Buick. Philip Weyerhaeuser, George's father, was directed to say nothing to anyone, to keep the news out of the papers, to gather five thousand old $20 bills, five thousand old $10 bills, and ten thousand old $5 bills. When he had the money ready, he was to place an ad in the personals column of the classified section of the *Seattle Post-Intelligencer*. It was to read: "We are ready. Percy Minnie."

The other man remained on guard. On Friday evening the first man returned with a picnic lunch, consisting of sandwiches, cookies and hard-boiled eggs. After they had all eaten, the men drove away, leaving George in the pit with two blankets for warmth and the light of a kerosene lantern for companionship.

One of the men was Harmon Waley, a tall, handsome, twenty-four-year-old from Hoquiam, Washington, a descendant of a pioneer family. In and out of jails and reform schools from the time he was seventeen years old, he had met and married Margaret Thulin, a pretty, placid, blonde girl from Salt Lake City who was wandering through the Northwest. In prison in Walla Walla, where he was confined after being shot in an attempted holdup of a sporting-goods store in Tenino, Washington, Waley became friendly with William Mahan, also known as William Dainard and Swede Davis, who had five bank holdups on his record, including a $100,000 bank robbery in Idaho. Waley, Margaret and Mahan were living in an apartment in Spokane, waiting for something to do, when Margaret happened to read in a newspaper that John Philip Weyerhaeuser Senior, George's grandfather, had died. The account made it clear that the family had both wealth and family devotion. Three days later Margaret, Waley and Mahan were in Tacoma, studying George's movements. They did not intend to capture him when they did; they were merely observing the route he followed going to and from school when he happened to walk up to their car.

The position of the Weyerhaeuser family in the Northwest could hardly be comprehended in less thickly settled regions. I once met my Uncle August Hanson, a logger in the Northwest for most of his eighty years, and he asked me what I was doing. I said I was writing an article about hunting and fishing in the Weyerhaeuser woods.

"That's about all there is around here," he said.

"What, hunting and fishing?"

"No, Weyerhaeusers."

Frederick Weyerhaeuser, the founder of the family fortune, was a German-American lumberman who could never resist buying timber. He said he liked to buy trees when it was raining and sell them when the sun shone. But, said his son, "I cannot remember that he ever sold any, no matter what the weather was." In 1900 Frederick Weyerhaeuser bought 900,000 acres of forest in the Northwest from the Northern Pacific Railway, then the largest single private land transfer in American history. The Carlisle-Pennell Lumber Company bought an enormous stand of Northern Pacific timber shortly before that time, as did another purchaser, William Boeing, to move the family fortune to the Northwest, but their acquisitions were small compared to Weyerhaeuser's.

Frederick Weyerhaeuser reached the United States from Germany in 1852. He prospered as a sawmill operator in Illinois and made industrial history when he combined a number of small operators like himself into an organization that could buy logs in quantities large enough to secure a steady supply and good prices. In 1891 he moved to St. Paul, Minnesota, then the lumber center of the country. He was a round, gray, quiet individual, painfully shy because of his German accent. His only hobby was beekeeping. He reached his small office in St. Paul at seven fifteen each morning and left it only when he went out in the woods to look over new stands of timber to buy.

In 1893 he bought a house on Summit Avenue in St. Paul, its fashionable street, almost entirely occupied by lumber barons, though the family of F. Scott Fitzgerald later settled on Summit Avenue.

The story was that Frederick Weyerhaeuser did not know that his next-door neighbor was James Hill, the builder of the Great Northern Railroad. In view of Hill's fame, this seems unlikely, but in view of Weyerhaeuser's habits it was possible. Hill had secured control of the Northern Pacific; he wanted to get rid of some high-interest indebtedness, and he also wanted to develop industry in the Northwest to provide return freight loads for his trains that carried grain east to Pacific ports. He offered Weyerhaeuser an immense chunk of the Pacific Northwest: the land around Mount Rainier, the land around Mount St. Helens, the land west of the Cascades from Snoqualmie Pass to Stevens Pass, extending from the mountains to Puget Sound, the land along the White River and the Greenwater where the emigrant trains had come after crossing Naches Pass, the land near Yacolt prairie down to the Columbia River, the dense forests in the southwest part of Washington near the mouth of the river, and even more scenic parklike stands of ponderosa pines in the mountain-lake country of central Oregon, together with other properties along the coast and in southern Oregon and northern California.

Hill wanted $7 an acre. Weyerhaeuser offered him $5. They compromised for $6. The sale aroused little comment at the time. Weyerhaeuser's board of directors complained that he might have got it for less. This was apparently true, for similar Northern Pacific land sold for less than a dollar an acre. In 1905 at a forestry conference President Theodore Roosevelt departed from his prepared speech to let fly with some spontaneous remarks about people who cut down the forests—"who skin the country and go somewhere else!" he said. It was felt that his remarks were directed at Frederick Weyerhaeuser, who was present. The President's blast horrified Gifford Pinchot, who considered it a triumph that he had persuaded Weyerhaeuser to attend. But there was worse to come. "That man," the President continued, "that man whose idea of developing the country is to cut every stick of timber off of it, and leave it a barren desert . . . That man," he concluded simply, "is a curse."

Weyerhaeuser did not live up to his billing as a full-time, dues-paying curse. But his enormous fortune and his seclusion led to legends. *The Mysterious Octopus* was one exposé written about him, and in *Weyerhaeuser—Richer than Rockefeller*, a researcher claimed to have discovered that he was the richest man in the world. Lincoln Steffens, at the height of his fame as a muckraker, decided to investigate Weyerhaeuser (Steffens exposed timber grabs in Oregon with the assistance of C. J. Reed of Portland, the father of John Reed), but after talking with the old man in his office at seven-fifteen one morning, Steffens decided there was nothing interesting to write about: Weyerhaeuser was honestly perplexed at the criticism directed against him. "What did we do wrong?" he asked.

Compared with the attacks on the Rockefellers, the Goulds, the Harrimans and other great families, the Weyerhaeusers got off lightly. Weyerhaeuser personally was at ease only with his family or in his woods. His six children and fifteen grandchildren never made news. They did not build yachts, buy castles or marry actresses or noblemen; they lived quietly even by the standards of St. Paul, which were pretty quiet. Then they moved to Tacoma, which was even quieter. Among timber companies, they were up to the standard of their time, perhaps a little better than most. They never operated company towns, the feudal baronies of smaller operators. The sons of the family went to Yale. On graduation they trained in the small family-owned subsidiary companies. They supported charities, endowed schools of forestry and aided civic-opera companies. Frederick Weyerhaeuser, a son of the founder and the literary member of the family—an art collector, Skull and Bones at Yale, an airman in the First World War—wrote in his *Trees and Men:* "I hope that it will bring you the faint cry of 'timber' on the slope of some deep canyon in the Cascades, and a picture of the snowy peak of Mount St. Helens towering above heavily forested foothills against the deep blue of the western sky." But the book was privately printed for his family.

Like all timber company lands, the Weyerhaeuser forests were barred to visitors. Hunting and fishing were prohibited. Camping was unheard of. And the Weyerhaeuser family ruled them from a seclusion as deep as the forest.

II

When George Weyerhaeuser did not arrive home for lunch, a search was started, and by the time the ransom note arrived, the police were at the house, so the instructions with regard to them could not be followed. The local newspapers, at George's father's request, reported that George was lost. But word that he was kidnapped was sent to the family in St. Paul, from which it reached Midwestern papers and then spread over the country.

On Saturday afternoon Waley and Mahan became alarmed, apparently at the sound of someone shooting at something in the woods. Also, they could not continue to drive back and forth without arousing attention in the tense atmosphere that was building up. Mahan's planning had a demented ingenuity. After dark on Saturday they lifted George from the pit and took him to a second pit, near the village of Kanasket, on the western edge of a Weyerhaeuser forest. He was again fastened by handcuffs to posts and left overnight.

Back in the Fir Apartments, in the red-light district of Seattle, Margaret and Mahan and Waley read the ad they had ordered in the Sunday *Post-Intelligencer*, saying Percy Minnie was ready, but with it was another: "Due publicity beyond our control please indicate another method of reaching you. Hurry." That night they locked George in the trunk of Mahan's gray 1935 Ford coupe and drove all night across the state to Spokane, 200 miles east, in 1935 a hard trip even in the front seat of a car. Mahan occasionally yanked George around; Waley occasionally rescued him. In the woods near the Idaho border they left George chained to a tree all day while they rented a furnished apartment in town, explaining to the landlady that they were salesmen. They returned that night with a big Uneeda Cracker carton, packed George into it and carried him into the apartment. The men put hoods over their heads, let him out and ordered him to write another letter to identify him to his family.

Mahan raced back to Seattle to collect the ransom. George was locked in a closet, Waley sleeping on a mattress outside the closet door. Mahan seemed to George to be a dangerous character, but Waley, wearing his hood and playing his ukulele, impressed him as odd.

In Tacoma, George's father received a special-delivery letter implying that George would be done away with unless the money was paid that night. He was ordered to register at the Ambassador Hotel in Seattle under the name of John Paul Jones and to await instructions. These came over the telephone, and directed him to a point near the Rhinelander Brewery on the road between Seattle and Tacoma. There he found a stake with a cloth tied on it. A tin can in the weeds directed him to a second stake on a side road. But there was no stake there. At dawn he returned to the Ambassador. The phone rang; he was directed to go home and send a different emissary. George's uncle Rod Titcomb was phoned at the Ambassador the next night and directed to a dirt road near Halfway House, where the Seattle-Tacoma airport was later built. Here a note at the stake directed him to a second stake at Angle Lake, a deep, mile-long trout lake in the woods.

Margaret and Mahan were parked on an unfrequented road by the lake—there was nothing unusual about a couple in a parked car. When Rod Titcomb drove up, Margaret remained in the car in the darkness; Mahan hid in the brush beside the road. Titcomb read his orders, turned on the dome light, placed a suitcase containing the twenty thousand bills on the front seat and walked down the road.

Mahan drove away in the car Titcomb had left. Margaret drove the Ford back to the Fir Apartments. Mahan hid the $200,000 in an abandoned shack on the outskirts of Seattle, left Titcomb's car on a side street, picked up the Ford at the Fir, and was headed for Spokane while Titcomb was still walking down the road.

George and Waley had come to an understanding of sorts. When there was no danger of anyone's coming by, George was let out of the closet, and Waley, still wearing his hood, played his ukulele and sang popular songs. George's relatively good treatment ended when Mahan returned. He was packed back into the cracker box and locked in the trunk of the car. They reached Seattle that night. Mahan and Waley picked up Margaret, drove to the shack, divided the money and put Margaret on a train for Salt Lake. Some time between midnight and dawn they stopped the car, got George out of the trunk, gave him a dollar and two blankets and left him beside a woods road. Rain started to fall. About daylight George picked up his blankets and walked out of the woods.

Presently he came to a cabin inhabited by Louis Spiers, who was cutting wood on Tiger Mountain nearby. There was no answer when George knocked, so he rapped on the window. Spiers had been annoyed by boys trying to get into his cabin, and growled, "Go away." George resumed his walk. In the morning, when it had grown light, he saw a shingled house on a lonely knoll several hundred feet from the road. Mrs. John Bonifas, the wife of a stump farmer, was preparing breakfast for her husband and their four children. George went around to the back and knocked on the kitchen door. Thus he returned to civilization. "I'm George Weyerhaeuser," he explained.

III

A scholarly work published in 1955, *Timber Concentrations in the Pacific Northwest*, concluded that the kidnapping of George Weyerhaeuser "did more to jostle the family from their seclusion than any single event since the muckrakers attacked the family interests." That was exaggerated: the Weyerhaeusers never read the muckrakers. But George's disappearance made a big difference. As a tentative gesture of friendliness toward the modern world, Philip Weyerhaeuser, who had become president of the company, opened its woods to hunters and fishermen. The action prompted Miss Helen Leonard, a young kindergarten teacher in Longview, Washington, to write to Philip Weyerhaeuser and ask why the company did not also open campgrounds for people who wanted to get out in the woods but who were not hunters and fishermen. She liked to hike along the Toutle River that flows through Weyerhaeuser lands, an exceptionally beautiful stream even in this land of rushing waters. "I got a nice answer the next year," Miss Leonard said. Things move slowly if your life is geared to the speed of growing trees. "Later on I was invited to a dinner to celebrate the opening of the first campground. I didn't know it had anything to do with me. The superintendent got up and said, 'Young lady, you have cost the Weyerhaeuser company $28,000.'" Presently, in its deliberate fashion, the company had six free campgrounds on the Toutle, and others on Coos Bay in Oregon, on the Satsop, the Greenwater, the Deschutes, and on Elbow Lake and Bald Hills Lake. No improvements were made beyond a sign reading, "Welcome," and a request that visitors be careful about fire.

A far bigger innovation was the first tree farm, started in 1941. The plan envisaged setting aside a large block of forest and logged-off land, and taking from it no more timber than was being newly grown there, to provide a steady supply of logs for the Weyerhaeuser mills —not merely for the next year or the next decade but for the next century. That meant the end of the practice of clear-cutting an entire area of all the forest growth on it.

The area chosen for the experiment was near Grays Harbor in western Washington, a region of deep, dark rivers, low hills, steep ravines, heavy rainfall and dense vegetation. Before reforesting started, it was as desolate a country as could be found in North America, and almost completely logged off. Clear-cutting had left vast areas where there was not a green stalk left standing, mile after mile of bleached stumps and bony snags. The tree-farm tract of 120,000 acres combined virgin timber, second-growth stands and logged-off land.

The logged-off area was planted with fir seedlings, and no more timber was taken from the tract than was replenished by new growth. It was a stair-step operation: sixty-year-old trees, in twenty years' time, would be ready for cutting, by which time the forty-year-old trees would be sixty and the seedlings would have grown to substantial size. That involved constant planting and cultivating, the thinning of dense stands as the trees grew, and the cutting of only small tracts at a time. It incidentally left the country green again, the streams clear and the wildlife multiplying.

Primeval forest contains little game. Big trees block out the sunlight from plants that provide forage; the sort of undergrowth that flourishes has little food value. Tree farms, however, with their clearings and different stages of tree growth, provide an ideal range. After the first tree farm was established, Philip Weyerhaeuser turned over the office and the bunk house of the tree-farm employees to the Washington State Game Commission for a ten-year study of wildlife. That was in 1946. The study resulted in a standard work, *The Blacktail Deer of Western Washington.*

The combination of tree farms, reforesting practices and game management resulted in increased hunting on the company lands. In 1937 hunters in what became the tree-farm area around Mount St. Helens bagged 326 deer. In 1968, in the tree farms there, they got 9,130 deer.

The tree farms were not planned as landscaping projects, but they transformed the appearance of the Northwest. They were straight business propositions, intended only to produce a steady supply of logs. In the process, green hills, not so majestic as when forest giants covered them but at least green, replaced the universal gray and brown of logged-off hills. The speed with which the farms were adopted by the timber business could hardly be credited. By 1957 there were 9,500 tree farms. By 1967 there were 32,000 of them. David Lavender, in *The Land of Giants,* called the first tree farm a stroke of genius in public relations. It may have been that. Certainly the promotion of reforesting, which the novelist James Stevens handled for the West Coast Lumbermen's Association, was conducted in a masterly fashion. It was also suggested that the tree farms were an ingenious effort on the part of big business to curry favor with President Franklin D. Roosevelt by imitating in private enterprise his own tree farm at Hyde Park. Whatever the reason, the tree farms flourished. Thousands of square miles, once so terribly blighted that the worst roadside junkyard was idyllic compared with them, became green and parklike, until suddenly, by 1960 or thereabouts, one could at last understand in the Northwest what George Vancouver and Theodore Winthrop had been talking about—the country's appearance was being restored.

IV

The Weyerhaeuser kidnapping was a peculiarly Northwestern operation, not in the sense that the crime of kidnapping was more common there but because the persons involved and the setting of logged-off land, stump farms, wood roads and back-street furnished rooms gave it a character that could be found nowhere else. In particular, the logged-off country where the Weyerhaeuser boy was hidden gave the crime a distinctive Northwestern character. It was all but impossible to find anyone in logged-off land. There were no trails and no roads except an occasional stretch of what had once been a logging railroad or a dirt road or a plank road to a logging camp. The deepest forest was easy going compared to land that had been clear-cut and abandoned. All that was left was a maze of crisscrossed and splintered wood. Even after the trees began to come back, and after stump farms began to be cleared here and there, the great expanse of logged-off terrain remained empty. Nowhere else were there such enormous blocks of uninhabited terrain. Any kind of cabin or shack was conspicuous in such country. But the Weyerhaeuser boy was not hidden in a shack; he was buried in an underground vault where discovery was all but impossible.

In the summer of 1969 I made a trip from one Weyerhaeuser tree farm to another, starting with the White River Tree Farm of 290,000 acres in the Cascades just north of Mount Rainier National Park. The purpose of the trip was pure idleness, merely to camp and loaf in the tree-farm campgrounds and fish in the rivers that run through those carefully tended woods. The White River Tree Farm was chosen as a starting place because of its literary associations. The farm spanned the valleys of the White and Greenwater rivers and ended, on the east, at the summit ridge of Naches Pass. It enclosed the trails that Theodore Winthrop described in *The Canoe and the Saddle,* the way that Lieutenant Robert Johnson of the Wilkes Exploring Expedition followed in first crossing Naches Pass, the country traversed by Dr. Tolmie on his way to try the first ascent of Mount Rainier, the scene of the near tragedy of the first party of emigrants who tried to reach Puget Sound over Naches Pass in 1853. The White River Tree Farm was about 15 miles north and south and 35 miles east and west, extending from Naches Pass to the Puyallup River near Puget Sound.

The town on its westernmost extremity was Kanasket. Kanasket? The name was vaguely familiar. After a time one remembered the circumstances: that was the place where George Weyerhaeuser had been secreted in the second plank-lined underground crypt. His kidnappers made such effective use of the emptiness of logged-off land that they nearly got away with the entire $200,000 ransom. The ransom bills were not marked. The numbers of as many as possible were recorded, but since the bills were old, and of different dates, and with no sequences, there was little hope of tracing the kidnappers through them. However, Margaret Waley in Salt Lake City left the hideout there to buy a pair of stockings, and paid for them with one of the bills whose number happened to be recorded. It was almost the first money spent from the ransom. Arrested and questioned, she confessed at once. She and Waley led authorities to a spot on Emigrant Pass where they had buried most of their half of the money. Mahan was tougher. He was traced to Butte, Montana, but broke out of a police trap and managed to keep going with his $100,000 share for two years, until he was finally caught in San Francisco. Margaret was sentenced to twenty years in prison, Waley to thirty years and Mahan to sixty years.

It was surprising, in 1969, to find the kidnapping that had been the nation's biggest crime story thirty-four years before was still very much alive. Little was known about it; in spite of all the newspaper stories at the time, there had never been a connected or even a chronological account of what had happened. Around Tacoma people told me not to ask George Weyerhaeuser about it. Anyone who heads a company that owns 5.5 million acres of forest, as the Weyerhaeuser Company did then (its lands were later increased to 7.3 million acres), does not want to remain in the public eye as the victim of a kidnapping at the age of nine. There was so much publicity directed at him then and when he had to testify at the trials of the kidnappers that he grew up in the midst of a kind of community conspiracy never to mention the subject. He was graduated from junior high school in Tacoma, went east to preparatory school at Taft and interrupted his schooling at Yale at eighteen to enlist in the Navy during the war. After the war and his delayed graduation from college, he worked as a choker setter on Weyerhaeuser logging crews, as a laborer, and then as kiln foreman and shift superintendent in a Weyerhaeuser pulp mill. He married, fathered six children, shot ducks for recreation and lived quietly in the pleasant residential suburb of Gravelly Lake near Tacoma, where so many Weyerhaeusers lived that the body of water became known locally as Weyerhaeuser Pond. At thirty-nine he became the youngest president of the Weyerhaeuser Company.

"No, I don't mind talking about it," he said of the kidnapping. "It didn't bother me unduly. I was just a kid, and I didn't know what was happening."

When he became president, there was some talk as to whether his independence stemmed from his desire to prove himself individually, simply because his kidnapping and his court appearance made him so famous as a nine-year-old. He doubted it. "A nine-year-old boy is a pretty adaptable organism," he said. "He can adjust himself to conditions in a way no adult could. It didn't affect me personally as much as anyone looking back on it might think."

After a pause he added, "But a family—I think a kidnapping is one of the worst things that can happen to a family."

What about those pits in which he was buried?

"Quite an excavation," he said.

And that ride across the state in the trunk of Mahan's car?

"I was just glad to get out of that hole in the ground. I slept most of the time. I had blankets, and it was warm back there."

What he wanted to talk about was the changed attitude of the timber industry toward conservation and the use of timber lands for recreation. The timber companies were under constant attack from conservationists for destroying the last remaining vestiges of the American wilderness, and he said that he could share some of the emotion they expressed. If he read that a dam was to be built that would change forever some area that he had known and appreciated, he regretted it and wondered if the structure was necessary; and if a building project threatened some shoreline of Puget Sound that had been important in his own life, he reacted even more strongly. In his boyhood his father had taken him and his brother duck shooting—sections of the Sound were great duck country in those days—and the places were so deeply embedded in his memory and so much a part of his life that he doubted that he could be objective about the value of the proposed improvements. He recognized the need for economic progress, but in such cases he wished it would take place somewhere else. So in a sense he could sympathize with the attacks of conservationists on the timber companies. But he believed there was a basic distinction to be made. Sometimes the changes that were proposed—a dam on a wild canyon, for example—changed the environment for all time; once the change was made, it could never be brought back to what it had been before. But the effect of other changes was not so lasting. Timber is a renewable resource, and the cutting of trees does not necessarily alter a region permanently. It seemed to him that wherever the changes involved a unique natural resource, whenever they destroyed a natural wonder which, once lost, could never be restored, there should be a careful and searching examination to determine whether the economic gain could really compensate for what was lost.

Weyerhaeuser gave the impression of wishing that trees grew faster than they do. His was a slow-paced business, one in which you plant now and plan to cut the trees down sixty years from now. Or in eighty years, or even after a century. Or perhaps never. Land for outdoor recreation had become so valuable that it might be worth more with trees growing on it than the trees would be worth if they were harvested. The Weyerhaeuser Company owned so many trees that if they were transplanted along the Atlantic coast they would make a belt of forest 20 miles wide extending from New York City to Atlanta, Georgia. The scenery was not carried on the company books as an asset. There was too much of it. What value could be placed on the scenery in the Skykomish Tree Farm, for example, which extended 30 miles east from Puget Sound into the mountains? How could you appraise the lovely green foothills around Drunken Charlie Lake, on the south border of the farm, or the deep black-rock gorge of the Stillaguamish River on the north boundary? How much were the 19,000 steelheads taken in a year from the Stillaguamish, or the 14,600 taken from the Skykomish, rivers that crossed the tree farm? Or the deer in the untenanted country north of Haywire Ridge, counted at twenty-two per square mile? Or the old trails and miners' cabins dating from the 1870 gold rush on the Sultan River? (The miners called it the Sultan because they could not pronounce the Indian name, which was Tsuel-tud. The Indians had comparable difficulty with the miners' place names, such as Quartz Creek and Swede Heaven Saloon.) The land in the eastern part of the Skykomish Tree Farm was at a steady slant. You looked either up or down. The big trees were cut half a century before tree farms were heard of. Stands of tall, skinny, second-growth Douglas firs rose 70 to 100 feet. Higher in the mountains were ragged red peaks like Mount Index, alpine meadows, and the boulder-strewn beds of foaming creeks—a country that suggested Switzerland but still, in its rough, wild, empty air, suggested Indian country more strongly.

South of this Weyerhaeuser tree farm was the company's Snoqualmie Tree Farm, whose eastern border took in the lakes on the western side of the Cascade lake country, a region sometimes quietly described as the most beautiful in the world, where some seven hundred lakes lie among the mountains, fanning out on both sides of a 25-mile stretch of the summit ridge. West of the Snoqualmie Farm was a backyard wilderness, half an hour from the city of Tacoma, called McDonald Tree Farm, a region of glacier-formed valleys alternating with narrow, river-cut canyons, covered with second-growth fir and hemlock and dotted with pondlike lakes and beaver ponds, some still unknown to map makers. Southwest was the enormous St. Helens Tree Farm, covering 567,000 acres and enclosing almost the entire length of the Toutle River in its 25-mile, 3,175-foot descent from Spirit Lake to the Cowlitz River—a parklike tree farm, with the terraced look of tree-farm forest, long stretches of waist-high infant trees; darker stands of ten-year-old trees, 20 to 30 feet high, dense and hedgelike, with a ragged, uneven skyline, with Mount St. Helens looming nearly 10,000 feet, a flawless white geometrical shape whose vast snow slopes were marked with the delicate thin icy lines of ridges.

Nearer the Columbia River was the Vail Tree Farm, a managed forest intermixed with the lands of Crown Zellerbach, the Northern Pacific Railway, and the State of Washington. This tree farm ranged from Willapa Harbor south to the Columbia, and inland from the Pacific Ocean to the Cowlitz River, in a country of sharp ridges, deep valleys and almost impenetrable thickets between low hills. The region was celebrated by James Gilchrist Swan in *The Northwest Coast* for its noble streams flowing through fine prairie land, and for its abundance of swans, geese, brant, loons, mallards, canvasbacks, redheads, snipe, plover, quail and pigeons. Swan was too enthusiastic, and he had a vested interest in the region, but in fact it always appealed to ornithologists despite its heavy, lowland character. James Graham Cooper, for whom the Cooper hawk is named, was there with Governor Stevens's survey in 1853, observing (along with more familiar birds) the Northwestern yellow-bellied sapsucker, the short-tailed albatross, the whistling swan, the marbled godwit (now rare) and the Coast pygmy owl. In another century George Cantwell of the United States Biological Survey combed the country, studying the Northwestern double-crested cormorant, the harlequin duck, the snowy plover, the glaucous-winged gull, the Oregon jay, the Oregon black-capped chickadee, the Washington purple finch and many others, and trying unsuccessfully to trap the Northwestern fish crow in a steel trap.

James Gilchrist Swan noted Long Island in Willapa Harbor, 1½ miles wide, 8 miles long, low and sandy, and expressed his belief that some good use could be made of it. Some good use was eventually made of it; a part of the Weyerhaeuser lands, Long Island became a national wildlife refuge, a great wintering ground for the imperiled black brant in its migration from Alaska. Where the forest approached the coast were the haunts of the Northwestern crow, *Corvus caurinus* Baird, commonly called the fish crow or the tidewater crow, the only bird known to practice racial discrimination. The Northwestern crow loves Indians and hates white people. The bird will play with Indian children without fear but flies off in alarm if a white man approaches. "The Indians of the Northwest do not molest the crow," the authoritative *Birds of Washington State* reported in 1953, "which has, in consequence, become astonishingly abundant and tame. The Indians claim to know many individual birds, and some have even received names. The crow, while friendly with Indians, is very suspicious of whites."

South of the Columbia are two large Weyerhaeuser tree farms near Coos Bay, one enclosing most of the flow of the Mackenzie River. Another, the largest forest in the Weyerhaeuser domain, covers some 700,000 acres in south-central Oregon. This farm extends into California near Mount Shasta. Largely ponderosa pine, the Klamath forest lay outside old Frederick Weyerhaeuser's original purchase of the Northern Pacific land grant. He bought it after he had already acquired more timberland than it seemed possible to consume, and it was this acquisition that led to government investigations and charges of fraud. The Klamath forest turned out to be the richest and most beautiful of his many great bargains, open woods without the dense undergrowth of fir forests, blue subalpine lakes that harbored magnificent flights of waterfowl on the Pacific flyway, a wooded park tilted toward the sharp peaks of Three Sisters mountains in the Cascades and the Blue Mountains farther east.

V

One of George Weyerhaeuser's first acts when he became president of the Weyerhaeuser Company was to set up a recreation department in the corporate-management structure, instructed to study all the company forests to see what their recreational possibilities were. Presently the company issued a long-pondered statement of its recreation policy. Officially entitled "Policy No. 60.1, Procedure 60.14, revised March 28, 1968," the document carefully pointed out that the main purpose of the tree farms was to provide a continuous and profitable supply of raw material, but it went on to state that, when recreation needs were compatible with this primary purpose, "the lands shall be made available for public enjoyment." It was further spelled out that sites of historic interest and outstanding scenic beauty should also be preserved for public enjoyment. Under some circumstances "the recreational value may exceed the value of other land use."

The prose of Policy No. 60.1 was hardly more stirring than its title, but it was nevertheless a historic document, not quite a Declaration of Independence but an amazing reversal of traditional timber-company practice. It could hardly be expected to satisfy wilderness enthusiasts, and for that matter tree farms, with their network of roads to prevent forest fires and their constant activity of planting and thinning stands, are at the opposite pole from the ideal of a wilderness forever wild. Policy No. 60.1 did not go far enough, even by less exacting standards. No criteria were established for classifying lands of outstanding scenic beauty, and the qualifications for sites of historic interest were vague. A woods boss whacking away at the trees on a hillside was not likely to be dissuaded from one particular stretch of the woods because Hazard Stevens passed that way on the first ascent of Mount Rainier. The Weyerhaeuser Company set aside 25 acres at the summit of Naches Pass where the wagon train of Asher Sargeant was trapped in 1853, and where the wagons were lowered on cords made of oxhide down a 1,000-foot decline to the Greenwater River, but along the river itself the logging crews were at work even while the words of Policy No. 60.1 were being so carefully chosen. Not that there was a great loss of scenic beauty. The big trees along the rivers were taken out generations ago in pioneer days, and the spindly remnants high on the hills were scarcely bigger than telephone poles. But they were the last remaining portion (except for the 25 acres) of a wilderness that deserved to be called historic if any in the Northwest could be so called.

As limited as it was, the new policy of the company had an impact that could be appreciated and understood only by someone who had known the Northwest before the tree farms existed, when unrestricted clear-cutting was the ordinary practice of all timber companies. A part of Theodore Winthrop's belief that a new civilization would come into being there was based on the notion that the scenery would be a civilizing influence; in fact there was no scenery. The mountains and the forests and the rivers would enhance "the daily development of the finer and more comprehensive senses," Winthrop wrote, hard to believe if one saw only snags and blackened waste. Towns were built on lowlands, or by the railroads that followed low ground. If some forest remained, the big trees blocked any view of the wild setting as a whole. Here and there, on high ground or at openings formed by a valley, the landscape opened out, and one could see Rainier or St. Helens astonishingly near at hand. The summit ridge of the Cascades, usually a bluish haze in the distance, suddenly became etched on the horizon one day each fall with the first snowstorm, while the days were still warm in the lowlands, the entire range materializing all at once in a gleaming white wall that seemed to have been manufactured and installed overnight. Only a singularly unresponsive individual would fail to be moved by such visions, but they were infrequent, and it was a work of some consequence merely to reach a point where they were visible.

I went from the headwaters of the Greenwater in the White River Tree Farm to the headwaters of the Sultan in the Skykomish Tree Farm to the headwaters of the Toutle in the St. Helens Tree Farm without experiencing a moment of regret that woods roads and fire trails laced the managed greenery. It was not wilderness, it was certainly not forever wild, but it was so immeasurably superior to what the logged-off land had been that one could only be grateful for it. There were, to be sure, some odd items in the woods. The newly planted trees are periodically sprinkled with nutrients in the form of pellets dropped from helicopters. From the air it is hard to distinguish where one patch of forest ends and another begins, and so in order to avoid fertilizing the same ground the pilots drop small yellow balloons at the corners of each tract. The sight of one of these in the middle of nowhere, floating like a child's circus balloon above the branches, was invariably startling. But it is a mistake not to think of the tree farms as wild. The woods seem strange, dense and uniform, trees of the same girth and height, and in stands of the same species—unlike the primeval forest where fir and spruce and cedar were indiscriminately scattered— all contrived, tended, watched, cared for, thinned and protected, but moving in the wind with the same sound and motion, and never tame.

I went from the tree farms to the logged-off land I had known in my childhood. My grandfather Cantwell built a town he called Little Falls (from the falls on the Olequa River) located midway between Portland and Seattle on the Northern Pacific Railway. It became a sizable place, with a sawmill and a big brick and clay-pipe factory to which the clay was hauled on a narrow-gauge railroad that ran before my grandfather's house. He had been a Civil War veteran of some heroic reputation, and after the war he commanded a company of freed slaves at Fort Union, New Mexico, during the Indian troubles in the Southwest, but his town of Little Falls became filled with emigrants from the Southern states as its industry expanded, and he scarcely enjoyed being known as the founding father of the place. After his death in 1912 the Northern Pacific Railway, on the grounds that there were too many towns named Little Falls, changed the name to Vader, after a recent settler of German extraction—who, however, did not appreciate the honor and departed for Florida and never returned. The forest nearby was logged, and the sawmill burned to the ground; the clay factory burned about the same time, and Vader became known as an extreme example of the featureless, rundown lumber town that continued to exist after its industry ceased. The hills above the town commanded a magnificent view of a great expanse of the Cowlitz River valley to the mountains, but what one actually saw, unless one climbed the hills, were a store and a saloon still open among buildings with boarded-up windows, with treeless slashings all around. In 1968 a group of real-estate promoters in Seattle discovered the superb view of the mountains from the hills behind the town and, giving the place still another name—Enchanted Valley—sold home sites around a residential park which was to have, along with swimming pools and riding paths and shopping centers, the benefit at last of the scenery.

And was it true that people would have benefited if the scenery had been preserved? Winthrop could easily believe that Puget Sound and the wild Cascades would inspire others as they inspired him; a timber owner hiring a crew of loggers was not likely to think of his men as sensitive to natural beauty. But if magnificent surroundings did not make people better, was the opposite true? No one defended unrestricted clear-cutting that devastated the land. Even at its worst there were occasional attempts to keep the natural features of the country unchanged.

From Little Falls we moved in the summer of 1914 to an unspoiled wilderness that was only beginning to be logged. The Carlisle-Pennell Lumber Company owned large stands of timber in eastern Lewis County, extending from the Newaukum River to the foothills of Mount Rainier. Shortly before the start of the First World War, the company built a sawmill, one of the largest in the United States, in the middle of its woods. We lived in tents while the mill was built to saw lumber for the houses. The owner, William A. Carlisle—known as old W.A., to distinguish him from his son, young W.A.—had esthetic interests and wanted to avoid the worst features of the blight of logged-off land around the town. My father, who had been a school principal before he became a builder, was Carlisle's superintendent of construction and a favorite adviser of the old gentleman. Ordinarily the forest near a mill was logged first, so a mill town existed from the start as the center of an area of desolation, but Carlisle built his mill and logging railroads first, began cutting the trees at the far end of his holdings and gradually worked in toward the town. He named his town Onalaska and wanted to make it a showplace among company towns. The trees that enclosed it were huge even by the standards of that land of big trees. The forest was continuous, starting just behind the church and extending to the Cascades. Otherwise the town was a typical lumber town, with houses of identical design, four-room, five-room, and six-room, all painted a shiny gray and trimmed with white, with a company store, a company movie house, a company pool hall and a big recreation center, and with its own company money that could be spent only in company-operated businesses.

Nevertheless, old man Carlisle put up a constant struggle to keep up its appearance. He conducted competitions with cash prizes for the best lawns and the best flower gardens to counteract the architectural monotony of the dwellings. Each summer he hired the kids to pick up nails, railroad spikes, bolts, nuts, chunks of broken machinery and other industrial debris that could be used as scrap iron to aid the war effort and keep the place tidy. As a result the town during his lifetime was more than ordinarily attractive and, when approached by the dirt road that ran between the trees, suddenly opened up as a neat, compact and secluded little island of busy and thriving enterprise hidden away in a forest as deep as could be found anywhere. But to get from that island to the mountains through the woods was impossible. Camping in a lumber company's forest was unthinkable. The nearby woods were a playground for children, and the banks of the Newaukum were Sunday picnic grounds, but exploring beyond the fringes of the forest was too expensive for people who worked in the region. People came from the East to take the stage to Longmire Springs on Mount Rainier, not people who lived near the base of the mountain. Native Northwesterners grew up in the shadow of firs that were 200 feet high or higher, and in a sense it was harder to reach the mountains than it had been in Winthrop's time.

After old man Carlisle's death my father became the superintendent of the mill and the company town of Carlisle, a much older company town, located near the coast north of Grays Harbor. Carlisle was the epitome of the worst lumber town, in the way that Onalaska had been a relatively good one. At Carlisle the primeval cedar forest had been leveled so thoroughly there was scarcely any green growth in sight. The enormous stumps, cut high above the swampy ground, were bleached white and stretched away in endless rows like so many tombstones. The natural drainage was halted and stagnant pools formed a morass over what had once been earth under the trees. The rivers turned the color of tannic acid. A cut finger exposed to this fluid became inflamed with what was called cedar poisoning, a mysterious ailment that killed fish and dogs and, it was believed, people as well—an all-encompassing disease apparently unknown to medical science but compatible with the lethal appearance of the terrain. During the salmon runs the town loafers used to sit on the highway bridge outside town and shoot the salmon trying to leap the falls over the mill dam—highly illegal, and wasteful as well, since the dead fish merely washed downstream—a dreary pastime somehow in tune with life in a country so logged-off, ruined, desolate and otherwise blighted. The natural beauty of a region might not make people any better; a blighted area certainly made them worse.

In country not greatly different from this the kidnappers of the Weyerhaeuser boy hid their victim, and it was knowledge of this sort of terrain that made the kidnapping a peculiarly Northwestern crime. There was also perhaps something distinctively Northwestern about the sequel. While Harmon Waley was serving his thirty-year term in the Federal penitentiary at Leavenworth, Kansas, he began writing to the boy he had kidnapped. George Weyerhaeuser answered his letters. By the time Waley finished serving his sentence—the full thirty years—Weyerhaeuser had become president of the Weyerhaeuser Company. Through a friend in Kansas he helped Waley get a job there without letting anyone know that he had done so. "Why did I do it?" he asked, looking annoyed. "I went through all sorts of sensations when I was kidnapped, from fear and concern to the point where I felt sorry for him. I guess I thought he had paid his debt. . . . No, I don't want to say that," he said in exasperation, meaning that he did not want to use a stereotyped phrase.

Some part of the Northwest inheritance is a sense of the psychic consequences of life in a logged-off world. Whether or not new habits of thought and life come into being there, so much is certain: life in a logged-off wasteland is intolerable, equally intolerable if you own the wasteland or if you merely work there.

VII

The Columbia:
New Systems of Thought

I

Outside the village of Canal Flats, British Columbia, a large billboard depicted an uprearing grizzly bear with bloody jaws. The beast was pictured by a primitive artist of considerable graphic power, and the sign below it, in shaky lettering, read "Welcome to Canal Flats." It appeared to be the least hospitable invitation to a town ever placed beside a road. Closer examination revealed that there was a wooden cutout figure of a hunter beside the road some distance from the sign. He was kneeling, the gun at his shoulder, and the idea was that he had just shot the bear. Weeds, however, had grown over the hunter. He could hardly be seen without a search. Canal Flats, as it turned out, was trying to advertise itself as the world's greatest center of grizzly-bear hunting. The billboard had not been designed to intimidate tourists and frighten them into driving by without stopping. It was intended to promote what the people of Canal Flats believed to be the greatest attraction of their community and the region.

Canal Flats was a town with a population of 356 people, located on a small gravel plain about 80 miles north of the boundary between the United States and Canada. The town had a one-block business district, a little sawmill, a railroad siding and the ruins of a timbered canal lock. Nothing remained of the canal itself except a ditch, about 10 feet wide and 1 foot deep, filled with water as clear as glass. Small pines grew along its bank, adding an incongruously landscaped air. The water in the canal seeped from the Kootenay River, less than a mile away across the gravel plain, and flowed into Columbia Lake, the source of the Columbia River. This was the place where, in 1807, David Thompson discovered the source of the Columbia. His house was at the southernmost point of the lake, about where the canal emptied into it. In the summer of 1963 the plain was not greatly different from the way Thompson described it a century and a half earlier, except for the few houses in Canal Flats, the road and the picture of the grizzly.

The canal, however, was once a major change in that unchanging landscape, and very nearly a great change in the geography of the entire region. It was the creation of William Adolph Baillie-Grohman, a sportsman who had wandered into the area searching for mountain goats. Baillie-Grohman was the foremost English hunting writer of his time. He had an unparalleled following among British aristocrats. He was the sort of writer who contributed serious articles to sporting journals, advising his readers not to take their valets with them on hunting trips, in particular not to the Wind River mountains of Wyoming. He argued sensibly that valets also had to eat, so more food would have to be packed in. That would require another pack horse and perhaps another handler, who would also require supplies. Also, if you took a portable bathtub along and expected your valet to prepare your bath after a day's hunt, you might find that some Wyoming joker had shot holes in the bottom of your bathtub. Theodore Roosevelt once wrote that wherever he hunted, no matter how difficult the terrain, when he was worn out and exhausted some guide invariably told him that Baillie-Grohman had been there and had made his way easily over the same country.

A peppery little man with spiked mustaches and a combative disposition, Baillie-Grohman had prepared for his life work by memorizing the measurements of virtually every trophy head in the world. No small part of the correspondence columns of English periodicals was filled with his denunciations of the errors of other authorities. He was particularly severe with an unfortunate Tacoma taxidermist who claimed an elk head with antlers measuring 70 inches. Baillie-Grohman was certain that the record was 62½ inches, and that his own best head, shot in the Wind River mountains, was second at 60½. When he was told that an elk head on the wall of a firehouse in Portland, Oregon, measured 73 inches, he was sure it was a fake. He journeyed to Portland, secured the assistance of people he described as some of the leading citizens of the city, climbed a ladder in the firehouse with them as witnesses, tapped the antlers with a hammer and concluded they were fabricated from two separate pairs carefully joined by plaster. "I instantly communicated my suspicions," he said. He suggested that an American investigator should "tap the upper length of either antler with a hammer, which would cause particles of cement to become dislodged." This was done, and to his immense satisfaction chunks of concrete fell from the bogus trophy to the firehouse floor.

One of Baillie-Grohman's many conflicts with rival authorities on wildlife led to his historic trip to the upper Columbia region in 1882. At that time scientists doubted that the creature known as the Rocky mountain goat (*Oreamnos americanus*) really existed. They said it was a product of hunters' folklore. Hunters in the Rockies and the Cascades were sure these animals existed, for they were frequently shot. David Thompson had included a long report on them in his *Narrative*, telling how he had sent to the North West Company the skins of a hundred of them that his men had shot in the mountains back from the Columbia in this very region of Canal Flats. But Thompson's book was still unpublished in 1882. A stuffed mountain goat was on display in a Philadelphia museum, but it was so badly put together that reputable naturalists were sure that it was a fake. A situation of this sort aroused Baillie-Grohman's hunting ardor to the pitch of a crusading mission. He was willing, he said, to stake his life that mountain goats existed. Making his preparations with great care, he hinted at many dangers lying in wait for him in an unknown country, and departed with a ringing statement: "My expedition has only one purpose, to find goat, or perish in the attempt!"

Now, his expedition really was perilous, but not in the way that he had anticipated, not in the sense of physical danger, though that existed also, but in the threat to his mind. When Baillie-Grohman came to the place where Canal Flats was later established, he was astonished to discover, as had David Thompson before him, that there were two great rivers there, flowing side by side but in opposite directions. He noted also that the Kootenay River, though only a short distance from the Columbia across a level plain, was much higher than the Columbia—as much as 11 feet higher in high water. Why not dig a ditch across the plain and start the Kootenay flowing into the Columbia? Once started, the Kootenay would obviously create a new channel for itself, and its very large volume would be added to the water of the Columbia. Precisely what Baillie-Grohman hoped to accomplish by his scheme was never altogether clear. It was the idea, the opportunity, that fascinated him. As nature had designed it, the Kootenay wasted miles in its erratic flow. It flumed away in fast water 80 miles to the boundary with the United States and then wandered 182 miles through

Idaho and Montana, before circling back into Canada to unite with the Columbia at last. How much simpler it would be if the two rivers were joined near their headwaters! If anyone ever demonstrated that the wild Northwest would generate new systems of thought and life, it was Baillie-Grohman. The trouble was that his new system was too imaginative and intoxicating; he was possessed by his vision, and a kind of irresponsibility, a certain facetious spirit of enterprise, took hold of him in place of the rigorous discipline that a new civilization would demand. His life was transformed. So were the lives of his friends who joined his enterprise.

Back in London, in the map room of the British Museum, Baillie-Grohman was startled to learn that no one knew anything about the proximity of the Kootenay and the Columbia. "I found that while the travelers who had visited the spot and left any record behind (their number could be counted on one's fingers) and had noticed and expressed surprise at this singular configuration, none appeared to recognize the importance of a canal between the rivers." But why a canal? Baillie-Grohman's stated reason was that by diverting the Kootenay into the Columbia he would save the land that was lost by the Kootenay's annual floods. There was a good deal of gold mining on the Kootenay River at that time, far downstream from Canal Flats, and it might be that Baillie-Grohman dreamed of picking up nuggets from the dry bed of the Kootenay after its waters had been diverted, but if so he never mentioned the possibility in his extensive writings on the subject.

Baillie-Grohman was thirty-one years old in 1882. He was the son of an Irishwoman who had made a morganatic marriage with a member of the ruling family of the Austria-Hungary empire and, had the qualifications for royalty not been so severe, would have been in line for the throne of the Hapsburgs. He found goats in the Canadian Rockies and so did not perish, but he scarcely bothered with his triumph over scientific skeptics. Instead he founded Kootenay Syndicate Limited and began signing up titled Englishmen to join his company. His aristocratic lineage—or half-aristocratic, in any event, for his mother was admittedly a commoner—as well as the romance of his parents' life, and his personal magnetism combined with his exploits with rod and gun, made him a popular figure with the nobility. Obviously, he was the ideal person to start a large engineering project in a remote wilderness area.

He easily persuaded the legislature of British Columbia to give him a grant of 47,500 acres to repay him for digging the canal. In addition, he received every inch of the land between the international boundary and Kootenay Lake, a stupendous chunk of beautiful real estate. This was because it was believed he would save the land lost by the Kootenay's annual floods. With these assets, Baillie-Grohman hurried back to England to sell shares in Kootenay Syndicate Limited and line up investors and hunters to return to Canal Flats with him.

He arrived with his party in the summer of 1884, to find that the government of Canada had put a stop to the digging of a canal between the Kootenay and the Columbia. In his eagerness to secure the land that would otherwise be inundated by the Kootenay, he had not given sufficient thought to the land that would be flooded by the Columbia. The Canadian Pacific Railway was even then being built through the Rockies, and the flow of the Kootenay, added to that of the Columbia, would wash away the bridges and tracks of the railroad. Apart from the railroad engineers, no one cared what happened to either river. There were then only fifteen settlers in a region as big as England and Wales combined, and several of these were people connected with Baillie-Grohman's enterprise.

He lighted into the government of Canada and the Canadian Pacific Railway with the energy he had formerly devoted to exposing false claims to hunting records. He accused them of treachery, deceit, fraud, theft, graft, high freight rates and the appropriation of articles from a box of clothing sent to him by his tailor in London. The political and commercial agencies quickly capitulated. They worked out a compromise. Baillie-Grohman could not dig a drainage canal which would divert the Kootenay into the Columbia, but he could build a navigation canal, with locks, across Canal Flats, and would therefore control shipping on both rivers. Since he could not get the flood lands he expected to reclaim, the British Columbia legislature granted him another tract of 67,600 acres.

To add to his trials, he was pursued by a wealthy and eccentric American named Robert Sproul, who vowed to shoot him on sight. Sproul believed that Baillie-Grohman had defrauded him in a deal involving a gold mine on Kootenay Lake. On one occasion Sproul jumped from behind a tree only three feet in front of Baillie-Grohman's horse and fired at him with a rifle. But he was too close; Baillie-Grohman's horse was so startled he reared and bolted, and Sproul missed. On another occasion Baillie-Grohman was riding in a train in Idaho, on his way to seek a warrant for Sproul's arrest, when Sproul suddenly appeared behind him in the smoking car and pressed his revolver against the back of Baillie-Grohman's head. They rode along for several miles in this fashion, until the conductor persuaded Sproul to wait until they got off so as not to have the killing on his train. Baillie-Grohman avoided Sproul when they reached the station, as Sproul was afraid he would be arrested if he shot Baillie-Grohman there. Sproul then shot and killed another man involved in the mine dispute and was eventually hanged, though his wealthy California family tried to get him pardoned. President Chester A. Arthur intervened with the Canadian government in his behalf, and many prominent Canadians urged a commutation of the death sentence as Sproul's case became an ugly international dispute.

"The experiences of that summer," said Baillie-Grohman, "in spite of the hard work and the sinister events, were of the pleasantest kind." His colony had become fashionable. Lady Gwendolyn Rous and Mrs. Algernon St. Maur, who later became the Duchess of Somerset, were among the early visitors. Lord Norbury, who settled on the Kootenay River not far from the home of the two ladies, invested in Baillie-Grohman's project. Lady Adela Cochrane, whose husband was a cousin of the Earl of Dundonald, a power in Canadian affairs, was an intrepid woman who not only joined Baillie-Grohman's enterprise; she also operated a placer mine on Findlay Creek, about 4 miles from Canal Flats, that lay between the Columbia and the Kootenay.

Baillie-Grohman secured additional support from Frank Lascelles, a son of the Earl of Harewood, "who climaxed his many eccentricities by shooting and killing his Chinese servant at his home on Columbia Lake." A little later Captain Northcote Cantile, a nephew of Lord Mount Stephen, another powerful figure in Canadian affairs, joined the colony on the upper Columbia. He was a striking figure in any company, always drinking champagne for breakfast and accompanied everywhere by his personal attendant wearing Highland costume and playing the bagpipe.

Arthur Clutterbuck and James Lees, a pair of fashionable writers, the authors of travel books with occasional Gilbert-and-Sullivan-like flashes of wit, arrived for a round of visits between trips to the mountains to hunt mountain goats. They found old friends everywhere around them. Even when they went deep into the wilderness they found fashionable acquaintances, Count Ernest Hoyes and Count Ferdinand Truttsman-dorff—a close friend of Edward, Prince of Wales—from the Imperial Court in Vienna, who were hunting there also. One of the owners of Tiffany's in New York was located nearby. The Duke of Somerset bought his Indian moccasins in Baillie-Grohman's store in Canal Flats, and a remittance man whose name was never revealed was pulling slabs from the head rig of Baillie-Grohman's sawmill.

It was a brilliant society. An improvised steamboat, the *Duchess*, ran the 113 miles of the Columbia from Canal Flats to connect with the railroad at Golden. The upstream trip was made in two days, the downstream in one. Soon really fine steamers, with baths and comfortable staterooms, were in use; the river voyage became a popular side trip for transcontinental passengers on the railroad. In 1889 the *Isabella* made the run down the river in only six hours, or 17 miles an hour, an almost incredible speed in view of the sharp bends and the places where the river narrowed to 20 or 30 feet across.

Baillie-Grohman eventually completed his canal across Canal Flats. Since it did not start at the point nearest the two rivers, it was 6,700 feet long. But the building of canal locks for steamers proved to be expensive. There appeared to be no bottom to the gravel under Canal Flats, nothing on which a foundation could be laid. After sinking more and more timber without success, Baillie-Grohman gradually scaled down the size of the locks to save weight. The result was that when the locks were finally constructed they were not large enough for the river boats of either the Kootenay or the Columbia. Only two boats ever passed through the locks. One of these, the *Northern Star*, which ordinarily sailed on the Kootenay, was too wide for the locks. An improvised dam of sand-filled ore bags was piled around the boat. The Kootenay River was sealed off behind. The ore sacks in front were blown up with dynamite. The *Northern Star* scooted across the flats like a surfboard on the crest of a wave. But it was not a practical method of steamboating. Baillie-Grohman retired to his ancestral estate in Austria, adjoining the shoot of the Duke of Coburg-Gotha, and the locks gradually sank into the gravel and the canal filled up.

II

Our reason for visiting Canal Flats was the proposed dam at Mica Creek farther down the Columbia. Negotiations were under way for the Columbia River treaty between the United States and Canada, providing for changes on the Kootenay and the Columbia beyond anything contemplated by Baillie-Grohman in his most extravagant imaginings. The water problems of the two nations were so confused by the erratic flow of rivers across the international boundary that it was impossible to make sense of them when reading the treaties: you had to go look at the rivers. The trouble was that the boundary was a straight line, and rivers do not flow in straight lines. When the British government capitulated in 1846 and unexpectedly agreed to fix the boundary at the 49th parallel, it surprised everyone. The Americans had not even asked for it. Many years before, as a bargaining point, the Americans had suggested the 49th parallel, but it was instantly rejected, and no one had thought of it since, until the British suddenly brought it up as a better solution than 54° 40' or fight. The sudden fixing of the boundary at the 49th parallel terminated the promising venture in dual or triple citizenship that was working very well in the provisional government of Oregon, and it also created innumerable points of dispute over water rights because so many rivers—the Similkameen, the Pend Oreille, the

Marias, the Milk, the Souris and others—wandered back and forth along their ancient watercourses from one country into the other.

Disputes arose because people on one side of the boundary diverted water that deprived people on the other side. A private citizen cannot sue a foreign government, so each dispute had to be taken up by the United States Department of State or the Department of External Affairs in Canada. The statesmanship of Elihu Root worked out a solution in the Boundary Waters Treaty. This provided that a citizen downstream in one country had the same rights and privileges in the courts of the other country as he would have if he were in fact a citizen of that country. It was a new application of the same principle of the treaty of joint occupancy that had worked so well a century before. A farmer in Montana whose water supply was cut off by a Canadian irrigation project had the same rights in Canadian courts with respect to such questions as he would have if he were a Canadian subject. A Canadian farmer whose water was diverted by a water diversion in North Dakota had similar rights in American courts, as much as if his land were in the United States and both parties in the disputes were American citizens.

Canadian legal experts were not enthusiastic about the Boundary Waters Treaty. It conflicted with ancient concepts of sovereign rights, the rights of the sovereign, the basis of the rights of government. All international law, apart from the treaty, as well as all past practices in Europe, including the many disputes over the waters of the Danube, indicated that a country could do whatever it wished with the rivers in its lands. The Canadian experts also held that the United States was inconsistent. In its dealings with Mexico over the Colorado River, the United States followed the traditional practices of international law. It was only with respect to Canada that the United States agreed to make no changes in rivers flowing into the other country without consultation and agreement. Also, it was held in Canada that the Boundary Waters Treaty was violated in Franklin Roosevelt's administration, because the Canadian government was never informed that Grand Coulee was to be built on the Columbia. In the case of navigable streams, the consent of the Canadian government was required. The building of Grand Coulee Dam was scarcely secret, and no doubt the Canadian government would have given its permission—still, it had never been notified, or asked.

And each year the Kootenay flooded enormous areas in both Canada and the United States as it had done in the days of Baillie-Grohman. Grand Coulee was built with provisions for additional generators that would nearly double the power output of the dam if the annual overflow could be contained and released as needed. At last, in 1954, negotiations began for the Columbia River Treaty that was to provide for American-financed dams to be built in Canada to control those flood-waters. In one early session the American negotiators placed on the table twenty-five ancient maps to support the American position. The Canadians stared at them in astonishment. They were David Thompson's original maps of the Columbia. The Canadians did not know they existed, the Americans were uncertain as to who David Thompson was, and no one was able to explain how they happened to be in the archives of the United States government.

Aside from this momentary embarrassment, negotiations proceeded smoothly, at the usual speed of such affairs, for the next eight years. The project provided for two dams on the Arrow Lakes section of the Columbia, just north of the international boundary, a dam on a tribu-tary of the Columbia high in the Selkirks, an enormous dam on the Kootenay, on the American side of the border, which would back water 40 miles into Canada and, finally, for the immense Mica Creek Dam on the Columbia itself, just downstream from David Thompson's old cabin at Boat Encampment, which would back water 120 miles up the Canoe River and the Columbia itself. The dam at Mica Creek, while eventually producing power at the site, would at first merely store the water produced by the snow melt each year and release it to provide for maximum use of the generators at Grand Coulee. The United States would pay most of the cost of the Canadian dams, under a formula which was calculated on the savings to the United States of the cost of the annual floods of the Kootenay and the Columbia (estimated at $5.7 million a year) and the value of the increased power of Grand Coulee. Part of the additional power would be returned to Canada.

While the treaty was being discussed in the United States Senate, the Senators were informed that Canadian enthusiasm for the project had declined, and the government of that country was considering an alternate plan. This involved drilling a short tunnel through the moun-tains north of Revelstoke and diverting the overflow of the Columbia into the valley of the North Thompson River and thence into the valley of the Fraser to provide water for irrigation there. The Columbia at the point where the tunnel would be dug is 500 feet wide, 12 feet deep, and its current flows 7 to 12 miles an hour. The elevation of the river there is 1,700 feet above sea level. But only a short distance west, about 4 miles through the rock wall of the mountains, the North Thompson flows at only 1,000 feet above sea level. The Canadians did not propose to take all the water of the Columbia through the tunnel (although, under international law, apart from the Boundary Waters Treaty, they had the right to do so) but only the 15 million acre-feet annually wasted by the floods.

The thought of the Columbia's possible diversion startled the Senate hearings on the treaty, all the more because Grand Coulee's full potential had never been developed. "That would," said Senator Stuart Symington (Democrat, Missouri), "largely nullify the heavy investment we have made in our own country; is that correct?"

"Yes, that is precisely the point," said Secretary of the Interior Stewart Udall.

The United States Army chief of engineers, General Emerson Itschner, was summoned to give details on the Canadian diversion tunnel. He demonstrated to the alarmed statesmen how short a tunnel would be needed. In Canada a committee of the House of Commons called an expert from the Department of External Affairs to discuss the legality of the project. He informed the committee that Canada had a perfect right to divert the waters of the Columbia if it desired to do so, or the waters of the Kootenay, or any other Canadian river, under international law. "Whether it would be a wise or friendly thing to do," said the expert, "is another matter."

The United States Senate ratified the Columbia River Treaty by a vote of 90 to 1. A new clause was added to the treaty, by which Canada agreed not to dig any tunnels or ditches or otherwise siphon off the Columbia into some other Canadian river during the next sixty years. Agreement was reached during the administration of President Eisenhower in the United States, and the government of Prime Minister John Diefenbaker in Canada, but Canadian approval was then delayed by a dispute between the federal government of Canada and the province of British Columbia. Some time later a second celebration, with another signing, was held during the administration of President Kennedy and Prime Minister Lester Pearson.

At last, on September 16, 1964, President Lyndon Johnson, in a ceremony held at the United States–Canadian border, handed to Premier William Andrew Cecil Bennett of British Columbia a check for $273,291,661.24, an advance payment for benefits in the way of flood control and increased hydroelectric power which would accrue to the United States from a dam to be built across the Columbia a few miles downstream from Boat Encampment. Work started that afternoon. Chain saws began to whine into ancient cedar trees; electrical crews began scaling mountains that had never been climbed to erect shiny new micro-wave relay towers on their summits. Large-scale construction work had become a gigantic loudspeaker operation: an unbroken torrent of sound accompanied by the shriek of saws, an undertone made up of the dull thud of explosives, the broken beat of air compressors, the sound of bulldozers, earth movers, pumps, jack hammers, helicopters, trucks and gritty voices over public-address systems.

III

All this commotion disturbed the animal kingdom. Deer, moose, grizzlies, marten, mink, lynx, black bear and other creatures were on the run. The only way for them to go was up the Canoe River valley. In the season after work began on the Mica Creek Dam hunters killed 1,400 moose in the area around Valemount, 100 miles north. And at that time it was impossible for hunters to get very deeply into the valley itself.

In the summer of 1965 we decided to take a canoe trip the length of the Canoe River to the dam site for a last look at the valley before it disappeared. The Canoe forms in icefields at the 9,000-foot level of Mount Sir Wilfred Laurier, some 20 miles northwest of Valemount. Just west of that town the river jetted out of a gorge only 70 feet wide and began its southward flow through the valley to the Columbia. Above the point where the river came out of its rock walls it was hemmed in between sheer cliffs; below, it curved back and forth across a deeply wooded valley that was from 1 to 5 miles wide, with snow-covered peaks on both sides. A Canadian National railway bridge crossed the Canoe River at the head of this valley. A splintery wooden bridge spanned a gravel road only a few yards downstream from the steel railroad bridge. The water curled and braided as it came out of the canyon—cold, fast, impenetrable, gray-green, white-flecked, carrying the scent of rocks and ice.

We spent a lot of time on that highway bridge. We had two canoes, 17-foot aluminum Grummans, rented from the Hudson's Bay Company at Winnipeg. The original plan was that four of us would take a slow run down the valley to record its last wilderness days. One member of the party was a scientist, an authority on antibiotics. One was a staff member of a wilderness foundation. The others were an outdoor writer and me. The scientist became involved in conferences in Washington, D.C., and could not make it. Bil Gilbert, the outdoor writer, was spilled while covering a jeep race in northern California and was slow in arriving. That left Bob Waldrop, from the foundation, a skilled white-water canoeist. He stood on the bridge studying the Canoe River with dismay. It was not dangerous enough. That was the opposite of the way I felt about it; we did not have much in common.

Unbelievably, we were too late to reach an unchanged wilderness. The Mica Creek Dam was to take nine years in building. The water would not begin to back up until 1973. It was only in the late fall of 1964 that work started on the dam, but in the summer of 1965 logging operations to clear the valley of the Canoe of all its trees were under way, with Valemount the center of operations. The logging operations were in three stages. The first would take out all the big trees, the forest giants. When this was completed, the small trees, all those more than 11 inches in diameter, would be logged, each tree cut off 8 inches from the ground. In the final stage everything else would be cut down and processed. By that time the dam would be finished, and water would flood the valley floor that had been scraped clear of all greenery.

Seven small logging companies were working along the river, though they were still near Valemount. A road was being cut down the east bank of the river. Fortunately, only one bulldozer was at work, and it was stalled with a broken transmission, so the road had not gone very far. The people of Valemount regarded us and our canoes with a certain wonderment as the days passed. Bil Gilbert, the most experienced member of the party, had prepared a large fiberglass box to be carried in one canoe, containing provisions which were to be added to in Valemount. The box was stocked with dried eggs, dried milk, dried mush, dried potatoes and other nourishing fare. Gilbert impressed on us that these foods were sufficient to sustain life for an almost indefinite period, but lacked variety. We were to add such appetizing items as cheese, raisins, sandwich spread, chocolate bars and food that could be eaten at lunch stops without making it necessary to unpack. We stood on the bridge, and pondered the river as we waited, and neglected to buy these delicacies. The truth is that I was afraid the people of Valemount would be even more perplexed if they saw us buying a lot of cookies and sandwich spread and then loitering around town, instead of starting down the river.

Valemount was a duplicate of the lumber towns of Oregon and Washington half a century earlier: a sawmill on the far side of the railroad tracks, a rectangular two-story wooden hotel, a store, a gravel road, a school, and that characteristic Northwestern air of busy growth and impermanence. The Continental and the Super-Continental of the Canadian National stopped for ten minutes at Valemount, long, gleaming trains, bright with stainless steel, with rich black and gold and red interiors of the cars visible in the soft indirect lighting seen through the wide windows. The passengers stared dully at the rough, rusty side tracks, the scattered houses, the weeds along the road and the distant mountains all around. Or they walked up and down the station platform during the ten-minute stop, pacing with unhurried importance, with something old-fashioned about them, as though their tickets entitled them not to passage to Vancouver or Montreal but back to 1910 or thereabouts, to a vanished and unhurried world. The eastbound trains pulled away from the long climb to the resort town of Jasper, 75 miles away. The westbound trains left small packets of two-day-old newspapers from Montreal and Toronto lying on the platform and hurtled downgrade, settling up a rumbling roar that could be heard for miles as they crossed the high bridge over the Canoe. They then raced down the valley of the North Thompson River to Kamloops and continued on to Vancouver, 354 miles distant.

The days passed. The Super-Continental was discontinued while we waited. But the date on which the train was discontinued did not include trains that had started the previous night, and early one morning Gilbert arrived when we did not expect him or the train. We hurried to get the canoes on a hired truck, pay the hotel bills, check our waterproof supplies and get on our way. The morning was gray, warm and still. At the bridge the river was so charged, aerated, foamy and bubbling where it shot out of the chasm that it appeared to be carbonated.

The truck driver helped us unload the supplies. Then he turned his truck around and, before driving away, leaned out of the cab and said, "You fellows might keep your eyes open for a body when you're going down the river."

I assumed, of course, that somebody had been lost trying to go down the Canoe to the Columbia. "Was he trying to run the river?" I asked.

"No," said the driver. "He jumped off the bridge."

"Who was it?" Gilbert asked. "A stranger?"

"No," said the driver, rather sadly. "He was a prominent man."

The idea of coming upon the body of a prominent man as we floated down the Canoe somewhat dampened whatever enthusiasm we still felt at starting out. But there is always a moment of concentrated excitement at starting down a new river, something compounded of fresh air, wind, the noisy current and the attention demanded by the ceaseless changes of the racing water. We went sliding away fast, with just time enough to think, "Some current!" or "What a river!" or some equally profound thought. Waldrop, alone in the other canoe, was already far ahead of us down the river, weaving around boulders like someone trying to learn to ride a bicycle. There were occasional long *bang! bang!* sounds, like muffled revolver shots under the water as we scraped over boulders. The surface was choppy, turbulent, disorderly, a sputtering, incoherent passage, with standing waves in some places and spurts and jets of foam in others, the water so opaque it was impossible to see rocks under the surface before the canoe was upon them. The river dropped in a long uniform slope between banks lined with cedars and lodgepole pines. Near the east bank, where it was deeper, resonant submarine boomings rose from the bottom as we banged over rocks. A little over a quarter of a mile from the bridge the river turned sharply at a high, haystack-shaped log jam and suddenly deepened with a big creek coming in from the right. There were no more shallows.

The water was still fast, but now deep and smooth, with tiny eddies and swirls racing downstream as soon as they formed. Except for shoals at each bend of the river, it was silent. The channel narrowed at each bend and cut a deep passage close to the bank, but part of the river continued flowing over the gravel at the higher level until, suddenly discovering that it had neglected to make the turn, it dropped to the main channel in innumerable diminutive waterfalls; we looked from one side of the canoe and saw them at a level with our eyes. The shoals hummed and buzzed in the summer woods.

Sometimes a splash made one think a fish had jumped nearby. But the sound came from trees seesawing in the hurrying water. They were mostly small saplings washed from the banks. The roots caught on rocks at the bottom, and the trunk and the branches, moving up and down in a wind-blown, water-blown way, were polished like ebony.

No one said anything. At a wide place in the river, as we rounded a bend, a hawk dropped on a kingfisher, only a few feet in front of the canoe. The two birds seemed to hang suspended in the air as the canoe drifted nearer. Then they exploded in a flurry that ended when the kingfisher broke free. They both hit the water. Almost at once they were in the air again, separated. The hawk seemed to spring upward before it struck. This time it hit slantingly, the kingfisher plainly in its claws.

"A goshawk," Gilbert called to the other canoe. "He got a kingfisher."

The hawk had paid no attention to the canoes, but at the sound it turned in the air. The kingfisher dropped free and skimmed very low across the water to land on a stick projecting from a tangle of driftwood. I thought it would go for cover, but it did not. The hawk turned in a low half circle to look us over and then perched on a gray snag across the river from the kingfisher, watching us with morose dislike as we drifted away.

Around another bend two deer poised on a sun-washed gravel bank as we approached. One shifted uneasily in the green shadow of small birch trees. The other stood almost negligently in the open at the edge of the water. We stopped paddling and drifted straight toward them. There was no sound except the drowsy wash of the water and the splash of minute waves against the canoe. We seemed to be too unfamiliar to be alarming, merely some strange shape, gleaming, clawless and unthreatening. We were not more than a hundred feet away when the deer turned unhurriedly and went into the woods.

Around another bend, farther down the river, a moose stood on a small grassy knoll, its head down, looking at the water, undecided about crossing the river. When it finally saw the canoe, we were within the distance of a "Don't Walk" sign across a busy street. The moose turned and stumbled into the woods in an awkward, embarrassed fashion, like someone trying to avoid meeting an acquaintance he does not want to see.

Or were there animal eyes watching us from behind trees and under brush all along the river? Every hundred yards or so there were sandbanks, smooth as boat-launching ramps, sloping down from the forest floor, and these were covered with tracks—raccoon, moose, deer, otter, mink, bear, fox, lynx—everything except the tracks of human beings. We were only a few miles from town. But it was still wild enough. We went back and forth across the narrow valley, sometimes facing the Rockies in the east and then the confusion of rocks and snow and knife-edged pyramids that made up the Monashee Mountains—so named from a Gaelic term meaning "peace"—reaching southwest to the Columbia. At each hairpin turn the current speeded up and there were stretches of fast water. Then at the next stretch it was possible to see the river slanting down a real grade, like a gentle hill of water, the trees on its banks looking as if they were planted in rows. We came to the first rapids: Yellowjacket Rapids, so named for a creek that flowed in above them. These were the ones that people in Valemount said you were in before you knew they were there. It was true. The current ran faster, the canoe accelerated, the river narrowed until big cottonwoods nearly joined overhead. Then there was a turmoil of small standing waves, marbled with white lines that seemed to promise real white water ahead. That was all. That was Yellowjacket Rapids. You were in them before you knew they were there, and out of them before you knew you had been in them. It was easy, too easy, a sort of joke, and yet pleasant and a little unreal, a touch of magic, so that one wondered what had really happened. The Canoe was dropping fast. It should have been leaping over rocks, twisting in narrow clefts between boulders, and driving and probing with the ceaseless power of mountain streams. Instead it raced along quietly, the Rolls-Royce of rivers, never foaming and churning around those innumerable bends. The morning grew warm, and in the still air and under the cloudless sky the blue-green surface of the river was smooth and seemed motionless, as if the river were a solid that glided at the same speed along the bottom and on the surface. And bright and clear as the haze lifted, white and gold in the sunlight, the incredible profusion and grandeur of the mountains.

"I don't see how you guys could have forgotten to bring the food," Gilbert said. We had neglected to buy those staples that were to add variety to our dehydrated diet. How could we have done so? We had a week in Valemount which we could have devoted entirely to the task. We could offer no explanation or defense. On his trip with the jeep racers, Gilbert had bought a new kind of Norwegian survival ration that had just been put on the market. Each wafer supposedly contained as much nourishment as a full meal. Each was about the size of a Fig Newton and was laminated with various layers of compressed meat extracts. We stood on the bank of the river, silently munching one wafer apiece.

"Cheer up," said Waldrop. "There'll be a Howard Johnson's around the next bend."

We floated on into the afternoon. The map showed a little lake, called Beaverpelt, in the woods about half a mile from the river, and we decided to stop there to fish. The Canoe was too busy a river to provide likely looking fishing spots. We camped on a small level tract of hard-packed sandy ground, thinly covered with grass and dried moss. The sun was behind Mount Thompson, an 8,000-foot peak on the west. The river looked grayish in the sunless light. A big graywashed driftwood log masked the place where the creek that flowed out of Beaverpelt Lake entered the river, the creek itself almost invisible in the brush of the cavelike woods. It was hard going through the woods along the outlet, into deep sand and clay and over crisscrossed logs left by old floods. The lake—on the map—lay at the base of a sharp ridge, almost a cliff, and it appeared that one could walk directly across to it from the river. But huge fallen logs, with bigleaved weeds growing around them, blocked the way. We gave up the attempt to make a meal of the fish in Beaverpelt Lake and ate a nourishing meal of powdered chili.

Rain fell during the night, a pleasant resonant splatter on the low roof of my tent. In the morning the snow was far down the slopes of Mount Thompson. I built a fire, put on a pot of coffee and tried to catch a fish in the Canoe River. How could Thompson have said, "The water clear over pebbles and small stones?" The water looked old, faded, mildew-colored, glacial-green, clay-green, mud-green. On close examination innumerable flakes and clay-colored particles were moving up and down, rising and falling with the current as they raced along. It was hopeless. I decided to go to Beaverpelt Lake and make up for having forgotten to buy food by catching a lot of fish. Gilbert and Waldrop got up before I got away, and we filed into the underbrush. The brush was so wet it was like walking into shoulderhigh rain. We wore rain suits, the fluorescent red and plastic green shimmering like neon signs through the leaves. The land was chopped into steep rises of 20 or 30 feet, overgrown and bleached with splintery fallen trees. Between these ridges, over the black watery soil, devil's clubs grew 5 or 6 feet high. We climbed over logs at 45-degree angles down a slope and slid over the other side of the logs, puffing and sweating, picking up needles from devil's clubs and landing in ankle-threatening holes in the ground. Beaverpelt Lake was a stupendous disappointment after the labor required to reach it, an expanse of marshy, dead-looking gray-black water backed up behind an ancient beaver dam. The dam was so old that trees half a foot through were growing on it. Not only were there no fish; there was no life of any kind, no birds, not even any insects. The morning grew intensely hot as we fished from banks lined with bony snags, without a hint of action; the water was lifeless.

At that time the Canoe River valley seemed so inhospitable that one could hardly regret that it was to be filled with the water from the Mica Creek Dam. But back in the canoes that feeling vanished and never reappeared. A canoe never seems as wonderful as after breaking through underbrush. The silence and the motionless speed, the windless spaces of the mountains rising above the trees, the spell-bound air of the woods along the banks made the river seem part of a higher order of nature than the thickets. The water was clearer, flowing green and blue in the cool bright air. A bird that seemed to be a great blue heron, insofar as it could be identified from an angle, flew low and unafraid over the water.

A high rock wall appeared on the west side of the valley. The river no longer curved back and forth but ran straight along the base of the wall. A lower ridge began to show above the trees on the west, and the wall and ridge gradually came together until the valley was less than a mile across. A good-sized little river called Bulldog Creek came in from the east. It flowed from the Selwyn Range of the Rockies, dropping 6,000 feet in 10 miles. Long before we reached it, we could hear the high ringing, almost metallic, sound of cascading water. Where Bulldog Creek joined the Canoe there was a wide, still pool, almost circular, perhaps a hundred yards across, and below this the Canoe dropped 40 feet in continuous rapids.

We drifted slowly across the still water, Gilbert and Waldrop standing up to ponder the current. They picked a channel on the east side, away from the rocks at the base of the cliff. Alone in the first canoe, Waldrop rounded the turn and shot ahead out of sight. When we came around, he was far down the rapids. We raced into criss-crossed chop and then into standing waves that were 3 feet high. The river became very narrow. The channel was so close to the trees we could see drops from the spray glistening on the leaves. It was like coasting down a shaded drive in a park, except that the sunlight through the trees was tinted by the green water and had a vague submarine look. The sound of the rapids was a hollow echo-chamber roar. There were no rocks or obstructions in the rapids. The canoe accelerated and then was checked as it bucked in the standing waves. Water shot over us in these waves, no longer as spray but in bucketsful. The erratic rhythm of the waves gave a kind of lurching cadence to the run.

Halfway through the rapids there was a long, smoothly flowing, silent stretch. The water was still fast, but the surface was unbroken. It was exhilarating—uncomplicated, fast, magical. As we raced along, I could see grass and small trees beyond the bank, patterns of shadow and sunlight that suggested French Impressionist painting. But that went by in a few moments, and then we were in even faster water, with standing waves that were higher than those near the start of the rapids. A good deal of water came over the bow. The canoe was bucking, the bow going up and down as if it were being wrenched, and I tried to get more leverage by digging the paddle deeper to see if I could keep the bow up, but we suddenly careened into smooth, dry water before I could find out.

We stopped to put on dry clothes and bail out the canoes. The woods had changed. We were coming into a cedar forest, flat tablelands beside the river, widely spaced trees, parklike groves that were almost free of underbrush. About 2 miles below Bulldog Rapids, on a terrace 10 or 12 feet above the river, a timber was nailed between two cedar trees. We thought it might be some kind of marker, but it was merely part of a shelter put up long ago for some hunter's camp.

The place looked familiar. It was here, or about here, that David Thompson reached the highest point when he ascended the Canoe River from Boat Encampment in 1811. He gave the location of his last camp as 52° 36′ 42″ north and 118° 15′ west. On the detailed maps that were made when the Mica Creek Dam was planned, our location was 52° 37′ 42″ north and 118° 57′ west. Thompson's calculations were essentially accurate, though modern surveys have revised his figures slightly, and he was always stupendously in error when he estimated the heights of mountains. He wrote in his *Narrative* that he ascended the Canoe River 48 miles, by which he must have meant 48 miles up the valley, not the wandering river miles, and that, too, indicated he might have stopped at this point. He was there on the afternoon of September 21, 1811; we were there on September 15, 1965, and there was no essential difference in the country in the intervening years. The Canoe River had never been mapped or explored before the Mica Creek Dam was proposed. Nothing ever happened along its banks. No roads were built, no farms cleared, no towns started, no battles fought. Antiquarians knew of the existence of the river because they knew about Boat Encampment, but aside from Thompson himself, and a few hunters and prospectors, no one visited it. Its fate was unique; nothing would ever happen along its banks. It would not have any banks. It was going to disappear before it had been discovered.

But in all likelihood Thompson had camped at this place. "Turned about," he wrote, "as 2 men come up with word that Mr. Wm. Henry and men had arrived this end of the Athabasca Portage." The reason he stopped here, despite the difference in his calculations and those of modern mapmakers, was that the big rapids were just above this natural campground, and he normally stopped at the foot of a rapids rather than begin a portage around it late in the evening. In any event, it was a beautiful compass point. Looking around at the far side of the grove, Gilbert discovered a trail leading into the woods. He and Waldrop hurried to explore it before dark; I remained with the canoes. In a few minutes they reappeared in the same part of the woods into which they had vanished. "We took the wrong trail!" Gilbert yelled back. "We're trying the other fork!"

It began to get a little cold, and my water-soaked legs were getting stiff. When I left New York, my wife gave me some small waterproof containers of wax-covered matches so I could start a fire and get warm after being overturned in the rapids. I had never used them and felt some doubt that they would ignite. Now I pulled some dried twigs from the bank and started a fire. It felt comfortable. I climbed up the bank and built a real fire in the fire pit where the hunters had built their lean-to. Gilbert and Waldrop were gone so long it was obvious we would not have time to look for another campsite before dark. Except for the lack of a small stream flowing into the Canoe, which meant we would have to use the river's muddy water, this site was ideal. I unloaded the canoes and lighted the gasoline lantern and hung it on the crosspiece; it appeared that Waldrop and Gilbert might have trouble locating the trail in the shadows on their way back.

Darkness came fast and they emerged at last, looking perplexed and interested; there was a good trail leading away from the river; they had followed it for nearly a mile, and then it ended—a well-beaten path that led nowhere. We had a drink of whiskey mixed with Canoe River water. Then we ate heartily of soup and Italian noodles, with canned plums for dessert, brought to the surface from some hidden recess of the fiberglass box. After dinner we drank coffee laced with whiskey, smoked cigars and turned our drying clothes and water-soaked shoes to the fire.

We talked about explorers who somehow always managed to write their diaries in the wilderness. They would arise before dawn, tramp through the woods all day, or push upstream against raging torrents,

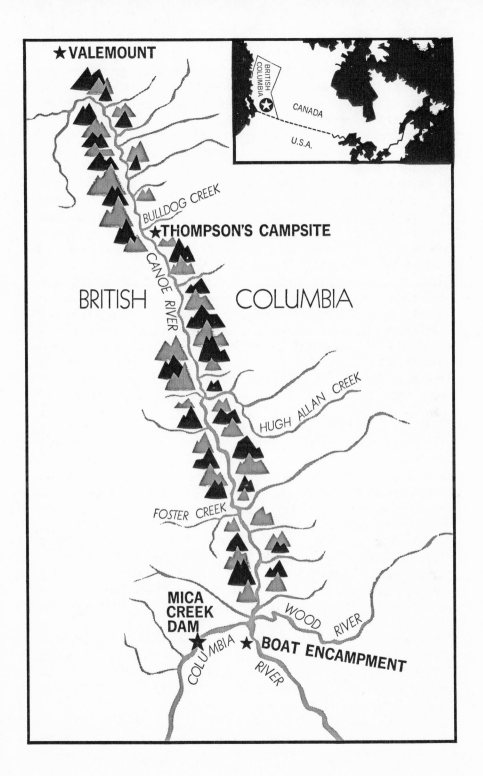

or climb steep mountains, perhaps pausing to interrogate a few Indians on the way, and at night, when their trusty voyageurs were snoring, they took out their quill pens and carefully wrote out everything that had happened. Sometimes they wrote so much at the end of a day of such travel that a man in an office at a desk could hardly hope to match it, and Gustave Flaubert would have spent a month over the passage.

We talked about Sir John Franklin, Sir Alexander Mackenzie, Samuel Hearne, rapids, jeeps, rivers and fish. Waldrop strung a line near the fire and hung his drenched clothes on it to dry. At every stop we all dried out the socks, shirts and underwear that had been soaked in the rapids and turned our shoes toward the fire to dry out the insides. But Waldrop was much more careful in this respect than Gilbert and I were; he walked back and forth, constantly tending the fire and turning his clothes on the line with the patience of a customer at a laundromat. He and Gilbert compared the rapids of the Canoe with those of the rivers in the East—the Cheat, the Jackson, the Smokehole, the Youghiogheny, the Potomac; they had run them all. This or that stretch of the Canoe was perhaps like something on the upper Potomac. In fact, the Canoe ranked nowhere among rivers for good white water. Canoeists rank rapids on a scale from one to six, with six being the most difficult that can be negotiated and out of which experienced canoeists have a chance of emerging alive. The rapids of the Canoe ranked at number four, at best. They were deficient in all those dangerous falls, chutes, chasms, rock dams and boulder-strewn cascades that give rivers their reputation among white-water enthusiasts. "This is going to be a hard story to write," Gilbert said sympathetically. "Nothing happens."

I had been thinking about that.

"You can say you found the prominent man," Waldrop suggested. "Nobody could contradict you."

"It wouldn't work."

I had brought with me three books, picked because they were easy to carry: *Native Trees of Canada,* published by the Queen's Printer; Thoreau's *A Week on the Concord and Merrimack Rivers;* and Paul Morand's *Open All Night,* this last because I noticed that it fitted in my pocket as I was leaving New York. Thoreau managed to make a week of nothing happening a matter of considerable interest. In fact, his book was absorbing as a wonderful chronicle of continuous unhappenings. He made camp in a farmer's field:

> For the most part there was no recognition of human life in the night, no human breathing was heard, only the breathing of the wind. As we sat up, kept awake by the novelty of our situation, we heard at intervals

foxes stepping on dry leaves, and brushing the downy grass close by our tent, and once a musquash fumbling among the potatoes and melons in our boat; but when we hastened to the water we could detect only a ripple in the water riffling the disc of a star. At intervals we were sere-naded by the song of a dreaming sparrow or the throttled cry of an owl; but after each sound which near at hand broke the stillness of the night, each crackling of the twigs, or rustling among the leaves, there was a sudden pause, and deeper and more conscious silence, as if the intruder were aware that no life was rightfully abroad at that hour.

Native Trees of Canada revealed that hereabouts we could expect to find aspen, white birch, juniper, Alpine fir, mountain alder, hawthorn, chokecherry, blueberry alder, maple, as well as spruce, cedar, fir and ponderosa pine. Lodgepole pine grew to 100 feet, Engelmann spruce to 150 feet. Red-cedar trees were here, as much as 200 feet high and 800 years old. *Open All Night* was not much more useful as a source of inspiration. Forty years before, when Paul Morand was a sophisti-cated young French writer in that innocent pre-Vichy world, he wrote a story about a six-day bicycle race, the title story, and it became so popular that he followed it with "Baltic Night," "Hungarian Night" and so on, until he had covered most of Europe. In the machine-gun-scarred cities in the Balkans, the hero and his friend picked up a young Jewish refugee, a café singer, and took her to Budapest. There she was kidnapped by members of the Iron Guards, those primitive forerunners of the Nazis, who chloroformed her and dropped her in the Danube. Morand's stories were not very consequential works in an age when Joyce and Proust were still alive and writing, but they were distinctive and they had some sort of flavor that gave one a sense of the shell-shocked life in the cities he wrote about.

But what about a work called *Canoe River Nights?* The trouble was that it would be a remarkably quiet work. Compared to the adven-tures of the young Frenchmen and their girl in Budapest, the Canoe River was a dull place. And soon it would not even be a place at all. Soon it would be entirely under water. Over these branches that were still faintly light there would be waves springing up under the wind blowing from the mountains. The rapids we had coursed down would be gravel slopes at the bottom of a lake 100 feet below the surface. Still, it was curious. In *The Buffalo Head* a British Columbia writer, Raymond Patterson, wrote something applicable. He crossed the val-ley of the Kootenay to the Columbia, just before the snows began, and watched the elk moving through a mountain pass below him:

> They streamed steadily around the point of the mountain, coming from God knows where, and they kept on coming. I counted up to about 70 and then I gave up. I just sat there, entranced, watching them. . . . Late

that evening I made my usual round of the horses. If, I thought, this valley had been in the mountains of Europe, it would have seen so much: ambushes and raids, the journeyings of princes and merchant caravans, the passage of armies. These things would have been part of the history of our own people and we should have known of them. And so, upon this camp, with its horse bells and its crackling stove and the candlelight that glowed so warmly through the tent walls, the past would have come crowding in on us and we would have felt, all around us, the quiet pressure of the vanished centuries. But here nothing had ever happened.

My pockets were filled with small pieces of water-soaked notepaper bearing cryptic notations that I had trouble reading—"red-tailed hawk . . . indifferent . . . the chopped-up look of shoal water." I decided to sit up all night and think about the river. Perhaps something would happen. But what would there be to record? The woods were even quieter than they were by day. There were no night birds, no frogs, crickets or animal sounds. Nothing happened—nothing but the river flowing as it had flowed in the night through the centuries. Its sound too had changed; it was now a low, quiet purring. The sky was brilliant with low stars and then golden with a full moon, but the trees concealed the sky, except over the river that gleamed with a faint, luminous glow.

Waldrop disappeared. He was arranging his socks on the clothesline at the side of the fire when he vanished silently into the night. At one instant he was busy with his task; at the next there was only darkness where he had been. It happened so suddenly we sat for several seconds in stunned silence. We just wondered where he was and how he could have disappeared without our noticing that he was gone. Then his head slowly came into the firelight, as though by some feat of levitation it was floating above the earth. In the darkness he had stepped back too far and dropped down into the river. He hoisted himself up on the bank, looking so angry at himself that no one said anything. He went on putting wet clothes on the line as if nothing had happened. It was not, perhaps, a very momentous occasion to record, but in a country where there had previously been no human happenings, and which was soon to vanish for all time, you could not expect too much.

IV

In the daylight it was easy to see why Gilbert and Waldrop lost the trail. It was masked. At the edge of the cedar grove it turned abruptly, but the brush had been left growing, not trodden down at all, and after a space of ten or twenty yards the trail resumed again as a well-beaten path.

A mile back from the river the trail led directly to an old log cabin, bolted, locked, nailed shut, and with heavy hinged slabs fastened over the windows. Two hawthorn bushes 8 or 10 feet high grew on a grassy slope before the cabin. The high weeds indicated that no one had lived there for some time, certainly not this summer or the one before.

The cabin faced a lake a mile long and not quite that wide. The far side was hidden by reeds. Immense beaver houses were visible through the reeds, gray old domes like aquatic beehives.

Directly before the cabin the water was clear, sometimes broken with slow, widening circles where fish were feeding, or when tiny satin riffles formed as a breeze touched the surface.

About a hundred feet in the woods to the right of the cabin, and about the same distance from the shore of the lake, steam rose from a narrow V-shaped ravine. Bright shining green vegetation surrounded it in tropical growths. Weeds grew higher than one's head. Vapors rose through the cedars whose branches joined above the ravine. A stream of boiling water, 4 or 5 feet wide, flowed toward the lake, sending up steam all along its course. Little logs that were lying in its channel looked as if they were cooking.

Gilbert and Waldrop went back to the Canoe to put away the canoes and bring supplies for camp, leaving me at the lake. An old rowboat was lying under water near the cabin. It was the work of an unskilled craftsman and was almost triangular, the stern board almost as long as the sides. I bailed it. The water had been standing for a long time and contained small, gummy, dustlike particles when the sediment was stirred.

The water of the lake near the place where the hot spring entered it was silver with minnows, thousands and thousands of them, or hundreds of thousands, spinning and swimming in prehistoric abundance, tiny ones near the surface, larger minnows near the bottom. Each time I emptied the bailing can a frenzy started among the minnows; they ate the dustlike specks, or tried to, and larger minnows darted up to take them away. I wondered what the sediment contained that pleased the fish so much and wondered if it might not appeal to bigger fish also. I emptied one of my waterproof containers of matches and filled it with water from the hot spring, hoping to have it analyzed and perhaps find out what fish in a state of nature, untroubled by fishermen and without hatchery experience, really like to eat. (Jumping ahead a little, I cannot say the experience was enlightening. The Associated Analytical Laboratories in New York, after a spectrographic search, reported that the following elements were found to be present, in roughly this order of plenitude: silicon, sodium, calcium, lithium, potassium, magnesium, iron, boron, aluminum, nickel, strontium, copper, manganese, titanium, silver, chromium, antimony, lead, molybdenum and tin—and sent me a bill for $60. "It is evident that this water is good hard water," said the scientists, "rich in various minerals. The relativity of the mineralogic picture to fish could best be interpreted by a qualified marine biologist." I sent a copy of the report to a qualified marine biologist, and he replied that there were always too many mosquitoes around hot springs to provide good fishing.)

What there was in those minerals that the minnows liked to eat remained a mystery. But there was no question about what the big fish liked to eat. They liked to eat the minnows that ate the minerals.

I managed to empty the boat, and pulled it up on the shore and turned it over, but when I got it back in the water and put my weight in it, innumerable holes appeared high on the sides; it could be kept afloat only if one bailed constantly. So I built a fire and examined the area. The trail was a masterpiece. It was masked at both ends. The cabin was not even visible from the lake—the knoll and the hawthorn bushes concealed it—and dry cedar wood, such as was stacked in the shed opposite the front door, makes almost no smoke when it burns.

A couple of hundred feet from the cabin, and on the opposite side of the stream of hot water flowing into the lake, there was an improvised bath, constructed with small logs forming the sides, three walls buried in the hillside. Or rather, there were two baths, each about 7 feet square; the one nearer the hot-water stream had partially filled up, and the second one was built beside it. The hot water flowed into them through a small trough formed by a hollow log that had been split in half, the water entering the trough near the point where the hot spring emerged from the earth. Pouring from the trough, the hot water was clear and free-flowing, a ribbon of bubbling water that was about 6 inches across and a quarter of an inch deep. The bottom of the bath was made of white sand, and the hot water that flowed into it from the trough, and then drained over the side into the lake, looked sparkling and carbonated. (It had a salty medicinal taste, but no odor, though a laboratory report found a high bacteria count as well as coliform organisms that originate in organic waste. "This sample," said the scientists, "is grossly contaminated with bacteria and not fit for drinking purposes.")

The stillness of the place was uncanny. Except for the occasional keening when one cedar tree scraped against another if the breeze caught it right, there was no sound at all. It was the stillness of a place where nothing had ever happened, and here it was not difficult to imagine all this country lying 200 feet below the waters of the lake that soon would be formed. A couple of camp robbers and a Steller's jay suddenly flew in and began moving around the small trees and the hawthorn bushes. They were a sign that Gilbert and Waldrop would soon be back. Camp robbers can tell the difference between people carrying a pack, and thus planning to camp, and people who are merely hunting or fishing for the day. These two were the first camp robbers we had seen on the Canoe. They were more cautious than most of their kind; some of these birds will come into a camp and steal pancakes off a breakfast table.

These two moved nervously around in irregular circular flights from one hawthorn bush to the next, then to a small dead tree beside the lake, some 30 feet away, then to the lower branches of a big tree near the cabin, then to the top of a thin young cedar closer to the hot spring, then back to the hawthorn bushes. They were never still. The Steller's jay was a magnificent bird, a deep luminous purple, and was plainly following the camp robbers, trying to emulate them, but was afraid and was constantly orbiting at a greater distance, barely landing on a bush and taking off again. No, it was not difficult to imagine all the land around here deep under water, and fish darting around a submarine growth the way the birds moved around the trees.

V

In the afternoon Waldrop managed to get a small raft, made of poles wired together, out to the edge of the reeds. The poles sank beneath his weight, but he found near the cabin an old Campbell's Soup box that he used for a seat; if placed exactly in the center of the raft, it kept him reasonably above the water. I walked along the shore to the end of the lake opposite the hot spring, to fish where a cold-water inlet came down from the mountains, but marshy ground, and muddy shallows some distance from shore, made it impossible to get to the inlet.

When I got back to the other end of the lake, Gilbert was sleeping in the improvised hot-spring pool. He seemed to be really sleeping, his head resting on a mossy log. He opened his eyes and said, "This is the greatest place in the world." He jumped from the hot spring into the tepid lake water near the shore, and then into the cold lake water farther from shore. After he dressed he hurried back to the campfire where he was preparing some dish of dried food.

I climbed into the pool. The water was extremely buoyant. I had to hold myself down or I would float and turn on the surface. The water was more than warm, almost hot, despite that long passage through the trough in the mountain air.

With no great knowledge of hot springs, it was nevertheless possible

to claim that this was the finest in the world; it was impossible for
it to be bettered. I looked up through a screen of young cedar boughs
into depthless blue sky. A big red-rock mountain to the southeast across
the lake, with a crumpled look to its saddle summit, was gradually
thinning of snow as the afternoon grew warm; I could almost see the
snow retreating above the timberline. Now and then a faint breeze
reminded one of the freshness of the air.

When I climbed out of the pool and dressed, Waldrop was labori-
ously scooping his makeshift raft back across the lake. It seemed to
be even more unwieldy than when he took it out, the poles spreading
apart when he paddled. He propelled it forward a few feet and then
was forced to pause and pull the logs together again. He reached shore
and stood breathing heavily, pale and exhausted, like an actor after
a triumphant opening night.

"Well?" Gilbert asked.

Waldrop separated the logs in the front of the raft and lifted a wire
fastened there. That was why the raft was so hard to handle; he had
taken off some of the wires holding the poles together and used them
to string together five big trout, a 16-inch rainbow, a Dolly Varden
about the same size, and three magnificent fish, one 18 inches and
the others a shade smaller, which we could not identify. They were
brilliantly but delicately colored, each with a distinct red band from
head to tail down the sides, and the lower half, below the band, a
bright yellow color that faded to white. That description fitted golden
trout but it was hard to imagine golden trout that large. Waldrop had
hooked a dozen more but with no net could not get them on the
raft. He had finally solved the problem to some extent by using the
Campbell Soup box for a net. He worked the fish to the raft, held
the box under the water with one hand and gradually worked the
fish into it.

The sun had gone down and the air was getting cold. Beaver began
to appear in the mirror-still water by the reeds. Gilbert filleted a couple
of big fish into chunks about three inches long and dropped the
chunks into a deep frying pan filled with Wesson Oil. We piled our
plates high with the chunks, salted them and stood around the fire
eating until we were full.

Gilbert took a flashlight and made his way to a point of land that
projected into the reeds to watch the beaver. I washed the dishes in
the streams of hot water that flowed from the hot spring. A couple of
heat-blackened poles lay across it and formed a limber footing. It
seemed strange to be washing dishes in hot water flowing from the
earth, soaping and rinsing them, and then stacking them on the grass
by the fire, an odd and humdrum use for a natural wonder.

In the moonlight the mountains took on a subdued old rose and copper color. I found they were not to be looked at steadily; it was better to glance at them from time to time and then look at the fire, or the cabin, or something that seemed ordinary and familiar and less transformed by enchantment. The night grew very cold, and I crawled into my sleeping bag to keep warm. In the morning locomotive clouds of steam were billowing over the lake from the hot spring. The fog did not have the soft featurelessness of fog in general; it was dynamic, driving, pumping ceaselessly from the natural fog factory. The water on the tin plates had frozen into thin sheets of ice.

When the fog lifted, we could see that the snow had moved far down the mountain slopes. Every morning the snow was below the timberline, covering the caribou meadows, and every afternoon it faded away toward the summits, but each morning it reached farther down and each evening had retreated less. Gilbert said he had watched the beaver until nearly midnight. A fawn came down to the point of land near the camp, he said; you should have seen it.

We left that place on a warm, windless midmorning. The Canoe River widened into a broad expanse of still water. We floated for half a day through a drowsing, motionless world, animated only when we disturbed different bank beavers and high-speed ducks. For the first time it was necessary to paddle to make any progress; the Canoe dropped only 20 feet in 20 miles. It was here that Thompson, going upstream, wrote, "River good." To the west was Mount Albreda, much like Mount Thompson near our starting point but higher, nearer and steeper. The caribou meadows above the tree line were very distinct in the clear air; the caribou were coming down the mountains because the snow no longer melted during the day.

We had no glasses, and argued whether the shapes we saw were really caribou. For some distance above the timberline, but well below the sheer rise to the summit, were the big, pale-green, sharply tilted caribou meadows, bordered with grassless gray rock. The lower portion of these meadows ended in the scattered clumps of trees at the highest point of the timberline; at their highest reach the grass faded away among the rocks. Near the tree line were isolated shapes, distinct as cattle feeding but blurred by distance until they seemed to take on or to lose life as one watched, as though animals were suddenly transformed into rocks, or rocks into animals. And then, farther south toward the Columbia, the caribou meadows themselves disappeared from the mountains. The escarpment on the west rose until it formed a rock wall. In its slow curving progress across the valley, the Canoe alternately ran directly toward it and directly away from it. Where the woods opened up in front of us on these westward runs we saw the most spectacular scene in the course of the river, a thousand-foot cascade that poured over the rock wall to the valley floor. It fell in a ribbon of vapory white against the dark rock. Two thirds of the way down the cliff the water struck some rocky projection and thinned into two falls. It looked as though we were going straight to the base of the falls, but the river turned, and a couple of miles of thick woods lay between the river and the cliff, the falls appearing to evaporate among the treetops.

The valley still extended due south, but the mountains were now nearer on both sides. Beyond the Columbia, still 50 or 60 river miles south, the valley continued due south as the valley of the Columbia, the great trench between the Rockies and the Selkirks. That trench was sometimes visible directly ahead of us, a narrow opening, a notch, a line of light between massive slanting ranges that finally vanished in haze—a passageway between mountains, but one that had always been impassable to man because of the wild rivers, and that was now to be smoothed and stilled for all time.

The character of the Canoe River changed as we approached the Columbia. The snow mountains began to close in on both sides of the river. Something chill and changeable came into the air. The places where the tributary creeks joined the Canoe were now usually boulder-strewn deltas, sometimes with splintered trees wedged among rocks and level fields of small stones giving evidence of the power of the spring floods. Often the deltas had the wrecked look of logged-off land; among the battered tree trunks and the skulls of moose and deer and the heaps of debris piled in dry and clay-caked confusion, one could soberly think of coming upon the body of a prominent man.

Ptarmigan Creek came in from the east, dropping 9,000 feet in 22 miles, from its headwaters in the Rockies, one branch heading only half a mile from one of the headwaters of the Fraser River. Where the Ptarmigan joined the Canoe, it formed a spongy triangle of white sand and low banks of gravel. At this low-water period Ptarmigan Creek was only 30 feet wide, but the flood marks indicated it was 200 feet wide at high water. The water was clear and cold, agate colored, with the sand slightly gummy underfoot. We stopped there to pan for gold, sometimes isolating shining yellow specks in the intense black sand but, so far as any practical result was achieved, gaining nothing more than a sense of how lonely and frustrating panning for gold on the Canoe River must have been for the miners who really worked at it.

Grouse Creek came in about 20 winding river miles below Ptarmigan, formed somewhere in unreachable highlands near the 10,900-foot peak of Mount Albreda that rose 12 miles west of the Canoe. We camped at Grouse Creek, about 2 miles from where Thompson camped on the night of September 20, 1811. Grouse Creek was also clear, flowing through beds of white sand like the sand on an ocean beach above the summer tide mark. Camp was about 200 feet from the creek, on a grass-covered terrace that had remained intact, although all around it the birch groves had been crushed and broken by floods, and small stones had washed through the woodland and sometimes were piled high around the trunks of trees that were still growing.

We were entering a part of the river where there were faint historical associations, fragments of legends, the elusive traces of people who had come up the river in the days when the Columbia was the main route of travel. In the east the close-packed peaks of the Rockies rose 2 miles high against the skyline, so awesome it was hard to believe that anyone could get through them at any time and incredible that Thompson had found a pass in the middle of winter. Alexander Ross, a fur trader, came upon the Canoe River about where we had put our canoes on it and called it a small and insignificant stream. Sir George Simpson, when he reorganized the Hudson's Bay posts in the Northwest, wanted to use the Canoe as a main trade route, the parties to go up the Canoe from the Big Bend of the Columbia and cross to the Fraser instead of going down the Columbia. The artist Paul Kane, who passed through Boat Encampment in 1850, wrote that the Canoe River was being used by the Company to move furs north for shipment to Russia. Ranald MacDonald, a legendary Northwestern character—he was a grandson of Concomly, the Indian chief who dealt with Lewis and Clark, and was one of the first Americans to visit Japan—went out of his way, in his autobiography, to describe the Canoe River. Because of its name, he said, people thought that the Canoe was good for canoe travel. But it was not, nothing more than "a continuous mountain torrent, not navigable, even in an Indian canoe."

The legends came nearer in time with stories of gold hunters. Gold was discovered on the upper Columbia near the Big Bend, and in 1866 Walter Moberly, a Canadian government surveyor, passed through the region searching for a route for a wagon road to the goldfields. He heard that four hundred men were working near the Big Bend and that some of them had gone up the Canoe River. They were said to be satisfied with their return, though averaging only 50 cents a pan. They left the region soon after, drawn away by reports of $100-a-day diggings on the Fraser.

Two decades later the Canoe River acquired its only permanent resident. Alphonse Emonds appeared at Boat Encampment in 1884. David Thompson's old cabin had washed away, and Emonds built another on the site. He also built a string of five cabins, a day's travel apart, up the Canoe River, and spent his life going from one to the other, keeping up his trap lines. The Canadian Pacific railway was built in 1884, the old Hudson's Bay trail by Boat Encampment was no longer needed and Emonds had the country to himself. He lived there alone for thirty-eight years.

Emonds was a sociable, well-built man of medium height, well-informed and intelligent. He prospered as a trapper. Each spring he took a boatload of furs—beaver, marten, mink, lynx, fox and bear—down the Canoe and the Columbia to Revelstoke, the nearest town, some 90 miles down the Columbia from Boat Encampment. He bought real estate in Revelstoke with his earnings and became well-to-do. After selling his furs he went north, to where Valemount was later built, and rode down the Canoe to Boat Encampment. Madison Lorraine, an engineer from California who floated the length of the Columbia in 1921 (in a rowboat he built at Canal Flats), spent three weeks with Emonds, hunting and exploring up the Canoe; it was the high point of his 1,246-mile journey from the Columbia headwaters to the sea. Emonds was then serving as a government fire warden. Lorraine found him an able and sensible man, free of any eccentricities connected with his lonely life, except for an occasional unguarded revelation of his belief that, as a descendant of the Bourbon kings, he was the rightful heir to the throne of France. In the spring of 1922 Emonds was found floating in a boat among the ice floes on the Columbia. He was conscious but was paralyzed and could not speak. He had somehow drifted safely through the Columbia rapids and was approaching the worst of these, called Death Rapids—a short distance above Downie Creek—when his boat was seen by a miner. It took the miner eighteen days to get Emonds to the hospital at Revelstoke, and he died there without recovering the power of speech or the ability to write. It was theorized that he had suffered a series of strokes and had managed to get into his boat and to cast off into the current before he became completely helpless. But it was never revealed what his background was or why he had spent his life alone on the river.

Such were the substance of the legends of the Canoe, and they were the only ones. On the scene they were made more melancholy by the images of loneliness they evoked. Their mystery was pervasive, akin to other puzzles of the area, like the loss of Thompson's maps and diaries. But in the forest the mysteries began to be taken for granted, a part of some great never-to-be-known land that was doomed to be flooded and forgotten. What remained was a ghostly presence along the river of a few people whose lives were drowned in solitude beyond measurable depth.

Hugh Allan Creek appeared, beyond a big rapids. Thompson noted on his page of figures: "Grand rapids." He was right, for the river dropped 30 feet there and the water was wild and violent; but there were no obstructions and it was a fast, short run, thrilling but not difficult. Below these rapids, where the river was 200 feet wide or wider, there was a wide, level expanse of flat gravel, laced with tiny streams threading through the stones and leaving the huge gravel bed wet and shining in the gray light. This was the way Hugh Allan Creek came into the Canoe. It was an eerie place. Another cabin stood far back from the river in a clearing overgrown with waist-high grass. It was bolted and nailed shut, with slabs over the windows and a huge spread of antlers over the door. On one side of the cabin, where there had once been a fenced-in vegetable garden, Hugh Allan Creek was gnawing at the dirt bank far below. The creek was a big river by the standards of the valley, bigger than the Canoe had been at the point where we entered it near Valemount; but the outlet was divided into two rivers, with the cabin standing in the diminishing island they formed, and these two main outlets in turn filtered in innumerable rivulets through the stones before they joined the Canoe.

Howard Creek came in from the west, forming the strongest rapids we had met, with a 20- or 30-foot drop in the length of a long city block. But rapids were now continuous, not in the sense of unbroken white water but in the sense that there were now no long stretches without rapids. Time became deceptive; a watery haze and a uniform gray threat of rain lay over the river and the endless trees. Sometimes on the mountains patches of yellow light opened high on the peaks, while on nearby slopes the gray vapor indicated that rain or snow was falling. We seemed to be in a drowned world, drenched by one rapids after another. They began to seem alike, each bend like the one we had rounded before, the same submerged trees dodged again and again. There was a stair-step pattern to the rapids. I estimated that we would be in white water for perhaps five minutes, and then have a rest period of smooth water for ten minutes or more before the next rapids. But when I timed the actual alternations of speed and calm they went like this: at 4:37 P.M. a fast stretch that lasted until 4:41; at 4:46 a smooth passage that ended in another short rapids; at 4:50, calm water again. If the runs lasted too long, one's neck and shoulder ached from the bucking of the canoe in the standing waves, and occasionally it seemed that one more wave would be too much to endure. But then the alternations of smooth water gave one relief again, and the Canoe raced on, big and fast, tremendously powerful, wild and remote, ceaselessly changing, but with a kind of tranquillity, a busy harmlessness to its hurry.

For the first time boulders began to appear in the rapids. In a stretch of smooth water I was leaning over the bow and suddenly saw, 5 or 6 feet below, white and gray and yellowish shapes racing past, dimly visible. It took me a moment to realize the water had cleared and was transparent: there were pockets of gravel visible and patches of white sand, and again and again I could see the river growing shallow and the submarine shelves that indicated rapids ahead. We had grown so used to the opaque water that it seemed unbelievable: Thompson had said that the water was clear over pebbles and small stones, and he was right, though upstream where the river was opaque it was impossible to credit it.

On our last day on the river, late in the morning, rain started with such violence that we had to get to shore. A cabin, presumably one of Emonds's, stood in a partial clearing, hidden in reeds and weeds up to its eaves. The windows were out and the door open. The wreckage, more than anything else, made it uncomfortable, and though the rain continued we started out again. Toward evening, near the Columbia, rain was spraying in sheets across the river; merely sitting in the canoe was as drenching as running a rapids. A long way ahead, where the river was 200 feet across, two large red disks appeared over the water. A metering cable, to register stream flow, crossed the Canoe there, and the red disks were hung on it so that any bush pilot, coming to land on the river, would not hit the cable. They looked like decorations left over from some street fair, and they came as a shock with the knowledge that the Columbia was only a short distance ahead.

We came out of the Canoe in the rainy twilight and were in the Columbia before we knew it. The current of the bigger river caught the canoe and shot it diagonally halfway across the river. It felt as if someone had grabbed it under water and thrown it like a javelin. Going into midstream was like mounting a hill of water that was rushing along sideways. The Columbia rounded a 90-degree turn just above the mouth of the Canoe, and the current was so powerful the river seemed to be doubling up and folding over as it rounded the point. We were carried downstream for some distance before we landed on a huge plain, covered with gravel and boulders and cut with small channels, over which the Columbia flowed at all seasons except in the lowest water. Working our way back upstream by wading along the bank, we went above the mouth of the Canoe to get back to the opposite shore—a logging road ran there to Boat Encampment. We set the canoes across the Columbia, holding them quarteringly against the current, like a ship tacking into the wind. There was a big dead snag on the far bank, and we steered by it, paddling hard on the downstream side to keep the canoe in the same position; heading too directly across would have swept us broadside in that current. It was now nearly dark, and that gray snag drew nearer and nearer, like some cherished landmark of home.

We dragged the canoes up on shore, stuffed dry clothes into our packs and hiked upstream along the shore. Fresh-cut logs were piled beside a muddy road, ready to be hauled away. A bridge of wooden timbers, the cross planks broken, crossed the Wood River where it entered the Columbia a quarter of a mile above the Canoe. The Wood was a pale bluish gray, roaring with lethal violence through a narrow gap. More piles of logs were ranged along the road; a loaded truck stood at a log landing. There were the sound of a pump, the hum of a gasoline-driven generator, the gleam of an unshaded light over the door of a work shed. Those splintery logs and the bark and debris that had spilled over the black, oily-looking soil made more immediate the flooding of the land; it looked like a land being cleared of valuables before an invasion.

But why take out only the trees? Who knew what else might be buried under the water? And why stop with an unknown river? If something had to be flooded, why not places whose every inch had been explored of all they contained? The familiar lament of conservationists about the loss of some wilderness area did not have much force in this particular doomed wilderness; in a century and a half only a handful of people had even known of the river. For that matter, even the accessible wilderness would not be reduced. The Canoe would be destroyed, but out of the lake that would be formed the unknown streams that flowed into the Canoe—Dawson Creek, Hugh Allen Creek, Foster Creek, Baker Creek, Grouse Creek—would come within reach as the water backed up to the entrance of their canyons. The lake that was going to come into being was also going to open the way to a greater wilderness area than any wilderness destroyed by it.

So the loss was not of any known value. On the eve of the Civil War, Nathaniel Hawthorne wrote that he feared our institutions might be destroyed before we had realized the best of the possibilities they contained, and what one felt was that something whose value was not yet known was going to be destroyed in the ending of this small, wild, unknown valley. We had a long walk to the prefabricated luxury of a motel at Boat Encampment, a metal structure built, like all the buildings to house workmen on the Mica Creek Dam, in segments that could be taken down and carted away when the dam was finished. Waldrop and Gilbert began singing "We Are Marching to Pretoria." For some reason the Anna Livia Plurabelle passages of Joyce's *Finnegans Wake* kept coming to my mind—"My ho head halls. I feel as old as yonder elm"—and I thought of how much the River Liffey meant to Joyce and how persistently its image was woven into his work. The passage was not really applicable. My ho head did not really hall. I did not feel as old as yonder elm; I had never felt better. The sight of that old gray snag across the Columbia, the roar of the river against the metal sides of the canoe, the recollection of green tablelands along the riverbank and the frosty heights above them, the vagrant sights and sounds all along the way had become realities of a tangible value whose existence I had not even suspected and the possession of which, even in the rain, even with the weight of the pack, the uneven ground, the dirt, the wet clothes, meant even then a sense of permanent enrichment. Night fell on the River Liffey: "My ho head halls. Can't hear the water of. The chittering water of. I feel as old as yonder elm. Night now! Beside the rivering waters of. The hitherandthithering waters of. Night!"

VIII

Arts and Letters

Don Francisco Antonio Mourelle was a pilot, not a man of letters, but his book, *Voyage of the Sonora in the Second Bucareli Expedition*, translated into English in 1781, was a lucid, direct, forceful report, such as an experienced professional writer might have produced from a pilot's story; as the first book dealing with the Pacific Northwest, it placed Northwestern literature with modern writing from the start. There was nothing mysterious or cryptic about Mourelle's book, as there so often was in the earliest explorers' writings about the New World. He saw the land from the deck of the *Sonora*, and he evoked it with a matter-of-fact exactitude, a windswept, rain-darkened world, sometimes brightened with brief sunlit sky clearings, with broken off-shore rocks, surf, sand and gray cliffs in the foreground, and beyond these the tiers of tree-covered cliffs ending in the haze and snow of mountains.

In literary terms it was a good beginning. Compare it with the puzzlements of Spaniards in Florida, or Cabeza de Vaca in Texas, or the French in Quebec and Indiana, or Father Escalante in Arizona, and it is as clear as the works of Northwestern history published a hundred years later—clearer, in some respects. The high point of Mourelle's book is his report of the killing of the men of the *Sonora*'s boat crew by Indians. In this, also, the writing is spare and unadorned and devoid

247

of melodrama, a simple, stoical account, yet not heartless or unfeeling, the work of a man concerned only to communicate: this is what happened.

What was true of Mourelle's book characterized many of the explorers' works that followed it, less convincing though some of these were. A region whose literary heritage included John Meares's *Voyages to the Northwest Coast of North America*, Alexander Mackenzie's *Voyage from Montreal on the River St. Lawrence through the Continent of North America*, the journals of Lewis and Clark, Captain George Vancouver's *A Voyage of Discovery to the North Pacific Ocean*, David Thompson's *Narrative of His Explorations in Western America, 1784–1812*, Washington Irving's *Astoria*, Theodore Winthrop's *The Canoe and the Saddle*, James Gilchrist Swan's *The Northwest Coast*, Peter Skene Ogden's *Traits of American Indian Life and Character*, Jesse Applegate's *A Day with the Cow Column in 1843*, the journals of William Fraser Tolmie, Paul Kane's *Wanderings of an Artist*, Gustavas Hines's *Wild Life in Oregon*, the histories of Frances Fuller Victor and the historical studies of Edmond Meany was exceptionally favored, richly endowed if only in the vivid and controversial documentation of its brief but recorded past.

Among books that were historically less important, but still of great interest in their fragmentary glimpses of hidden sides of Northwestern life, the literary heritage was even more varied. It encompassed such works as *Narrative of the Adventures and Sufferings of John R. Jewitt*, the autobiography of a sailor, a village blacksmith in less venturesome hours, held captive by Indians near Nootka in 1803; *Ranald MacDonald, the Narrative of His Early Life*, the autobiography of a half-Indian adventurer who, in his boyhood, went to school with Japanese sailors cast up on the Northwest coast; and William Baillie-Grohman's somewhat eccentric *Fifteen Years Sport and Life in the Hunting Grounds of Western America and British Columbia*. In later years there were engaging and unpretentious personal narratives, Guy Waring's *My Pioneer Past*, for example, the story of a ranch in the Cascades near the Canadian border that gave Owen Wister—Waring's friend at Harvard—the material and the setting for *The Virginian*; or Madison Lorraine's *The Columbia Unveiled*, the work of an engineer who at the age of sixty-eight built a rowboat at Canal Flats, British Columbia, and rowed all the way down the Columbia River to the Pacific Ocean, "to record my protest," he said, "against the theory that men are no longer efficient after 50 years of age."

There were no trailing medieval legends to burden the writing of the Northwest from the start. But like much modern writing, a quality of considered hindsight, or second guessing, pervades the major works.

Meares's *Voyages* was not only a beautifully printed and magnificently illustrated report of his bold enterprise: it was a part of Meares's campaign to pressure the British government to pressure the Spanish government to recompense him for his losses. The very first books on the Northwest were late arrivals in terms of modern history. People could read, and public opinion influenced political action. Public relations and ideological considerations shaped the written history and even the physical descriptions of the region, so much so that the literary works were often as much contributions to then-current ideological questions and public relations as they were records of the time and place.

Even Mourelle's *Voyage of the Sonora* had something of this essential Northwest ambiguity, as though it were part of some undisclosed project, as though interested parties sometimes deflected its narrative or interpolated material into it. The questions began with its publication. No explanation was given as to how Mourelle's manuscript reached his English translator. The Spaniards in those days kept their voyages secret. The book appeared in England at a time when backers were sought for the fur-otter trade. It was a selling point in this trade that the Indians of the Northwest Coast valued metal so highly they would trade a fortune in skins for a few pieces of old iron. In Mourelle's account of the death of the men in the *Sonora*'s boat he mentioned that the Indians, after the murder, tore the boat apart for metal scraps. Mourelle was on the *Sonora*, far from shore, and yet he could, even in that moment of intense confusion and danger, clearly distinguish what 300 savages were doing.

A curious form of special pleading and slanted description existed in Northwestern writing along with its candor and accuracy. The result was the ideological and political library already described, with the books of one party presenting the region as bleak and inhospitable and not worth struggling for, and the works of another party picturing it as favored by nature beyond any other. The authority of so honest a book as Swan's *The Northwest Coast* was weakened because the author was interested in selling real estate in the area he described, and Edmond Meany could step aside from his scrupulous and sagacious scholarship in his *History of the State of Washington* to add such press-agent boosting for the state as "The crops of grain, hay, hops and potatoes are important. . . . The 284 creameries produced over eight million pounds of butter in 1907."

In one sense it is misleading to speak of a Northwestern literary heritage. The books were so hard to come by (especially in the Northwest), or were so long delayed in reaching the public, that they remained semiconfidential, if not actually hidden, and in any case were not a part of the common cultural life of the region. Mackenzie crossed the continent in 1793; his book was published in 1801, and was almost unobtainable a century later. When the ship *Boston* was lost in 1803 and the crew murdered, John Jewitt survived; the Indian chief responsible for the slaughter had seen Jewitt work as a blacksmith and kept him alive to shape iron. Jewitt was rescued in the summer of 1805 and his *Narrative*, which he sold door-to-door in the Eastern states, was published in 1816. The journals that Lewis and Clark kept in the dreary Northwestern winter of 1805–1806 appeared in a digested form in 1814, in a version that made that winter seem even more miserable than the explorers pictured it as having been. The complete text of their journals was not published until 1904. David Thompson's account of life on the upper Columbia in 1807 finally appeared, as has been said earlier, in 1916. The Wilkes Expedition explored the Northwest in 1841, and the final volume of the report of the expedition appeared in 1874. Not that its appearance made much difference to the reading public, in the Northwest or elsewhere. Only one hundred copies were printed by the government.

Legends about the Northwest persisted, and especially in the Northwest itself, in the absence of what might have been the standard source books of its history. One example was the controversy concerning Japanese junks wrecked on the coast. About the middle of the seventeenth century, roughly in the period when Cromwell was opposing King Charles I in England, the Emperor of Japan tried to prevent his subjects from voyaging beyond Japanese shores. It was decreed that all junks should be built with open sterns and large square rudders that made them unfit for the open sea. If any junk so constructed was driven out to sea, it was quickly disabled. Half a hundred cases were recorded of such vessels drifting helplessly or driven ashore on the North American coast. In 1833 a junk carrying a cargo of porcelain was wrecked on the Olympic Peninsula south of Cape Flattery. Fourteen of the original crew of seventeen died. Two sailors and a boy survived and were kept as slaves by the Indians. When pieces of pottery appeared in trade with the Indians, traders of the Hudson's Bay Company investigated and heard of the wrecked ship. (Tom McKay, a figure in many Northwestern mysteries, led an expedition to the Olympic Peninsula to rescue the Japanese but had to turn back.) Eventually the captain of a Hudson's Bay trading vessel bought the slaves and took them to Vancouver. Overestimating the scientific ardor in London, the local Company officials thought British experts would be interested in the voyage they had made.

For the Japanese sailors the entire experience must have been extremely disagreeable. They were blown across the Pacific, kept in servitude by savages and, when they were rescued, trained in the singing of hymns in a language they could not understand. There were many half-Indian children in Oregon born of the union of traders and Indian girls, and the Company had temporarily retained a young American missionary, Cyrus Shepherd, to teach thirty of these. The teaching included religious instruction, and each Sunday night the students gathered in the main hall of the post and sang hymns they had memorized to the assembled officers, traders and employees. The Japanese were added to the classes of children and learned to sing hymns along with them. A century later the thought of these weekly gatherings bemused Judge Charles Carey, author of *A General History of Oregon*, as he brooded about Shepherd's "difficulties with the Indian dialects, plus the Japanese language, recast into evening hymns."

Among the half-Indian students was Ranald MacDonald, then eleven years old. His father was a Scottish trader of some importance in the Company. His mother was a daughter of Concomly, the leading chief of the tribes near the mouth of the Columbia, a figure whose real importance was questioned by later students but who in any event always claimed great importance, and who presented himself as a friend of the white people with considerable advantage to himself. Ranald MacDonald was proud of his half-Indian ancestry. He also acquired an interest in Japan that lasted throughout a long life. His three Japanese schoolmates were sent to London on a Hudson's Bay ship. The members of the Royal Society had no interest in them; the Company at last shipped them to the Far East at its own expense. The Japanese government refused to let them into Japan on the grounds that they had been contaminated by their intercourse with foreigners. They were finally deposited in the Portuguese port of Macao, across the harbor from Hong Kong, where they acted as interpreters in the limited trading with the rest of the world that Japan then allowed.

Meanwhile Ranald MacDonald had been sent to Scotland by his father to be trained to become a banker. He ran into slights there that he thought were reflections on his half-Indian ancestry, so he ran away and became a sailor on whaling vessels. As a young man he arranged with the captain of a whaler to cast him ashore on a remote northern coast of Japan. The Japanese would not permit Europeans to visit the country, but they returned shipwrecked sailors to trading vessels. Ranald MacDonald lived in ceremonious captivity, teaching English to a few carefully screened Japanese students. He was still engaged in this when an American naval officer, Lieutenant James Glynn, on duty in the Far East, heard that American citizens were held in slavery in Japan. Glynn boldly sailed into the harbor of Nagasaki under the guns of the fort and demanded their release. Most of the captives were South Sea Islanders from the crews of wrecked whale ships, and when they were turned over to Lieutenant Glynn, Ranald MacDonald was among them. Back in the United States, the lieutenant used his experience to try to persuade the firm of Howland and Aspinwall to establish coaling stations in Japan. He failed in that, but his campaign helped promote Commodore Perry's visit to open Japan to the West. Ranald MacDonald disappeared into the wilds of the upper Columbia and eventually wrote his autobiography. It was not a very good book, confused by his attempts to identify his Indian ancestors as royalty and to make chiefs and their daughters the equivalent of European kings and princesses, but it certainly had some bearing on the question of whether Japanese mariners had really reached the North American mainland; it might have contributed to the discussion, but it was not published until 1923.

II

Captain Vancouver was an exception among the explorers; he reached Puget Sound in 1792, and his great book, *A Voyage of Discovery to the North Pacific Ocean,* was published only six years later. He was eager to get it finished; he was excited about his discovery, he loved the country, he had no hidden ax to grind, and the delay in his case was caused by long service at sea. He was working on the book when he died in 1798 at the age of forty, and his brother and Peter Puget put the finishing touches to the manuscript. But Vancouver was exceptional in many respects. There was nothing like Meares's cunning in his case, or any intimation that, while pretending to be describing a new land, he was furthering the projects of some hidden financial associates.

It is true that Vancouver gave names to gigantic Northwestern landmarks with untroubled generosity, naming mountains, including Rainier, for old naval associates—as well as twenty-three places for prominent individuals in England, such as Sir William Bellingham, who had control of storekeeper accounts for the Royal Navy and whose friendship might be useful—but most of his place names were spontaneous gestures of esteem, including nine places named for members of his crew and twenty places for personal friends in humble positions in life. Vancouver, however, was most exceptional in his appreciation of the region he had found, and perhaps alone among explorers in his reasons for pride in his discoveries. Explorations in his day were undertaken for the promise of gold or other forms of wealth, and the value of a newfound land was measured in terms of what the homeland might gain from it. Vancouver merely attested that the Northwest was beautiful. His pride in his discovery was that he had found a region more beautiful than had any of his predecessors, rivals or colleagues. The wealth of the Northwest was scenery, and he felt the new land he had found was infinitely valuable simply for its appearance. He had come upon a parklike region so perfectly fashioned by nature that it seemed to have been cultivated by generations of gardeners. "I could not possibly believe that any uncultivated country had ever been discovered," he wrote, "exhibiting so rich a picture."

That was the true wealth of the Northwest, a picture, a scene, a setting, something immeasurable in terms of material standards. Two persistent themes in early Northwestern writing bore on Vancouver's belief. One was the notion that the benign climate and the physical beauty of the country would influence human behavior and make the people who lived there better than they otherwise would have been. A second persistent theme was British and American relations, not in the sense of formal diplomatic arrangements but as a part of ordinary daily life. Both these themes, however, were seen in the Northwest literary heritage from an oblique angle. They reached the readers, insofar as they were generally publicized, through the writings of the early American missionaries, refracted, in a sense, or scaled down in importance by the missionaries' belief that these were temporal matters or incidental happenings along the fringes of their own great enterprise. The hope that motivated them was that the Christian education of the Indians would forestall in Oregon the Indian wars that darkened history in all other parts of the continent. In 1834 the Reverend Jason Lee, a Canadian who had trained in New England for the ministry, his nephew Daniel Lee, and two Methodist lay brethren set out for Oregon with Nathaniel Wyeth's party. Wyeth stopped on the way to build Fort Hall on the Oregon Trail. The missionaries were guided on to Vancouver by the ubiquitous Tom McKay. In 1836 Dr. Marcus Whitman and his bride, and the Reverend Henry Spaulding and his wife, established their missions at Waiilaptu, near Walla Walla, and at Lapwai in what became Idaho, settlements that were remarkably successful in terms of the times and the conditions under which the missionaries worked. In response to a call by Jason Lee for reinforcements, a second party, headed by Dr. Elijah White, reached Oregon in 1837. Still another appeal by Lee led to a third party in 1839, this one of twenty-seven men, nineteen women and sixteen children who arrived in Oregon by ship.

At that time Washington Irving's *Astoria* was the only popular book about the region (though the Reverend Samuel Parker's almost unreadable *Journal of an Exploring Tour Beyond the Rocky Mountains* was published soon after his return to the Eastern states following his Northwest visit of 1835), and the work of telling the story of Oregon's early years came down to men who were members of these parties.

Their point of view was exceptional, and their experiences were hardly representative of the pioneers generally. They wrote in varying degrees of bitterness as their hope of converting the Indians faded. Perhaps Winthrop had been right, perhaps the beginning of a new system of thought and life was implicit in their struggle to prevent a reenactment of the old, savage Indian tragedy, but if so the meaning of it was not communicated in their halting, painful and interrupted narratives. Even more the political experiment involved in the joint occupancy of Oregon was subordinated in their books to their defenses of the missionary work; they pictured it as largely a matter of the intrigues of self-seeking men on both sides.

The filaments that connected the books written by the missionaries were too tenuous to be discussed in terms of individual works; a clearer impression was gained by examining the threads that linked them. The authors knew one another. They had taken part in the same events. They were co-workers, friends and sometimes rivals. Sometimes their books gave an impression of being a single multivolume work written by different people. The first in point of time was *Ten Years in Oregon, the Travels and Adventures of Doctor E. White and Lady*, published in Ithaca, New York, in 1850. (The Reverend Mr. Parker's book, in 1838, was not part of these related volumes.)

Other matters were dealt with in *Ten Years in Oregon*, but the interconnections of the books can be illustrated by Dr. White's relations with one individual who appeared also in the books of other missionaries. Soon after he arrived in Oregon, Dr. White became associated with William Bailey, whose background was obscure. He was reportedly of English birth, had studied to be a physician and was exiled to the United States by his family because of his drunkenness. Bailey reached California as a common sailor, jumped ship and eventually joined a party bound overland for Oregon. The party was attacked by Indians, and Bailey, who was one of five survivors, reached Vancouver with his face horribly disfigured where he had been gashed by an ax.

But he survived. He was at odds with Jason Lee, though he went to California in 1837 with the Willamette Cattle Company party backed by Ewing Young and William Slacum, in which Jason Lee played a part. On the overland trip back to Oregon, Bailey endangered the entire party by murdering two Indians in revenge for the injury he had suffered. He was held in very low regard when Dr. White befriended him. White persuaded him to renew his study of medicine and to stop drinking, and as a result Bailey became known as a physician.

Despite the distrust of others in the mission, Dr. White remained on close terms with him. In February, 1839, during a revival meeting, Bailey became a convert to the Methodist Church. He was courting

Margaret Jewett Smith, a teacher in the mission school. They were married the following month, despite efforts by Miss Smith's friends to dissuade her. After two days of wedded life, Bailey announced that he no longer believed in the Bible or had any connection with the church. Margaret's confusion and distress led her to write the first novel of Oregon, *Grains, or Passages in the Life of Ruth Rover*, in which the bride sets the tone of the book by asking herself, "*What* have I married?"

It may be that her novel (written after she secured a divorce) overstated the miseries of her married life. The couple had many visitors, including Lieutenant Wilkes, who found their cabin one of the best he had seen in Oregon. They also made two long journeys to the Eastern states. But Bailey—and Dr. White, also, for that matter—seemed to have been unfortunate in the practice of medicine. The school was taught by young Cyrus Shepherd (previously the teacher of the shipwrecked Japanese sailors), who had arrived in Oregon with Jason Lee's first party and whose health, along with that of his students, was rapidly failing. As many as forty Indian children were in the school, "notwithstanding the fearful mortality that reigned among the children," as Gustavus Hines wrote tersely. "About one-third of all that had been received up to this period had died, and most of the remainder were in a sickly condition."

Shepherd's health grew worse. "A swelling appeared on one of his knees," Hines wrote, "which at first created but little concern, but at length assumed a very alarming aspect." Dr. White and Dr. Bailey decided to amputate the leg, and "death ensued a short time after the amputation."

Dr. White's career was characterized by his bold and independent actions. During a trip to the Eastern states he managed to be appointed Indian agent for the region west of the Rocky Mountains. Since there were no other United States government officials in Oregon, Dr. White believed himself to be authorized to decide on governmental matters also.

His most startling venture was to introduce flogging into the Indian tribes, and this is one aspect of their story that casts over the early books of Oregon an air of melodrama and makes occasional passages sound like something out of Krafft-Ebing. With chilling personal bravery Dr. White journeyed far into Idaho (guided by Tom McKay), where he departed from the usual practice of the Hudson's Bay Company in the area by appointing individual chiefs to represent the tribes in their relations with the United States government and with the white men generally. This alone might not have been disastrous, but Dr. White imposed on his appointed chiefs a penal code which they applied vigorously. The penal code provided that anyone stealing anything worth more than a beaver skin should receive fifty lashes, with twenty-five lashes for injuring crops, for tearing down a fence, for riding a horse without permission of the owner and for other offenses.

Dr. White was much pleased by the enthusiasm of the chiefs, who even suggested additional crimes to be punished. He returned to the settlement in the Willamette Valley. A wave of floggings swept over the Indian country. The new practice, while heartily endorsed by the chiefs who did the flogging (and who claimed it would win them the approval of the white authorities for their acceptance of the white man's ways), was not approved by the braves who were flogged. These grew increasingly dissatisfied, until, as Gustavus Hines reported with alarm, some resisted even to the knife.

With the Indian country in an uproar, Dr. White was summoned to straighten things out. A story had grown that the Indians had decided to exterminate all the white people. Dr. White found that Tom McKay was unable to guide him into the Indian country again. No Hudson's Bay employee was willing to go along, and Gustavus Hines was drafted to accompany White on the long journey up the Columbia to a council grounds near Walla Walla. Hines had reached Oregon with the party that responded to Jason Lee's second call for reinforcements. His book, originally called *Life on the Oregon Trail*, later *Wild Life in Oregon, Being a Stirring Recital of Actual Scenes of Daring and Peril Among the Gigantic Forests and Terrific Rapids of the Columbia River*, and first published in 1851, was a superior work among missionary books, but like others it was marked by a disjointed narrative, characters appearing and disappearing without the reader knowing who they were, and local conflicts alluded to without explanation as to what they were about. But isolated scenes were of graphic power. One such came on Sunday, April 30, 1843, when Hines and Dr. White stopped at The Dalles on their way to calm the Indians. "After a comfortable night's rest," Hines wrote, "we arose, and enjoyed our humble repast, consisting of ham, bread, butter and tea. We prepared to spend the day as profitably as we could." The scene inspired gloomy reflections. After reading the Scriptures and praying, Hines walked alone through the woods and rested on a wild apple tree that leaned over the water. The country was frightening, the shores rocky and abrupt, the precipices above so steep they caused one to cringe involuntarily if he looked up, the great basalt masses in wild confusion on the cliffs and in broken fragments in the river itself.

Hines had been in Oregon for more than five years. The hope of the missionaries had been broken; their Indian schools failed; the Eastern authorities of the Methodist Church found it hard to understand that

there had been no accounting of the considerable sum of money—
$40,000—raised to further the good work. A kind of hallucination came
over Hines as he sat by the river. He found memories of home becoming more real to him than the country around him. He remembered his
parents, from whom he had not heard for years; he could vividly imagine
his schoolmates and friends; he could see the towns and cities where
he had lived; he seemed to hear the sound of wheels and hooves on
the pavement, and the ringing of church bells. So real was the vision
that when it ended he did not know what had happened: "starting up,
I found myself surrounded by the stillness of death." When, he asked,
would this land be like the beloved land of home? "This is truly a
land of darkness."

Some seven hundred Indians, with a thousand horses, had assembled
for the council. They were led by Joseph, then second in command to
Ellis among the Nez Percé chiefs. A day passed while they waited for
Ellis and his party, reportedly 50 miles away. The stage was then set
for a sham battle on a colossal scale to impress the visitors. Dr. White
and Hines joined Joseph and his warriors in a line of battle drawn up
on a narrow plain.

> We were requested to take our places in the front ranks of Joseph's
> band, in the center, and soon appeared, coming over the mountain, be-
> hind which they had been waiting, a cloud of Indians that spread itself
> over its sides. The mountain seemed alive, as hundreds of Indians came
> moving toward the valley. They were all mounted on their best horses
> and these were ornamented with scarlet belts and head dresses, while
> tassels dangled from their ears. They arrived on the borders of the plain,
> and the two bands were separated from each other about 50 rods, and
> now the scene that presented itself beggars description. A thousand sav-
> ages rushed into all the maneuvers of a deadly fight, while the roar of
> musketry, the shrill sound of the war whistle, the horrible yelling, and the
> dashing to and fro upon their fiery steeds, which continued for half an
> hour, and approached us nearer and nearer until the froth from their
> horses' nostrils would fly into our faces as they passed—these, with the
> savage pomposity with which they were caparisoned, and the frightful
> manner in which they were daubed with paint, their fiery visages being
> striped with red, black, white and yellow, were all calculated not only to
> inspire terror, but a dread of savage fury in the mind of every beholder.
> At the very height of the excitement, when it appeared that the next
> wheel of the cavalry charge would trample us beneath their feet, Ellis
> stretched himself up to his utmost height upon the back of his splendid
> charger, and waving his hand over the dark mass, instantly all was quiet,
> and the terrifying yell of the savage was succeeded by profound silence.
> All dismounted, and the chiefs and principal men shook hands with us
> in token of friendship.

Hines was less informative about the outcome of discussions of the whipping system. He mentioned a meeting with chiefs less important than Ellis and Joseph during which it was discussed.

> The chiefs who were appointed through the influence of Dr. White were desirous that these regulations should continue. But the other influential men who were not in office desired to know of Dr. White of what benefit this whipping system was to be to them. They said they were willing it should continue, provided they were to receive blankets, shirts and pants, as a reward for being whipped. They had been whipped a good many times, and had got nothing for it.

III

At least seven hundred emigrants kept diaries of their crossing of the plains, and probably a great many more; that many, published and unpublished, existed a century after the great period of travel over the Oregon Trail. It would take a bold commentator to claim to have read them all, but even those published and fairly available reveal a change in tone before and after the cession of Oregon by the British in 1846. One change was that during the treaty of joint occupancy the hardships tended to be attributed to the weather and other natural causes; after the treaty was abrogated, the difficulties were often attributed to the departing British. Even more than the treaty, the Whitman massacre that followed in 1847 marked a dividing point in the tone of pioneer writing. The Whitman massacre, and the career of Dr. Whitman, accounted for more of early Northwestern literature than any other subject, but this work is concerned with overlooked or hidden aspects of Northwestern life rather than with those which shaped its image, as did the Whitman tragedy, and consequently will not follow the event in detail. A library of books and pamphlets did that, most of which, as Edmond Meany wrote, "charged the Catholics and the Hudson's Bay Company with having incited the Indians to their atrocious deeds." In outline, the event took place as follows. Late in 1847 Dr. Whitman was warned by a friendly Indian of a plot to murder him. There had been a good deal of sickness, rumors in the Indian country held him to be responsible, the presence of a Catholic mission nearby led to denominational discord, and Dr. McLoughlin advised Whitman to abandon his mission for a time for his own safety. Whitman refused. He spent the night of November 28, 1847, caring for a number of Indians who were sick, his home having become almost a hospital. The following morning he was discussing the illnesses with one Indian when another came up behind him and killed him with a blow of a tomahawk. During the day, at long intervals, ten people were butchered. Because there were captives as well as survivors, each killing was known in bloody detail. On the day following the first assault, two who had escaped were discovered and killed. A week later the Indians returned and killed two men in their sickbeds. Forty-three women and children were taken captive, the women brutally mistreated, and three young children died of exposure and neglect.

To the old gloom of the explorers' accounts of constant rain, and to the stoic dejection of the missionaries' records, there was now added a dark element of conspiracy and cunning. One example was a story that swept the Northwest that Peter Skene Ogden, on his deathbed, confessed that he had organized the massacre. Likewise it was believed that the priests at the Catholic mission had refused to admit a family that had escaped the slaughter and asked for refuge. William Gray's *History of Oregon* was discredited because of his intense bias against the Catholic Church after the massacre, with a loss to historical literature, for Gray, who had been a lay member with the first Whitman mission party, had been one of the organizers of the provisional government and had personally started the wolf meetings that preceded it. There was a new pattern in the emigrants' diaries. They began with a note of interest and excitement in the first entries as they started across the plains, an interest that grew to awe as they reported the immense herds of buffalo on the prairies or the wilderness of the Rockies, an awe that gave way to fear when they at last reached the promised land of Oregon and met the shock of stories of the massacre.

The diary of Mrs. Elizabeth Smith is typical of a progression found in many others. She left Indiana with her husband and seven children in April, 1847, and was 258 days on the way before she reached Portland. She was a keen observer, her animation evident in brief and sometimes searching passages. "June 22—Made 15 miles. See antelope every day. June 23—Made 18 miles. At present there is 140 persons in our company. We see thousands of buffalo. June 25—Made 18 miles. Our road is like a floor. June 29—This morning eight of our largest and best work oxen were missing, besides two yoke of Welch's, three yoke of Adam Polk's, and about 30 head belonging to the company. We hunted every direction without success." She reported baking bread, an accidental death, picking gooseberries, giving gifts to begging Indians, and noted places where the ground was so strong with lye that after a rain one could wash linen in the pools without soap. Her interests were domestic, and she savored the strangeness of the country while looking up from doing the laundry—"Here we have a good time for washing, which we women deem a great privilege"—or picking berries to add to her family meals at the foot of South Pass: "Passed over one mountain. Here we found some gooseberries, and they were as smooth as currants and tasted much like fox grapes. . . . Found some currants. Better than tame currants. They were yellow."

She was so interested, and had so little time, that she rose at night after the children were asleep and jotted down her diary entries by candlelight:

Aug. 1—Passed over the Rocky Mountains, the backbone of America. It is all rocks on top and they are split into pieces and turned up edgeways. Oh, that I had the time and talent to describe this curious country.

Part of the company turned aside to Whitman's mission, and some of these were later killed in the massacre. Mrs. Smith's party found the mountains beyond The Dalles closed by snow, so the wheels were taken off the wagons and they were placed on rafts for the remainder of the journey.

Nov. 1—Finds us still in trouble. Waves dashing over our raft and we are already stinting ourselves of provisions. My husband started this morning to find provisions. Left no man with us except my oldest boy. It is very cold. The icicles are hanging from our wagon bed to the water. Tonight about dusk Adam Polk expired. No one with him but his wife and myself. We sat up all night with him while waves were dashing below.

Nov. 18—My husband is sick. It rains and snows. We start this morning around the falls with our wagons. We have five miles to go. I carry my baby and lead, or rather carry another through snow, mud and water almost to my knees. When I got here I found my husband lying in Welch's wagon, very sick.

Nov. 19—My husband is sick and can have but little care. Rain all day.

Nov. 20—Rain all day.

Nov. 29—Landed at Portland, on the Willamette, 12 miles above the mouth, at 11 o'clock last night.

Nov. 30—Raining. This morning I ran about trying to get a house to get into with my sick husband. At last I found a small leaky concern with two families already in it. My children and I carried up a bed. I got some men to carry my husband up through the rain and lay him on it.

Jan. 15—My husband is still alive, but very sick. There is no medicine here except at Fort Vancouver, and the people there will not sell one bit.

Jan. 20—Cool and dry. Soldiers are collecting here from every part of Oregon to go and fight the Indians in middle Oregon in consequence of the massacre at Whitman's mission. I think there were 17 men killed at the massacre, but no women or children, except Whitman's wife. They killed every white man there except one, and he was an Englishman. They took all the young women for wives. Robbed them of their clothing and everything.

Feb. 1—Rain all day. This day my dear husband, my last remaining friend, died.

Feb. 2—Today we buried my earthly companion. Now I know what none but widows know, how comfortless is that of a widow's life, especially when left in a strange land, without money or friends, and the care of seven children. Cloudy.

Mrs. Smith survived; some emerging community spirit carried her along, together with the help of strangers and neighbors who were almost as much in need as she was. She married again, this time a farmer who had lost his wife, and raised two families as she lived to old age, a moderately prosperous and respected figure who was considered typical of the pioneer women. The presence of a background of emigrant literature, and even more the presence of a body of readers whose experiences, to some extent, paralleled those of Mrs. Smith, often made the more conscious literary productions of Oregon seem high-flown and unreal.

Dr. White's *Ten Years in Oregon* and Gustavus Hines's *Wild Life in Oregon* were published in the years that saw the publication of Melville's *Moby Dick*, Hawthorne's *The Scarlet Letter*, Dickens's *David Copperfield*; if nothing else they indicated what it meant to be writing in a world so far removed from the centers of culture. And yet in 1857, only three years after Margaret Bailey's *Grains*, James Gilchrist Swan wrote in *The Northwest Coast* a clear and candid report of the same world that remained readable and informative a century later; and only four years later Winthrop's *The Canoe and the Saddle* appeared, one of the finest adventure stories in the English language. In both these works some signs of a distinctive Northwestern literature could be said to appear, not so much in their content as in their authors' attitude toward existence, their recognition of human trials against a backdrop of scenic grandeur, their elemental democracy in the appraisal of men where class and social distinctions had been largely erased and, above all, their consciousness of the inapplicability of much of their literary background to the world in which they lived. One result was a habit of deliberate understatement, of perils recounted in a casual or even breezy manner, and not without notes of parody of the travelers' tales that were then stock literary fare, a practice that reached an extreme point in Winthrop's writing, where genuine dangers were recounted with a half-ironic self-consciousness so persistent that even when he was about to have his scalp lifted he was embarrassed to discover the experience was so much like the inferior literary accounts he had read of it.

James Gilchrist Swan was a member of an old Boston family, sea captains and booksellers and publishers being among his relatives. One of his kinspeople was the purser on the ship *Quatamozin*, of Boston, that ventured up the Columbia River in 1807, when David Thompson was building Kootenay House on the upper Columbia. In 1850 Swan was in San Francisco acting as an agent for Boston shipowners. An Indian chief named Chetzamokha, who became known as the Duke of York (and who became a character in *The Canoe and the Saddle*), arrived in San Francisco on a lumber schooner. The Indian was frightened and lonely in the city, and Swan befriended him and taught him English. After Chetzamokha returned to the Northwest, Swan was surprised to receive a beautiful Indian canoe sent by Chetzamokha on another ship in gratitude for Swan's kindness.

One of Swan's friends was Charles Russell, who made the mistake of investing in Pacific City, a nonexistent metropolis on the north side of the Columbia River near its mouth. Pacific City was the creation of Dr. Elijah White after events had removed him from his position of authority in Oregon. "He was the original town-site boomer of the Northwest," Edmond Meany wrote of White. "He plotted Pacific City, and began to sell lots to numerous dupes. He claimed his city had schoolhouses, handsome residences, and other attractions." (Dr. McNulty, the physician of the Pacific Mail Company and Winthrop's host at the time Winthrop got smallpox, was a salesman of Pacific City real estate.) As one of the victims of the Pacific City swindle, Russell left the site and moved a few miles north to Willapa Harbor, where he began rebuilding his fortune shipping oysters to California. The oysters were raked from the bottom of the bay at low tide and sold to traders who operated schooners racing back and forth to San Francisco. The price was around a dollar a basket over the side; each schooner carried around 2,000 baskets, paid for in gold on the spot, and shipments averaged about 50,000 baskets each season.

Swan accordingly sailed to the Northwest in 1852, at the age of thirty-four, and remained there until his death around the turn of the century. He did not prosper in the oyster trade, or in any of his later commercial ventures, but he became an accomplished naturalist, artist and map maker, as well as the author of the best and most lifelike account of the region and the times in *The Northwest Coast*. Swan contributed the material on Indians of the Northwest to Henry Schoolcraft's monumental study of North American Indians; he wrote papers for the Smithsonian Institution and other scientific agencies; he served in the national capital as the private secretary to Governor Stevens when the governor was in conflict with Jefferson Davis and Captain McClellan over the railroad route; he was a customs agent watching for Russian smugglers along the Olympic Peninsula. After he left Willapa Harbor, Swan settled at Port Townsend, the home of his old friend Chetzamokha, and by way of this connection, and his later duties as Indian agent at Neah Bay, he came to be the best-informed American on Indian life and to possess among the Coast tribes more influence than any individual before or after him.

The Northwest Coast is an excellent work, though flawed; its vivid scenes give way too often to guidebook reports of places, or extended quotations from less gifted writers than Swan himself. He excelled at accounts of fishing and duck shooting or paddling up unknown rivers. As he lived in one of the places with the heaviest rainfall, he became a masterly describer of weather:

> Now the storm raged fiercer, and was accompanied with thunder, and lightning and hail. This music of the elements increased from forte to fortissimo—accompanied with the crashing of the trees, which had been partially burned, on the cliff opposite, and were falling with a tremendous noise—till near midnight, when, the constant torrent of rain having loosened the chimney, it fell down with a crash; and at the instant a squall of wind whistled into the fireplace, blowing about a couple of bushels of coals and ashes into the middle of the room.

Swan did not complain about the weather. "It does not, as has been asserted," he said in passing, "rain without intermission." He rather individualized each storm:

> As night closed in the wind began to rise, and before I had reached half way home it blew violently, accompanied with a drizzling rain that served to nearly blind me, and it was with difficulty that I stumbled along over the trees and avalanche of earth that the storm had hurled down from the cliffs above. I had now to pass round a precipitous point which projected into the Bay, and around which the water was about two feet deep, although the tide was rapidly ebbing. The wind dashed the waves against this cliff so that the spray flew higher than my head, and wet me through. Suddenly I heard an uproar overhead, and felt a trembling of the earth, which plainly indicated a landslide. There I was, pinned between the cliff and the water, with no alternative but to wade along. At length down came a portion of the cliff behind me, and with a splash that completely covered me with muddy water. I did not know where it was coming next, but had every reason to believe the whole face of the cliff was falling.

The contrasting accounts of the Duke of York in Swan's book (and in other Northwest histories) and that in *The Canoe and the Saddle* suggest that Winthrop encountered the Indian at a low point in his career. But *The Canoe and the Saddle* is so distinctive a work that more than an ordinary degree of distinction is included in summarizing it. The action is concentrated into the ten days between August 21 and August 31, 1853. The narrative is limited to Winthrop's trip the length of Puget Sound and over the Cascades by horseback to the Columbia River. Winthrop did not tell the reader who he was, or how he happened to be in the Northwest, or what he was doing there. The geography was confusing to people who did not know the region, and the publisher, ordinarily more conscientious—he was James Fields, the discoverer of Hawthorne—neglected to provide a map and indeed, seemed a little uncertain as to where the Pacific Northwest was in relation to Boston.

Winthrop nowhere makes things easier for the reader. His approach was always elliptical, indirect, consciously unexpected. The strangeness and remoteness of the scene were compounded by Winthrop's use of Indian speech: he gave the conversations in the Indian language first, followed by a highly fanciful translation. Thus an old chief, bargaining for the services of his son to serve as Winthrop's guide, began a long palaver: "*Hale she cooocks nika tenas*; no breeches hath my son." Winthrop refuses to pay more. The old chief goes on: "*Pe halo shirt*; and no shirt." Winthrop is unmoved. "*Pe woka yaha shoes*," says the old chief; "and no shoes hath he." These bilingual exchanges are usually funny, sometimes grotesque, and also contain a note of literary commentary: they have a high-flown literary elegance that makes them, in effect, parodies of the lofty translations of the Greek and Roman classics of the time. But they scarcely contribute to the clarity of the action.

Winthrop could not escape topical allusions. The first of his books to be published after his death was *Cecil Dreeme*, a melodrama of society and high finance in New York. Its villain is Densdeth, cynical and worldly, a millionaire and Wall Street operator. Densdeth is a master at inducing vain and conservative merchants to join him in reckless ventures—railroad to nowhere, supported by enormous land grants—then eroding their position and self-respect by involving them in his own schemes to get the property at the expense of small investors. Densdeth is a social favorite who finds his way with mystifying ease into the lives of daughters of great families. He is a criminal, perhaps a murderer, but he is also personally powerful. "What does it mean," the young narrator asks himself, "this man's strange fascination? I begin to dread him. Will he master my will? What is this strange potency of his? . . . If I resist, I am my own man; if I yield, I am Densdeth's."

The original of Densdeth was William Henry Hurlbert, remembered principally for the many novels in which he appeared as a character, including Thomas Wentworth Higginson's *Malbone*. Hurlbert was a Southern-born graduate of Harvard Divinity School, the descendant of a military family—his brother became a famous Union general—who after being ordained as a minister left his church, was briefly a Catholic convert, and became famous as a sensational dramatist.

Hurlbert appears and reappears in the diaries of Winthrop's cousin, George Templeton Strong, during an agonizing period in which he attempted to blackmail the Strong family on the strength of indiscreet letters written by the wife of one of the members. During the Civil War Hurlbert became the chief editorial writer of the *New York World*. He was violently opposed to Lincoln, and in his tributes to McClellan went out of his way to praise what he called McClellan's magnificent accomplishment in exploring the Cascade Mountains. "The vast extent, the magnificent possibilities, the grand unity in variety of our great national dominions," Hurlbert wrote, "which are but sounding forms of work on the lips of so many a blatant orator, became simple realities to the intelligent American officer. . . ." Hurlbert survived the many attacks of novelists, lived down his lurid past, and as the editor of the *New York World* became renowned as a pillar of journalism.

In *John Brent,* the second of Winthrop's novels to be published, he returned to the West for such inspiration as the story possessed. The book is the prototype of innumerable Western novels, dramas, movies and television shows: it revolves around the friendship of a flawless and accomplished outdoorsman, John Brent, and the young narrator. In a sense the novel was an intellectualized version of the dime novels that were then beginning to appear. The episodes involve the rescue of an emigrant girl from Mormon kidnappers and the escape of a runaway slave. Jesse Applegate appears, thinly disguised as Armstrong of the Umpqua, in time to save the company in a moment of peril.

The narrator of *John Brent* buys a gold mine so unproductive he called it Damn Fool Owner Mine. He has a chance to sell it and does not want to admit it is known as the Fool Owner; he calls it the Fooloner. A legend of ancient Spanish diggings boosts the price of a mine, so the mine becomes the Don Fulano, an easy transition from Damn Fool Owner by way of Fooloner. Now in the oscillations in Winthrop's novels from farce to tragedy the narrator acquires a magnificent horse that he calls Don Fulano because the sale of the mine gave him money for the purchase. After Brent and the narrator help a runaway slave to escape, the horse is seized by the authorities to pursue the Negro, and as it is swimming a river the narrator shoots it to let the slave get away. *John Brent* was the only one of Winthrop's novels that could have been published in his lifetime. A publisher offered to bring it out if Winthrop would remove the scene of the shooting of the horse, but Winthrop refused to do so.

These books were almost dime novels, but Winthrop's sardonic humor would not let them remain only that. Casual jokes and current topics pop in and out of the melodrama. One favorite subject was family pride. The hero of Winthrop's novel *Mr. Waddy's Return* is one Ira Waddy, the last holder of a great New England name, whose venerated ancestor, the first Ira Waddy, had come over on the *Mayflower*. He was the ship's cook. He put too much pepper in Miles Standish's soup. The result was a family curse that haunted each generation of Waddys. "My father rather scoffs at these old legends," says the aristocratic Boston heroine of the novel, when the last surviving Waddy confesses the family secret and, in spite of it, asks her to marry him.

Winthrop's inventiveness was tumultuous and uncontrolled; conversations become distractions in the exchanges of puns and parodies of prevailing literary clichés; characterizations are blurred by momentary impulsive comments that were generated by the intellectual interests at the time he wrote rather than by the drive and direction of the story he was trying to tell. When Winthrop started east after his Northwestern adventure, he felt a sinking of heart. "I feared I was retreating from the future into the past," he wrote, and insofar as he was leaving the scene of a great native drama that was still to be written for a scene so familiar that he wasted his time trying to rework it, that was what he was doing. The novels that he later wrote of New York society always seemed to be incomplete, and with all that they reveal of the gifts and the promise of their author they suggest even more a lack of direction, or the absence of something that would have checked their ceaseless drift with the crosscurrents of immediate intellectual interests. "Nothing is so easy as improvisation," Henry James wrote, "the running on and on of invention. . . ." and Winthrop's inventions ran on at the expense of everything else. The wit of his comments that seemed so alert in their own time, when what they opposed or ricocheted from was commonly understood, was lost as new interests arose in the literary world to supplant those he parodied; his novels were dated as soon as they appeared.

If Winthrop had wanted only the approval of the literary crowd, there would have been no loss in his concentration on the kind of subjects they understood. But his purpose was serious; even in *Cecil Dreeme* he was trying to show the corruption of society, and in fact the novel at its best reveals a knowledge of shadowed areas in social life that could only be guessed at by people not of Winthrop's social position. But he lacked some sense of a common human reality outside the sophisticated world he described. His character modeled on Jesse Applegate was a cardboard cutout compared to Applegate himself. He made only one passing reference in a letter to the emigrant women—"always captivated talking of the trip across the plains, which almost all the Oregon women have made"—and nowhere showed an understanding of what had been involved in that experience. One turns with relief from so much wasted literary artifice to the artless honesty of the emigrant journals. Sometimes it is not too much to see foreshadowings of a new civilization coming into being, and new habits of thought and life, in their records of infinite casual kindness and the habit of mutual assistance engrained as a normal part of community life.

IV

In 1862, a year before *The Canoe and the Saddle* was published, Mrs. Frances Fuller Victor and her husband moved from New York to Sacramento, California, but within two years they settled in Portland, Oregon, where Mrs. Victor began a lifelong study of the history of the Northwest. Almost all Northwestern histories stem from the work of this remarkable woman. She was born in Rome, New York, on May 23, 1826, the first of five daughters, and her literary career began when she was a fourteen-year-old student in a girls' school in Wooster, Ohio. Her sister, Metta Victoria Fuller, four years younger, was even more precocious. Both girls became locally known for their verse published in newspapers, but Metta at fifteen wrote a full-length novel, *The Last Days of Tul, a Romance of the Lost Cities of Yucatan*, which was published by a Boston firm in 1847.

Meanwhile the poetry of both girls appeared in national magazines, and as literary prodigies they became known as the Sisters of the West, in emulation of the sisters Alice and Phoebe Cary of the Eastern seaboard, whose poetry was better but who were a good deal older. Metta Fuller attracted the attention of Nat Willis, then editing the *Home Journal*, and he serialized her second novel, *The Tempter*, in which she carried on the story of Sue's *The Wandering Jew*. After it became "a decided literary sensation," the sisters moved to New York. Metta was seventeen and Frances was twenty-one years old. They were attractive girls. Rufus Griswold, the anthologist and tireless screener of all new talent, became their sponsor for a time, publishing their joint work, *Poems of Sentiment and Imagination*. At that particular moment in literary affairs the Astor Place riot and the Forrest divorce case had brought the intellectuals into uncomfortable public attention, and the Fuller sisters promised to bring a fresh note of youthful simplicity to the scene.

The Sisters of the West did not make it with the literary crowd, even though Metta's third novel, *The Senator's Son*, went through ten printings and sold another 30,000 copies in England. Their parents had settled in Pontiac, Michigan, and after two years in New York the girls rejoined them there, later settling on their own in Ypsilanti. While Frances lived with her parents, Metta married a Dr. Morse, who vanished from her life sometime in the next five years. In 1853 in Pontiac Frances married a man named Jackson Barritt, who presently vanished from her life also.

Both sisters continued to write through this unclear period, but they no longer cultivated the literary world. Metta contributed to *The Saturday Evening Post*, wrote cookbooks and romances under the pseudonym of Rose Kennedy, and sensational novels, such as *Fashionable Dissipations* and *Mormon Wives*, under her own name. Her most popular book was *Maum Guinea; or Christmas Among the Slaves*, widely publicized by claims, never verified, that Abraham Lincoln liked it.

In 1856 Metta married Orville Victor, a reserved, austere editor whose scholarly manner gave no outward indication of a drive comparable to that of a captain of industry. Victor was born in Sandusky, Ohio, in 1827. He studied at the seminary in Norwalk, Ohio, and gained some notice as a poet. In 1851, at twenty-four, he became the editor of the *Sandusky Daily Register*, which had been bought by Henry Cooke, a native of Sandusky, the younger brother of Jay Cooke, the financier and backer of the Northern Pacific Railway; Jay Cooke put up part of the money for the purchase of the newspaper.

Metta wrote for her husband's paper for two years. Victor had also become the editor of the *Cosmopolitan Art Journal*, which was somewhat mysteriously published in both New York City and in Sandusky. In 1858 the couple moved to New York, but on this occasion the situation was not what it had been when Metta and Frances were known as the Sisters of the West. They were now both working journalists. The firm of Beadle and Adams had moved from Buffalo to New York, and in December, 1858, Metta became the editor of its magazine, called *The Home*. Frances was also a writer and editor with the publishing house, though her relationship with it was less clear. Orville Victor began as a writer, with a life of Garibaldi, but presently was fully occupied as the firm's chief editor, a position he retained from 1861 to 1897.

The growth of the firm began with the publication of *Seth Jones*, the work of Edward Ellis, a twenty-year-old schoolteacher in Red Bank, New Jersey, who modeled his Indian stories on the works of James Fenimore Cooper but kept them short. The book was so sensationally popular that it began the boom in dime novels that lasted more than three decades. There were never enough good adventure stories, and Orville Victor's contribution to American culture was to find people who could write some sort of fast-moving tale without being concerned whether it was good or bad, so long as it kept moving and so long as it pleased an undemanding audience of young readers. He published the works of well-known writers such as Mayne Reid and Joseph Ingraham, the author of *The Prince of the House of David*, but his major innovation was to develop heretofore unpublished authors from all walks of life: farmers, carpenters, sailors, adventurers, housewives, schoolteachers, physicians, restaurant operators, telegraphers, actors, lawyers, clergymen, soldiers and common laborers. He paid them well for the time, usually $75 to $100 for a novel. In this way he accumulated a stable of bright and capable people who could turn out their short novels, a hundred pages or so, in a few days or a week, and who were uninhibited by common sense or elementary probabilities in their stories. Victor maintained a high standard of narrative speed in the dime novels, and he demanded a lot of dialogue, usually in a dialect found nowhere else on earth; he kept on hand a staff of artists who could produce vivid, grotesque and generally imaginative illustrations; and he kept up a schedule of weekly publication that was not equaled until mass-produced magazines flourished three quarters of a century later. Almost all the heroes of dime novels—Deadwood Dick, Buffalo Bill, Texas Jack, Wild Bill and even Frank Merriwell—were the creations of writers Victor hired.

Frances's second marriage was to Victor's younger brother, Lieutenant Henry Clay Victor, an engineer in the Navy, soon after the start of the Civil War. He was transferred to the Pacific Coast in 1863, and she followed him there, writing for San Francisco and Sacramento newspapers. At the end of 1863 he resigned his commission, and when the Civil War ended, the couple were in Portland. It is possible that work for Orville Victor had something to do with her presence there.

The firm of Beadle and Adams published many books about the Northwest. The first of these was *Our New States and Territories: Oregon and Washington*, by Albert Richardson, which appeared in 1866. Richardson had been the chief war correspondent of the *New York Herald*, in which capacity he also worked as a spy for the Northern army. He was the first reporter to recognize Grant's genius, and Grant's first biographer. Captured at Vicksburg, Richardson spent a year in a Confederate prison and after his escape wrote *The Secret Service, the Field, the Dungeon and the Escape*, another enormously popular book.

Richardson's interest in the Northwest—if, indeed, he ever felt any, for he had never been there—was very brief. He had fallen in love with Mrs. Daniel McFarland, a prominent actress who was the wife of a Tammany politician in New York, and about the time *Our New*

States and Territories was published, Mrs. McFarland divorced her
husband to marry Richardson. On the day the divorce was granted,
McFarland charged into Richardson's office and shot him. The writer
lingered for some time, and the Reverend Henry Ward Beecher performed the ceremony that united him to the former Mrs. McFarland
on what proved to be his deathbed, Richardson dying when the wed-
ding was over.

Meanwhile, in Portland, Mrs. Victor had become associated with
Joe Meek, the former mountain man, and her relations with this legendary figure in Northwest history influenced her view of its past, and
perhaps shaped dime novels as well, as he became the prototype of
the heroic trappers and Indian fighters who figured in them. Her husband was lost at sea, and Mrs. Victor made no attempt to conceal
her fascination with this huge, bearded, outspoken frontiersman, with
his fine appearance and buoyant temper, his courage and his personal
knowledge of historic events and people. Meek was a great ladies' man
and, after his long years in the wilderness and his many affairs with
Indian girls, was fascinated with white women. He was also a fine
storyteller. He was not bashful, she said, and told her his stories "in
his soft, slow, yet smooth and firm utterances, with many a merry
twinkle in his mirthful dark eyes."

Meek was born in Virginia of slave-owning parents in 1810. He
spent his boyhood playing with Negro children in the slave quarters.
He rarely went to school and was sixteen before he learned to read.
At eighteen he left home and wound up trapping beaver in the Rockies. He became a partner of William Sublette, another historic figure,
though Meek was associated at one time or another with Joseph
Walker, Ewing Young and most of the celebrated mountain men. He
remained in the wilderness, making fewer trips to civilization than
most of them; it was eight years after he entered the mountains before
he tasted bread again.

Meek reached Oregon in 1840. He told Mrs. Victor that he moved
there because beaver were becoming scarce in the Rockies. In any
event he was one of a number of former trappers who, like Ewing
Young, arrived when the missionary movement was struggling for its
life. He had the good-natured contempt of a veteran Indian fighter
for the missionaries' hope of civilizing the Indians. For years he had
been with the American trappers in the Rockies who were opposing,
forestalling, baiting or dodging parties of British trappers (often with
Peter Skene Ogden in charge on the opposite side) and who were
sometimes believed to be trying to provoke conflict to involve the
two governments. Meek consequently had little interest in British
and American cooperation under the treaty of joint occupancy. These

two questions—the education of the Indians and the relations of British subjects and American citizens—were the crucial ones before the people of Oregon. On both matters Mrs. Victor absorbed Meek's views. "Joint occupancy was a polite word," she wrote, "masking a Hudson's Bay monopoly." But she was too intelligent and appreciative to accept Meek's prejudices and said of the British in the Northwest: "fine foes, the author firmly believes them to have been in those days, yet foes nevertheless."

Meek was the American who called for a division at the meeting at Champoeg that voted to establish the provisional government. He guided the Wilkes Exploring Expedition. He led a rescue party after the Whitman massacre, and he also raced to Washington to plead with President Polk for help for the Oregon country after the massacre, wangling $7,400 from the President. His name, signed with a beautiful penmanship remarkable for a man who learned to read at sixteen, validated the census returns of 1850, since he was the United States marshal. There was surely something askew in Meek's life story, perhaps most strikingly evident in his naming his half-Indian daughters after the heroines of the novels of Sir Walter Scott, and it was not surprising that Mrs. Victor, with an intellectual curiosity added to her emotional interest, set herself to write it.

She called her biography *The River of the West*, a misleading title, for most of the book deals with Meek's mountain adventures before he reached Oregon. She told much of the story in Meek's own words as he told them to her. She paraphrased long sections of his recollections, and she introduced dialogues, such as conversations between Meek and Sublette, or between Meek and President Polk, in which all the parties talked like characters in dime novels. She informed the reader that she had a hard time keeping Meek on a subject. He came to her home and she prepared to take notes. "Tell me about a buffalo hunt," she said. He started, but he soon wandered far afield. Meek had known many Indian women, in addition to the seven he married. Each Indian wife was more beautiful than the last. One of them was the wife of his partner Sublette. Meek took her over when Sublette was injured. She bore Meek a daughter. Then she herself was killed by Indians. Mrs. Victor probed endlessly for the details of Meek's love life. She wanted to know what each wife had been like. One in particular, one who wanted to return to her own people—why had she wanted to leave him? Why did the Indians kill Sublette's ex-wife? She did not get satisfactory answers. "The writer of this veracious history," she said, "has never been able to obtain a full and particular record of our hero's earliest love adventures."

She sometimes gives the impression of wanting to disclose her own love adventures, stopping just short of informing the general reader of the details of her relationship with Joe Meek. Sometimes she idealizes him. In other passages she is fretful and complaining. In the middle of an admiring chapter she might insert cutting comments about his bragging and his crude conduct. Once he told her about a harmless Digger Indian he had killed. (He had killed many Indians in fights over trapping grounds or women, but this was unprovoked and took place without a struggle.) Why had he done it? Well, the Indian looked as though he might at some future time disturb one of Meek's beaver traps. He had not done so, but he looked as though he might. So Meek shot and killed him. But Meek insisted that he had scruples. He was once present when Joseph Walker's band killed twenty unarmed Indians who were cultivating a garden, and he took no part in the slaughter. "I didn't belong to that crowd," he said. "I sat on a fence and saw it, though. It was a shameful thing."

She was jealous of him. She was jealous of the Indian women he had known before her, and she was even jealous of Mrs. Narcissa Whitman because of Meek's admiration of her. In *The River of the West* she stepped aside from the narrative to repeat something of what Meek told her of his meeting with Mrs. Whitman. He had been in the wilderness a long time when he came to the Whitman mission. Dr. Whitman was away, and Meek could not keep his eyes off the frail, beautiful, fair-skinned young wife as she busied herself around the house, blushing at his attentions, a scene that Mrs. Victor could imagine vividly, and which might even have suggested scandal, had Mrs. Whitman not been so venerated as a noble, heroic and tragic figure. But in spite of her feminine quirks Mrs. Victor soon acquired a knowledge of Northwestern history that no one of her time could equal. When Hubert Howe Bancroft operated his history-writing factory in San Francisco, she became an editor and the principal writer of his staff. Bancroft published the books of his authors under his own name. He sold his books by subscription before publication, offering various editions and bindings at prices ranging from $175 to $350 a set, the purchasers of the higher-priced editions receiving, in addition to the many volumes, the satisfaction of finding their ancestors praised in all the editions.

Mrs. Victor wrote the entire text of Bancroft's *History of Oregon*, a meticulously detailed two-volume work, and all of Bancroft's *History of Washington, Idaho and Montana*. She wrote much of the seven-volume work published as Bancroft's *History of California*, and she contributed extensively to his histories of Texas, New Mexico and Arizona. Meanwhile, in New York, the dime-novel writers were running out of locales and subjects for their books, and Oregon became a favorite setting for their stories because of the factual background she provided.

None of Orville Victor's many authors knew anything about the Oregon country at first hand. *The Lost Cache, a Tale of Hid Treasure,* the first dime novel of Oregon, appeared early in 1866. It was laid in the Blue Mountains of Oregon, in mythical goldfields, and was signed by J. Stanley Henderson. The story concerned three separate parties searching for the same gold cache. Albert Johannsen, in *The House of Beadle and Adams,* a work so carefully researched that it is impossible to write anything about dime novels without drawing on it, identified J. Stanley Henderson as Edward Willett, editor of the *Brooklyn Daily Eagle.*

The second was *Sol Ginger, the Giant Trapper, or the Flower of the Blackfeet,* dealing with Old Sol, the giant trapper (who surely suggested Joe Meek), a story laid in Elk City, Oregon, published in 1869. The author was given as Lewis W. Carson. Mr. Johannsen's researches established that Carson was the pen name of Albert Aiken, an actor who turned out several dime novels laid in Oregon, between his theatrical engagements.

The third apparently was *The Phantom Princess, or Ned Hazel, the Boy Trapper,* laid in Washington Territory near the Canadian border and signed Captain James Fenimore Cooper Adams. This was one of many pen names used by Edward Ellis, whose *Seth Jones* started the dime-novel industry on its way. *The Phantom Princess* was part of a whole series laid in Oregon that included *Nick Whiffles Pet, or In the Valley of Death,* as well as *The Blackfoot Queen, or Old Nick Whiffles in the Valley of Death.* Under the name of Charles La Salle, Ellis also wrote *Burt Bunker, the Trapper, a Tale of the Northwest Hunting Grounds,* and as Bruin Adams he was the author of *Little Rifle, the Boy Trapper, or the Young Hunters of Oregon.*

In one six-month period in the fall and winter of 1873 and early 1874 dime novels laid in Oregon appeared at the rate of one a month. *Rattling Dick, the Mountain Outlaw, or the Mystery of Diamond Gulch,* a tale of kidnapping near the border between Oregon and California, was followed by *The Antelope Boy, or Smokeholler, the Medicine Man,* a story involving ventriloquism and Indian lore, laid on the Yakima River. It was signed Bernard Clyde, which was one of the pen names of George Aiken, a well-known New York playwright, the older brother of Albert Aiken. George Aiken made his place in American theatrical history with his adaptations of *Uncle Tom's Cabin* and *The Old Homestead.*

Next came *The Spy Squaw, or the Rangers of the Lava Beds,* concerning the Modoc Indian war of California, signed by Charles How-

ard. Howard was really Thomas Harbaugh, a house painter of
Casstown, Ohio, who abandoned his trade when his books sold, and
who turned out some thirty volumes, including others laid in the
Northwest, such as *Fighting Fred, or the Castaways of Grizzly Camp,*
set in the Cascades of Washington.

The Pacific Northwest was an ideal locale for the tireless hacks who
wrote dime novels. Oregon was so far removed from the world of dime-
novel readers that factual accuracy was not necessary, and the reputation of the region was such that almost anything said about it would
be believed. Roger Starbuck, who began his Northwestern books with
*Kentucky Ben, the Long Rifle of the Cascades, or the Boy Trappers
of Oregon,* pioneered in setting his tales on the Olympic Peninsula
of Washington, about which almost nothing was then known by the
general public, with his *Oregon Josh, the Wizard Rifle,* having to do
with the rivalry of British and American trappers for the furs of the
region, and with *Hunter-Pard Ben, or the Wakash's Blind Lead,*
doubtless the first fiction to be located near Mount Olympus. Starbuck
was really Augustus Comstock, a former sailor on whaling vessels.

Edward Wheeler's *Sealskin Sam, the Sparkler, or the Tribunal of
Ten, a Tale of the Mines,* was laid in some vague terrain in Washington Territory, and Wheeler also took Deadwood Dick into the
Northwest in *Deadwood Dick's Danger Ducks, or the Owls of Oregon,*
a part of the Deadwood Dick series that became one of the most
valuable properties of dime-novel art. But one of the most unlikely
figures in the gallery of dime-novel authors was William Manning.
He was a descendant of an old family of Salem, Massachusetts; Nathaniel Hawthorne's mother was Betsy Manning. William Manning
lived in Staten Island in New York and devoted much of his life to
compiling a lengthy book, *The Genealogical and Biographical History
of the Manning Families of New England.* While laboring on it, he
supported himself by writing dime novels, several with Northwestern
settings, including *Hotspur Hugh, or the Banded Brothers of Giant's
Army,* and *Texas Tartar, the Man with Nine Lives,* laid in the Columbia River and on the border with British Columbia.

Mrs. Frances Victor wrote no dime novels; her writings inspired them.
The eleven years she spent doing Bancroft's historical work fixed the
permanent concept of the past of the region. The period of time she
had to deal with was brief. Many of the leading figures from the early
days were still alive when she wrote. She hunted up the survivors on
their isolated farms. She pieced together the history of tiny settlements
as well as of cities, carefully assigning to each homesteader his precise
place in the order of arrivals in Oregon. She covered Indian wars, mission disputes, Hudson's Bay Company history, mining, agriculture,

transportation, exploration and education, and to round things off she acquired an impressive knowledge of Northwestern trees, berries, plants, animals and fish, sometimes pleasantly intermingling scientific information with her own experiences in planting and raising flowers.

Because of the microscopic detail in her books, the names of so many landowners, the detail of the biographies, the attendance at political meetings, the specific sequences in Indian troubles or religious disputes, history was recorded in the region as it was nowhere else, and documented with the thoroughness of papers in a lawsuit. Almost no independent history writing was done after Mrs. Victor's books appeared; later writers simply amplified and expanded what she had written. Such scrupulous historians as Charles Carey, in his *General History of Oregon*, published in 1936, repeated again and again in summarizing complex situations that Mrs. Victor's book "may be relied on for general reference." Even Bancroft wrote that in "heavy as well as light branches of literature . . . she stands unapproached among the female authors of the Pacific Coast." Alfred Powers in his history of Oregon literature said of her:

> She was poor and widowed and kinless and childless. . . . Oregon historians have for half a century taken her vast beneficences for granted, and have not turned aside in warmth and gratitude for tribute or a biography. In life she gave much and received little. After her death the complacency of acceptance has largely continued. . . . She was the perfect observer, living quietly and moving unobtrusively in a colorful and historic land, all of which she saw, and all of which she knew.

Not only professional historians quarried her books. The popular studies of the Northwest, David Lavender's *The Land of Giants*, Archie Binns's *The Roaring Land*, Nard Jones's *Evergreen Land*, Henry Lenoir Davis's novel *Honey in the Horn*, the logging stories of Stewart Holbrook and the Puget Sound histories of Murray Morgan, took off from the historical base she established. And in fact it was almost impossible to write of any aspect of the Northwest without being in her debt; she had been there before.

Bancroft himself was not remembered warmly. With his tremendous acquisitive drive and energy he roamed through the Oregon country, picking up diaries, deeds, letters, documents and papers of all sorts, promising to return them when his histories were finished and never remembering to do so. Mrs. Victor said that his actual rewriting and editing were irresponsible, which seems to have been the case. Far from refining his original versions of his books, Bancroft added comments so coarse and irrelevant she was ashamed to think of them. In one famous passage in *History of Oregon*, where she had patiently unearthed the troubles of the emigrants in 1841, Bancroft added a sentence: "Men are such preposterous pigs!" so foreign to her own way of thought, and so violently at odds with her feeling about the pioneers, that she could only excuse it as his effort to add what she called chic to the narrative. Such additions might startle the reader, she admitted, but "in my humble opinion they add nothing to the value of history."

The value of history was in the knowledge of human affairs it communicated for its measure of guidance in what would otherwise be only and forever the unreflecting stir around us. The laws were real, as inescapable as the law of gravitation; actions had consequences, and if we tried to avoid knowledge of past happenings to liberate ourselves for activities in the present, we only prepared for those unacknowledged consequences to take their toll of us. The recording of history was no more than the most exact relation of what had been. But historians were as human as the subject of their studies, and Mrs. Victor was the most human and feminine of historians.

It was only by accident that the amount of work that she had done became known. Bancroft's operations scandalized historians (among them Henry Adams, who exposed him in *The North American Review*) and he became irritated at reports that Mrs. Victor had contributed a great deal to his books. He was vain and foolish enough to publish an account disparaging her and praising his own accomplishments, claiming that Mrs. Victor merely prepared rough factual outlines for the books which he then wrote. She replied with a detailed accounting of the precise extent of her labors. She was a far better writer than Bancroft, and she knew it; her pride of craftsmanship was outraged, and she wrote to defend it, rather than in the hope of benefiting from the books.

She did not benefit. When her work with Bancroft ended, she was without resources. Her sister Metta died in 1885, the dime-novel business ended a few years later, and Orville Victor, who would not allow his authors to use typewriters because he feared they would lower the quality of dime-novel prose (he really thought it was high), spent his last years selling insurance. Frances Victor supported herself in Oregon selling face cream and toilet articles from door to door. But this was Oregon, and presently it was recollected that a great historical researcher was ringing doorbells. She began a new career and worked her way back from extreme poverty, writing articles and guidebooks and lecturing in different communities about their past. She continued to collect information, extraordinarily detailed, on each town, mine, salmon cannery or other enterprise in the Northwest, up to the time she died, at the age of seventy-five, in a boardinghouse in Portland.

There were contradictions in her books. Some of these were the result of Bancroft's editing, she said, but more deeply they came from a suspension of judgment in the face of such physical reality as Meek meant for her. Scrupulous as was her documentation of the trials of the missionaries, she could not escape a sort of feminine contempt for them—their foolish quarrels with one another, their querulous appeals for help, their lack of aggressive leadership, their grabbiness for personal financial security when the missionary movement began to fail. Her reports of Joe Meek's fights with grizzlies and with Indians were written with zest and were not bettered by the dime-novel writers who stole her stories. She described such fights without critical comment. An ambush of white men by Indians, or a massacre of Indians by white men, were happenings like facts of nature. So she accepted the reality of Indian warfare as an unpreventable fact of American experience, totally ignoring that the great dream of the missionaries in Oregon was to prevent what had happened everywhere else from happening there. As hidden as she was behind the screen of Bancroft's authorship, she did more to shape the national view of the Northwest than any other writer except Irving. Her labors and her resiliency and her political sophistication were unaccountable in any other way than as expressions of genius, incomplete and ill-proportioned though the final works were. Yet with all one's sense of awe at her work and her learning there remains a sense of perplexity as well, and a question of what the history of the Northwest might have been—the works of history, that is, not the events themselves—if dime novels had never been written.

V

Frances Victor did not experience the gnawing concern of writers who came after her: their distance from the centers of culture in the Eastern states. The feeling that they were out of things was strong enough among literary men, but it was more clearly evident in the lives of Northwestern musicians. The first piano did not reach Vancouver until 1846, and in 1861 John Minto, an English-born sheep rancher and legislator, wrote the first Northwestern native composition, "The Oregon Farmer," which he introduced to the public by singing it himself at the first Oregon State Fair. A band appeared the next year. A German communist colony was established at Aurora on the banks of the Pudding River not far from Portland, the band was so much in demand it became one of the colony's most profitable assets. One member, Henry Theophilus Finck, summed up more than anyone else the dilemma of Northwestern searchers for culture; he idealized his Oregon childhood (all except its music), and in his later years, when he was a power in New York musical circles as the music critic of the *New York*

Evening Post, he remembered the joys of swimming in the Pudding River, the thrill of climbing Mount Hood, the intoxication with the Chinook winds, with a vividness never found in his harsh critical writing. He pictured an almost idyllic pioneer world that seemed to have everything but the power to inspire its artists.

His story was more typical than he seemed to realize. For every intellectual like Frances Victor who left the East to work in Oregon, a dozen went the other way. Homer Davenport, the great cartoonist of the *New York Evening Journal,* who was born in Silverton, Oregon, in 1867—nationally famous after his deadly pictures of Mark Hanna, covered with dollar signs, symbolizing the Trusts—looked back on his old home in *The Country Boy.* It seemed unbelievable. "I never saw so many picnics," he wrote, "and never went with so many pretty girls, and the ball games ran all through the summer." But Finck was more representative than Davenport. There were no ball games in his childhood. There was music at home, string quartets playing Haydn and Mozart, and band music at fairs and political rallies, the blare and rattle of which he hated, but still more powerfully there was the music of his imagination. When his father told him of hearing sixty-five musicians playing a Mozart overture, the mere thought of it overwhelmed him and made him fearful that he would never hear anything comparable. His own household was "an oasis in the howling wilderness of surrounding unmusicality," but he was possessed by what he called an almost insane longing to hear the great orchestras and the great symphonies that seemed hopelessly remote.

He heard them. Perhaps he heard too much, for he became known during his forty-three years as a critic for his stringent criticism and his savage attacks on performers, from Adelina Patti to Walter Damrosch, who did not come up to his exacting standard or who had otherwise irritated him. His first shock in the East was the appearance of Harvard itself: "It would have been impossible to find a more uninteresting, dreary locality for a university." He found himself looking around him for the sight of mountains. He walked and walked, expecting to find country, and reached only more suburbs. But music brought him many friends. Henry Wadsworth Longfellow's nephew lived in his hall, and after Christmas dinner with the poet's family, Finck was often in the Longfellow home, playing duets with his daughter. Longfellow treated him graciously, asking questions about Oregon, and Finck told him about "the wholesale slaughter of splendid trees." Finck and his musical friends began to play at the home of Oliver Wendell Holmes and William Dean Howells, and he became a favorite of Professor Charles Eliot Norton as well. After Finck graduated with the class of 1876, Howells assigned him to write about the Wagner

Festival at Bayreuth for the *Atlantic Monthly*, and thereafter Finck's career developed with almost dreamlike ease.

He soon knew everyone he wanted to know: Paderewski, Lillian Nordica, Ernestine Schumann-Heink, Fritz Kreisler, Geraldine Farrar, Mary Garden, Maria Jeritza, Caruso, as well as wealthy patrons of music such as Henry Villard. He gradually became a compulsive name-dropper: Mark Twain, his fellow critic James Huneker, Julian Hawthorne—anyone with a name. He admitted that he liked the power his position gave him. He was known as the critic who observed that a concert was not worth a paragraph and then devoted a column to attacking it. When the Metropolitan Opera House in New York was hastily built—he said it was because the newly rich society people were tired of waiting for boxes at the Academy of Music—he compared it to a warehouse or a prison. The *Evening Post* faced damage suits because of his slashing attacks on pianists who performed on pianos which Finck believed were inferior to those made by his friend William Steinway. He experienced no remorse if some temperamental artist was shattered by one of his articles. He enjoyed it. He believed it did the victim good. With satisfaction he reported that after an exceptionally adverse review of Jeritza's performance in *Thaïs* a friend found the great singer, tears streaming down her features, sobbing, "He is right! He is right!"

It was a heady existence for a boy from the Pudding River country of Oregon. Finck returned to the Northwest occasionally, where his brother Edward had become a composer of such pieces as "The Albany Oregon Gavotte," and "The Ashland Oregon Schottische," and he even wrote a guidebook about the scenery visible on railroad routes, but his interests were in the musical capitals of Europe. He was an outspoken admirer of many full-bosomed opera stars, each enjoying favorable reviews for a period before another star replaced her—"a born sensualist," he explained himself simply, "if there ever was one."

He was inclined to doubt that the sensualists of preceding ages amounted to much. In a bold venture into philosophy that might almost have been a burlesque of Winthrop's prophecy that new systems of thought would arise in the Northwest, Finck wrote *Romantic Love and Personal Beauty*, a two-volume work in which he applied the notion of progress and the theory of evolution to human love and lovemaking. He argued that love had progressed slowly from very crude beginnings to a high modern plane that was splendidly satisfactory, and of which previous lovers had been entirely ignorant. At times he skirted close to the character of the modern discoveries in lovemaking, but he never specifically described wherein it bettered the practices stumbled upon by accident in the past. He rather argued negatively, disparaging the famous love stories from antiquity and Biblical times and the medieval world, and he displayed considerable skill in writing about such a matter as homosexuality in ancient Greece without actually mentioning it. There were glimmers of sense in his book, which William James praised rather nervously, especially in his point on the relation between love and equality, and the impossibility of true love between men and women in the ancient world when women had been slaves. But such glimmers of sense were quickly blotted out by his elaborate catalogs, perhaps written to burlesque scientific works, in which he enumerated the beauties of women of different countries and races—feet, hands, noses, eyes, ears, legs, mouths, approaching, but never actually coming to grips with, other organs—and concluded that American women surpassed all others in all that he listed.

There were, of course, literary creations more responsible than dime novels or highbrow nonsense in the literary heritage of the Northwest. But we have been occupied with overlooked or neglected aspects of the cultural life of the region. A more official roster of recognized Northwest writers would include others: Ella May Higginson of Bellingham, Washington, whose sentimental poetry had moments of tranquil lyricism; Frederic Homer Balch, a minister who died in 1891 at the age of thirty after writing *The Bridge of the Gods,* a legend of the falling of an immense natural bridge that once spanned the Columbia; Joaquin Miller, a poet, showman and self-advertiser of ability, famous in his own time for *The Danites in the Sierras,* a melodrama dealing with a secret police force of the Mormons; Eva Emery Dye, the author of a violently partisan biography, *McLoughlin and Old Oregon;* John Reed, the son of wealthy Portland pioneers, whose impassioned *Ten Days That Shook the World* was one of the first eyewitness accounts of the Bolshevik Revolution in Russia; Edwin Markham, born in Oregon City in 1852, a poet known for "The Man with the Hoe"; Charles Erskine Scott Wood, an Army lieutenant in the Indian country of Oregon, author of *The Poet in the Desert* and *Heavenly Discourse;* Mary Caroline Davies, a Portland poet of graceful and generally light verse; James Stevens, a former logger, who wrote *Paul Bunyan,* a literary version of logging folklore, at the urging of H. L. Mencken; H. L. Davis, born in Jesse Applegate's old settlement at Yoncalla, Oregon, whose *Honey in the Horn* was a conscious attempt to use Northwestern history in a realistic novel; Vernon Parrington, a University of Washington professor who spent twenty years on his *Main Currents in American Thought.*

The work of such authorities as these, the recognized writers of the Northwest, nevertheless had something in common with the neglected, the forgotten, or the overlooked with which we have been concerned. Neither possesses any sharply defined characteristics that identify them as belonging to the region. A century after Winthrop's prophecy that a new civilization must inevitably come into being in this favored land, the one characteristic of its culture was that it had no distinguishing features that set it apart. The local contributions that were made in almost every field, in architecture, painting, in music or fiction, or even in contributions to government, were in the same patterns as those of the rest of the United States. There was nothing in the Northwest remotely like the regional quality which, however modified, could still be recognized as belonging to New England; still less were there distinctive usages like those that remained a part of the culture of the South, or the traces of Spanish inheritance that persisted even during the growth and changes in the desert country of California and the Southwest. No distinctive patterns evolved in the structure of Northwestern society, and in the lighter aspects of native culture, accents, speech, phrases, foods and costumes there were no exceptional features either: no Northwesterner would wear the sombreros that set apart the Texans celebrated in J. Frank Dobie's many books, or cultivate accents which, real or acquired, flavored Southern speech, or use the twangy country phrases that were supposed to be found among the hillbillies of Tennessee. No, the Northwesterner tried to be as much as possible like everyone else, only more so.

One result was that Northwestern writers experienced an unusual problem of identification, as though they were natives of an intellectual abstraction rather than a region. In *The Waist-High Culture* Thomas Griffith, a former Seattle police reporter who became the editor of *Life*, apologized for beginning his sociological and political book with an autobiographical introduction; he felt it necessary "because where I came from helps explain where I stand." But where one came from in the Northwest was as often as not a featureless common denominator of America. H. L. Davis once wrote that in the Northwest one could travel a hundred miles and seem to be in another country. He meant it in terms of climate and weather and scenery. Frances Victor described the history of one town after another, and they all seemed to be alike, following the same progress from donation land claim to cities, or to county seats, or merely to whistle stops on a railroad. They looked alike, with the unvaried main streets and frame houses. They varied in their settings, a paradox, uniform human patterns set in spectacularly different scenes. They varied also in their social life, variegated patterns, as shifting and as hard to follow as the checkerboard pattern of Northwestern weather that confused the first explorers as to what sort of land they had really found.

When Davis considered the country he had grown up in, the little towns with their old buildings overshadowed by garages and stores, and the civilized monotony against the endless variety of nature, he concluded that part of the trouble came because the initial achievement of the pioneers had not been followed up: "the country got off to a better start than it was able to live up to." In the absence of a genuine identity based on its own past, there rose the myth of a rip-roaring past of picturesque violence, the legend of a land of violent and aggressive independence, of mighty labors and whirlwind travels, a land of giants, a land of men to match mountains, a land where the treasured folktale was that Dr. Whitman had to race across the nation to save Oregon from the British, a land where even the most run-down, broken-down mill town in a logged-off wasteland could be held up as a surviving fragment of a mighty past.

That myth never fitted the scene. It led to a surfeit of books concentrated on the hard-drinking, hardworking lives of loggers and of the frontier generally, the mills, camps, docks, red-light districts, bunkhouses, logging camps, all concerned with creating an image of the Northwest symbolized by the logger in his mud-splattered tin pants. The best of these books, the logging histories of Stewart Holbrook, or such works as Murray Morgan's *Skid Road* or Nard Jones's *Evergreen Land* or Archie Binns's *Northwest Gateway*, were colorful and picturesque and contained local information hard to come by elsewhere, but they were still forced, or theory ridden, or dominated by the need to present a picture of a violent and unrestrained society that had influenced Northwest writing since the time of Frances Victor's portrait of Joe Meek.

And in any case they could not be said to prefigure that new civilization and those new systems of thought and life that Theodore Winthrop confidently predicted for their homeland. It seems to me that Winthrop's vision was justified. He had one great moment of illumination in his hurried and feverish life, an instant of simplicity when he saw more clearly than he ever did in his baffled struggles for illumination. His discovery was no different from that of Vancouver, recognizing that the greatest wealth of the world he had found was its scenery, but he carried it a step farther in considering what the effect of that land would be on its future population.

Nathaniel Hawthorne, in the troubled days before the Civil War, worked over the history of the country to try to see what had led to the growing rift between North and South, and in *Our Old Home* he suggested some new kind of union or reunion of the United States and England to dilute the political views of the United States that were hardening beyond flexibility. He seemed to have a dual citizenship in mind, an interchange of peoples, coexisting with the existing governments; and while he recognized the obstacles in the way, he still believed that the people of the United States and Great Britain had shown enough genius in the creation of democratic government, and enough ingenuity in adjustments and institutions, to overcome the problems if they had the will to do so. But in the past of Oregon some such interchange of people under dual sovereignties had actually been established. It is true that the framers of that unique venture in government did not hold it up as an example of a new system of thought and life, but that is what it amounted to. Modesty or prudence prevented them from advertising how unusual it was. They did not claim it a model for all mankind, or a cause that would liberate humanity and create a new world. It was merely a temporary device designed to meet local conditions. Those conditions were in themselves the result of a desire for peace on the part of the governments of the two countries that involved, temporarily at least, a cession of their traditional rivalries, and thereby made possible the spontaneous creation of a democratic government in a land they held in common. American rather than British initiative established it, but it had the support of the majority of the British as well, even Mrs. Victor admitting that the British subjects "held the American principles of legislation, in commercial and civil matters, were, generally speaking, just and humane, and from which even British legislation might derive some useful hints."

The new form of government was peacefully established and peacefully abandoned when the need for it seemed to have passed. It was even gratefully abandoned, for the pioneers were somewhat embarrassed by finding themselves simultaneously citizens of Great Britain, the United States and Oregon, and felt themselves to be under the suspicion of infidelity to all of them and puzzled as to what they were expected to be loyal to. But at the local level that new venture into human government involved a degree of adjustment that meant, for the common citizen, a kind of statesmanship in the ordinary routines of daily life. And the independent government of Oregon, despite the fact that it was not a sovereign state and despite the fact that all its citizens were also citizens of two different nations that were often at odds, functioned very well indeed, with an efficiency unmatched by any absolute tyranny.

It seems to me that there are aspects of the hidden life of the Northwest with their bearing on the problems of a later century. H. L. Davis said that the Oregon writers "in their search of the past must have missed something, since they failed to establish a unity between it and the world out of which they wrote." So they did, but the fault lay less in the world out of which they wrote than remote and derivative forms that shaped their art. Some part of the pioneer inheritance persisted. It would take an unusually bold Northwesterner to assert that he and his neighbors were being made better by the matchless influence of the scenic grandeur around them, and insofar as I understand Freudian and behavioral psychology such physical surroundings have no bearing on human actions: Pavlov's dogs responded to the ringing of the bell whether it rang in clear mountain air or in a smoke-polluted garbage dump, and infant sexuality operates on the adult equally among green trees and in the ghetto. Still, in the Northwest one felt a difference between the quality of life that was lived in a logged-off wasteland and that enjoyed in a land where the trees had not been cut down. And if a new system of thought and life was coming into being there, it was not one to maintain that the physical beauty of a place, and the conditions of life that went with it, were without influence on human psychology.

My own belief is that Winthrop was right, and the unspoiled world did exert its civilizing influence, but in a different sense than he expected. The adventures and the dangers that he deliberately hunted, and the hardships that he consciously imposed on himself, were for the dwellers in the land he passed through the ordinary stuff of daily living. It was a delusion to imagine that somewhere else in the world one would find life, adventure, self-testing; they were implicit in existence wherever one was, especially in the old Oregon country. But the intensity of his search was a measure of his rejection of the society in which he had grown up, and if he could imagine the Oregon of a magnificent future, with people molded by a great land to create a new civilization, it was because he was himself a product of the society he was trying to escape and sensed what he needed.

No new systems of thought and life; no easy pass through the Cascades. What then remained after a century that still retained the promise of a hundred years before? When one looks back on it, the lasting part of the Northwest inheritance was not that body of events preserved in its official history, but a treasury of personal experience: David Thompson on the Continental Divide in the middle of winter thinking of the brilliance of the stars overhead and the promise of a new world that lay before him; Jesse Applegate watching the wagons ahead and reflecting that no other men, with the means at their command, would undertake so bold a journey; Hall Kelley marveling at the skill of his Indian guide taking his canoe through the rapids. They had something in common: Theodore Winthrop, unconscious on the prairie, roused by the worried nuzzling of his horse; Edmond Meany tramping alone down the Olympic coast to find where the men of the *Sonora* had been killed. There was no question of literary artifice in the power of such passages. Elizabeth Smith's diary of 1848—"Rain all day. . . . If I could tell you how we suffer you would not believe it"—

was on a plane of equality with Mary McCarthy's account in *Memories of a Catholic Girlhood* of her parents' death in the lethal influenza epidemic in the Northwest in 1918—the simplest and most telling of her writing. Guy Waring's recollection of the Okanogan valley in the 1880s in *My Pioneer Past*—"As I recall the ranch flooded with the yellow sunlight my heart is stirred as by no other memory"—which was written for his friends, had the same authenticity in its sense of the country as did Betty MacDonald's *The Egg and I*, which told of pioneering a farm on the Olympic Peninsula and which sold by the millions of copies to become the Northwest's most popular book: "After Christmas it rained and rained and rained and dusk settled like a shroud a little after three o'clock. From the forlorn grayness of the burn would come the sharp crack of a falling snag. . . ." If they do not add up to a distinct regional character, they may imply something more valuable. It may be that the deepest wisdom of the Northwest consisted in *not* developing a unique regional society to set it apart from the rest of the country. Those new systems of thought and life could turn out to be something very simple and humane, and it is possible that a new examination of the history of the old Oregon country will reveal that its overlooked educational power—the scenery—has been exercising its influence from the start. No other part of the country has so little to live down.

Appendix
The Diary of Dr. David Maynard

Dr. Maynard's diary was first published in the *Washington Historical Quarterly*, Volume I, No. 1, October, 1906, pp. 50–62, and was incorporated in *David S. Maynard and Catherine T. Maynard, Biographies of Two of the Oregon Immigrants of 1850* by Thomas W. Prosch without comment beyond a few sentences of introduction. That Prosch worked from the original is indicated by a sentence: "It was evidently inconvenient to him to write, as the daily spaces were small, three to the page, and there was much to do on the way, but between the lines and the times much can now be seen and read that does not appear in letters and words upon the paper." The original could not be located, however, although Dr. Maynard's instruments and other possessions were preserved and displayed in the museum of the Seattle Historical Society. The first entry in the published version is that of Tuesday, April 9, 1850:

Left home for California. Passed through Norwalk to Monroeville. Took the cars to Sandusky.[1] Saw a large eagle on the prairie. Passage, 75

[1] The Toledo, Norwalk and Cleveland Railroad was in operation in 1850, with connections to Sandusky. (U.S. Railroads, D. McClellan. New York, 1850.) Carlisle,

cents. Paid to Drakeley, $4.[2] Dinner and horse feed, 75 cents. Total, $5.50.

April 20th.—Left Cincinnati at 4 o'clock on board the *Natchez.*

April 21st.—Arrived at Louisville at 10. Walked to New Albany in Indiana, a place of about 7,000 inhabitants—Lockville. Saw James Porter, the Kentucky giant, 7⅔ feet.

Thursday, May 16.—Crossed the Missouri river at Saint Joseph and encamped.

May 17.—Left camp about 11 o'clock, and went six miles. Passed the snake's den.

May 18.—Traveled about seventeen miles over the bluffs. Very little timber, but good water.

May 19.—Traveled about eighteen miles. Passed one grave. An Indian farm about four miles west of the toll bridge kept by the Sac and Fox Indians. Toll, 25 cents. Passed one of the most beautiful pictures of country I ever saw. Drove the team with Mason.

May 20.—Traveled about sixteen miles over beautiful rolling prairie. No timber. Passed some new graves. Passed one horse and one ox left to die at leisure.

May 21.—Tuesday. Passed the grave of A. Powers, of Peoria County, Illinois, died on the 20th inst. about 65 miles west of St. Joseph. Traveled about eighteen miles. Was called to visit three cases of cholera. One died, a man, leaving a wife and child, from Illinois, poor. He lived seven hours after being taken. No wood or water secured.

May 22.—Rainy. Traveled five miles, and came to wood and water in plenty. Went on about ten miles further, and put out for the night. Fleming and Curtis taken with the cholera. Wake all night. Called upon just before we stopped to see a man with the cholera, who died soon after.

May 23.—Curtis and Fleming better, but not able to start in the morning. Started at 12, and traveled about six miles. Plenty of water three-quarters of a mile north of the road. Stopped in camp with Dr. Bemis's company. Heard wolves during the night.

May 24.—Started early. Curtis and Fleming pretty comfortable. Traveled about nineteen miles. Passed the forks leading to Independence.[3] Camped

---

in Lorain County, Ohio, subsequently became part of the city of Elyria, 30 miles east of Monroeville. The train trip from Monroeville to Sandusky was approximately 25 miles. Prosch nowhere named Carlisle as Maynard's home. The 1850 census, Free Inhabitants of Carlisle Township in the County of Lorain in the State of Ohio, "enumerated by me on the 9th day of Sept. 1850, I. H. Saxon," lists no. 889, David Maynard, aged 43 male, physician, place of birth, Vt.; Lydia A. aged 45 (possibly 43), place of birth, Vt.; Henry, aged 19, school (written in another hand) born Vt.; Frances, 12, born Ohio.

[2] The Drakeley family were early settlers in Carlisle (*History of Lorain County, Ohio,* p. 247). Listed (17 members) in 1830, they had apparently moved away by the time the 1850 census was taken.

[3] In 1850 the Saint Joseph crossing was the main route to the gold fields, the popu-

at Blue river. One grave, child 11 years old. Forded the stream. Raised our loading. Got my medicines wet. Boys caught a meal of catfish. Fish were large and plenty, and included enough for tomorrow's breakfast.

May 25.—Started at Big Blue river. Took in company Samuel J. Hunter. Left the river at half past 3. Another grave. Traveled ten miles.[4]

May 26.—Traveled about five miles and rested. Had catfish for breakfast.

May 27.—Went in with John Child's train of ten wagons.[5] At night the company lacked water, having camped on a hill away from water and wood. Traveled eighteen miles. Saw an antelope.

May 28.—Started late. Traveled alone, about fifteen miles. Plenty of food and tolerable water. Passed four graves. Camped on a dry hill, a few rods from the Childs train.[6]

May 29.—Started at 6 o'clock, going about eighteen miles. Water scarce and poor. Curtis gave the milk away. Went without dinner. A drove of buffaloes were seen by a company ahead. Left the team and went on ahead. Saw one buffalo and one antelope. Took sick with the cholera. No one meddled or took any notice of it but George Moon.[7]

May 30.—Feel better. Start on foot. Continue to get better. Travel up the Little Blue twenty miles. Wood, water and feed tolerable.[8]

May 31.—Started at 6. Followed up the Blue. Passed one good spring. Feed short. Traveled twenty miles. Hunter left, and I took the cooking line.[9]

June 1.—Left the range of the Blue. Traveled twenty miles. Saw three antelopes.[10]

---

lation of the town reaching 3,000, with some 10,000 emigrants waiting to be ferried over the river. The intersection with what was then the lesser route, from Independence (Kansas City), was near present-day Marysville, Kansas. (Merrill Mattes, *The Great Platte River Road*, pp. 112–114); Nebraska Historical Society, *Platte River Routes*, Vol. I. No. 14.

[4] This camp was near present-day Oketo, Kansas.

[5] I was unable to identify John Childs definitely. A householder of that name is in the 1840 census, living at Elyria, Ohio, with his wife and three children, but not in the census of 1850. Maynard's figures make this camp near the present-day Fairbury, Nebraska, airport. A marker indicates the route of the Oregon Trail at that point.

[6] About three miles northeast of Hebron, Nebraska, and one mile west of the historical marker of the Oregon Trail.

[7] Almost on the county line between Thayer and Nuckolls County, Nebraska, a little more than four miles east of the town of Oak, Nebraska.

[8] Maynard's figures place this camp on the border between Nuckolls and Clay County, Nebraska, two miles east of Deweese.

[9] By Maynard's estimate of distances and the known route of the Oregon Trail, this camp was about four miles south of Hastings, Nebraska.

[10] On the county line between Adams County and Kearney County, Nebraska, just south of the Chicago, Burlington and Quincy Railroad, five miles northeast of Heartwell, Nebraska, and approximately five miles south of the south channel of the Platte River.

June 2.—Started late. Rode all the forenoon, and read. Traveled eleven miles. Put up on the Platte. No wood or good water.[11]

June 3.—Started at half past 6. Traveled five miles to Fort Kearney. Saw tame buffaloes. The fort buildings are built of wood, brick and mud. The country is flat and rather low. Two miles southeast are sandhills in sight. Went about twenty-two miles, and fell in with innumerable hosts of immigrants. Rained throughout the night.[12]

June 4.—Traveled up the Platte river twenty miles. The road was low, level and muddy. The river is about a mile wide. At 2 o'clock it began to rain and blow tremendously, continuing all night. Camped without a spark of fire or warm supper, with our clothes as wet as water. A man died with the cholera in sight of us. He was a Mason. I was called to see him, but too late.

June 5.—It rains yet. Got as wet as ever in getting the team. I got a chance to cook some meat and tea with Dr. Hotchkiss's stove. In company with Mr. Stone from Mansfield. Have a bad headache; take a blue pill. Start at 9; travel to a creek, twelve miles.[13]

June 6.—Start at 9. Unship our load, and cross a creek. One death, a Missourian, from cholera. Go eighteen miles. Pass four graves in one place. Two more of the same train are ready to die. Got a pint and a half of brandy. Earn $2.20. Left Krill with a dying friend.

June 7.—Start late. Find plenty of doctoring to do. Stop at noon to attend some persons sick with cholera. One was dead before I got there and two died before the next morning. They paid me $8.75. Deceased were named Israel Broshears and William Broshears and Mrs. Morton, the last being mother of the bereaved widow of Israel Broshears. We are 85 or 90 miles west of Fort Kearney.[14]

June 8.—Left the camp of distress on the open prairie at half past 4 in the morning. The widow was ill in both body and mind. I gave them slight encouragement by promising to return and assist them along. I overtook our company at noon twenty miles away. Went back and met the others in trouble enough. I traveled with them until night. Again over-

[11] On the south bank of the Platte, one mile east of Highway 10.

[12] Merrill Mattes (*The Great Platte River Road*, p. 201) quotes a letter written from Fort Kearney on June 1, 1850: "About 30,000 have passed already this side of the river, and probably one fourth as many on the north side. While resting here yesterday probably 1,000 wagons passed. . . ." Mattes estimates that 50,000 travelers to California passed Fort Kearney in 1850.

[13] Plum Creek fits the description, but is about five miles nearer Fort Kearney than the distances indicated in Maynard's diary, through most of which his estimates are remarkably accurate.

[14] There is a marker of the Oregon Trail on the south bank of the Platte, near the entrance of the bridge (Highway 21) which leads to Cozad, Nebraska, on the north side of the river. The distances and the descriptions of the country indicate that Maynard's meeting with the stricken Broshears party was in the area between this point and one slightly east of Gothenberg (also on the north side), ten miles west.

took our company three miles ahead. Made my arrangements to be ready to shift my duds to the widow's wagon when they come up in the morning.

June 9.—Started off in good season. Went twenty miles. Encamped on a creek. Wolves very noisy, keeping us awake all night.

June 10.—Traveled eleven miles, and crossed South Platte at the lower crossing. Stream three-fourths of a mile wide, with a heavy current.[15]

June 11.—Traveled twenty-one miles. Waded for wood for self and Rider. Got small ash poles.

The diary breaks off at this point, resuming on June 25, and thereafter continuing with daily entries until the party reached Tumwater on September 25.

[15] The Oregon Trail crossings of the Platte varied considerably as the channel shifted, but the lower crossing in 1850 was slightly east of the highway bridge at the city of North Platte. (*History of Lincoln County*, edited by Ira Ball and Will H. McDonald, American Historical Society, Vol. I, pp. 322–323.) Thus in tracing Maynard's movements westward 85 or 90 miles west of Fort Kearney, or tracing them back east some 50 miles from the Platte crossing, his estimates of the distances traveled are generally confirmed—except, of course, in his account of his 60 miles of riding back and forth between the Broshears' party and the party he left, on June 7 and 8, 1850.

Notes and References

Chapter I. The Rain

I (pages 11–15)

INDIANS AND CEDAR BOARDS: James Gilchrist Swan, *The Northwest Coast*, p. 110; Edmond S. Meany, *Mount Rainier: A Record of Explorations*, p. 16.

SALMON: Personal observation, Newaukum River, Washington, 1914–1922 and 1965; Francis H. Ames, *Fishing the Oregon Country*, p. 164; Enos Bradner, *Northwest Angling*, p. 172; Swan, *The Northwest Coast*, pp. 103–104.

BARTOLOMÉ FERRELO: Edmond S. Meany, *History of the State of Washington*, p. 9. RAINFALL: on the coast of Oregon, United States Weather Bureau, *Climatic Summary of the United States, Section 3, Western Oregon*, pp. 12–19.

DRAKE'S VOYAGE: Meany, *History of the State of Washington*, pp. 11–13. RAINFALL: off the Olympic peninsula, U.S. Weather Bureau, *Climatic Summary of the United States, Section 1, Western Washington*, p. 19.

JUAN DE FUCA: James McCurdy, *By Juan de Fuca's Strait*, p. 4; Charles H. Carey, *A General History of Oregon*, Vol. I, p. 6. LUIS DE VELASCO, Viceroy of Mexico: Henry Bamford Parkes, *A History of Mexico*, pp. 94–95; *Encyclopaedia Britannica* (10th ed.), Vol. XVIII, p. 337; *Encyclopedia Americana*, Vol. XVIII, p. 825. RAINFALL: in Santiago, Spain; *Encyclopaedia Britannica* (10th ed.), Vol. XXV, p. 530; in Seattle, Washington, U.S. Weather Bureau, *Climatic Summary of the United States, Section 1, Western Washington*, p. 19.

Voyage of the Santiago: Meany, *History of the State of Washington,* p. 22.

Voyage of the Santiago and Sonora: Don Francisco Antonio Mourelle, *Voyage of the Sonora in the Second Bucareli Expedition,* pp. 34–42; Edgar Stewart, *Washington, Northwest Frontier,* Vol. I, pp. 72–73.

Weather: Olympic Peninsula rainfall, U.S. Weather Bureau, *Climatic Summary of the United States, Section 1, Western Washington,* p. 23; also Department of Commerce bulletin, *Climate of the States, Washington.*

Forest on the shore: Edmond Meany in 1905, when the Olympic Peninsula was inhabited only by Indians, explored alone to the site where the men of the *Sonora* were killed and described the woods. Meany, *History of the State of Washington,* p. 23.

II   (pages 15–18)

Cook's opinion of the Northwest: In all accounts; see Margaret Ormsby, *British Columbia, a History,* pp. 9–14; Edmond Meany, *Vancouver's Discovery of Puget Sound.*

Meares's voyages: John Meares, *Voyages to the Northwest Coast of North America, 1788–1789:* Ormsby, pp. 14–29; Carey, Vol. I, pp. 66–68. The disguised Portuguese are in Meany, *History of the State of Washington,* p. 26.

Gray's voyages: Frederic Howay, "Voyages of the Columbia to the Northwest Coast." Death of Marcos Lopius: pp. 31–35; also, Meany, *History of the State of Washington,* pp. 40–44.

III   (pages 18–23)

Kendrick's dishonesty: Howay, p. vi. Kendrick's death: Howay, *Oregon Historical Quarterly,* Vol. xxlll, December, 1922, pp. 277–302. Kendrick's family: *Vital Records of Rhode Island,* Vol. IV, p. 83; *Dictionary of American Biography,* Vol. X, p. 329; *Massachusetts Soldiers and Sailors in the Revolutionary War,* p. 109; Josiah Paine, *Edward Kendrick and His Descendants,* p. 6.

Point Grenville. Meany, *History of the State of Washington,* p. 23, locates the site of the massacre of the men of the *Sonora* at 47° 30′ from the original documents and his personal investigation, near the mouth of the Hoh River, some 30 miles north of Point Grenville. Later accounts, as in *Washington, A Guide to the Evergreen State,* p. 559, give Point Grenville as the location without reference to Meany's work. From my personal observation it seems unlikely that anyone would land for water near Point Grenville. In my childhood we spent the summers near the resort town of Moclips, the nearest community to Point Grenville. Moclips was the westernmost point of the Northern Pacific Railway, planned to become a great summer resort akin to the New Jersey resort towns on the Atlantic, but the boom ended, and the town was then a collection of wooden hotels with boarded windows and sagging balconies, with sand dunes drifting in the streets. We went to Point Grenville to rake crabs from the clear pools left at low tides. From the window of our house we looked across a quarter of a mile of beach, smooth, packed, hardened, remarkably porous, draining and absorbing the water as the tide fell. The surf broke a quarter of a mile from shore. Landing anywhere near there seems unreasonable in view of more accessible rivers not far distant.

VANCOUVER'S MEETING WITH GRAY. The United States agreement with Britain not to aid Spain in the event of war between Britain and Spain over Nootka is, with different emphasis, in Carey, *A General History of Oregon*, Vol. I, p. 67, and Meany, *History of the State of Washington*, p. 31. Vancouver's encounter with Gray is in George Vancouver, *A Voyage of Discovery to the North Pacific Ocean*, pp. 31, 34, 36, 41, 60, and in Meany, pp. 34–39.

GRAY IN BULFINCH HARBOR: Howay, "Voyages of the Columbia," p. 396.

VANCOUVER IN PUGET SOUND: Vancouver, p. 56 and following; Edmond Meany, *Vancouver's Discovery of Puget Sound*.

IV (pages 23–28)

MACKENZIE'S EXPLORATION: Alexander Mackenzie, *Voyage from Montreal on the River St. Lawrence through the Continent of North America to the Frozen and Pacific Oceans in the Years 1789 and 1793*, pp. 136–190. T. H. McDonald, *Exploring the Northwest Territory*, pp. 3–24.

ALEXANDER McKAY: Washington Irving, *Astoria*, Vol. I, p. 26; Carey, *A General History of Oregon*, Vol. I, pp. 176–181; Catherine M. White, *David Thompson's Journals Relating to Montana and Adjacent Regions*, p. 237; J. A. Hussey, *Champoeg: Place of Transition*, p. 93.

SHALER'S VOYAGE: William Shaler, *Journal of a Voyage between China and the Northwest Coast of America, Made in 1804 by William Shaler*, p. 27. Shaler's career is in *The Dictionary of American Biography*.

RAIN IN LEWIS AND CLARK JOURNALS: The original journals, in different editions edited by Reuben Gold Thwaites and by Elliott Coues, are difficult to secure. I have used the Keystone Western Americana paperback edition (Lippincott, 1961) as more readily available. This is a reprint of the first 1814 edition. The material on the rain is in Vol. II, pp. 470–505. Bernard De Voto, *The Journals of Lewis and Clark*, pp. 279–336, gives many of the original passages. Lewis and Clark's fort is well described in Albert and Jane Salisbury, *Two Captains West*, p. 145.

V (pages 28–35)

LEWIS'S FIRST REPORT OF THE EXPEDITION. John Bakeless, *Lewis and Clark*, p. 377. Irving, *Astoria*, p. 20. I have used the Keystone Western Americana edition, edited by William H. Goetzmann, as most readily available. White, *David Thompson's Journals*, as above, notes that Lewis's report reached Canada soon after Lewis's return, p. vii. Russian interest in the Columbia River is in Hector Chevigny, *Russian America: the Great Alaskan Venture, 1791–1867*, reporting an expedition under Nikolai Bulygin sent from Alaska to build a Russian fort at the mouth of the Columbia in 1808. The expedition's ship went ashore near Destruction Island. The survivors, including Bulygin's eighteen-year-old wife, were enslaved by Quillayute and Quinault Indians. Fifteen survivors were eventually ransomed by the captain of the American trader *Lydia* and returned to Alaska. In Chevigny's account the wife of Bulygin was taken by a local Indian chief, became of influence in the tribe, and refused to rejoin the Russians, Bulygin himself dying before the ransom was paid. His wife, passed from chief to chief, killed herself. Chevigny's source was an untranslated work, *Krushenie-Rossiiskage-Amerikanskoi Kompanii sudna Sviatoi Nikolai* (*Wreck of the Russian-American Ship Saint Nicholas*), by Vasilii Tarakanov, included in a collection of works by V. M. Golovnin published in Saint Petersburg in 1853.

Chevigny was an authority on Russian history in Hollywood. He was also a prolific author of movie scripts and radio dramas. His strong pro-Russian sympathies, extending over both Czarist and post-Czarist Russia —as president of the Radio Writers Guild he was under frequent attack for reported Communist activities—and the movie-script tone of his writing weakens the historical authority of his books. At my request my son-in-law, Lars-Erik Nelson, a Reuters' correspondent in Moscow, tried to locate the original documents on which the report in the 1853 volume was based, but was unsuccessful—"although an inability to discover historical sources in Russia," he wrote, "does not mean they may not exist."

Ross Cox NARRATIVE: Edgar I. and Jane R. Stewart, *The Columbia River*, is an annotated edition of Ross Cox's book; pp. 63–69.

Irving and Astor: Robert Cantwell, *American Men of Letters*, pp. 25–33; William H. Goetzmann, biographical introduction of *Astoria* (Keystone edition), pp. vii–xii.

The Ogden family: William Ogden Wheeler, *The Ogden Family in America*, p. 640; also, *Dictionary of American Biography* entry, Josiah Ogden Hoffman.

Treaty of joint occupancy: Carey, *A General History of Oregon*, Vol. I, p. 231; Meany, *History of the State of Washington*, pp. 87–90. The Russian ukase of 1821, barring vessels from the Northwest coast, Meany, p. 91.

Oregon experiences under joint occupancy: "A happy people," J. A. Hussey, *Champoeg: Place of Transition*, p. 141.

Loss of the Tonquin: Irving, *Astoria*, Vol. I, pp. 84–91.

Chapter II. The River

I (pages 36–43)

Public Archives of Canada: The history of the Public Archives is in *The Beaver: A Magazine of the North*, Winter, 1967, pp. 48–53.

David Thompson's birth: His birth record is in the Register Book of Births and Baptisms belonging to the Parish of St. John the Evangelist,

Westminster, in the County of Middlesex, Vol. II, beginning January 14, 1755, and ending the eighth day of January, 1791. David Thompson's birth and baptism are on page 137. John Thompson's birth is on page 153. The death of David Thompson senior is in St. John, Smith Square Burials, 1757–1775.

GREY COAT SCHOOL: J. B. Tyrrell, editor, *David Thompson's Narrative of His Explorations in Western America, 1784–1812*, includes Thompson's account of his schooling. The existing records of the Grey Coat School: personal observation. The material on Thompson's admission is in the Report of the Annual Meeting of the Directors, Tuesday, April 29, 1777. The salary of the instructor of mathematics is in the entry for July 1, 1777. The flight of Samuel M'Phearson to avoid service with the Hudson's Bay Company is in the entry for March 30, 1784. Thompson's apprenticeship to the Company is in the entry for May 20, 1784.

THOMPSON'S RECORD WITH THE HUDSON'S BAY COMPANY: The two editors of *Thompson's Narrative*, J. B. Tyrrell (1916) and Richard Glover (1961), arrived at directly opposed views of Thompson's relations with the Company. Tyrrell accepted Thompson's own account. Glover concluded that Thompson had behaved ungratefully. Glover's comments are in *David Thompson's Narrative, 1784–1812*, edited by Richard Glover, pp. xvi–xxx.

THOMPSON AND THE NORTH WEST COMPANY: The best account is in Catherine White, *David Thompson's Journals Relating to Montana and Adjacent Regions*. Thompson's marriage to Charlotte Small is on p. lxix. However, Sandford Fleming, in "Expeditions to the Pacific," *Transactions of the Royal Society of Canada*, Vol. VII, Sec. 2, May, 1889, page 108, gives Charlotte's age as eighteen years at the time of her marriage, not fourteen.

THOMPSON'S ACHIEVEMENTS: Thompson's record is well summed up in Tyrrell's edition of *Thompson's Narrative*, though this work, having been superseded by Glover's disparaging edition of the same book, is now almost unobtainable. Catherine White, in *David Thompson's Journals Relating to Montana*, summarizes professional opinion: "He was the greatest practical land geographer the world has ever produced" (p. cxxix) and notes that Thompson's map of Canada, the first complete work of the sort ever made, "should have won him recognition as the foremost geographer of his time" (p. cxxvi).

THOMPSON'S FATHER-IN-LAW, PATRICK SMALL: White, *David Thompson's Journals Relating to Montana*, p. 243.

THOMPSON'S BROTHER-IN-LAW, JOHN McDONALD: He figures prominently in Ross Cox's *The Columbia River* (edited by Edgar I. and Jane R. Stewart, pp. xxviii, 156, 348–349, and in White, *David Thompson's Journals Relating to Montana*, p. 236, as well as in Thompson's own *Narrative*.

MERIWETHER LEWIS'S ENCOUNTER WITH INDIANS: *Lewis and Clark Expedition*, Vol. III, pp. 730–732. Thompson's mistaken view of the fight is in Tyrrell's edition of *Thompson's Narrative*, p. 375.

II   (pages 43–48)

THOMPSON AND LEWIS'S REPORT: That Thompson read Lewis's letter on the expedition is in White, *David Thompson's Journals Relating to Montana*, p. vii, as is the discovery of Thompson's handwritten copy of Vancouver's writings on Puget Sound, which was found in the Public Library in Vancouver, Canada in 1901. The journey through the mountains is largely from Tyrrell's edition of *Thompson's Narrative*.

THOMPSON'S ROUTE THROUGH THE ROCKIES: The place names are variously given. "Wapta" for "Sunwapta," etc. I have used the names as given on the Canadian Department of Mines and Technical Surveys, Sheet 82 N.W., Vernon-Golden, British Columbia–Alberta. That Thompson followed along the Continental Divide (or the Height of Land, in Canadian usage) might seem to contradict that his route was through a pass, but in fact the passage was between high peaks, though much of it was on a ridge that divided waters flowing east from those draining west to the Columbia.

MOUNT NELSON: Thompson always misjudged the height of mountains. The peak later named Mount Nelson, west of Kootenay House, is 10,772 feet but could hardly have been the one he had in mind, as it is 14 miles distant. A smaller peak 5 miles west of Lake Windermere is 7,350 feet and matches Thompson's description.

THOMPSON'S COMMENTS ON THE COLUMBIA: Tyrrell's edition of *Thompson's Narrative*, pp. 448, 458.

COLUMBIA TRIBUTARIES: The rivers and creeks flowing into the Columbia are taken from the Canadian Department of Mines and Technical Surveys maps of the Columbia River Basin.

THOMPSON ON THE KOOTENAY: Tyrrell's edition of *Thompson's Narrative*, p. 385. The course of the Kootenay and the Columbia are in Robert Cantwell, "The Columbia, a Gem of a River," *Sports Illustrated*, February 24, 1964, pp. 56–66, and William Baillie-Grohman, *Fifteen Years Sport and Life in the Hunting Grounds of Western America and British Columbia*. Madison Lorraine, *The Columbia Unveiled*, pp. 38–56.

III   (pages 48–51)

KOOTENAY HOUSE AND THE INDIANS: Tyrrell's edition of *Thompson's Narrative*, p. 375 and following.

IV   (pages 51–53)

LETTERS OF ZACHARY PERCH: Thompson C. Elliott, "The Strange Case of David Thompson and Zachary Perch and Jeremy Pinch," *Oregon Historical Quarterly*, Vol. XL, 1939, pp. 188–189. Also Carey, *A General History of Oregon*, Vol. I, p. 144. Elliott noted speculation that Perch and Pinch were assumed names for someone acting for General James Wilkinson, in command of the United States Army, who was subsequently discovered to be an agent for the Spanish government, and who was financially interested in the fur-trading ventures of Manuel Lisa.

THOMPSON'S RETURN OVER THE ROCKIES: Tyrrell, *Thompson's Narrative*, p. 385 and following; also, personal observation of part of Thompson's route, summer, 1965.

V (pages 53–59)

THOMPSON AND THE FOUNDING OF ASTORIA: The trading posts which Thompson established in Montana and elsewhere are in White, *David Thompson's Journals*, pp. ci–cv. That Thompson's twenty-four men were turned back by Indians is in all accounts, with varied interpretations, though generally without notice that he was not personally present.

White (p. cviii) points out that no orders to Thompson to establish a base at the mouth of the Columbia were ever located. His own *Narrative* gives no indication that he thought of himself in a race to reach the mouth of the river before the Astorians. His journal for 1811 has disappeared, but in his notes he speaks of planning to reach the mouth of the Columbia by August, 1811.

Washington Irving, in *Astoria* (Vol. I, p. 75), called Thompson a spy in the camp of Astor's men. He held that Thompson was frustrated in his effort to claim the lower Columbia for Great Britain "by the desertion of his men." His description of Thompson planting flags and informing the Indians that the country belonged to the King of England is wildly exaggerated in terms of the known documents.

Thompson's actual trip over the mountains and down the Columbia has been pieced together from the fragmentary field notes on which he figured latitude and longitude and made occasional comments to be added to his journals later. See Elliott Coues, *The Manuscript Journals of Alexander Henry and David Thompson, 1799–1814*, and "New Light on the Early History of the Northwest," *Oregon Historical Quarterly*, Vol. XXVI, No. 1, 1925, pp. 33–49.

Thompson's field notes are in photostatic copies in the Public Archives of Canada, Ottawa, Vol. XI, Book No. 26, *Columbia River to the Sea and up the Columbia from Illthayapa* [indecipherable] *Falls to the Athabasca Mountains, Canoe River to* [indecipherable] *Falls*, etc., 1811. Course and latitude worked, pp. 95–155; Canoe River, pp. 147–153.

Thompson's own account of his winter crossing of the Rockies is in Tyrrell, *David Thompson's Narrative*, p. 441 and following. The region in summer is well described in Raymond Patterson, "We Clomb the Pathless Pass," *The Beaver: A Magazine of the North*, Winter, 1968, pp. 33–49.

THOMPSON AT BOAT ENCAMPMENT: Thompson's expedition is summarized in O. B. Sperlin, "Explorations of the Upper Columbia," *Transactions of the Royal Society of Canada*, Vol. IV, No. 1, January, 1913. Tyrrell's edition of *Thompson's Narrative* remains the most objective account of Thompson's achievement; Glover's edition is marred by the intrusion of his critical comments, as (p. lxiii): "Thompson did not choose to go down the Columbia; instead he went upstream to the river's source . . . the enormous detour left him traveling away from his objective from 17 April at least until he left Spokane House on 16 June." Glover credits Thompson with great ingenuity in constructing a canoe of cedar sheets and implies that the makeshift craft possessed fine qualities for negotiating fast water, an opinion evidently not shared by Thompson's men or by Thompson himself.

Thompson's last trip over the Rockies, after his visit to Astoria, is in White, p. cxviii.

LORD SELKIRK: A most concise and illuminating account of the Hudson's Bay colonizing project is in the Stewarts' edition of Ross Cox's *The Columbia River*, pp. xxvi–xxx.

THOMPSON'S LATER YEARS: The best account is in White, *David Thompson's Journals Relating to Montana*, p. cviii and following.

VI (pages 59–65)

THOMPSON'S REPUTATION: The conflicting views of Thompson's character and work are principally drawn from a comparison of the edition of *Thompson's Narrative* as edited by Tyrrell and that later edited by Glover. "A tissue of falsehood and misrepresentation" is in Glover's edition, p. xxii. His discussion of the Hudson's Bay payments to Eliza Evans is on p. xliii and following.

MICA CREEK DAM AND BOAT ENCAMPMENT: Robert Cantwell, "The Columbia, a Gem of a River," *Sports Illustrated*, February 24, 1964, pp. 56–66.

Chapter III. *The United Government of Oregon, Great Britain and the United States*

I (pages 66–78)

SCOTT FITZGERALD ON THE WILDERNESS: See *The Great Gatsby*, closing paragraphs.

HALL KELLEY: Fred Wilbur Powell, "Hall Jackson Kelley, Prophet of Oregon," *Oregon Historical Quarterly*, Vol. XVIII, Nos. 1–3, 1917.

EWING YOUNG: Frank Lockwood, *Pioneer Days in Arizona*, pp. 67–70; Powell, "Hall Jackson Kelley," pp. 116–121; Frances Fuller Victor, *The River of the West*. Joseph Walker's reputation as an Indian killer is in Washington Irving's *Adventures of Captain Bonneville*.

AMERICAN VISITORS AT VANCOUVER: The visit of Thomas Nuttall and John Kirk Townsend is in Stanley G. Jewett and others, *Birds of Washington State*, pp. 26–27, and in J. A. Hussey, *Champoeg: Place of Transition*, pp. 63, 73, 81.

JOHN MCLOUGHLIN: His background is in Richard Gill Montgomery, *The White-Headed Eagle*, pp. 6–20; his marriage, pp. 26–27; his wife's background, p. 29; his arrest for murder, p. 32. Stewart, *The Columbia River*, pp. xxvi–xxx, reports the battle of Seven Oaks.

PHILOSOPHERS AND PATRIOTS: The division of opinion in the Hudson's Bay post regarding the Americans is in Frances Victor, *The River of the West.*

II (pages 78–85)

BOOKS IN THE NORTHWEST: James Gilchrist Swan, *The Northwest Coast*, p. 65; "The Multnomah Circulating Library," *Washington Historical Quarterly*, Vol. XXII, pp. 261–262; Edmond Meany, *History of the State of Washington*, p. 141. Charles Carey, *A General History of Oregon*, Vol. 1, p. 324, attaches less importance to the library.

TRIAL OF HUBBARD: Hussey, *Champoeg: Place of Transition*, p. 83; also, the Reverend Gustavus Hines, *Wild Life in Oregon*. Hubbard's marriage to the Indian girl, supposedly the one he had rescued from Thornburg, is noted in his marriage to Mary Somata, Hussey, p. 83. When Hines left Oregon by ship (*Wild Life*, p. 248), he was surprised to find Hubbard a fellow passenger and reported that with eating, sleeping and gambling nearly all the time, Hubbard had evidently become "neither wiser nor virtuous from the history of the past."

EWING YOUNG AND THE GOVERNOR OF CALIFORNIA: General Figueroa, the Mexican governor of California is in Carey, Vol. I, p. 261. His retraction of the charge that Young was a horse thief is in *Oregon Historical Quarterly*, Vol. XVIII, March, 1917, p. 127.

YOUNG'S DISTILLERY: Frances Fuller Victor, *The River of the West*, p. 293. Mrs. Victor understated the importance of the projected distillery as a source of contention between the British and the Americans; see also Carey, Vol. I, pp. 264–265. Lee's background in Canada is in William B. Sprague, *Annals of the American Pulpit*, p. 972.

PETER SKENE OGDEN: Alfred Powers, *History of Oregon Literature*, pp. 49–51; William Ogden Wheeler, *The Ogden Family in America; Dictionary of American Biography*; Meany, *History of the State of Washington*, p. 121; Archie Binns, *The Roaring Land*, pp. 197–204.

PUGET SOUND AGRICULTURAL COMPANY: Frederick Merk, "The Oregon Pioneers and the Boundary," *American Historical Review*, Vol. 29, pp. 681–699.

DEATH OF EWING YOUNG: Hines, *Wild Life in Oregon*, p. 418 (Hines was secretary of the graveside committee); Victor, *River of the West*, p. 294; Hussey, pp. 136–138; Carey, Vol. I, p. 319.

WILKES EXPEDITION: Robert Johnson's exploration through Naches Pass is in Meany, *Mount Rainier*, pp. 13–33.

WOLF MEETINGS: Meany, *History of the State of Washington*, pp. 141–145.

FORMATION OF THE PROVISIONAL GOVERNMENT: Carey, Vol. I, p. 317 and following; Meany, *History of the State of Washington*, pp. 138–145; Hines, pp. 418–437.

WAGON TRAIN OF 1843: Jesse Applegate, *A Day with the Cow Column in 1843*. The foreign relations of the provisional government, and the question of loyalty to the United States and Great Britain, are in Meany, *History of the State of Washington,* p. 144.

III   (pages 85–91)

WAGON TRAIN OF 1844: John Minto, *Transactions of the Fourth Annual Reunion of the Oregon Pioneers Association,* May 4, 1876; General Gilliam, p. 39; Michael Troutman Simmons, p. 39.

SIMMONS BACKGROUND: Evelyn Crady Adams, "The Troutman Families of Kentucky," *Filson Historical Club Quarterly,* Vol. 24, No. 3, pp. 199–226; John Minto, "Reminiscences of the Honorable John Minto," *Oregon Historical Quarterly,* Vol. II (1901), pp. 118–212.

GEORGE WASHINGTON BUSH: John Edwin Ayer, "George Washington Bush," *Washington Historical Quarterly,* Vol. VII, No. 1, 1916, p. 40 and following; Jalmar Johnson, *Builders of the Northwest: Michael Troutman Simmons and George Washington Bush,* pp. 64–81; Meany, *History of the State of Washington,* p. 224; Carey, *General History of Oregon,* Vol. II, p. 489.

SIMMONS AT WASHOUGAL: William D. Welsh, *A Brief History of Camas, Washington,* pp. 10–11; Washington Centennial Commemoration, 1854–1954, *Arrival of Michael Simmons Party at Tumwater to Establish the First Community in Washington,* pp. 4–9.

JOHN ROBINSON JACKSON: Meany, *History of the State of Washington,* p. 224; Washington Centennial, p. 5; Margaret R. and Fred E. Carver, *Michael Troutman Simmons and Andrew Jackson Simmons,* p. 23. Theodore Winthrop, *The Canoe and the Saddle* (Tacoma edition, pp. 260–261), contains Winthrop's account of Jackson's farm.

SIMMONS MILL: Meany, *History of the State of Washington,* p. 226. The daily output of 3,000 board feet is in Elwood Evans, *The State of Washington,* p. 300.

DR. WILLIAM TOLMIE: William Tolmie, *Physician and Fur Trader: The Journals of William Fraser Tolmie;* Meany, *Mount Rainier, a Record of Explorations,* pp. 6–12; William J. Betts, "Route to Mount Rainier," *The Beaver: A Magazine of the North,* Summer, 1965, pp. 14–23.

SIMMONS: Gatherings of the descendants of Michael Troutman Simmons are described in *Michael Troutman Simmons and Andrew Jackson Simmons,* by Margaret R. and Fred E. Carver, and in *The Ancestors and Descendants of Jonathan Simmons and Mary Troutman and of Their Children Who Settled in Washington and Oregon,* by the same authors.

THE LOSS OF SIMMONS'S FORTUNE: Meany, *History of the State of Washington,* p. 226.

IV   (pages 91–97)

BROSHEARS PARTY: Thomas W. Prosch, *David S. Maynard and Catherine T. Maynard,* pp. 10, 11, 20, 21, 66, 67. (Prosch's biography was also printed in the *Washington Historical Quarterly,* Vol. I, No. 1, 1906.)

DR. DAVID MAYNARD: J. Tate Mason, "Seattle's First Physician," pp. 2–29. Archie Binns, *Northwest Gateway,* p. 54, says: Maynard "might have been a great man. . . . There were delays and counterattacks and in the confusion he was done to death."

MAYNARD'S BACKGROUND: Maynard's past before his meeting with the Broshears party is found only in Prosch, *David S. Maynard.* I was unable to verify any of the biographical facts given by Prosch, who knew Maynard personally and who wrote while the second Mrs. Maynard was still living. From Prosch's statement that Maynard lived in Ohio "near Cleveland," I eventually located him in the 1850 census, *Free Inhabitants of Carlisle Township in the County of Lorain in the State of Ohio.*

MAYNARD AND MRS. BROSHEARS: Maynard's diary, printed in Prosch, entries of June 7 through September 25, 1850.

THREAT TO MAYNARD: Mrs. Ryder's threat to shoot Maynard on sight is in Prosch's biography, p. 70.

SENATOR WELLER AND MAYNARD: Prosch, pp. 25-26.

EDMUND SYLVESTER, SIMMONS AND MAYNARD: Meany, *History of the State of Washington*, pp. 226-227; Prosch, p. 27.

MAYNARD'S POSITION IN SEATTLE: Prosch, *A Chronological History of Seattle*, p. 258 and following; Mason, "Seattle's First Physician"; Archie Binns, *Northwest Gateway*, pp. 31-42. The baptism of Chief Seattle is in Jalmar Johnson, *Builders of the Northwest*, p. 104.

MAYNARD'S LAND CLAIM: His original title is recorded Certificate No. 440 of the Donation Land Claims, notification No. 461, General Land Office, Olympia, Washington Territory, approved, March 14, 1869; cancelled, August 12, 1872; cancellation affirmed by the Secretary of the Interior, March 1, 1875.

Prosch, *David S. Maynard*, p. 37, gives a map of Maynard's town plan.

The example of Maynard's gift of land is in Binns, *Northwest Gateway*, in the letters of Catherine Blaise, wife of a clergyman, to whom Maynard gave two acres of shoreland, p. 83.

OREGON LAND LAWS: Their application in Maynard's case is in Prosch, pp. 54-55.

MAYNARD'S DIVORCE: Provisional and Territorial Government Papers, on microfilm, Oregon Historical Society. No. 4780, petition for divorce, filed by David S. Maynard, December 10, 1852; character reference by I. N. Ebey, December 15, 1852. The first Mrs. Maynard's reply to the divorce is not included in Prosch's biography. The quotation on her position is in Report of the Decisions of the Supreme Court of Washington Territory, July term, 1880, page 7 and following. The development of Maynard's land claim in Seattle's red-light district is traced in Murray Morgan's *Skid Road.*

V (pages 97-102)

SIMMONS: He is described as "the Daniel Boone of the Territory" in Swan, *The Northwest Coast*, p. 396. Governor Stevens on Simmons is quoted in Philip Henry Overmeyer, "George B. McClellan and the Pacific Northwest," *Pacific Northwest Quarterly*, Vol. 32, No. 1, January, 1941, p. 13.

SIMMONS AND PATKAMIN'S ATTACK: Meany, *History of the State of Wash-*

ington, p. 149. Shortly after Maynard arrived at Puget Sound, he employed Patkamin as a guide in his search for coal deposits; Prosch, p. 23.

INDIAN TREATIES: Meany, *History of the State of Washington*, pp. 165–175; Swan, *The Northwest Coast*, pp. 330–350. The text of the treaties have been published in facsimile editions by Shorey Publications, Seattle. All Indian treaties up to 1873 were included in *A Compilation of the Treaties between the United States and the Indian Tribes*, published by the U.S. Government Printing Office, Washington, 1873.

The investigations of J. Ross Browne in the Pacific Northwest that included his investigation of Simmons is in Richard H. Dillon, *J. Ross Browne, Confidential Agent in Old California*, pp. 170–183. David Michael Goodman, *A Western Panorama*, based on the writings of John Ross Browne, includes other material on Browne in the Northwest, including an interesting picture of the Duke of York published in *Harper's Magazine* in February, 1862, to illustrate Browne's text. The sketch is of the Duke of York and two of his wives (including one identified as Jenny Lind) in an awful condition of stupefied half-nakedness. According to Dillon (p. 175), the Duke of York became an alcoholic, though Northwestern defenders of the chief denied this. Browne's articles infuriated Northwesterners, especially his devastating account of the town of Port Townsend: "From what I saw during my stay there, I formed the opinion that the Duke of York and his amiable family were not below the average of white citizens. . . ."

SIMMONS DURING THE INDIAN WAR: Simmons's work as an Indian agent is in a report by Lieutenant W. B. Gosnell to Governor Stevens, dated December 31, 1856, in the *Washington Historical Quarterly*, Vol. VIII, p. 298:

> At this stage of affairs it is proper to refer to the prompt and efficient action of M. T. Simmons, Indian Agent, in breaking up the combination of the Sound tribes. Immediately after the White River massacre he went to work to remove the friendly Indians to a distance from the scene of hostilities. . . . He told them the war ground was on the east side of the Sound, and that all who remained on that side would be considered hostiles by the whites and treated accordingly— and that all who desired to be regarded as friendly must remove to the west side. To effect such an object at such a time was no trifling undertaking, but by indefatigable exertions and at great personal risk, he at length succeeded in removing all the Indians who were in danger of becoming disaffected, except a few who remained in Seattle. . . . Thus those removed were placed on Reservation under the charge of the Local Agents whose business it was to give notice of any suspicious movements. The hostiles saw that it was impossible to receive assistance from the friendly Indians so long as they remained on Reservation, and Leschi made no attempt, except in the case of his descent on Fox Island, to break up the whole system. Having met with but little success in that attempt, he never repeated it.

VI (pages 102–111)

MAYNARD LAWSUITS: *Report of the Decisions of the Supreme Court of Washington Territory*, Lydia A. Maynard vs. Thomas B. Valentine, July term, 1880, pp. 3–19; Henry C. Maynard et al appellant vs. W. C. Hill, et al, appellees, p. 321; George W. Bullene vs. Abraham Garrison (concerning Maynard's donation claim), p. 588, etc.

MAYNARD'S ROUTE ALONG THE PLATTE: This section is drawn from Maynard's diary, as printed by Prosch, and from my own observations in following the Oregon Trail. I used maps prepared by the Nebraska Historical Society, *Platte River Routes*, Vol. I, Nos. 14–32, and Nebraska Department of Roads maps of Jefferson, Thayer, Marshall, Clay, Adams, Kearney, Phelps, Gosper, Dawson and Lincoln counties. Joseph Steele, *Across the Plains in 1850*, follows the route at the time of Maynard's trip. (He was at Fort Kearney on June 14, 1850; Maynard was there on June 3, 1850). Merrill Mattes, *The Great Platte River Road*, contains an exhaustive report of all the routes.

Chapter IV. The Easterners

I (pages 112–114)

WINTHROP IN PANAMA: Laura Winthrop Johnson, *Life and Poems of Theodore Winthrop*, pp. 92–136.

WINTHROP AND JESSE APPLEGATE: Winthrop's letter to his sister Laura, from Portland, April 30, 1853, in the Tacoma edition of *The Canoe and the Saddle*, p. 246.

WINTHROP'S FAMILY BACKGROUND: Lawrence Shaw Mayo, *The Winthrop Family in America*; Richard Dunn, *Puritans and Yankees, The Winthrop Dynasty of New England*; Elbridge Colby, *Theodore Winthrop*; Laura Winthrop Johnson, *Life and Poems of Theodore Winthrop*. Winthrop is described in his sister's book, p. 4, and in George William Curtis's biographical introduction to Winthrop's novel, *Cecil Dreeme*. Winthrop's comment on the Oregon people is in *The Canoe and the Saddle*, p. 104.

MALCOLM BRECK: Winthrop's letter to Laura, *The Canoe and the Saddle*, Tacoma edition, p. 246.

II (pages 114–120)

BRECK AND ASPINWALL RELATIONSHIP: Samuel Breck, *Genealogy of the Breck Family*, p. 55. Malcolm Breck as mayor of Portland is in H. W. Scott, *History of Portland, Oregon*, p. 194. Breck's partner in his Portland store is identified by Scott as W. S. Ogden of New York, a nephew of Peter Skene Ogden. See William Ogden Wheeler, *The Ogden Family in America*.

WINTHROP AND THE ASPINWALL FAMILY: Letters of Theodore Winthrop, New York Public Library: July 26, 1849; April 1, 1851; April 14, 1851; June 16, 1851; and others.

THE ASPINWALL AND ROOSEVELT FAMILIES: Algernon Aiken Aspinwall, *The Aspinwall Genealogy*, p. 110; Franklin Delano Roosevelt, p. 168.

WINTHROP AT YALE: Colby, pp. 22–25; Laura Johnson, pp. 5–6. TRAVELS IN EUROPE, Johnson, p. 42, Colby, pp. 27–32; Winthrop letters, New York Public Library.

MEETING WITH ASPINWALL IN PARIS: Laura Johnson, p. 42, says the meeting came during a visit with "Dick Hunt, an old schoolmate. . . ."

PACIFIC MAIL STEAMSHIP COMPANY: Winthrop, letter of April 14, 1851, gives the figure of a profit of $70,000 on a single voyage.

ASPINWALL AND GEORGE LAW: Joseph P. Schott, *Rails Across Panama*. A contemporary view of Law is in Junius Henry Browne, *The Great Metropolis*, p. 642, "one of the most unpopular men."

JOHN LLOYD STEPHENS: Stephens's original mission is in his introduction to *Incidents of Travel in Central America, Chiapas, and Yucatan*. His career is related in Victor Wolfgang Von Hagen, *Maya Explorer*. The business of the railroad is in F. N. Otis, *History of the Panama Railroad*, and in William R. Scott, *The Americans in Panama*.

WINTHROP'S DUTIES: Letter of April 14, 1851; his journey to Switzerland with Aspinwall's son, Johnson, p. 73; buying pictures for Aspinwall, letter, April 29, 1852.

GOLD ROBBERIES IN PANAMA: Schott, *Rails across Panama*, pp. 60–63, 99, 145.

WINTHROP'S RESIGNATION: Inquires about coal, letter March 10, 1852; offers his resignation to Aspinwall, letter, August 19, 1852.

CONDITIONS IN PANAMA: Schott, p. 145.

WINTHROP IN PANAMA: His office, Johnson, pp. 94–95; guard of $2 million gold shipment, p. 105; works on a salary without doing anything, p. 105; gold shipment of the *California*, p. 113; his sixth trip across Panama, p. 128.

III   (pages 120–127)

WINTHROP AND DR. McNULTY: Georgia Willis Read and Ruth Gaines, *Gold Rush, the Journals, Drawings and Other Papers of J. Goldsborough Bruff*, Vol. I, pp. 468–469.

WINTHROP AND COLONEL BONNEVILLE: Johnson, p. 139. The letter was from General Ethan Allen Hitchcock. *Washington Historical Quarterly*, Vol. II, October, 1907, states that General Hitchcock was in command of the Pacific division with headquarters in Benecia, California.

MEETING WITH PETER SKENE OGDEN: Letter, May 1, 1853, in the Tacoma edition of *The Canoe and the Saddle*, p. 248.

SMALLPOX: Letter of June 13, 1853, p. 250 of Tacoma edition. Grant on smallpox, *Personal Memoirs*, p. 104. Winthrop's trip down the Columbia is in his letter of June 13, 1853. His visit to Applegate is in his letter of June 28, 1853, in the Tacoma edition.

RELIGION: Winthrop's admission that he has neither faith nor religion is in his letter to his mother, August 19, 1852. Comments on Winthrop are throughout George Templeton Strong's diary, especially January 31, 1851; October 22, 1854; July 16, 1856; July 23, 1857; January 13, 1861; May 11, 1868.

POETRY OF LAURA WINTHROP JOHNSON: Laura Winthrop Johnson, *Poems of Twenty Years*. The kinship of John Winthrop and the poet William Alabaster is in Leander Bishop's *History of American Manufacturers, 1608 to 1860*, in the discussion of Winthrop and his iron works, and appears also in the *Encyclopaedia Britannica*, 10th ed. Alabaster appears in Winthrop's letters to Laura Winthrop Johnson.

WINTHROP AND APPLEGATE: Letter of June 28 and July 11, 1853, in Tacoma edition, pp. 255–259. Applegate's farm and library are in Powers, *History of Oregon Literature*, pp. 368–372, and in Works Progress Administration, *Oregon*, pp. 317–318. Winthrop's consideration of settling in Oregon is in his letter of July 12, 1853, Tacoma edition, pp. 257–258.

IV (pages 127–142)

BONNEVILLE: Meany, *History of the State of Washington*, p. 59, calls Bonneville "a history-made man," confirming the judgment of H. M. Chittenden in *The American Fur Trade*.

CAPTAIN WILLIAM HOWARD: *Herringshaw's Library of American Biography*, Vol. III, p. 232. Howard's service in the Marine Revenue Service is in the official records of the Coast Guard. See also *Alaska and Its History*, by Morgan Sherwood, pp. 253–270.

NAT WILLIS: His position in New York literary life is in Van Wyck Brooks, *The Times of Melville and Whitman*. A bitter portrait is in the novel *Ruth Hall* by Fanny Fern, the pseudonym of Willis's sister. Junius Henry Browne, in *The Great Metropolis*, described Willis at the age of fifty-eight "as vivacious as an eighteen-year-old girl." Willis's poem to Laura Winthrop is in Laura Winthrop Johnson, *Eight Hundred Miles in an Ambulance*, reprinted from Willis's first book of poems, *Sketches*.

RICHARD STORRS WILLIS: Winthrop's letter of February, 1849, in the New York Public Library.

CAPTAIN HOWARD AND MRS. FORREST: *Report of the Forrest Divorce Case, Containing the Full and Unabridged Testimony of all the Witnesses*, by the Law Reporter, *New York Herald*. Howard's unknown whereabouts is on p. 152. The official court records of the Forrest divorce case are in the Law Library of New York University.

HOWARD IN THE NORTHWEST: His coal mine at Bellingham is in Lelah Jackson Edson, *The Fourth Corner*, p. 22; also Tacoma edition, pp. 241, 259, 264.

EDWIN FORREST AND HOWARD: Richard Moody, *Edwin Forrest, First Star of the American Stage*. Forrest's career, pp. 11–15; friendships with men, pp. 47, 72, 113; dissipations in Europe, pp. 121–139; his earnings, p. 185; conflicts with Macready, pp. 251–267.

DIVORCE CASE: The details are drawn from *Report of the Forrest Divorce Case* . . . for the most part, with some additional details from contemporary newspaper accounts; and other sources for identification of individuals, i.e., A. H. Messiter, *A History of the Choir and Music of Trinity Church*, p. 31, for identification of Mrs. Forrest's sister.

ASTOR PLACE RIOT: Forrest's part in the riots is in Moody, pp. 292–297; his assault on Willis, pp. 320–326.

WINTHROP AND HOWARD: Howard is mentioned in Winthrop's letter of August 23, 1848. On the Cowlitz: *The Canoe and the Saddle*, Tacoma edition, pp. 259–263; Jackson's farm, p. 260.

WINTHROP ON PUGET SOUND: His view of Steilacoom is in the Tacoma edition, p. 262; the Hudson's Bay comment on Howard is on pp. 241 and 263. Dr. Tolmie's canoe, pp. 263–264. Tolmie's Indian legends, pp. 274–279; also, William Tolmie, *Physician and Fur Trader: The Journals of William Fraser Tolmie*. Winthrop at Victoria, Tacoma edition, pp. 279–280. Howard's coal mine, Edson, *The Fourth Corner*, p. 23. Contemporary opinions of the Indians are drawn from Swan, *The Northwest Coast*, Hines, *Wild Life in Oregon*, Ogden, *Traits of American Indian Life*, etc. The resolution of the Washington legislature thanking the Hudson's Bay Company for its action on Ebey's death is in the *Washington Historical Quarterly*, Vol. I, No. 1, 1906.

FROM PORT TOWNSEND TO NISQUALLY: This section is entirely from *The Canoe and the Saddle*, pp. 22–44, aside from minor additions for clarity. The song "Malbrook," which Winthrop mentions the Indians sang, is a French folk song, supposedly dating from the Crusades, whose full title is "Mort en Convoi de l'Invincible Malbrough." It was a favorite song of Marie Antoinette, and Napoleon is reported to have hummed it as he crossed the Nieman River to invade Russia. An adaptation of the tune is in *Le Mariage de Figaro*. What the Indians were singing was the tune generally known to Americans as "We Won't Go Home Until Morning." The *Winnipeg Free Press*, May 16 and 19, 1966, related the history of the song in articles by Gene Telpner.

V   (pages 142–156)

WINTHROP'S RIDE OVER NACHES PASS: This section is based on *The Canoe and the Saddle*, pp. 61–141, except for minor details, as in the identification of Edward Jay Allen as the person in charge of the road builders, and the material on McClellan's failure to find a railway pass through the Cascade Mountains.

McCLELLAN ON THE CASCADES: Lillian Alice Dease Crane, *McClellan in Washington State*, p. 24; Isaac Stevens, *Report of Explorations of a Route for the North Pacific Railroad*, Vol. I, p. 387. Much of McClellan's report is incomprehensible because he used his own names for places, but the distances traveled each day can be worked out from it.

Other sources used: Philip Henry Overmeyer, "George B. McClellan in the Pacific Northwest," *Pacific Northwest Quarterly*, Vol. 32, No. 1, January, 1941; Thomas W. Prosch, "The Military Roads of Washington Territory," *Washington Historical Quarterly*, Vol. II, No. 2, pp. 118–126; Louis LeGrand, *Geo. B. McClellan, General-in-Chief*. Oscar Winthur, *The Old Oregon Country*, pp. 129–130, gives McClellan's orders, with additional detail in LeGrand, pp. 44–47. Joseph T. Hazard, *Pacific Crest Trails from Alaska to Cape Horn*, pp. 100–103, says, "McClellan found the task beyond his liking, and failed to complete it. . . ."

GRANT AND McCLELLAN AT VANCOUVER: Grant, *Personal Memoirs of U. S. Grant*, Vol. I, p. 102.

WINTHROP'S MEETING WITH LIEUTENANT HODGES: In 1913 John Williams of Tacoma, Washington, published a fine edition of *The Canoe and the Saddle* as part of a campaign to change the name of Mount Rainier to Mount Tacoma. The appendix, pp. 323–326, contains the recollections of Brigadier General Henry C. Hodges of his encounters with Winthrop. Winthrop's own account of "Lieutenant H." is on pp. 86–87.

MEETING WITH THE ROAD BUILDERS: Allen's career is in Blanche Billings Mahlberg, "Edward J. Allen, Pioneer and Roadbuilder," *Pacific Northwest Quarterly*, Vol. 44, No. 4, 1953, pp. 157–160. Allen's recollections of Winthrop are in the Tacoma edition, pp. 326–331. Allen arrived in the Northwest in 1852, at twenty-two, took part in the Monticello convention, promoted the Naches Pass road and raised money for it from the settlers, was placed in charge of the work and accomplished the results described by Winthrop and by George Hines's *First Trip by Immigrants through the Cascades*. Allen (Tacoma edition, p. 328) said McClellan in 1854 gave him "the contract to expend what remained of the $20,000." He reported that a road over the pass would cost $500,000 and "hence that idea was abandoned." Allen is said to have been one of the party that made the first ascent of Mount Adams (Nard Jones, *Evergreen Land*, p. 104) in August, 1854. He then traveled to San Francisco and returned to Pittsburgh in 1855, having been in the Northwest slightly over two years. He served in the Civil War and was an able writer. He died in 1915. No other pioneer figure became as prominent in Northwest history on the strength of so little actual experience in the region. His recollections are generally dubious.

WINTHROP'S MEETING WITH McCLELLAN: Winthrop's account is in *The Canoe and the Saddle*, pp. 141–145. For the nature of the country near Naches Pass, see American Alpine Club, *Climber's Guide to the Cascade and Olympic Mountains of Washington*, pp. 239, 308, and Robert Cantwell, "High Path to a Wild Paradise," *Sports Illustrated*, August 5, 1963, pp. 48–55. Essential to an understanding of the danger to emigrants caused by McClellan's failure is the address by George H. Himes, "An Account of Crossing the Plains in 1853, and of the First Trip by Immigrants Through the Cascade Mountains via Natchess Pass," printed in *Transactions of the Thirty-fifth Annual Reunion of the Oregon Pioneers Association, June 19, 1907*, pp. 134–152. A party of 155 persons, with thirty-six wagons, became trapped in the pass, having taken the route under the mistaken belief that the road had been completed, and a disaster comparable to that of the Donner Party was narrowly averted. Thomas Prosch, "The Military Roads of Washington Territory," *Washington Historical Quarterly*, Vol. II, No. 2, January, 1908, pp. 118–126, summarized McClellan's work: "Of the task McClellan made an entire failure. He expended in unknown ways much of the money [$20,000] but as far as the citizens and immigrants were aware, not a dollar in actual road construction." See also Overmeyer, "George B. McClellan and the Pacific Northwest," *Pacific Northwest Quarterly*, January, 1941, p. 35; Lillian Alice Dease Crane, *McClellan in Washington State*, p. 30; Meany, *History of the State of Washington*, pp. 60, 160–161.

After McClellan's failure to find a railroad pass through the mountains,

Governor Stevens sent Frederick Lander, a member of his surveying party, with another exploring expedition, and Lander (later McClellan's intelligence officer during the Civil War) also reported there was no way through them, both reports made ridiculous by Abiel Tinkham's successful crossing—a costly success for Stevens, for McClellan's enmity lasted until Stevens's death early in the Civil War. Louis LeGrand, *Geo. B. McClellan, General-in-Chief, U.S.A.* pp. 47–52, records McClellan's disparagement of Tinkham's achievement: "I do not think that any important conclusions should be based on the results of Mr. Tinkham's trip." William Henry Hurlbert, *General McClellan and the Conduct of the War*, contains a vehement denunciation of blatant orators and vague and passionate men (unidentified) who exaggerated the value of the wilderness or who criticized McClellan's work there. Hurlbert was a character in Theodore Winthrop's novel *Cecil Dreeme* (Van Wyck Brooks, *The Times of Melville and Whitman*, p. 197). He has been identified as the hero of the novel, the painter Cecil Dreeme, certainly erroneously, for Hurlbert's views were at the opposite pole from those of Winthrop in all respects, and Hurlbert had been the center of a scandal in the Winthrop family through his attempts to blackmail the wife of one of its members.

VI   (pages 156–166)

WINTHROP AND STRAIN: Laura Winthrop Johnson, *Life and Poems*, pp. 172–190, quotes Winthrop on the disaster of the Strain party: "It is difficult to see how any men in their senses could have been so totally deceived with regard to the whole character of the Isthmus." Lieutenant Strain is reported (LeGrand, p. 31) to have been an associate of McClellan's in an earlier exploring venture.

WINTHROP IN NEW YORK AND ST. LOUIS: Johnson, p. 261 and following.

WINTHROP IN THE CIVIL WAR: Johnson, pp. 280–296; Curtis, biographical introduction to *Cecil Dreeme*, pp. 14–16; Colby, pp. 65–78.

DEATH OF WINTHROP: Johnson, pp. 91–96; Colby, pp. 74–78. Colby disparages Winthrop's part in drafting the plan of the attack on Little Bethel, as did Curtis. Winthrop wrote home (*Life and Poems*, p. 291) a few hours before the battle. He reported estimates of the number of Confederates in the outpost as ranging from 400 to 2,500—quite a difference, and a characteristically ironic commentary by Winthrop regarding military intelligence. Winthrop also remarked that "if we find them where we expect"—another typical comment—some prisoners should be taken. He anticipated "a sharp scrimmage, or half a battle." He added that if he returned he would send home his notes of "the Plan of Attack, part made up from the General's notes [Butler], part from my own fancies. We march at midnight." Appleton's *Annual Cyclopedia*, 1861, pp. 343–346, gives a detailed account of the fiasco and its shock to the North.

SUBSEQUENT CAREERS OF PERSONS IN WINTHROP'S ACCOUNT: Loolowcan is spelled Qualchin in most histories of the Indian wars of the Northwest. His murder of Bolon that started hostilities is in Meany, pp. 179–180 and 215, although his record and that of his father Owhi are in all accounts of the war. Owhi's death is described in the Tacoma edition, p. 61. The Duke of York, in addition to the note in J. Ross Browne's article in *Harper's Magazine*, is in Elwood Evans, *History of the Pacific Northwest*, in Swan's *The Northwest Coast*, and in most accounts of pioneer days. Captain Howard's record after leaving the Pacific Northwest is in the official records of the Coast Guard, and his part in the Davidson expedition to Alaska is in Morgan Sherwood, *Alaska and Its History*. Mrs. Forrest's career on the stage is in Moody, p. 327 and following.

WINTHROP'S BELIEF: Winthrop's conviction that the grandeur of the scenery and the beauty of the country would gradually work an influence on men to generate new systems of thought and life is grained too deeply into the text of *The Canoe and the Saddle* to permit isolated quotations. The belief that the country was in itself a force in modifying conduct and shaping character was quite frequently expressed in early Northwestern writing, and it is true that such people as Joe Meek and Ewing Young appeared to change, as, for that matter, did Dr. John McLoughlin and others. But Winthrop's comment was subtler. It dealt with the content of experience, with the nature of images lodged in the memory, to form there a reservoir on which the individual could draw, or would inevitably draw. The creative spirit, or the poet, as he sometimes called him, was that part of society especially vulnerable to "the multitude of agents" always at work to dwarf and to poison him. That dwarfing and poisoning, as it was exemplified in the life of Hall Kelley and perhaps in the life of Winthrop himself, would go on, but resistance was strengthened in a new land, as he felt himself to be strengthened, and he suggested that the multitude of agents would also be influenced to moderation and calm—to civilization—by the same strengthening agencies. More deeply he implied that the country and the wilderness rescued him from despair, and it is this aspect of *The Canoe and the Saddle* which, with all its mannerisms and facetiousness and self-conscious independence, still links it with Proust, the Proust who wrote, in *Within a Budding Grove*, in terms almost identical with those of Winthrop, of "that desire to live which is reborn in us whenever we become conscious anew of beauty and of happiness."

Part Two

Chapter V. Salmon

I (pages 169–174)

NORTHWESTERN ARTS: Applegate's library is in Joseph Schaffer, "Jesse Applegate: Pioneer, Statesman and Philosopher," *Washington Historical Quarterly*, Vol. I, No. 4, July, 1907, p. 228. The family background of Edward Finck is in Henry Theophilus Finck, *My Adventures in the Golden Age of Music*. Other Edward Finck compositions, "Ashland Schottische,"

"Astoria Waltz," "Baker City March," "Dalles Polka," "Portland Waltz," "Roseburg Caso," celebrate Oregon places. "The Umpqua Is Calling for Me" was composed by Z. M. Parvin. "Dear Little Webfoot Girl," by E. A. Borm and J. H. Courtienne-Dworzak, was published in Portland in 1908.

Alfred Powers, *History of Oregon Literature*, reported in 1935 that he could locate only eighty songs written in the area in the preceding seventy-five years. The statement is misleading in an otherwise invaluable book, for an examination of titles and Oregon and Washington composers in the catalogue of copyright entries in the Library of Congress reveals more than three hundred in that period, and a more thorough search would undoubtedly turn up more. In view of the small population of the region, it probably produced more songs of local patriotism or feeling than any other section of the country. Unfortunately, they were not very good, and few became popular. Such titles as "Watch Tacoma Grow," "Sounds from Bellingham Bay," "She Is Sleeping where the Silent Tilden Flows," "Seattle," "Dear Seattle," and "Queen City of the Sound" are typical. Two Northwestern writers of song lyrics produced popular favorites, Ballard MacDonald of Portland, who wrote the words to "Beautiful Ohio" and "The Trail of the Lonesome Pine," among many others, and Stoddard King of Spokane, who as a student at Yale wrote "There's a Long Long Trail A-Winding" to music by Zo Elliott, a World War I favorite that became one of the most widely sung of popular songs. Harold Weeks and Oliver Wallace of Seattle produced an immensely popular work, "Hindustan" (whose success inspired George Gershwin to write "Swanee"), but on the whole the popular and concert music of Northwestern composers failed to take hold, nationally or in the Northwest. (Interview, Harold Weeks, Seattle, 1965.)

YACOLT BURN: Stewart Holbrook, *Burning an Empire*, pp. 115–120; Ralph Hidy, *Timber and Men*, pp. 229–231. Fred Becker of Ukiah, California, gave me his recollections of logging in the burned-over area long after the fire.

POPULATION: Details from the 1850 census are in Elwood Evans, *The State of Washington*, p. 40.

ELIZABETH CHAMPNEY: *The New York Times*, October 14, 1922; *Who Was Who*, 1897–1942.

II (pages 174–182)

HORSEFLY RIVER SALMON RUNS: Robert Cantwell, "Melodrama on the Horsefly River," *Sports Illustrated*, October 21, 1961, pp. 70–80; International Pacific Salmon Fisheries Commission Annual Report, 1962.

SOCKEYE SALMON: J. W. Jones, *The Salmon*. There are many references to their abundance in early Northwestern literature; e.g., Walter C. Moberly, *The Rocks and Rivers of British Columbia*, p. 30. See also James Gilchrist Swan, *The Northwest Coast*, p. 140: "From the last of August to the first of December these salmon come into the Bay in myriads, and every river, brook, creek or little stream is completely crammed with them."

FRASER RIVER: The background of the Quesnel River dam is from research by Mrs. Dolly Connolly. The slides on the Fraser are in Bruce Hutchinson, *The Fraser*, and C. P. Lyons, *Milestones on the Mighty Fraser*. Other sources are Loyd Royal, *The Effect of Regulating Selectivity on the Productivity of Fraser River Sockeye*, and interviews with Loyd Royal, director, International Pacific Salmon Fisheries Commission, and Clarence Pautzke, then head of the United States Fish and Wildlife Service.

III (pages 182–186)

INDIANS AND EXPLORERS: Ruth Underhill, *Indians of the Pacific Northwest*; John Jewitt, *Narrative of the Adventures and Sufferings of John R. Jewitt*; Ross Cox, *The Columbia River*. The failure of the salmon run on the Columbia in 1827 is mentioned in Cox's book.

COMMERCIAL FISHING: The figures on the annual catch on the Columbia in early years are from Evans, *The State of Washington*, pp. 92–97.

FOREST FIRES AT THE SPAWNING GROUNDS: The material on this section is almost entirely drawn from personal observation on the Horsefly River, August, 1961, together with interviews with old residents of the area, including Frank Jones, the original homesteader at the spawning grounds, and Mrs. Gibbons, the local historian.

The effect of the increased water temperature on the 1961 salmon run is in the International Pacific Salmon Fisheries Commission report for 1962.

Chapter VI. Tree Farms

I (pages 193–197)

WEYERHAEUSER KIDNAPPING: The material in this section has been drawn from the day-by-day accounts in the *Seattle Times*, *Seattle Post-Intelligencer* and *The New York Times* during the period in which George Weyerhaeuser was held and during the trials of his kidnappers. This chapter is expanded from an article, Robert Cantwell, "The Shy Tycoon Who Owns One Six-Hundred-and-Fortieth of the United States," in *Sports Illustrated*, August 18, 1969. Additional material was provided by Bernard Orell, vice president of the Weyerhaeuser Company, and by George Weyerhaeuser, president. The historian Murray Morgan of Tacoma contributed material on the background.

WEYERHAEUSER FAMILY: Ralph W. Hidy, *Timber and Men*, pp. 4–6, 212–217; Frederick Weyerhaeuser, *Men and Trees*, pp. 8–13, 14–16. Sarah Jenkins Salo, *Timber Concentrations in the Pacific Northwest*, p. 5, says: "This family has been and is the most important family in American lumber history, and as such the Weyerhaeusers' contribution to our culture should be discussed in general historical works as well as in special biographical studies."

WEYERHAEUSER AND HILL: Joseph Gilpin, *Life of James J. Hill*, Vol. I, pp. 383–462; Vol. II, pp. 31–73. Hidy, *Timber and Men*, pp. 212–250;

Frederick Weyerhaeuser, *Men and Trees*, pp. 13–14. George Leighton, "Seattle," *Harper's Magazine*, February, 1939, reported that Weyerhaeuser chose a home in St. Paul next door to Hill by accident. The extent of the Weyerhaeuser purchase of Northern Pacific lands is in United States Department of Commerce and Labor, Bureau of Corporations, *The Lumber Industry, Concentration of Timber Ownership in Selected Regions*, *July*, 1914, Vol. I, pp. 228–267; Vol. II, pp. 13–45.

WEYERHAEUSER AND THE MUCKRAKERS: Lincoln Steffens, *Autobiography*, pp. 365–368; Hidy, *Timber and Men*, pp. 301–305.

II   (pages 197–199)

KIDNAPPING OF GEORGE WEYERHAEUSER: The material in this section has been drawn from contemporary newspaper reports, with minor corrections and additions supplied by George Weyerhaeuser.

III   (pages 199–201)

THE WEYERHAEUSERS AND PUBLIC RELATIONS: David Lavender, *The Land of Giants*, calls the establishment of the first tree farm a master stroke in public relations. That the impulse had deeper origins was stated by Bernard Orell, a former professor of forestry at the University of Oregon, in his recollections of John Philip Weyerhaeuser (interviews with the author) and in fact represented a trend visible in Northwestern history from the start in the conflict between economic exploitation and the desire to preserve the scenic beauty of the region. The shock to the family caused by the kidnapping of George Weyerhaeuser is in Salo, *Timber Concentrations in the Pacific Northwest*, p. 60. The growth of the tree farm movement is in Hidy, *Timber and Men*, pp. 502–508; the effect on wildlife, *Washington State Game Bulletin*, Vol. 17, No. 1, 1965.

The establishment of the first Weyerhaeuser campground: interviews, Bernard Orell and Miss Helen Leonard, Longview, Washington.

IV   (pages 201–207)

TREE FARMS AND RECREATION: The hunter's maps supplied by the Weyerhaeuser Company outline the tree farm areas and list campgrounds, roads, rivers and trails. The material in this section is largely drawn from my own notes made during visits to the tree farm campgrounds in Washington, supplemented with interviews, especially with Howard Millan of Puyallup, a forester, and B. F. Franklin of Enumclaw, who cruised much of the area in the Cascade Mountains.

Statistics on the elk herds and the fish and wild life in the tree farm areas were supplied by Clar Pratt, of the Washington Fish and Game Commission. The ornithological work of George Cantwell for the United States Fish and Wildlife Service in the areas appears throughout Stanley Jewett, *Birds of Washington State*; there is interesting material on James Graham Cooper (the naturalist with Governor Stevens's railroad survey) in the same volume and also in Edgar Erskine Hume, *Ornithologists of the United States Army Medical Corps*, pp. 38–51.

V (pages 207–211)

HISTORIC AREAS: The most familiar source on the near destruction of the first emigrant train to cross Naches Pass is Ezra Meeker, *The Busy Life of Eighty-Five Years*. It is, however, confusing because Meeker's own trip through the pass was made later, and the most coherent account is George Himes's in *Transactions of the Thirty-fifth Annual Reunion of the Oregon Pioneers Association*.

COMPANY TOWNS: The timber holdings of the Carlisle-Pennell Company are in the Department of Commerce and Labor, *The Lumber Industry, Standing Timber, Washington*, Vol. II, pp. 34–35. The contrast between the towns of Carlisle and Onalaska is drawn from the personal recollections of the author. Carlisle is also briefly described in Works Progress Administration, *Washington, A Guide to the Evergreen State*, p. 551: "a ghost logging town, forlorn cottages on both sides of the road, mingling with weather-beaten business buildings."

Chapter VII. The Columbia: New Systems of Thought

I (pages 212–218)

CANAL FLATS: This section is expanded from an article, Robert Cantwell, "The Columbia, a Gem of a River," *Sports Illustrated*, February 24, 1964, pp. 50–56. The place is described in Tyrrell's edition of *David Thompson's Narrative*; William Baillie-Grohman, *Fifteen Years Sport and Life in the Hunting Grounds of Western America and British Columbia*; Madison Lorraine, *The Columbia Unveiled*, pp. 25–57.

BAILLIE-GROHMAN: His biography is included in *English Sporting Authors*. His disputes over trophy head measurements are included in *Fifteen Years Sport and Life*, as is his fight with Sproul, pp. 225–240.

SOCIETY FIGURES ON THE UPPER COLUMBIA: Norman Hacking, "Steamboat Days on the Upper Columbia and Upper Kootenay," *British Columbia Historical Quarterly*, January–April 1, 1951. Mrs. Algernon St. Maur and Lady Gwendolyn Rous, p. 15; Lady Adela Cochrane, p. 16; Frank Lascelles, p. 34. Additional details are in Arthur Clutterbuck and James Lees, *A Ramble in British Columbia*, pp. 94, 154, 172.

STEAMBOATS TO CANAL FLATS: Hacking, "Steamboat Days," pp. 10–12, 15, 18, 21, 34. The passage of the steamer *North Star* across the flats from the Kootenay to the Columbia is in Lorraine, *The Columbia Unveiled*, p. 50, with additional material in the later account by Hacking.

II (pages 218–221)

UNITED STATES–CANADIAN TREATY: There is no detailed study of the relations of the two countries over the boundary waters. Ernest Watkins, "The Columbia River: A Gordian Knot," in *International Review*, Vol. XII, No. 4, 1957, summarizes the history of the treaties from the Canadian point of view. The late General Andrew McNaughton, former chief of staff of the Canadian army and for twelve years chairman of the Canadian section of the International Joint Commission, provided much of the background in an interview with the author at his home in Ottawa in October, 1961.

DAVID THOMPSON'S MAPS: The appearance of Thompson's long-lost maps during negotiations for the Columbia River Treaty in 1954 is described in Kerry Wood, "Two Notable Explorers of the Canadian West," *Winnipeg Free Press*, 1964.

MICA CREEK DAM: Personal interviews, Mica Creek, September 14–15, 1965. The *Seattle Argus*, June 24, 1966, describes the transformation of Boat Encampment and the building of the town of Mica Creek. *Winnipeg Free Press*, "Boom Town to Ghost Town," June 11, 1965, describes the expansion of the town to a population of 4,000 and its planned removal to restore the wilderness when the dam is completed.

III   (pages 222–234)

CANOE RIVER: This section is an expanded version of Robert Cantwell, "Riding Down a Dying River," *Sports Illustrated*, November 21, 1966, pp. 80–94. The description of Valemount is from the author's observations, September 1–7, 1965.

CANOE RIVER RAPIDS: The descent of the Canoe River is traced on the maps drawn in preparation for the building of the Mica Creek Dam by the Canadian Department of Mines and Technical Surveys, on a scale of one inch to one half-mile. A series of six maps shows the river and short portions of its tributaries, as follows: M.S. 79 (below Valemount); M.S. 78 (Bulldog Creek area); M.S. 76 (Hugh Allan Creek); M.S. 75 (Foster Creek); and (in the Columbia Basin Series) M.S. 31 (Boat Encampment).

THOMPSON'S CAMP: The latitude and longitude of Thompson's camp-sites are in his unpublished field notes, Vol. XI, Book No. 26, pp. 147–153. Photostatic copies are in the Public Archives of Canada at Ottawa.

IV   (pages 234–237)

CANOE RIVER HOT SPRINGS: This section is drawn from the notes of the author on the Canoe River, September 9–15, 1965.

V   (pages 237–246)

HISTORICAL REFERENCES: E. E. Rich, *History of the Hudson's Bay Company*, Vol. II, p. 579; Ross Cox, *The Columbia River*, p. 280; Paul Kane, *Wanderings of an Artist*, p. 222 and following; Ranald MacDonald, *The Narrative of His Early Life*. An edition of *The Expedition of Lewis and Clark* printed by Harper in New York in 1842 includes a considerable section on the Canoe River, which is identified as the North Fork of the Columbia in the introduction to the volume.

GOLD MINING NEAR BOAT ENCAMPMENT: Walter C. Moberly, *Columbia River Exploration*, 1865 (entry for September 10, 1865); also Walter Moberly, *The Rocks and Rivers of British Columbia*, p. 76 and following.

ALPHONSE EMONDS: Madison Lorraine, *The Columbia Unveiled*, pp. 163–171. Freeman Lewis, in *Down the Columbia*, referred disparagingly to Emond's practice of returning to Boat Encampment by way of Valemount and down the Canoe River, after taking his furs to Revelstoke, rather than by the shorter run down the Columbia to Boat Encampment from the railroad at Golden, but Lewis was obviously unfamiliar with the Canoe and knew nothing of the chain of Emond's cabins described by Lorraine.

Chapter VIII. Arts and Letters

The material in this chapter is derived from the books that are discussed in it and from the biographies of their authors.

Bibliography

Books

Applegate, Jesse. A *Day with the Cow Column in 1843*. Edited with an introduction and notes by Joseph Schafer. Chicago: printed for the Caxton Club, 1934.

Aspinwall, Algernon Aikin. *The Aspinwall Genealogy*. Rutland, Vt.: 1901.

Baillie-Grohman. *Fifteen Years Sport and Life in the Hunting Grounds of Western America and British Columbia*. London: Horace Cox, 1907.

Bakeless, John. *Lewis and Clark*. New York: William Morrow and Co., 1947.

Beckey, Fred. *Climber's Guide to the Cascade and Olympic Mountains*. New York: American Alpine Club, 1961.

Binns, Archie. *Northwest Gateway*. Garden City, N.Y.: Doubleday, Doran & Company, 1945.

———. *The Roaring Land*. New York: Robert M. McBride, 1942.

Breck, Samuel. *Genealogy of the Breck Family*. Omaha, Neb.: by the author, 1889.

Brooks, Charles Wolcott. *Japanese Wrecks Stranded and Picked up Adrift in the North Pacific Ocean*. San Francisco: California Academy of Sciences, 1876. (Facsimile edition Fairfield, Wash.: Ye Galleon Press, 1964.)

Browne, Junius Henry. *The Great Metropolis: A Mirror of New York*. Hartford, Conn.: American Publishing Company, 1869.

316

Bruff, J. Goldsborough. *Gold Rush, the Journals, Drawings and other Papers of J. Goldsborough Bruff.* Edited by Georgia Willis Read and Ruth Gaines. New York: Columbia University Press, 1944.

Buchanan, A. Russell. *David S. Terry of California, Dueling Judge.* San Marino, Calif.: Huntington Library, 1956.

Cantwell, Robert. *The Land of Plenty.* New York: Farrar and Rinehart, 1934.

————. *Laugh and Lie Down.* New York: Farrar and Rinehart, 1931.

Carey, Charles H. *A General History of Oregon Prior to 1861.* Two volumes. Portland, Ore.: Metropolitan Press, 1936.

Carver, Margaret R. and Fred E. *The Ancestors and Descendants of Jonathan Simmons and Mary Troutman and of Their Children Who Settled in Washington and Oregon.* Yakima, Wash.: By the author, 1970.

————. *Michael Troutman Simmons and Andrew Jackson Simmons.* Yakima, Wash.: By the author, 1967.

Case, Robert and Victoria. *Last Mountains, the Story of the Cascades.* New York: Doubleday, Doran & Company, 1945.

Clarke, Clinton G. *The Pacific Crest Trail.* Pasadena, Calif.: Vista del Arroya, 1935.

————. *The Pacific Crest Trailway.* Pasadena: Pacific Crest Trail System, 1945.

Clarke, S. A. *Pioneer Days in Oregon History.* Chicago: Clark, 1909.

Colby, Elbridge. *Theodore Winthrop.* New York: Twayne Publishers, 1965.

Coman, Edwin T., Jr., and Gibbs, Helen M. *Time, Tide and Timber: A Century of Pope and Talbot.* Palo Alto, Calif.: Stanford University Press, 1949.

Coues, Elliott. *The Manuscript Journals of Alexander Henry and David Thompson.* New York: Harper & Brothers, 1897.

Cox, Ross. *The Columbia River.* Edited with an introduction by Edgar I. and Jane R. Stewart. Norman, Okla.: University of Oklahoma Press, 1957.

Cutright, Paul Russell. *Meriwether Lewis, Naturalist.* Portland, Ore.: Oregon Historical Society, 1968.

Davis, H. L. *Honey in the Horn.* New York: Harper & Brothers, 1935.

————. *Kettle of Fire.* New York: William Morrow & Co., 1959.

DeVoto, Bernard. *The Journals of Lewis and Clark.* Boston: Houghton Mifflin, 1953.

Dillon, Richard H. *J. Ross Browne, Confidential Agent in Old California.* Norman, Okla.: University of Oklahoma Press, 1965.

————. *Meriwether Lewis: A Biography.* New York: Coward-McCann, 1965.

Dunn, Richard S. *Puritans and Yankees: The Winthrop Dynasty of New England 1630–1717.* Princeton, N.J.: Princeton University Press, 1962.

Edson, Lelah Jackson. *The Fourth Corner: Highlights from the Early Northwest.* Bellingham, Wash.: Cox Brothers, 1951.

Einarsen, Arthur S. *Black Brant: Sea Goose of the Pacific Coast.* Seattle, Wash.: University of Washington Press, 1965.

Emmons, Della Gould. *Nothing in Life Is Free: Through Naches Pass to Puget Sound.* Minneapolis, Minn.: The Northwestern Press, 1953.

Evans, Elwood. *History of the Pacific Northwest.* Portland, Ore.: North Pacific History Co., 1889.

———. *The State of Washington.* Tacoma: Washington World's Fair Commission, 1893.

Finck, Henry Theophilus. *My Adventures in the Golden Age of Music.* New York: Funk and Wagnalls Company, 1927.

———. *Romantic Love and Personal Beauty.* Two volumes. New York: Macmillan Co., 1887.

Gray, William Henry. *History of Oregon.* Portland, Ore.: Harris and Holman, 1870.

Griffith, Thomas. *The Waist-High Culture.* London: Hutchinson, 1960.

Grumbach, Doris. *The Company She Kept, a Revealing Portrait of Mary McCarthy.* New York: Coward-McCann, 1967.

Haig-Brown, Roderick. *Return to the River.* New York: William Morrow and Co., 1965.

Harper, J. Russell. *Paul Kane's Frontier.* Austin, Texas: University of Texas Press, 1971.

Hazard, Joseph T. *Pacific Crest Trails from Alaska to Cape Horn.* Seattle, Wash.: Superior Publishing Co., 1946.

Higginson, A. Henry. *British and American Sporting Authors.* Berryville, Va.: Blue Ridge Press, 1949.

Hill, Douglas. *The Opening of the Canadian West.* New York: John Day Company, 1967.

Hines, Gustavus. *Wild Life in Oregon.* New York: Worthington, 1881.

Holbrook, Stewart. *Burning an Empire: The Story of American Forest Fires.* New York: Macmillan Co., 1943.

———. *Far Corner.* New York: Macmillan, 1952.

Howay, Frederick. *Voyages of the Columbia to the Northwest Coast, 1787–1790, and 1790–1793.* Boston: Massachusetts Historical Society 1941.

Hult, Ruby El. *Lost Mines and Treasures of the Pacific Northwest.* Portland, Ore.: Binfords and Mort, 1960.

Hume, Edgar Erskine. *Ornithologists of the United States Army Medical Corps.* Baltimore, Md.: Johns Hopkins Press, 1942.

Hurlbert, William Henry. *Americans in Paris, or A Game of Dominoes.* New York: Samuel French, 1858.

———. *General McClellan and the Conduct of the War.* New York: Shelton and Company, 1864.

Hussey, J. A. *Champoeg: Place of Transition.* Portland, Ore.: Oregon Historical Society, 1967.

Innis, Harold A. *The Fur Trade in Canada.* New Haven, Conn.: Yale University Press, 1962.

Irving, Joseph. *The Annals of Our Time.* New York, n.d.

Irving, Washington. *Astoria*. Edited with an Introduction by William H. Goetzmann. Two volumes. Philadelphia: J. B. Lippincott Company, 1961.

Jacobs, Melvin C. *Winning Oregon*. Caldwell, Idaho: Caxton Printers, 1938.

Jewett, Stanley G., and others. *Birds of Washington State*. Seattle, Wash.: University of Washington Press, 1953.

Jewitt, John R. *Narrative of the Adventures and Sufferings of John R. Jewitt, only Survivor of the Ship* Boston. Ithaca, New York: Mack, Andrus and Cooper, 1816.

Johnson, Jalmar. *Builders of the Northwest*. New York: Dodd, Mead & Co., 1963.

Johnson, Laura Winthrop. *Eight Hundred Miles in an Ambulance*. Introduction by George William Curtis. Philadelphia: J. B. Lippincott Company, 1889.

———. *Poems of Twenty Years*. New York: De Witt C. Lent, 1874.

Jones, Nard. *Evergreen Land*. New York: Dodd, Mead & Co., 1947.

———. *Swift Flows the River*. New York: Dodd, Mead & Co., 1940.

Judson, Katherine. *Myths and Legends of the Northwest*. Chicago: McClurg, 1910.

Kane, Paul. *Wanderings of an Artist*. Toronto, Ont.: The Radisson Society, 1925.

Kelsey, Vera. *British Columbia Rides a Star*. New York: Harper & Brothers, 1958.

Kesey, Ken. *One Flew over the Cuckoo's Nest*. New York: Viking Press, 1962.

———. *Sometimes a Great Notion*. New York: Viking Press, 1963.

Lamb, Martha J. *History of the City of New York*. New York: Barnes, 1877.

Lavender, David. *The Land of Giants*. New York: Doubleday & Company, 1958.

Lees, J. A., and Clutterbuck, W. J. *B.C. 1887, A Ramble in British Columbia*. London: Longmans & Co., 1888.

LeGrand, Louis, M.D. *Geo. B. McClellan, General-in-Chief, U.S.A.* New York: Beadle and Company, n.d.

Leslie, Robert F. *High Trails West*. New York: Crown Publishers, 1967.

Lewis, Meriwether. *The Lewis and Clark Expedition*. Edited by Archibald Hanna. Philadelphia: J. B. Lippincott Company, 1961.

Lockwood, Frank. *Pioneer Days in Arizona*. New York: Macmillan Co., 1932.

Lorraine, Madison Jackson. *The Columbia Unveiled*. Los Angeles: Times-Mirror Press, 1924.

Lyman, William Denison. *The Columbia River*. New York: G. P. Putnam's Sons, 1909.

Lyons, C. P. *Milestones on the Mighty Fraser*. Vancouver, B.C.: Evergreen Press, 1950.

McCarthy, Mary. *A Charmed Life*. New York: Harcourt, Brace, 1954.

——. *The Humanist in the Bathtub.* New York: Harcourt, Brace, 1947.

——. *Memories of a Catholic Girlhood.* New York: Harcourt, Brace and World, 1957.

McCurdy, James. *By Juan de Fuca's Strait.* Portland, Ore.: Metropolitan Press, 1937.

MacDonald, Ranald. *The Narrative of His Early Life on the Columbia River under the Hudson's Bay Company Regime; of His Experiences in the Pacific Whale Fishery; and of His Great Adventure in Japan; with a Sketch of His Later Life on the Western Frontier. 1824–1894.* Spokane, Wash.: Eastern Washington Historical Society, 1920.

McDonald, T. H. *Exploring the Northwest Territory: Sir Alexander Mackenzie's Journal of a Voyage by Bark Canoe from Lake Athabasca to the Pacific Ocean in the Summer of 1789.* Norman, Okla.: University of Oklahoma Press, 1966.

Mackenzie, Alexander. *Voyage from Montreal on the River St. Lawrence through the Continent of North America to the Frozen and Pacific Oceans in the Years 1789 and 1793.* London: Cadell and Davis, 1801.

Mattes, Merrill J. *The Great Platte River Road.* Lincoln, Neb.: Nebraska Historical Society, 1969.

Mayo, Lawrence Shaw. *The Winthrop Family in America.* Boston: Massachusetts Historical Society, 1948.

Meany, Edmond S. *Diary of Wilkes in the Pacific Northwest.* Seattle, Wash.: University of Washington Press, 1926.

——. *History of the State of Washington.* New York: Macmillan, 1909.

——. *Mount Rainier: A Record of Explorations.* New York: Macmillan Co., 1916.

——. *Origin of Washington Geographic Names.* Seattle, Wash.: University of Washington Press, 1923.

Meares, John. *Voyages made in the years 1788 and 1789, from China to the northwest coast of North America.* London: Logographic Press, 1790.

Meeker, Ezra. *The Busy Life of Eighty-Five Years.* Seattle, Wash.: by the author, 1916.

Moberly, Walter C. *Columbia River Exploration, 1865.* New Westminster, B.C.: 1866.

——. *The Rocks and Rivers of British Columbia.* London: H. Blacklock, 1885.

Montgomery, Richard Gill. *The White-Headed Eagle: John McLoughlin.* New York: Macmillan Co., 1934.

Moody, Richard. *Edwin Forrest, First Star of the American Stage.* New York: Alfred A. Knopf, 1960.

Morgan, Murray. *Skid Road.* New York: Viking Press, 1956.

Morison, Samuel Eliot. *The Maritime History of Massachusetts, 1783–1860.* Boston: Houghton Mifflin, 1925.

Mourelle, Don Francisco Antonio. *Voyage of the Sonora in the Second Bucareli Expedition.* From the translation of the Hon. Daines Barrington, 1781. San Francisco, Calif.: Thomas Russell, 1920.

Nicholson, George. *Vancouver Island's West Coast.* Victoria, B.C.: Morriss, 1965.

Ogden, Peter Skene. *Traits of American Indian Life and Character. By a Fur Trader.* London: Smith Elder and Company, 1853.

Ormsby, Margaret. *British Columbia, a History.* Toronto, Ont.: Macmillan Co. of Canada, 1958.

Patterson, Raymond M., *The Buffalo Head.* New York: William Sloane Associates, 1961.

————. *The Dangerous River.* London: Allen and Unwin, Ltd., 1954.

Peers, Wilson Kinsey. *And There Was Salmon.* Portland, Ore.: Binfords & Morts, 1949.

Phillips-Wolley, Clive. *A Sportsman's Eden.* London: Bentley, 1888.

————. *Trottings of a Tenderfoot.* London: Bentley, 1884.

Piers, Sir Charles Piggott. *Sport and Life in British Columbia.* London: Heath Cranton, 1923.

Platt, Rutherford. *The Great American Forest.* Englewood Cliffs, New Jersey: Prentice-Hall, 1965.

Powell, Fred Wilbur. *Hall J. Kelley in Oregon.* Princeton, New Jersey: Princeton University Press, 1932.

————. *Hall Jackson Kelley, Prophet of Oregon.* Portland, Ore.: Ivy Press, 1917.

Powers, Alfred. *History of Oregon Literature.* Portland, Ore.: Metropolitan Press, 1935.

Prosch, Thomas W. *David S. Maynard and Catherine T. Maynard, Biographies of Two of the Oregon Immigrants of 1850.* Seattle, Wash.: Lowman and Hanford, 1906.

————. *A Chronological History of Seattle.* Seattle, Wash.: Dr. Charles North, 1950.

Reid, Robert. *Puget Sound and Western Washington.* Seattle, Wash. Sherman Printing Co., 1912.

Rich, E. E. *History of the Hudson's Bay Company 1670–1870.* Three volumes. New York: Macmillan Co., 1961.

Ross, Nancy Wilson. *Farthest Reach.* New York: Alfred A. Knopf, 1940.

Saint Maur, Susan Margaret, Duchess of Somerset. *Impressions of a Tenderfoot during a journey in search of Sport in the Far North West.* London: J. Murray, 1889.

Salisbury, Albert and Jane. *Here Rolled the Covered Wagons.* Seattle, Wash.: Superior Publishing Co., 1948.

————. *Two Captains West.* Seattle, Wash.: Superior Publishing Co., 1950.

Scott, H. W. *History of Portland, Oregon.* Syracuse, N.Y.: Mason, 1890.

Shaler, William. *Journal of a Voyage between China and the Northwest Coast of America, Made in 1804 by William Shaler.* Claremont, Calif.: Saunders Studio Press, 1935.

Shaw, George C. *The Chinook Jargon and How to Use It.* 1909. (Facsimile edition, Seattle, Wash.: Shorey Publications, 1965.)

Sherwood, Morgan B. *Alaska and Its History.* Seattle, Wash.: University of Washington Press, 1967.

Steele, the Rev. Joseph. *History of Castleton, Vermont*. Clearmont, N.H.: 1877.

Stevens, Hazard. *Life of Isaac Ingalls Stevens*. Boston: Houghton, Mifflin & Co., 1900.

Strong, George Templeton. *The Diary of George Templeton Strong*. Edited by Allan Nevins and Milton Hasley Thomas. New York: Macmillan, 1952.

Stuart, Robert. *On the Oregon Trail, Robert Stuart's Journey of Discovery (1812–1813)*. Edited by Kenneth A. Spaulding. Norman, Okla.: University of Oklahoma Press, 1953.

Swan, James Gilchrist. *The Northwest Coast*. New York: Harper & Brothers, 1857. (Facsimile edition, Fairfield, Wash.: Ye Galleon Press, 1966.)

Symons, Thomas William. *Report on the Upper Columbia River and the Great Plains of the Columbia*. 1884 (reprint, Fairfield, Wash.: Ye Galleon Press, 1967).

Thompson, David. *David Thompson's Narrative of His Explorations in Western America, 1784–1812*. Edited by J. B. Tyrrell. Toronto, Ont.: The Champlain Society, 1916.

———. *David Thompson's Narrative, 1784–1812*. Edited by Richard Glover. Toronto, Ont.: The Champlain Society, 1962.

Tolmie, William Fraser. *Physician and Fur Trader: the Journals of William Fraser Tolmie*. Vancouver, B.C.: Mitchell, 1963.

Underhill, Ruth. *Indians of the Pacific Northwest*. Washington, D.C.: Department of Indian Affairs, 1944.

Vancouver, George. *A Voyage of Discovery to the North Pacific Ocean and round the World*. Two volumes. London: John Stockdale, 1801.

Victor, Frances Fuller. *River of the West*. Hartford, Conn.: Bliss & Co., 1870.

Von Hagen, Victor Wolfgang. *Maya Explorer, John Lloyd Stephens*. Norman, Okla.: University of Oklahoma Press, 1947.

Waring, Guy. *My Pioneer Past*. Boston: Bruce Humphries, 1936.

Welsh, William D. *A Brief History of Camas, Washington*. Camas, Wash.: 1941.

White, Catherine M. *David Thompson's Journals Relating to Montana and Adjacent Regions*. Missoula, Mont.: Montana University Press, 1950.

White, Dr. E. *Ten Years in Oregon*. Ithaca, N.Y.: Mack, Indrus and Co., 1848.

Williams, John H. *The Guardians of the Columbia, Mount Hood, Mount Adams and Mount St. Helens*. Tacoma, Wash.: John H. Williams, 1912.

———. *The Mountain That Was God, Being a Little Book about the Great Peak which the Indians named "Tacoma" but which is officially called "Rainier."* New York: G. P. Putnam's Sons, 1911.

Wills, Robert H. *High Trails: A Guide to the Cascade Crest Trail*. Seattle, Wash.: University of Washington Press, 1967.

Wilson, James Grant. *Memorial History of the City of New York*. New York: Historical Publishing Co., 1893.

Winther, Oscar Osburn. *The Old Oregon Country*. Palo Alto, Calif.: Stanford University Press, 1950.

Winthrop, Theodore. *The Canoe and the Saddle*. Boston: Ticknor and Fields, 1863. (Also *The Canoe and the Saddle, or Klalam and Klickatat*, by Theodore Winthrop, to which are now first added his Western Letters and Journals, edited, with an Introduction and Notes, by John H. Williams, with Sixteen Color Plates and More than One Hundred Other Illustrations (the Tacoma edition). Tacoma, Wash.: John H. Williams, 1913.

Wolle, Muriel Sibell. *The Bonanza Trail: Ghost Towns and Mining Camps of the West*. Bloomington, Ind.: Indiana University Press, 1953.

Wood, Robert L. *Across the Olympic Mountains*. Seattle, Wash.: University of Washington Press, 1967.

Works Progress Administration. *Oregon: End of the Trail*. Portland, Ore.: Binfords & Mort, 1940.

———. *Washington, A Guide to the Evergreen State*. Portland, Ore.: Binfords & Mort, 1940.

Yates, Edmund. *Recollections and Experiences*. London: Bentley, 1884.

Periodicals

Ayer, John Edwin. "George Bush, the Voyageur." *Washington Historical Quarterly*, Vol. VII, No. 1 (January, 1916).

Cantwell, Robert. "The Columbia, a Gem of a River." *Sports Illustrated*, Vol. 20, No. 8 (February 24, 1964).

———. "High Path to a Wild Paradise." *Sports Illustrated*, Vol. 19, No. 6 (August 5, 1963).

———. "Melodrama on the Horsefly River." *Sports Illustrated*, Vol. 15, No. 17 (October 21, 1961).

———. "Nemesis of the Black Brant." *Sports Illustrated*, Vol. 24, No. 20 (May 16, 1966).

———. "Riding down a Dying River." *Sports Illustrated*, Vol. 25, No. 21 (November 24, 1966).

———. "The Shy Tycoon Who Owns One-Six-Hundred-and-Fortieth of the United States." *Sports Illustrated*, Vol. 31, No. 8 (August 18, 1969).

———. "A Town and Its Novels." *New Republic*, February 24, 1937.

Coleman, A. P. "The Selkirks." *Transactions of the Royal Society of Canada*, Vol. VII, Sec. IV (1889).

Conover, C. J. "Cascade Crest Trail." *Mountaineer*, Vol. 28, No. 1 (1935).

Dawson, George. "Mineral Wealth of British Columbia." *Geological Society of Canada*, annual report, Vol. III (1887–1888).

Douglas, William O. "Pleasure Trails." *Washington Sportsman*, June–July, 1936.

Elliott, Thompson C. "The Discovery of the Source of the Columbia River." *Oregon Historical Quarterly*, Vol. XXVI, No. 1 (1925).

———. "The Strange Case of David Thompson and Jeremy Pinch." *Oregon Historical Quarterly*, Vol. XL, No. 2 (1939).

Fleming, Sandford. "Explorations to the Pacific." *Transactions of the Royal Society of Canada,* Vol. VIII, Sec. II (1880).

Hacking, Norman. "Steamboat Days on the Upper Columbia and Upper Kootenay." *British Columbia Historical Quarterly,* January–April, 1951.

Hanson, Howard A. "Michael Troutman Simmons." Masonic Papers. Research Lodge, No. 281, F. and A. M. Seattle, Vol. I, No. 15 (April, 1941).

Himes, George. "An Account of Crossing the Plains in 1853, and of the First Trip by Immigrants Through the Cascade Mountains via Natchess Pass." *Transactions of the Thirty-fifth Annual Reunion of the Oregon Pioneers Association,* June 19, 1907. Portland, Ore.

Hodgson, Maurice. "The Exploration Journal as Literature." *The Beaver: A Magazine of the North* (winter, 1967).

Johannsen, Robert W. "National Issues and Local Politics in Washington Territory, 1857–1861." *Pacific Northwest Quarterly,* Vol. 42, No. 1 (1951).

Kautz, A. V. "Ascent of Mount Rainier." *The Overland Monthly,* Vol. 14, No. 5 (1875).

Lokken, Roy N. "The Martial Law Controversy in Washington Territory." *Pacific Northwest Quarterly,* Vol. 43, No. 2 (1952).

Longmire, David. "First Immigrants to Cross the Cascades." *Washington Historical Quarterly,* Vol. VIII, No. 1 (1917).

————. "Narrative of James Longmire, A Pioneer." *Washington Historical Quarterly,* Vol. XXIII, Nos. 1 and 2 (January and April, 1932).

Magnusson, Elsa Cooper. "Naches Pass." *Pacific Northwest Quarterly,* Vol. XXV, No. 3 (1934).

Mahlberg, Blanche Billings. "Edward J. Allen, Pioneer and Roadbuilder." *Pacific Northwest Quarterly,* Vol. 44, No. 4 (1953).

Mason, J. Tate. "Seattle's First Physician: Dr. David Swainson Maynard." *Clinics of the Virginia Mason Hospital, Seattle,* Vol. XII (1933).

Merk, Frederick. "The Oregon Pioneers and the Boundary." *American Historical Review,* Vol. 29 (address at the meeting of the American Historical Association, December 28, 1923).

Minto, John. "Reminiscences." *Transactions of the Fourth Annual Reunion of the Oregon Pioneers Association,* May 4, 1876, Salem, Oregon. (1877).

Morris, Grace. "Wreck of a Japanese Junk, 1834." *Oregon Historical Quarterly.* Vol. XXXVIII, No. 1 (1937).

Overmeyer, Philip Henry. "George B. McClellan and the Pacific Northwest." *Pacific Northwest Quarterly,* Vol. 32, No. 1 (1941).

Powell, Fred Wilbur. "Hall Jackson Kelley, Prophet of Oregon." *Oregon Historical Quarterly,* Vol. XVIII, Nos. 1–3 (1917).

Prosch, Thomas W. "The Military Roads of Washington Territory." *Washington Historical Quarterly,* Vol. II, No. 2 (1908).

Schaffer, Joseph. "Jesse Applegate: Pioneer, Statesman and Philosopher." *Washington Historical Quarterly,* Vol. I, No. 4 (1907).

Scott, H. W. "The Foundation and Administration of the Provisional Government of Oregon." *Oregon Historical Quarterly*, Vol. II, No. 2 (1901).

Sperlin, O. B. "Explorations of the Upper Columbia." *Transactions of the Royal Society of Canada*, Vol. IV, No. 1 (1913).

Stevens, Hazard. "The Ascent of Takhoma." *Atlantic Monthly*, Vol. XXXVII (Nov., 1876).

Thorington, J. Monroe. "The Purcell Source of the Columbia River." *The Geographical Journal of Canada*, Vol. LXXVII, No. 5 (1931).

Thwaites, Reuben Gold. "William Clark: Soldier, Explorer, Statesman." *Washington Historical Quarterly*, Vol. I, No. 4 (1908).

Victor, Frances Auretta Fuller. "Hall J. Kelley." *Oregon Historical Quarterly*, Vol. II, No. 4 (1901).

Watkins, Ernest. "The Columbia River: A Gordian Knot." *International Review*, Vol. XII, No. 4 (1957).

Yesler, Henry. "The Founding of Seattle." *Pacific Northwest Quarterly*, Vol. 42, No. 4 (1951).

Documents

Charters, Statutes, Orders in Council, etc., Relating to the Hudson's Bay Company. London: Hudson's Bay Company (1957).

Index of Washington Territorial Records, Military Department, State of Washington, Office of the Adjutant General, Camp Murray, Wash., compiled by Colonel W. F. Field (1960), pp. 1–55.

Report of the Forrest Divorce Case, Containing the Full and Unabridged Testimony of All Witnesses. Law Reporter, *New York Herald.* New York: De Witt.

National Archives: *Records of the General Land Office, Oregon Donation Land Claims.*

Legal Aspects of the Use of Systems of International Waters, with Reference to Columbia-Kootenay River System under the Customary International Law and the Treaty of 1909. Memorandum of the State Department, April 21, 1958. 85th Congress. 2nd Session. Senate Document No. 113.

Index